EDITH WHARTON

GARLAND REFERENCE LIBRARY
OF THE HUMANITIES
(VOL. 1027)

EDITH WHARTON
An Annotated
Secondary Bibliography

Kristin O. Lauer
Margaret P. Murray

GARLAND PUBLISHING, INC. • NEW YORK & LONDON
1990

Library of Congress Cataloging-in-Publication Data

Lauer, Kristin O., 1943–
   Edith Wharton: an annotated secondary bibliography / Kristin O.
Lauer, Margaret P. Murray.
      p.   cm. — (Garland reference library of the humanities ; vol.
1027)
   ISBN 0-8240-4636-6 (alk. paper)
   1. Wharton, Edith, 1862–1937—Bibliography. I. Murray, Margaret
P., 1952–   . II. Title. III. Series.
Z8969.2.L38   1990
[PS3545.H16]
016.813'52—dc20   89–37067
                                                         CIP

Printed on acid-free, 250-year-life paper
Manufactured in the United States of America

For:

Karin Emily Olson, M.D.

who has the exceedingly rare gift of imperturbably taking the measure of a dream (then but harebrained scheme) in its infancy with a loving eye, and setting to work (as much sheer labor as only the authors know) and with intelligence, faith, self-sacrifice and patience transforming it into a reality. They call such people Dream Makers. Their value? Beyond measure. This bibliography is but one example of her bottomless generosity.

"For the Universe has three children, born at one time, which reappear, under different names,...but which we will call here, the Knower, the Doer, and the Sayer. These stand respectively for the love of truth, the love of good, and for the love of beauty. These three are equal....[E]ach of these three has the power of the others latent in him....The poet is the Sayer, the namer, and represents beauty. He is a sovereign, and stands on the centre."

Ralph Waldo Emerson

To our Brother, the *Sayer*, Wharton scholar *Lev Raphael*, the authors owe a great debt. His generous aid has immensely enriched this bibliography, as the wisdom of his new perspective has immensely enriched Wharton scholarship.

Contents

Acknowledgments

A bibliography of this scope necessarily rapidly becomes a team effort. One of the joys of the project was meeting and working with librarians and scholars who were invariably helpful and supportive, aghast at our courage, ever ready to offer sustenance.

Our first debt can never be repaid, for excellent Fordham Reference Librarian Anne Finnan, who taught us about on-line searches and directed those toddler steps four years ago, died recently. Patricia Middleton of the Yale Beinecke was enormously helpful, proving she well deserves her reputation as one of the world-class manuscript librarians in this country. We would also like to thank the superb librarians at Columbia University, Brooklyn Public Library and the New York Public Library. We owe a debt to Martha Swan at the University of Mississippi Library and to the librarians of the Newport Redwood Library for tracking down elusive material. Lowell Acola was invaluably helpful, providing us with much hard to find, older material.

One of the particular areas in which we needed expert help was the finding and translation of foreign articles and books. We were always particularly grateful to Jean Blackall at Cornell who tracked down and helped us sort out our Oriental titles and material. Teddi Oda translated several Japanese articles with expert commentary. Aulette Thiele spent grueling hours at the New York Public Library translating French references. Maurice Baroni was kind enough to take over a batch of French reviews which he translated beautifully. Fordham Professor Serafina deGregario graciously translated Italian for us. Professor Lester Figuerski was enormously helpful, with his wide expertise, in translating French reviews, and Rosalie Lamet brought her knowledge of French and French idiom and culture to her interpretations of the French reviewers. Ruth Brintz led me to Eva Sachs, and both were simply irreplaceable in their painstaking analysis of the German material. Irene Wachulewicz was kind enough to arrange Professor Figuerski's translations, and also found much of the German material we needed. Her nephew, Richard, spent hours in Hamburg looking up sources.

Many friends, hearing of our project, rushed to our aid. Reamy Jansen not only mentioned invaluable sources, but quickly provided copies of the material. Madelyn Miller perplexed customs officials and delighted us by returning from Europe with suitcases of tediously retrieved volumes. Harold Meyer brought Virago treasures. Arline Miller was ever watchful for sources. Barbara Pierce appeared one day with a heart-stopping gift: a first edition of *The Book of the Homeless*. Marianne Barrett found *Costerus* for us at the University of Virginia, and in a few days she had it in our hands.

Eminent Whartonians were the staunchest of allies. Alan Price, Mary Suzanne Schriber and Judith Sensibar all provided copies of their forthcoming material. Margaret McDowell, ever supportive, earned both our unbounded respect and our gratitude. Alfred Bendixen, bibliographer of the Edith Wharton Society, was willing to discuss the project in detail and offered numerous helpful suggestions along the way. Annette Zilversmit, then President of the Edith Wharton Society, furnished us with the old *Newsletters*. Professor Miyoko Sasaki called us from Japan in response to a frantic, last-minute plea and gave us treasured assistance.

Such a project as ours, however, does not only involve the laborious research and detective work. We had to gain expertise in many areas of computer technology. Without Robert Wasserman this bibliography might never have gotten to disk. His amazing expertise in all areas of academic computer technology is surpassed only by his patience in spending hours teaching neophytes the finer points of software, and, overall, calming the enormous anxiety of professor encountering machine. In terms of format and layout, Dr. Wasserman was the kind, tireless physician in attendance at the birthing of this bib. Dr. Gershen Kaufman, known for his supportive gentleness, made our proportional fonts workable at last. Chuck Bartelt at Garland has the same rare gift, and without her encouragement and aid this volume would have none of the polished appearance she so enthusiastically provided.

Certain people were so intimately involved with the project that it bears their stamp and could not be the same without their endeavors. One of these is a treasured friend--Georganne V. Brown--without whose devotion, sense of organization, painstaking attention to detail, hours of thought and planning, this bibliography would be far less than it is. Another is Laura Greeney, who first brought the proposal to Garland and, four years later, served as the final proofreader; she being the only one we would trust. Her intelligence, knowledge of bibliography and editorial acumen are unmatched in the business. We thank Pamela Chergotis, also, our first editor at Garland, who offered support, suggestion and encouragement. Another special friend of this bibliography is Ellen Ervin, who not only translated much difficult French and Italian material, but provided concise and informative annotations, and gave us the advantage of her vast linguistic knowledge.

Others cheered us along the way, kept up our courage at dark moments--Richard Daniel, loving host *extraordinaire*, offered an object lesson in "Whartonian country living" during our trips to the Beinecke. Dr. Dennis Perzanowski, a textbook in the art of friendship, steered us safely through the shoals of the Library of Congress.

Professor James W. Tuttleton deserves special mention, for he discussed our organization, gave us many invaluable tips, and from his bibliographical expertise made our bibliography much stronger and more useful.

In October 1988, we were finally able to meet our mysterious correspondent and scholarly soul-mate, Stephen Garrison. As true

Americanists, in our darkest hour we looked to the West, and there, from Oklahoma, rode our white-hatted benefactor. He placed his expertise, acquired through years of painstaking research on the Wharton primary bibliography, entirely at our disposal. His erudition, his counsel and his unstinting generosity are enriched by the wit and vigor which he brings to our shared discipline. Our debt to this gentleman and scholar cannot be overstated.

Careful Mary Kathrin Cook spent tedious hours proofing the data base materials, and Helen Elizabeth Olson brought her sharp editorial eye to the data base, willingly and lovingly proofing and just as willingly and lovingly offering sustenance to the bibliographer. Bert Olson housed the bibliography, paid for the night-long computer hours, placed the machine with the engineer's eye, housed and fed the bibliographer and friends and spent many mornings running about the county collecting express mail deliveries. The Olsons provided the Pearl of Great Price, the Hewlett-Packard Laser printer, on which this book was printed.

However, there could simply never have been a bibliography without Darrell Lauer. Any married academic woman with a small baby knows that the success of such a time-consuming project depends in large part on the hours of sacrifice and loving support of a good husband. Darrell Lauer is not only a "good husband" but an extraordinary human being. The list of meals he cooked, diapers he changed, hours he spent in the park, would be another volume of this size in itself. He also taught countless lessons in exchange for bibliographic assistance and, in a host of practical ways, was the ever-concerned father of this bibliography.

To Professor R.W.B. and Mrs. Lewis, we can only add another voice to all of those who speak of their legendary assistance to young scholars. They are ever accessible, kind and knowledgeable. And, in this particular case, for us, they made the magic.

Special gratitude, also, goes to Mark Sigerson, that remarkable, beloved secretary, not only for his intelligence but for his loyalty. Wonderful Kevin McBride simply turned up one morning bearing that first computer--his own--on his shoulder, and said, "Maybe this will help?"

Finally, this project was blessed with a kindly, humorous, patient and practical good uncle behind the scenes who lives in the real world and served in the invaluable capacity of keeping the bibliographers sane and as happy as possible with much good advice. He proves Emerson's wisdom: "Nothing astonishes men so much as common sense and plain dealing." We were incredibly lucky to have Jerry Crawford.

Preface

This selective secondary bibliography has been annotated and organized with the user's needs always the primary consideration. We have included all of the material from the invaluable Springer bibliography that runs from 1899-1973 and the material in James W. Tuttleton's bibliographical essays. Reviews included here that do not come from Springer come from Patricia Plante's dissertation. We have also included much of the material from the Brenni bibliography, in most cases to save the researcher valuable time rechecking sources that are often unreliable. We have depended on the Modern Language Association bibliographies, the Bendixen bibliographies in *The Edith Wharton Newsletter*, the updated Springer bibliography from and for material after 1975. If these previous secondary bibliographies have deficiencies, they usually arise in book mentions of Wharton. It is probably impossible to find *all* of the Wharton mentions in literary surveys. We have made every effort to track down the major ones. In some cases we have been more inclusive than the original Springer, again, to save the researcher time checking sources of little interest. We have also endeavored to include all the material cited in footnotes in the secondary bibliography and bibliographies included at the end of book-length studies. For

most of the French material we are indebted to Mary Suzanne
Schriber's bibliography of the French reception and E.K. Brown's
bibliography appended to his study of Wharton.

We have organized the bibliography, both primary and secondary,
with ease of access in mind. There is necessarily some overlapping.
For example, studies of literary relationships are often heavily
biographical, and contemporary surveys are entered under
contemporary evaluations, with surveys after 1939 incorporated
into another chapter. We chose to separate contemporary
evaluations and surveys from posthumous ones at 1939 in order to
include reevaluations immediately after her death with
contemporary studies. The indexes, however, should alert the
reader to material on any given work and subject.

We hope, by using a subject format, to make this bibliography as
useful and efficient a tool for the scholar as is practicable. Even
a cursory reading through the annotations listed in Chapter 5
provides an insightful summation of the critical reception during
Wharton's lifetime. Anyone researching a particular book need
only turn to the listings under the work in question to trace a
history of the issues raised by that work from its publication to
this day.

The reviews should prove particularly eye-opening for anyone
interested in literary history and the genesis of attitudes that have
been of paramount importance in Wharton scholarship.

Although we have endeavored to include everything of importance
(and any bibliography of a writer as extensively reviewed and
studied as Edith Wharton will necessarily have many unfortunate
oversights) through 1987, we have also included material from 1988
that was especially important and accessible.

The Primary Bibliography

The primary bibliography is intended to be an aid to the user of
the secondary, and is not an inclusive list, in any sense, of
reprintings and editions of her work. Stephen Garrison's *Edith*

Wharton: A Descriptive Bibliography, forthcoming from the University of Pittsburgh Press, must be consulted for full listings of first publication. We have listed, in the following order:

A. Titles of novels and novellas with first American printing information in chronological order. Other pertinent information occurs in annotation.

B. Titles of the short story collections with first American printings, including contents of each volume.

C. Titles of individual short stories in alphabetical order for ease of access, and first periodical appearance where indicated. However, the reader is cautioned to consult the forthcoming Garrison primary for full first periodical publication data.

D. Titles of poetry collections appear first, followed by an alphabetical listing of poems published individually (F4.), with first periodical publication noted. Again, the reader is referred to the forthcoming Garrison primary for full information.

E. Titles of nonfiction books in chronological order, including annotation where useful, to give the reader the latest reprinting information for volumes difficult to find.

F. Titles of Edith Wharton's essays, with first periodical publication information in chronological order within five separate sections as follows:

F1	Travel
F2	Reviews
F3	General Essays
F4	Personal Memoirs
F5	Introductions, Prefaces and Forewords

G. Titles of Translations, Collections, Editions and Adaptations in chronological order of publication.

H. Letters of Edith Wharton.

I. Selective list of manuscript materials and published fragments mentioned in the secondary bibliography. The Wharton papers at the Beinecke Library of Yale University contain hundreds of manuscript fragments, and this short list is only included to aide the user of the secondary bibliography.

J. Selective chronological list of major collections including contents and annotated introductions unless the introduction is relevant to another chapter. Such placement is noted in the Primary Bibliography.

Introduction

A Tale of Hobbyhorses Signifying Much:
Understanding Wharton Criticism 1899-1989

Approaching the crowded shelves of Edith Wharton's primary work--twenty novels and novellas, eleven short story collections, eighty-seven individual short stories, nine volumes of nonfiction, two volumes of poetry--the reader is understandably overwhelmed.

The secondary bibliography is equally staggering in sheer volume, running to over 1200 entries, and increasing at such an alarming rate every month the scholar is apt to take Henry James's attitude in the face of bibliographers: profound stupefaction.

The problem of understanding Wharton scholarship and her unique place in American Letters is doubly complicated for the apprentice (as well as the seasoned Whartonian, one must add) by a mystifying, odd assortment of stubborn, contradictory images. Wasn't Edith Wharton the conservative Grande Dame of American literature living outside Paris in one mansion with another elegant home on the Riviera? The well-born New York society hostess with a retinue of servants, often photographed with pearls and Pekinese? An acolyte of the man she addressed as *Cher Maître*, Henry James? The quintessential novelist of manners who wrote nostalgic, sedate and bloodless exposés of high society in the old Fifth Avenue brownstone world, the exclusive Parisian Faubourg, Newport and Monaco with settings lit by chandelier and candle? Was she not the formidable, conscience- and form-bound Grandmother of twentieth-century American fiction?

On the other hand, those images clash with her most culturally entrenched book, that chill little masterpiece, always a part of the American canon since its publication in 1911, which has weathered the many vicissitudes of Wharton's reputation. The tragic story of a poor New England farmer, *Ethan Frome*, sent critics back to Aeschylus.

Other, more recent, additions to the Wharton mythology after the publication of R.W.B. Lewis's definitive biography in 1975 and the advent of vigorous feminist criticism are even more disorienting. Professor Lewis exposed her mid-forties tempestuous affair with a bisexual, notoriously promiscuous American journalist, Morton Fullerton. He also unveiled a shocking fragment from her unpublished manuscripts: a detailed, pornographic scene of father-daughter incest, accompanying the outline of a short story, "Beatrice Palmato."

At about the same time, feminists elevated *The House of Mirth* to the status of a textbook on feminism. Lily Bart's tragedy in that novel as the victim of a patriarchal society in which women were raised to be beautiful, purposeless objects, became required reading in Women's Studies courses across America. Suddenly the author who advised American women in *French Ways and Their Meaning* to learn to keep their mouths shut and listen to men with the grace of their wiser French counterparts was adopted as the spokeswoman for enslaved women everywhere. The writer who began her career with a decorating book for millionaires, who had been the epitome of ladylike virtue and perfect, breathtaking white gardens, whom Vernon Parrington dismissed as "Our Literary Aristocrat," was seen as the champion of classless, non-capitalist, androgynous society.

At times her expatriation to France, her naturalistic pessimism and her sharp criticism of culturally arid America led scholars to feel they must defend her right to be a significant voice in American literature at all.

If we are to unscramble this collage of disjointed impressions, we must turn to the patient literary historians who point out that the problem of Edith Wharton is in many ways historical. She debuted with her first collection of short stories in 1899 and published much-reviewed fiction until her death in 1937. The dates of her career thus span the ascendance of naturalism, Theodore Dreiser, D.H. Lawrence, Ernest Hemingway, stream of consciousness writing, James Joyce and Virginia Woolf. In such a collection, the basically classical Edith Wharton was an anachronism. Only Sinclair Lewis and F. Scott Fitzgerald claimed strong affinities with Edith Wharton, the novelist of manners.

Edith Wharton herself lamented in one famous essay that it was the heyday of "the man with the dinner pail" fiction. As early as 1925, she was buried alive by the first full-length study of her work in which Robert Morss Lovett defined her as class-bound and old-fashioned--a Victorian out of time.

Unfortunately, she did not slip easily into the critics' pockets of her day, nor was she a visionary and technical innovator like Emily Dickinson. She looked backward to the classics for form and around her for material. In that respect, she is the American Jane Austen.

Yet her basic pessimism, the fatality that dogs her characters, the accidental and intentional suicides, the enormous, ill-spent wealth and leisure, the resignation, the incestuous overtones, the serious questions about marriage, the frequent adulteries, the satire of stable Old New York's infantilizing propensities, her disharmony with her social world and times, make her, not like Austen at work with a fine brush on ivory, but more akin to Thomas Hardy--carving her gallery of the damned in granite.

Technically, she is as assured of the value of form as Austen; thematically, she is as angry at convention as Hardy, as revolutionary as Nietzsche to whom she turned for justification of her one affair. Thackeray's dark moral social vision in *Vanity Fair* is perhaps the best analogue. Her great characters are crushed by circumstances, and the rhetoric of the text, until her very last novels, focuses the reader's attention on those circumstances so that the complex interplay between character and situation seems weighted in the scale of fatality. In Wharton, the social environment is *never* congenial to individual aspiration. That great line of Ellen Olenska's when Newland Archer wants to run away with her to a place where they can simply be themselves and love each other: "Oh, my dear--where is that country? Have you ever been there?" is the saddest, most telling line Edith Wharton ever wrote. Crippled Ethan and maimed Mattie Silver are its objective correlative.

Thus the student of Edith Wharton, taking even a shallow dip into the scholarship, encounters two basic approaches: attempts to defend and attempts to classify. The defensive phrase "Justice to" became instantly famous with Edmund Wilson's "Justice to Edith Wharton" when she died, but any student of the earlier criticism knows reviewers and scholars felt compelled to assume a martial attitude almost from the very beginning of her career. The charges? She was class-bound, minor James, dated, old-fashioned, narrow, uneven, merely clever, misogynistic, anti-Semitic, cold, aloof, un-American. Attempts to classify involved the question: In what respects is she classicist, realist, naturalist, American, novelist of manners, feminist?

Another very serious, puzzling, complicated question that faces the student of Edith Wharton is that the focus of scholarship centers on a very small number of her works as the influential biographical material is usually drawn from a small number of outstanding facts in a long, purposeful life. We read again and again of her upper-class, privileged family, her cold, rejecting mother, her marriage to the handsome, cheerful, unintellectual sportsman of her own class, Teddy Wharton, her affair with Morton Fullerton, her friendship with James and her lifelong devotion to the international lawyer who encouraged her writing, her soul-mate, Walter Berry. Everyone knows of her divorce from Teddy in 1913 after several nerve-shattering years in which he slowly receded into what sounds from a modern perspective like manic-depressive psychosis, involving such bizarre behavior for the formerly proper, congenial, sunny though dull Teddy as seriously mismanaging her money and setting up chorus girls in a Boston apartment. We gain, therefore, a very skewed portrait of Edith Wharton from much of the secondary material that ignores enormous stretches of her always energetic daily existence and her myriad interests and relationships.

Edith Wharton was a remarkably dynamic, sensitive traveller whose books on Italy and Morocco are still thought-provoking references. Unfortunately, the most dramatic image of Edith Wharton en route is that of the Angel of Devastation swooping down on James at Rye, scooping him into her chauffeured car and buzzing about the land. Much that she observed not only about society, but art and architecture as it reflects the basic temperament and historical development of a people, is overlooked. During World War I, Edith Wharton became a legend in France for setting up workrooms for the unemployed and rescuing refugee children. In 1916 she was given the highest honor the President of France could bestow, and was made a Chevalier of the Legion of Honor.

The thrust of criticism accents *The House of Mirth* (1905), *Ethan Frome* (1911), and *The Age of Innocence* (1920)--three novels out of twenty, fifteen years of a thirty-eight year career. Of the short stories, only "Roman Fever" has been frequently anthologized. *The Custom of the Country*, with its lethal, social-climbing Midwesterner, Undine Spragg, and its rich symbolic overtones, enormously influential in 1913, causing reactions as strong as those to James's *Daisy Miller*, another controversial portrait of the American woman abroad, is all but abandoned now. There is some new interest in the Jamesian *The Reef* with its compelling portrait of the restrained, ladylike woman yearning for a freer emotional life and *Summer* with its poignant detail of orphaned Charity Royall's sexual awakening. However, very few readers move beyond the famous trio, and therefore they miss Wharton's developing vision as she grew older. Most readers ignore the eight novels after 1920 completely.

The obvious reason is that the famous three have steadily remained in print. However, the more serious puzzling fact is that scholars abandoned them as well, or even before, publishers. The initial fault probably lies with Edmund Wilson who, in "Justice to Edith Wharton," soundly buried them, and admitted he stopped reading Wharton after *Twilight Sleep* (1927).

Objections to the fiction after 1920 complain of its shrill, uneven quality, of Wharton's rage at the modern world of flappers, uncultured millionaires, serial divorces and movie stars, of her distance from modern America, her lack of knowledge of the Midwest she satirizes. Astonishingly, on the other hand, critics of these novels also accuse her of sentimentality, lack of distance, and denounce her for making money writing women's magazine drivel.

Neglect of the short fiction is also a riddle. Few readers know she was a master of the ghost story, and therefore, although her supernatural tales are now available in paperback editions, so little attention is paid to them, the general reader misses the rich experience of "The Eyes," "Bewitched," "The Triumph of Night," "All Souls'" and "Pomegranate Seed." Again, the oversight exists because she was not an innovator in the short story form. She contended in *The Writing of Fiction* that the short story was "a shaft driven into the heart of experience," and her stories have often been analyzed as emphasizing situation at the expense of characterization. Several important Whartonians, significantly Margaret McDowell and R.W.B. Lewis, have built strong cases for the interaction of character and situation, and they should be consulted for insight into Wharton's work in the genre.

How, then, does the student of Edith Wharton best come to an understanding of the mass of Wharton scholarship with as unbiased and comprehensive a vision as possible?

The first pertinent warning is to keep the development of Wharton criticism clearly in mind. Chronologically, there are five major phases of Wharton secondary bibliography: (1) the reception of the very early work before *The House of Mirth* in 1905; (2) the years 1905-1920 when she was recognized as one of the leading-- in many cases *the* leading--American writer of her day; (3) 1920- 1937 when she was increasingly viewed within the Wharton formula as the *Grande Dame* of American Letters, perhaps prissy and dated, but still popular and widely reviewed; (4) 1937 (her death)--1975 and the publication of the Lewis biography, followed immediately by Cynthia Griffin Wolff's influential psychobiography employing the developmental model of Erik Erikson, *A Feast of Words: The Triumph of Edith Wharton*; (5) 1975--the present in which psychological and feminist studies predominate.

The first phase of Wharton criticism found, as early as 1900, William Dean Howells delighting from the Editor's Easy Chair at Harper's that a star of "literary conscience and artistic ideal" had risen. Nevertheless, journals and newspapers that reviewed her focused on her class and, especially, the influence of Henry James they found in the early collections and novellas. From these first critics stem what was to become the damaging formulaic accusation that she was class-bound and "clever" and--most harmful--merely minor James. One critic bluntly accused her of plagiarism, her "The Muse's Tragedy" only a thin transposition of *The Tragic Muse*.

On the other hand, her style, ever lucid and classical, and her epigrams--pithy and quotable--were widely admired. Her pessimism, however, even at this early date, for some, threw her vision into question.

We seldom turn to the early reviews of a writer's first work; in fact, the tendency is to study the latest questions and work backward. But in terms of Edith Wharton the foundation laid here from 1899-1905 is the basis for so many later prejudices, the conscientious scholar must be mindful of the evolution of criticism--and how it shaped a developing mythology. For example, modern charges in the popular press that she was a misogynist probably stem from the Genteel Tradition's demand for sympathetic characterization of women--particularly by women writers. Especially in the case of Edith Wharton, the scholarship has historically been an insightful tale of critical hobbyhorses. Her discipleship to James--then in growing disfavor for the density of his later style--was such a widely debated issue, one English reviewer pronounced it the King Charles' Head of Wharton criticism, eclipsing all other aspects of her work.

The second phase of Wharton criticism runs from the publication of the instantly famous *House of Mirth* (1905) through the Pulitzer Prize winning *The Age of Innocence* (1920). These fifteen golden years--at least professionally--saw publication of *Madame de Treymes*, *Ethan Frome*, *The Reef*, *Summer* and *The Custom of the Country*. A fascinating metamorphosis takes place here critically in this short time of enormous social and political upheaval. With *The House of Mirth* and the tragedy of Lily Bart, she was defined as prophet and moralist with a striking revolutionary social vision of the latent corruption and decadence in the highest society. From such appraisals stem modern analyses of her criticism of class and economic inequality. By 1920, however, *The Age of Innocence* was dubbed the work of a literary historian of a bygone age, and those reviewers solidified a Wharton code that termed her a class-bound conservative, a charming literary relic. Whichever view one adopts, to this day, strong arguments come from the other side.

Certainly there is a striking difference in narrative tone from the earlier novel to the later, rage giving way to nostalgic resignation, bitter, overt, epigrammatic satire mellowed to subtle symbol. But the response of critics was governed by prejudices about what Edith Wharton was and could and should do, and--centrally--massive ferment in the social, political and literary marketplace. How could the classical *salon* survive the divisive, horrifyingly prophetic Dreyfus affair? How could the Paris of *The Sun Also Rises* encompass Edith Wharton's Faubourg? Where, in a world electrified by *Ulysses*, does one place an Edith Wharton?

Such was the dilemma of the critic and reviewer from 1920 until her death in 1937. During those seventeen years literary tastes and standards changed so dramatically that if she was a respected historian in 1920, by 1937 she was--in much of the popular press--a fossil. Not only was the man with the dinner pail center stage, but so was James, and his bright sun threw her into a shadow from which she did not emerge until 1975 with the publication of Professor Lewis's biography and, at about the same time, the feminist Wharton revival.

This history that shaped her reputation was infinitely damaging to Edith Wharton because her developing vision was simply ignored--particularly when it fit nowhere within the established Wharton guidelines. Her farewell to the Life of Reason, for example, is objectified through Rose Sellars in *The Children* (1928). Her stark warning to the strikingly modern, overly committed, overly busy, unreflective woman is objectified in Pauline Manford in *Twilight Sleep* (1927). Her complex, insightful reworking of the difficult relationships between men and women lies in her searching analysis of Halo Tarrant and Vance Weston in her two monumental studies of artistic development, *Hudson River Bracketed* and *The Gods Arrive*. The hope she saw in the new young woman is dramatized in such later heroines as Nona Manford, Judith Wheater, Halo Tarrant, and Nan St. George.

We lose, in fact, an entire unfolding evolution of a type of woman emotionally very much like herself, introduced in Anna Leath in *The Reef*--the repressed lady yearning for sexual and emotional liberation. Anna, however, was far from her last word on the subject. We miss her searching, unforgettable portrait of war-time Paris in *A Son At the Front* simply because Edith Wharton, of all people, as one reviewer put it, "with her chill temperament" was the last person who should write a war novel.

To write of the women of Edith Wharton with only knowledge of Lily Bart, Gerty Farish, Zeena Frome, Mattie Silver, May Welland and Ellen Olenska is to neglect seventeen years of a mature woman's reflection on the troubled nature of male-female relationships and women's place in the social world.

After her death, in the years 1937-1975, scholars had to struggle against rigid attitudes, and the posture of the criticism was, overall, defensive. In the first place, these were the years of the memoirs, books by people who knew her, and, like Percy Lubbock's famous *Portrait of Edith Wharton*, they tended to reinforce images of the aloof, snobbish Grande Dame friend of James. Louis Auchincloss, of her class, with many family connections, always gave a more balanced account, but his very name and material still distanced her among the socially elite.

In the second place, any scholar dealing with Wharton necessarily had to temporize and look ahead because the Wharton papers at Yale were yet to be opened. Much of the biographical material from this time is unreliable. For example, the "Love Diary" was often quoted and attributed to an affair with Walter Berry until 1975 when Professor Lewis's biography revealed the lover as Morton Fullerton.

Blake Nevius's *Edith Wharton* was the first full-length posthumous study, and his careful lack of bias makes him still valuable. He also defined what scholars after him were to see as her major themes: the greater personality enslaved by the lesser, usually in marriage, and the exploration of the social responsibilities of the more magnanimous spirit. The thematic center of her work was defined as the conflict of the individual with society. When Irving Howe's influential Twentieth Century Views collection appeared, he formulated the problems of Edith Wharton as faced by the scholar in the sixties: her relationship to James, her pessimism, her unevenness, her class view. Millicent Bell's well-researched study of the relationship with James spurred Wharton interest, but also once again linked Wharton with him. Margaret McDowell and James W. Tuttleton emerged as important voices, consistently urging consideration of the neglected work and assessment without prejudices. The latter's solid bibliographical essays from this period are still the only reliable extensive analyses of Wharton scholarship anywhere.

Came 1975, and nothing would be ever again as it was. Professor Lewis's readable, thorough, scholarly, landmark biography won the Pulitzer Prize for that year. Much of the previous biographical material and most of the psychological speculation was now outdated. The Fullerton affair shot to the top of the mountain of documentation. The frigid Grande Dame reeled, and then toppled, with the surge of feminist interest and Cynthia Griffin Wolff's psychological study of the lonely young rich girl, starved for affection, who found fulfillment in a "feast of words."

Groundbreaking feminist studies followed quickly: Judith Fetterley's unforgettable "The Temptation To Be a Beautiful

Object," Elizabeth Ammons' eye-opening *Edith Wharton's Argument with America*, Carol Wershoven's *The Female Intruder in the Novels of Edith Wharton*. Many of Cynthia Griffin Wolff's and Elizabeth Ammons's galvanizing new readings of the Wharton classics were to uproot old interpretations, and the new book-length studies would at last urge the importance of the forgotten work and offer analysis of Wharton's developing vision.

Strong reactions to the proliferation of feminist criticism have just begun to surface with complaints that a feminist "takeover" has skewed Wharton studies once again. As we have seen, a one-sided orientation has always been a danger in Wharton scholarship, and the hobbyhorse of the day will influence what is published and which works dominate.

The publication of the Wharton letters in June of 1988 cast the Fullerton affair in far harsher light, and is certain to motivate more psychological digging. *The Letters*, with their invaluable annotations, are a goldmine for scholars of the future. Recent complaints by Marion Mainwaring and Mary Pitlick in the London *Times Literary Supplement* that Professor Lewis's biography contains errors--most notably that Edith Wharton did *not* have a nervous breakdown in 1895--which their own forthcoming books will correct, suggest that Wharton discussion will be lively in the future. Lev Raphael's revolutionary, gender-neutral psychological criticism which departs from the ubiquitous Freudian model promises there will be ever-new approaches to Edith Wharton and that she is not merely a fortunate favorite of the feminist tide as she was once a victim of modernism.

The bibliographer, however, rides a dull, old workhorse of a hobby with no specialization in prophecy. If we are to understand Wharton scholarship with its many contradictions it is well to keep our literary history in mind. It is also wise to remember that the basic tension in her work and her life arose because she was a lover of form and as equally passionate a lover of freedom. Form, to her, was beautiful and harmonious, but empty form without honor was vulgar. The picnic, one of her favorite activities, is an excellent example, for a picnic promises freedom of movement, view and dialogue, but her conception of the picnic with hampers, chauffeur, fine china, French wine and a constant flow of scintillating wit, could undoubtedly be both great joy and a trial.

She was sharp, acid, surgical, and she was intelligent, well-read, widely experienced, skeptical. Her universality lies in her warnings, her cautions--against self-effacement and self-sacrifice, most dramatically in *The Old Maid* and *Bunner Sisters*, against uncontrolled narcissism, in *The Custom of the Country*, against sterile detachment in all her cerebral men, against Utopian idealism, against rapid, unconsidered, mindless social change. Her warnings were taken up in the newspapers and journals of 1905 and are publicized by feminists with the same vigor today.

Edith Wharton's gallery of the damned is a sagacious scrutiny of the consequences of particular types of behavior in varied environments. In effect, like James and George Eliot, she dissected what goes wrong in human relationships and how those relationships are limited by the defined social structure. She herself never stopped loving, travelling, writing, reading, never became embittered. If anything, she mellowed with age and loved the young people around her, if not the shape of their world. Her very total, personal immersion in the daily rough and tumble of things, emotions and people--as her letters testify--was her own fulfilling answer to the moral dilemma of life in a fascinating world that broke her heart.

Kristin O. Lauer
Fordham University

Abbreviations

ABG	*A Backward Glance*
AofI	*The Age of Innocence*
BkofH	*The Book of the Homeless*
Buc	*The Buccaneers*
CC	*The Custom of the Country*
CI	*Crucial Instances*
CP	*Certain People*
DofM	*The Descent of Man*
EF	*Ethan Frome*
FF	*Fighting France*
FofT	*The Fruit of the Tree*
FW&M	*French Ways and Their Meaning*
GA	*The Gods Arrive*
GI	*The Greater Inclination*
GofM	*The Glimpses of the Moon*
H&WW	*The Hermit and the Wild Woman*
HofM	*The House of Mirth*
HN	*Human Nature*
HRB	*Hudson River Bracketed*
IB	*Italian Backgrounds*
IV&G	*Italian Villas and Their Gardens*
M'sR	*The Mother's Recompense*
MdeT	*Madame de Treymes*
NYPL	*The New York Public Library*
ONY	*Old New York*
SatF	*A Son at the Front*
TS	*Twilight Sleep*
VofD	*The Valley of Decision*
WofF	*The Writing of Fiction*
WO	*The World Over*
Yale	*The Yale Beinecke*

The *Edith Wharton Newsletter* is published twice a year under the auspices of the Edith Wharton Society. It contains book reviews, articles on all phases of Edith Wharton scholarship, news of forthcoming events of interest to Wharton scholars and annotated bibliographies of work on Edith Wharton.

Edith Wharton

Chapter 1

Primary Bibliography

A1-A22 *The Novels*

A1   *THE TOUCHSTONE.*
New York: Scribner's, 1900.
English edition, *A GIFT FROM THE GRAVE.* London:
John Murray, 1900.

A2   *THE VALLEY OF DECISION.*
New York: Scribner's, 1902.

A3   *SANCTUARY.*
New York: Scribner's, 1903.

A4   *THE HOUSE OF MIRTH.*
New York: Scribner's, 1905.

A5   *MADAME DE TREYMES.*
New York: Scribner's, 1907.

A6   *THE FRUIT OF THE TREE.*
New York: Scribner's, 1907.

A7   *ETHAN FROME.*

New York: Scribner's, 1911.
For French draft of the original manuscript see R7.40.
For bibliographical data see R7.44.

A8   *THE REEF.*
          New York: Appleton, 1912.

A9   *THE CUSTOM OF THE COUNTRY.*
          New York: Scribner's, 1913.

A10   *SUMMER.*
          New York: Appleton, 1917.

A11   *THE MARNE.*
          New York: Appleton, 1918.

A12   *THE AGE OF INNOCENCE.*
          New York: Appleton, 1920.
          See R12.54 for analysis of revisions.

A13   *THE GLIMPSES OF THE MOON.*
          New York: Appleton, 1922.

A14   *A SON AT THE FRONT.*
          New York: Scribner's, 1923.

A15   *OLD NEW YORK.*
          New York: Appleton, 1924.
          Boxed set included four volumes: *FALSE DAWN, THE
          OLD MAID, THE SPARK, NEW YEAR'S DAY.*

A15.1   *FALSE DAWN.*
          New York: Appleton, 1924.

A15.2   *THE OLD MAID.*
          New York: Appleton, 1924.

A15.3   *THE SPARK.*
          New York: Appleton, 1924.

A15.4   *NEW YEAR'S DAY.*
New York: Appleton, 1924.

A16   *THE MOTHER'S RECOMPENSE.*
New York: Appleton, 1925.

A17   *TWILIGHT SLEEP.*
New York: Appleton, 1927.

A18   *THE CHILDREN.*
New York: Appleton, 1928.

A19   *HUDSON RIVER BRACKETED.*
New York: Appleton, 1929.

A20   *THE GODS ARRIVE.*
New York: Appleton, 1932.

A21   *THE BUCCANEERS.*
New York: Appleton-Century, 1938.
Posthumous publication contains text, Wharton's synopsis, and Gaillard Lapsley, "A Note on *The Buccaneers.*" See R21.14.

A22   *FAST AND LOOSE.*
Subtitled: *A Novelette by David Olivieri.* Ed. Viola Hopkins Winner. Charlottesville: University Press of Virginia, 1977.
Edith Wharton's adolescent novel. See W12.

B1-B16 The Short Story Collections

B1   *THE GREATER INCLINATION.*
          New York: Scribner's, 1899.
          Contents: "The Muse's Tragedy"; "A Journey"; "The
          Pelican"; "Souls Belated"; "A Coward"; "The Twilight of
          the God"; "A Cup of Cold Water"; "The Portrait."

B2   *CRUCIAL INSTANCES.*
          New York: Scribner's, 1901.
          Contents: "The Duchess at Prayer"; "The Angel at the
          Grave"; "The Recovery"; "Copy"; "The Rembrandt"; "The
          Moving Finger"; "The Confessional."

B3   *THE DESCENT OF MAN, AND OTHER STORIES.*
          New York: Scribner's, 1904.
          Contents: "The Mission of Jane"; "The Other Two";
          "The Quicksand"; "The Dilettante"; "The Reckoning";
          "Expiation"; "The Lady's Maid's Bell"; "A Venetian
          Night's Entertainment."

B4   *THE HERMIT AND THE WILD WOMAN AND
          OTHER STORIES.*
          New York: Scribner's, 1908.
          Contents: "The Last Asset"; "In Trust"; "The Pretext";
          "The Verdict"; "The Pot-Boiler"; "The Best Man."

B5   *TALES OF MEN AND GHOSTS.*
          New York: Scribner's, 1910.
          Contents: "The Bolted Door"; "His Father's Son"; "The
          Daunt Diana"; "The Debt"; "Full Circle"; "The Legend";
          "The Eyes"; "The Blond Beast"; "Afterward"; "The
          Letters."

B6   *XINGU AND OTHER STORIES.*
          New York: Scribner's, 1916.

Contents: "Coming Home"; "Autres Temps ... "; "Kerfol"; "The Long Run"; "The Triumph of Night"; "The Choice"; "Bunner Sisters."

B7   *HERE AND BEYOND.*
New York: Appleton, 1926.
Contents: "Miss Mary Pask"; "The Young Gentlemen"; "Bewitched"; "The Seed of the Faith"; "The Temperate Zone"; "Velvet Ear-Pads."

B8   *CERTAIN PEOPLE.*
New York: Appleton, 1930.
Contents: "Atrophy"; "A Bottle of Perrier"; "After Holbein"; "Dieu D'Amour"; "The Refugees"; "Mr. Jones."

B9   *HUMAN NATURE.*
New York: Appleton, 1933.
Contents: "Her Son"; "The Day of the Funeral"; "A Glimpse"; "Joy in the House"; "Diagnosis."

B10   *THE WORLD OVER.*
New York: Appleton-Century, 1936.
Contents: "Charm Incorporated"; "Pomegranate Seed"; "Permanent Wave"; "Confession"; "Roman Fever"; "The Looking-Glass"; "Duration."

B11   *GHOSTS.*
New York: Appleton-Century, 1937.
Contents: "Preface"; "All Souls'"; "The Eyes"; "Afterward"; "The Lady's Maid's Bell"; "Kerfol"; "The Triumph of Night"; "Miss Mary Pask"; "Bewitched"; "Mr. Jones"; "Pomegranate Seed"; "A Bottle of Perrier."

B12   *THE BEST SHORT STORIES OF EDITH WHARTON.*
New York: Scribner's, 1958.
Edited, with an introduction by Wayne Andrews. See L2 for Introduction. Contains: "Roman Fever"; "Xingu"; "The Other Two"; "Pomegranate Seed"; "Souls Belated"; "The Angel at the Grave"; "The Last Asset"; "After Holbein"; "Bunner Sisters"; "Autres Temps ... ."

B13   *ROMAN FEVER AND OTHER STORIES.*
       New York: Scribner's, 1964. Rpt. with Introduction by
       Cynthia Griffin Wolff. New York: Collier Books, 1987.
       Contains "Roman Fever"; "Xingu"; "The Other Two";
       "Souls Belated"; "The Angel at the Grave"; "The Last
       Asset"; "After Holbein"; "Autres Temps ... ." For Wolff's
       Introduction see T37.

B13.1 *ROMAN FEVER AND OTHER STORIES.*
       Introduction by Marilyn French. New York: Berkley,
       1981.
       For short story titles see B13. Introduction is also her
       Introduction (minus the last section on *HofM*) to *The
       House of Mirth*, R4.28.

B13.2 *ROMAN FEVER AND OTHER STORIES.*
       Introduction by Marilyn French. London: Virago, 1985.
       For short story titles see B13. For Introduction see T9.

B14   *THE COLLECTED SHORT STORIES OF EDITH
       WHARTON.*
       Ed. R.W.B. Lewis. New York: Scribner's, 1968.
       See T17 for Lewis's introduction. Two volumes. Volume
       One contains all the stories from B1, B2, B3, B4 plus
       Chapter II of *The Writing of Fiction* and previously
       uncollected "Mrs. Manstey's View"; "The Fullness of
       Life"; "That Good May Come"; "The Lamp of Psyche";
       "The Valley of Childish Things, and Other Emblems";
       "April Showers"; "Friends"; "The Line of Least
       Resistance"; "The Letter"; "The House of the Dead
       Hand"; "The Introducers"; "Les Metteurs en Scène"
       (trans. Becky Nolan). Volume Two contains all the
       short stories from B5, B6 (except *Bunner Sisters*), B7,
       B8, B9, B10, "Writing a War Story" and the Preface and
       "All Souls'" from B11. For reviews see T12 and T15.

B15   *THE GHOST STORIES OF EDITH WHARTON.*
       New York: Scribner's, 1973. Rpt. New York: Popular
       Library, 1976.

Contains: "Preface" from *Ghosts*, "The Lady's Maid's Bell"; "The Eyes"; "Afterward"; "Kerfol"; "The Triumph of Night"; "Miss Mary Pask"; "Bewitched"; "Mr. Jones"; "Pomegranate Seed"; "The Looking Glass"; "All Souls'"; "An Autobiographical Postscript" (part of the original manuscript of *A Backward Glance*). For analysis of the collection see T34.

B16   *QUARTET.*
Kentfield, California: Allen Press, 1975.
Contains: "Roman Fever"; "The Other Two"; "The Last Asset"; "Afterward".

C1-C87 *The Short Stories*

C1   "After Holbein." *Saturday Evening Post* 200 (5 May 1928): 6.
In B8. Rpt. B12, B13, B14, J2. See T11, T19, T26, T30, T37.

C2   "Afterward." *The Century Magazine* 79 (January 1910): 321-339.
In B5. Rpt. B11, B14, B15, B16. See T20, T34.

C3   "All Souls'." From B11.
Rpt. B11, B14, B15. See T8, T18, T20, T34, T40.

C4   "The Angel at the Grave." *Scribner's Magazine* 29 (February 1901):158-166.
Rpt. B12, B13, B14. See T37.

C5   "April Showers." *Youth's Companion* 74 (18 January 1900):25-28.
Rpt. B14.

C6   "Atrophy." *Ladies' Home Journal* 44 (November 1927):
            8.
            In B8. Rpt. B14. See T30.

C7   "Autres Temps ... ." As "Other Times, Other Manners."
            The Century Magazine 82 (July 1911): 344-352; 82
            (August 1911): 587-594.
            In B6. Rpt. B12, B13, B14, J2. See T9, T37.

C8   "The Best Man." *Collier's* 35 (2. September 1905): 14.
            In B4. Rpt. B14.

C9   "Bewitched." *Pictorial Review* 26 (March 1925): 14.
            In B7. Rpt. B11, B14, B15. See T20, T26, T34.

C10   "The Blond Beast." *Scribner's Magazine* 48 (September
            1910): 291-304.
            In B5. Rpt. B14. See T16.

C11   "The Bolted Door." *Scribner's Magazine* 45 (March
            1909): 288-308.
            In B5. Rpt. B14.

C12   "A Bottle of Perrier."
             In B8. Rpt. B11, B14, J2, J5. See T20.

C13   "Bunner Sisters." *Scribner's Magazine* 60 (October 1916):
            439-458; 60 (November 1916): 575-596.
            In B6. Rpt. B12, B14, J2, J5, J7, J9. See T31.

C14   "Charm Incorporated." As "Bread Upon the Waters."
            Hearst's International-Cosmopolitan 96 (February 1934):
            28.
            In B9. Rpt. B14.

C15   "The Choice." *The Century Magazine* 77 (November
            1908): 32-40.
            In B6. Rpt. B14. See T24.

C16   "Coming Home." *Scribner's Magazine* 58 (December 1915): 702-718.
In B6. Rpt. B14.

C17   "Confession." From B10.
Rpt. B14.

C18   "The Confessional." From B2.
Rpt. B14.

C19   "'Copy': A Dialogue." *Scribner's Magazine* 27 (June 1900): 657-663.
In B2. Rpt. B14.

C20   "A Coward." From B1.
Rpt. B14.

C21   "A Cup of Cold Water." From B1.
Rpt. B14.

C22   "The Daunt Diana." *Scribner's Magazine* 46 (July 1909): 35-41.
In B5. Rpt. B14. See T26.

C23   "The Day of the Funeral." From B9.
Rpt. B14. See T30.

C24   "The Debt." *Scribner's Magazine* 46 (August 1909): 165-172.
In B5. Rpt. B14.

C25   "The Descent of Man." *Scribner's Magazine* 35 (March 1904): 313-322.
In B3. Rpt. B14. See T33.

C26   "Diagnosis." *Ladies' Home Journal* 47 (November 1930): 8.
In B9. Rpt. B14. See T30.

C27   "Dieu d'Amour." *Ladies' Home Journal* 45 (October
           1928): 6.
           In B8. Rpt. B14.

C28   "The Dilettante." *Harper's Magazine* 108 (December
           1903): 139-143.
           In B3. Rpt. B14. See T14.

C29   "The Duchess at Prayer." *Scribner's Magazine* 28 (August
           1900): 153-160.
           In B2. Rpt. B14. See T6, T7, T30.

C30   "Duration." From B10.
           Rpt. B14.

C31   "Expiation." *Hearst's International-Cosmopolitan* 36
           (December 1903): 209-222.
           In B3. Rpt. B14.

C32   "The Eyes." *Scribner's Monthly* 47 (June 1910): 671-680.
           In B5 and B11. Rpt. B14, B15, J5. See T18, T20, T34.

C33   "Friends." *Youth's Companion* 74 (23 August, 30 August
           1900): 405-406; 417-418.
           Rpt. B14.

C34   "Full Circle." *Scribner's Magazine* 46 (October 1909):
           408-419.
           In B5. Rpt. B14.

C35   "The Fullness of Life." *Scribner's Magazine* 14
           (December 1893): 699-704.

C36   "A Glimpse." *Saturday Evening Post* 205 (12 November
           1932): 16.
           In B9. Rpt. B14.

C37   "Her Son." *Scribner's Magazine* 91 (February 1932): 65.
           In B9. Rpt. B14. See T26.

C38   "The Hermit and the Wild Woman." *Scribner's Magazine* 39 (February 1906): 145-156.
In B4. Rpt. B14. See T35.

C39   "His Father's Son." *Scribner's Magazine* 45 (June 1909): 657-665.
In B5. Rpt. B14. See T26.

C40   "The House of the Dead Hand." *Atlantic Monthly* 94 (August 1904): 145-160.
Reprint *Atlantic Harvest*. Boston: Little, Brown, 1947. B14.

C41   "In Trust." *Appleton's Booklover's Magazine* 7 (April 1906): 432-440.
In B4. Rpt. B14.

C42   "The Introducers." *Ainslee's* 16 (December 1905): 139-148; 16 (January 1906): 61-67.
Rpt. B14.

C43   "A Journey." In B1.
Rpt. B14. See T30.

C44   "Joy in the House." From B9.
Rpt. B14. See T30.

C45   "Kerfol." *Scribner's Magazine* 59 (March 1916): 329-341.
In B6. Rpt. B11, B14, B15. See T18, T20, T38.

C46   "The Lady's Maid's Bell." *Scribner's Magazine* 32 (November 1902): 549-560.
In B3. Rpt. B11, B14, B15, J2.

C47   "The Lamp of Psyche." *Scribner's Magazine* 18 (October 1895):418-428.
Rpt. B14.

C48   "The Last Asset." *Scribner's Magazine* 36 (August 1904): 150-168.

In B4. Rpt. B12, B13, B14, B16, J11. See T37.

C49   "The Legend." *Scribner's Monthly* 47 (March 1910): 278-
         291.
         In B5. Rpt. B14.

C50   "The Letter." *Harper's Magazine* 108 (April 1904): 781-
         789.
         Added to the first English edition of B3. London:
         Macmillan, 1904. Rpt. B14.

C51   "The Letters." *The Century Magazine* 80 (August 1910):
         485-492; 80 (September 1910): 641-650; 80 (October
         1910): 812-819.
         In B5. Rpt. B14.

C52   "The Line of Least Resistance." *Lippincott's* 66 (October
         1900): 559-570.
         Rpt. B14.

C53   "The Long Run." *Atlantic Monthly* 109 (February 1912):
         145-163.
         In B6. Rpt. B14.

C54   "The Looking Glass." From B10.
         Rpt. B14, B15. In T30, T34.

C55   "Les Metteurs en Scène." *Revue des Deux Mondes* 67
         (October 1908): 692-708.
         Rpt. in English translation, B14.

C56   "Miss Mary Pask." *Pictorial Review* 26 (April 1925): 8.
         In B7. Rpt. B11, B14, B15. See T20, T34.

C57   "The Mission of Jane." *Harper's Magazine* 106
         (December 1902): 63-74.
         In B3. Rpt. B14. See T13.

C58   "The Moving Finger." *Harper's Magazine* 102 (March
         1901): 627-632.

In B2. Rpt. B14.

C59   "Mr. Jones." *Ladies' Home Journal* 45 (April 1928): 3.
       In B8. Rpt. B11, B14, B15. See T20, T34.

C60   "Mrs. Manstey's View." *Scribner's Magazine* 10 (July
       1891): 117-122.

C61   "The Muse's Tragedy." *Scribner's Magazine* 25 (January
       1899): 77-84.
       From B1. Rpt. B14.

C62   "The Other Two." *Collier's* 32 (13 February 1904): 15.
       In B3. Rpt. B12, B13, B14, B16, J2, J12. See T4, T9,
       T26.

C63   "The Pelican." *Scribner's Magazine* 24 (November 1898):
       620-629.
       Rpt. B1, B14, J5.

C64   "Permanent Wave." From B10.
       Rpt. B14. See T30.

C65   "Pomegranate Seed." *Saturday Evening Post* 203 (25
       April 1931): 6.
       In B10. Rpt. B11, B12, B15, J5, T3. See T20, T21, T34,
       T40.

C66   "The Portrait." From B1.
       Rpt. B14.

C67   "The Pot-Boiler." *Scribner's Magazine* 36 (December
       1904): 696-712.
       In B4. Rpt. B14.

C68   "The Pretext." *Scribner's Magazine* 44 (August 1908):
       173-187.
       In B4. Rpt. B14. See T2.

C69   "The Quicksand." *Harper's Magazine* 105 (June 1902):
           13-21.
           In B3. Rpt. B14.

C70   "The Reckoning." *Harper's Magazine* 105 (August 1902):
           342-355.
           In B3. Rpt. B14.

C71   "The Recovery." *Harper's Magazine* 102 (February 1901):
           468-477.
           From B2. Rpt. B14. See T26.

C72   "The Refugees." *Saturday Evening Post* 191 (18 January
           1919): 3.
           In B8. Rpt. B14.

C73   "The Rembrandt." *Hearst's International-Cosmopolitan*
           29 (August 1900): 429-437.
           In B2. Rpt. B14, J5.

C74   "Roman Fever." *Liberty* 11 (10 November 1934): 10-14.
           In B10. Rpt. B12, B13, B14, B16, J2. See T25, T30.

C75   "The Seed of the Faith." *Scribner's Magazine* 65 (January
           1919): 17-33.
           In B7. Rpt. B14.

C76   "Souls Belated." From B1.
           Rpt. B12, B13, B14. See T37.

C77   "The Temperate Zone." *Pictorial Review* 25 (February
           1924): 5.
           In B7. Rpt. B14.

C78   "That Good May Come." *Scribner's Magazine* 15 (May
           1894): 629-642.
           Rpt. B14.

C79   "The Triumph of Night." *Scribner's Magazine* 56 (August
           1914): 149-162.

In B6. Rpt. B11, B14, B15 and *Haunted New England.*
Ed. Charles G. Waugh, Martin H. Greenberg, Frank D.
McSherry, Jr. Dublin, New Hampshire: Yankee Books,
1988. See T20, T34.

C80   "The Twilight of the God." From B1.
Rpt. B14.

C81   "The Valley of Childish Things, and Other Emblems."
The Century Magazine 52 (July 1896): 467-469.
Rpt. B14.

C82   "Velvet Ear Pads." From B7.
Rpt. B14.

C83   "A Venetian Night's Entertainment." *Scribner's Magazine*
34 (December 1903): 640-651.
In B3. Rpt. B14.

C84   "The Verdict." *Scribner's Magazine* 43 (June 1908): 689-
693.
In B4. Rpt. B14.

C85   "Writing a War Story." *Woman's Home Companion* 45
(September 1919): 17-19.
Rpt. B14.

C86   "Xingu." *Scribner's Magazine* 50 (December 1911): 684-
696.
In B6. Rpt. B12, B13, B14, J2, J12. See T10, T26, T37.

C87   "The Young Gentlemen." *Pictorial Review* 27 (February
1926): 29.
In B7. Rpt. B14.

D1-D3   *The Poetry Collections*

D1   *VERSES.*
         Newport: 1878.
         Privately printed edition of Wharton's adolescent poetry.
         Contains: "Le Viol D'Amour"; "Vespers"; "Bettine to
         Goethe"; "Spring Song"; "Prophecies of Summer";
         "Song"; "Heaven"; "'Maiden, Arise'"; "Spring"; "May
         Marian"; "Opportunities"; "The Last Token"; "Raffaelle
         to the Fornarina"; "Chriemhild of Burgundy"; "Some
         Woman to Some Man"; "Lines on Chaucer"; "What We
         Shall Say Fifty Years Hence, of Our Fancy-Dress
         Quadrille"; "Nothing More"; "June and December";
         "October"; "A Woman I Know"; "Daisies"; "Impromptu";
         "Notre Dame des Fleurs."   German translations: Three
         Songs from the German of Emanuel Geibel; Longing
         (from the German of Schiller); A Song (Freely
         translated from the German of Rückert).

D2   *ARTEMIS TO ACTÆON AND OTHER VERSE.*
         New York: Scribner's, 1909.
         Contains: "Artemis to Actæon"; "Life"; "Vesalius in
         Zante"; "Margaret of Cortona";. "A Torchbearer"; "The
         Mortal Lease"; "Experience"; "Grief"; "Chartres"; "Two
         Backgrounds"; "The Tomb of Ilaria Giunigi"; "The One
         Grief"; "The Eumenides"; "Orpheus"; "An Autumn
         Sunset"; "Moonrise over Tyringham"; "All Souls'"; "All
         Saints"; "The Old Pole Star"; "A Grave"; "Non Dolet";
         "A Hunting-Song"; "Survival"; "Uses"; "A Meeting"; note
         on Vesalius.

D3   *TWELVE POEMS.*
         London: Medici Society, 1926.
         Contains: "Nightingales in Provence"; "Mistral in the
         Maquis"; "Les Salettes"; "Dieu D'Amour"; "Segesta";
         "The Tryst"; "Battle Sleep"; "Elegy"; "With the Tide"; "La
         Folle Du Logis"; "The First Year"; "Alternative
         Epitaphs."

D4.1-D4.48 Poems Published Individually

D4.1 "All Souls'." *Scribner's Magazine* 45 (January 1909): 22-23.
Rpt. D2.

D4.2 "Areopagus." *Atlantic Monthly* 45 (March 1880): 335.

D4.3 "Artemis to Actæon." *Scribner's Magazine* 31 (June 1902): 661-662.
Rpt. D2.

D4.4 "An Autumn Sunset." *Scribner's Magazine* 16 (October 1894): 419.
Rpt. D2.

D4.5 "Battle Sleep." *The Century Magazine* 90 (September 1915): 736.
Rpt. D3.

D4.6 "Botticelli's Madonna in the Louvre." *Scribner's Magazine* 9 (January 1891): 74.

D4.7 "The Bread of Angels." *Harper's Magazine* 105 (September 1902): 583-585.

D4.8 "Chartres." *Scribner's Magazine* 14 (September 1893): 287.
Rpt. D2.

D4.9 "The Comrade." *Atlantic Monthly* 106 (December 1910): 785-787.

D4.10 "Euryalus." *Atlantic Monthly* 64 (December 1889): 761.

D4.11 "Experience." *Scribner's Magazine* 13 (January 1893): 91.

D4.12   "A Failure." *Atlantic Monthly* 45 (April 1880): 464-465.
          Unsigned verse.

D4.13   "Garden Valedictory." *Scribner's Magazine* 83 (January
          1928): 81.

D4.14   "A Grave." *Current Literature* 46 (June 1909): 685.
          Rpt. D2.

D4.15   "The Great Blue Tent." *New York Times* 25 August
          1915, p.10.

D.4.16   "Had I Been Only." *Scribner's Magazine* 84 (August
          1928): 215.

D4.17   "Happiness." *Scribner's Magazine* 6 (December 1889):
          715.

D4.18   "High Pasture." See R2.14.

D4.19   "The Hymn of the Lusitania." *New York Herald* 7 May
          1915, p.1.

D4.20   "In Provence." *Yale Review* n.s. 9 (January 1920): 346-
          347.

D4.21   "Jade." *The Century Magazine* 49 (January 1895): 391.

D4.22   "The Last Giustiniani." *Scribner's Magazine* 6 (October
          1889): 405-406.

D4.23   "Life." *Scribner's Magazine* 15 (June 1894): 739.

D4.24   "Life." *Atlantic Monthly* 102 (October 1908): 501-504.
          Rpt. D2.

D4.25   "Lyrical Epigrams." *Yale Review.* 9 (January 1920): 348.

D4.26   "Margaret of Cortona." *Harper's Magazine* 103
          (November 1901): 884-887.

Rpt. D2.

D4.27   "Moonrise Over Tyringham." *The Century Magazine* 76 (July 1908): 356-357.
Rpt. D2.

D4.28   "Mould and Vase."
Atlantic Monthly 88 (September 1901): 343.

D4.29   "Ogrin the Hermit." *Atlantic Monthly* 104 (December 1909): 844-848.
See T35.

D4.30   "The Old Pole Star." *Scribner's Magazine* 43 (January 1908): 68.
Rpt. D2.

D4.31   "'On Active Service'; American Expeditionary Force (R.S., August 12, 1918)." *Scribner's Magazine* 64 (November 1918): 619.

D4.32   "The One Grief." *Scribner's Magazine* 24 (July 1898): 90.
Rpt. D2.

D4.33   "Only a Child." New York *World*, 30 May 1879, p. 5.
Rpt. *Yale University Library Gazette* 30 (October 1965): 67-69. See U10.

D4.34   "The Parting Day." *Atlantic Monthly* 45 (March 1880): 335.
Unsigned verse.

D4.35   "Patience." *Atlantic Monthly* 45 (April 1880): 548-549.
Unsigned verse.

D4.36   "Phaedra." *Scribner's Magazine* 23 (January 1898): 68.

D4.37   "Pomegranate Seed." *Scribner's Magazine* 51 (March 1912): 284-291.
Dramatic poem.

D4.38   "The Sonnet." *The Century Magazine* 43 (November 1891): 113.

D4.39   "Summer Afternoon (Bodiam Castle, Sussex)." *Scribner's Magazine* 49 (March 1911): 277-278.

D4.40   "Terminus." In Lewis, N17.
Believed to relate to a night Wharton spent with Morton Fullerton.

D4.41   "The Tomb of Ilaria Giunigi." *Scribner's Magazine* 9 (February 1891): 156.
Rpt. D2.

D4.42   "A Torchbearer." *Scribner's Magazine* 33 (April 1903): 504-505.
Rpt. D2.

D4.43   "Two Backgrounds." *Scribner's Magazine* 12 (November 1892): 550.
Rpt. D2.

D4.44   "Uses." *Scribner's Magazine* 31 (February 1902): 180.
Rpt. D2.

D4.45   "Vesalius in Zante." *North American Review* 175 (November 1902): 625-631.
Rpt D2.

D4.46   "Wants." *Atlantic Monthly* 45 (May 1880): 599.
Unsigned verse.

D4.47   "With the Tide." *Saturday Evening Post* 191 (29 March 1919): 8.

D4.48   "You and You." *The Pittsburgh Chronicle Telegraph*, 24 January 1919, p.6.

E1-E9   The Nonfiction Volumes

E1   *THE DECORATION OF HOUSES.*
            Edith Wharton and Ogden Codman, Jr. New York:
            Scribner's, 1897.
            Note reprint with introductory notes, New York:
            Norton, 1978. See V95 and V96.

E2   *ITALIAN VILLAS AND THEIR GARDENS.*
            Illustrated with Pictures by Maxfield Parrish. New York:
            The Century Co., 1904.
            See the 1988 Da Capo Press reprint with introductory
            notes by Arthur Ross, Henry Hope Reed and Thomas
            S. Hayes. Reed's essay, "Edith Wharton and the
            Classical Landscape of America" traces the history of
            gardening and classical design in America, as it relates
            to Edith Wharton's era. Hayes's "Edith Wharton's
            Italian Garden at the Mount" describes the planning
            and execution of the gardens at EW's home, The
            Mount, in Lenox, Massachusetts.

E3   *ITALIAN BACKGROUNDS.*
            Illustrated by E.C. Peixotto. New York: Scribner's, 1905.

E4   *A MOTOR-FLIGHT THROUGH FRANCE.*
            New York: Scribner's, 1908.

E5   *FIGHTING   FRANCE   FROM   DUNKERQUE   TO
            BELFORT.*
            New York: Scribner's, 1915.

E6   *FRENCH WAYS AND THEIR MEANING.*
            New York: Appleton, 1919.

E7   *IN MOROCCO.*
            New York: Scribner's, 1920.

Reprinted in London in 1984 as part of the Century Travellers Series with a brief biographical introduction and appreciation.

E8   *THE WRITING OF FICTION.*
New York: Scribner's, 1925.

E9   *A BACKWARD GLANCE.*
New York: Appleton-Century, 1934.
Scribner's paperback, 1985. Henry James material reprinted in Chinese, translated by Longyi Pu [P'ulung i], in *Foreign Literatures* 8 (1986): 77-87.

F1-F5.5 Articles

F1-Travel

F1   "A Second Motor-Flight Through France." *Atlantic Monthly* 101 (January 1908): 3-9; 101 (February 1908): 167-173; 101 (March 1908): 345-352; 101 (April 1908): 474-482.
Travel serial in four parts.

F2.1-F2.9 Reviews

F2.1   "The Blashfields' Italian Cities." *Bookman* 13 (August 1901): 563-564.
Review of Edwin H. and Evangeline W. Blashfield, *Italian Cities*.

F2.2   Review: *Ulysses: A Drama*, by Stephen Phillips. *Bookman* 15 (April 1902): 168-170.

F2.3   Review: *George Eliot*, by Leslie Stephen. *Bookman* 15 (May 1902): 247-251.

F2.4   Review: Mrs. Fiske's performance in *Tess*. *New York Commercial Advertiser* (7 May 1902): 9.
Review of dramatization of Thomas Hardy's novel *Tess of the d'Urbervilles*.

F2.5   "Mr. Paul on the Poetry of Matthew Arnold." *Lamp* 26 (February 1903): 51-54.
Review of Herbert W. Paul's *Matthew Arnold*.

F2.6   "Mr. Sturgis's 'Belchamber.'" *Bookman* 21 (May 1905): 307-310.
Review of Howard Sturgis's *Belchamber*.

F2.7   "Maurice Hewlett's '*The Fool Errant*.'" *Bookman* 22
        (September 1905): 64-67.
        Review of Maurice Hewlett's *The Fool Errant*.

F2.8   "The Sonnets of Eugene Lee-Hamilton." *Bookman* 26
        (November 1907): 251-253.
        Review of Eugene Lee-Hamilton's *The Sonnets of the
        Wingless Hours*.

F2.9   "Henry James in His Letters." *Quarterly Review* 234 (July
        1920): 188-202.
        Review of Percy Lubbock's *The Letters of Henry James*.
        Second half reprinted in *Henry James: A Collection of
        Critical Essays*, ed. Leon Edel. Englewood Cliffs, New
        Jersey: Prentice-Hall, 1963.

F3.1-F3.16   General Articles

F3.1   "More Loves of an Englishwoman." *Bookman* 12
        (February 1901): 562-563.
        Parody.

F3.2   "The Three Francescas." *North American Review* 175
        (July 1902): 17-30.
        "The almost simultaneous production of three plays on
        the subject of Francesca da Rimini, by playwrights
        [Phillips, d'Annunzio, and Crawford] of three different
        nationalities, illustrates in an interesting manner that
        impulse of the creative fancy which so often leads one
        imaginative writer to take up a theme already dealt with
        by another."

F3.3   "The Vice of Reading." *North American Review* 177
        (October 1903): 513-521.

F3.4   "George Cabot Lodge." *Scribner's Magazine* 47 (February
        1910): 236-239.

F3.5   "The Criticism of Fiction." *Times Literary Supplement*,
         14 May 1914, 229-230.

F3.6   "Jean du Breuil de Saint-Germain." *Revue Hebdomadaire*
         24 (15 May 1915): 351-361.

F3.7   "The Great American Novel." *Yale Review* n.s. 16 (July
         1922): 646-656. Rpt. *The Yale Review* 75.2 (Winter
         1986): 229-238.

F3.8   "William C. Brownell." *Scribner's Magazine* 84
         (November 1928: 596-602.
         Rpt. in *W.C. Brownell: Tributes and Appreciations*. New
         York: Scribner's, 1929.

F3.9   "A Cycle of Reviewing." *Spectator* 141 (3 November
         1928), supplement: 44-45.

F3.10   "Visibility in Fiction." *Yale Review* n.s. 18 (March 1929):
         480-488.

F3.11   "The Writing of *Ethan Frome*." *Colophon*, part II, no.
         4 (September 1932): n.p. Rpt. *Breaking into Print*, edited
         by Elmer Adler, 190. New York: 1937.

F3.12   "Confessions of a Novelist." *Atlantic Monthly* 151 (April
         1933): 385-392.

F3.13   "Tendencies in Modern Fiction." *Saturday Review of
         Literature* 10 (27 January 1934): 433-434.

F3.14   "Permanent Values in Fiction." *Saturday Review of
         Literature* 10 (7 April 1934): 603-604.

F3.15   "Reconsideration of Proust." *Saturday Review of
         Literature* 11 (27 October 1934): 233-234.

F3.16   "Souvenirs du Bourget d'Outre-mer." *Revue
         Hebdomadaire* 45 (21 June 1936): 266-286.

Written on Bourget's death. See Jean Gooder's article on *The Reef* (R8.12) for a discussion of Wharton's relationship with Bourget and commentary on article.

F4.1-F4.6 Autobiographical Articles

F4.1 "My Work Among the Women Workers of Paris." *New York Times Magazine*, 28 November 1915, 1-2.

F4.2 *Edith Wharton's War Charities in France.*
Mrs. Wharton's General Report from 1914-1918 and *Report of the New York Committee*. Microfilm. NYPL.

F4.3 "The French (As Seen by an American)." *Scribner's Magazine* 62 (December 1917): 676-683.

F4.4 "How Paris Welcomed the King." *Reveille* No. 3 (February 1919): 367-369.

F4.5 "Christmas Tinsel." *Delineator* 103 (December 1923): 11.

F4.6 "A Little Girl's New York." *Harper's Magazine* 176 (March 1938): 356-364.

F5.1-F5.5 Prefaces

F5.1 "Introduction." *A Village Romeo and Juliet*, by Gottfried Keller. Trans. by A.C. Bahlmann with an introduction by Edith Wharton. New York: Scribner's, 1914.

F5.2 Preface. *Futility* by William Gerhardi. Preface by Edith Wharton. New York: Ouffield, 1922.

F5.3 "Preface." *Speak to the Earth: Wanderings and Reflections among Elephants and Mountains*, by Vivianne de Watteville. London: Methuen, 1935.

F5.4   "Foreword." *Benediction* by Claude Silve. Trans. Robert
            Norton. Foreword by Edith Wharton. New York:
            Appleton-Century, 1936.
            Claude Silve was the pen name of Philomène de la
            Forest-Divonne.

F5.5   "Foreword." *Ethan Frome*: *A Dramatization of Edith
            Wharton's Novel* by Owen Davis and Donald Davis. New
            York: Scribner's, 1936.

G1-G4 Translations, Editions, Adaptations

G1   *The Joy of Living*. New York: Scribner's, 1902.
            Translation of Hermann Sudermann's *Es Lebe Das
            Leben*: *A Play in Five Acts*. See W7.

G2   *The Book of the Homeless*. Edited by Edith Wharton.
            New York: Scribner's, 1916.
            See W10.

G3   *Eternal Passion in English Poetry*.
            Selected by Edith Wharton and Robert Norton. New
            York: Appleton-Century, 1939.

G4   *The House of Mirth*: *The Play of the Novel*. Edith
            Wharton and Clyde Fitch. Edited, with an Introduction,
            Notes and Appendixes by Glenn Loney. Rutherford:
            Associated University Presses, 1981.
            Gives, along with the script, details of the Fitch-
            Wharton collaboration on the play of *The House of
            Mirth*, which closed after 14 performances. Analyzes
            differences between play and novel. Concludes that an
            oversimplified plot, simplified motivation and misplaced
            settings as well as audience desire for a comedy of
            manners accounted for dramatic failure. Includes
            appendices: Dresses and costuming directions, reviews,

Fitch correspondence, Wharton's discussions of the project, Fitch interviews. See R4.70 and R4.71.

H1 The Letters

H1   *The Letters of Edith Wharton.*
Edited with an introduction by R.W.B. Lewis and Nancy Lewis. New York: Scribner's, 1988.
Contains approximately 400 letters of EW, written between 1874 and 1937. Excellent annotations. Well-indexed, with photographs and lengthy introduction. Introduction discusses letter writing in her life, the masculine and feminine qualities of her mind, the finding of the Fullerton letters and the new aspects of the affair that emerge, her attitude toward feminism and notes pertinent aspects of her relationship with her various correspondents.

I.1-I.7 Manuscript Material

I.1   "Beatrice Palmato." Published fragment. In Lewis, N17, and Wolff, N28.

I.2   "Cruise of the Fleetwing." Unpublished short story fragment. Yale Beinecke. See W9.

I.3   "Life and I." Unpublished autobiographical fragment available Yale Beinecke.

I.4   "Literature." Unpublished manuscript. Yale Beinecke. See W8.

I.5   "The Love Diary." Unpublished manuscript.

Referred to as both the Fullerton journal and the Love Diary. Started in October, 1907, at Lenox, continuing into 1908. Written to Fullerton and titled "The Life Apart."   See Lewis, N17, for a complete discussion of the two overlapping diaries of 1908. Before the Lewis biography this diary was thought to concern Walter Berry. Indiana University Lilley Library.

I.6   "Mother Earth." Unpublished short story fragment. Yale. See W9.

I.7   "New England." Unpublished short story fragment. Yale. See W9.

J1-J14   The Major Collections

J1   *The Collected Works of Edith Wharton.*
          10 Volumes. New York: Scribner's, 1914.
          Contains *Crucial Instances, Sanctuary, Descent of Man, Madame de Treymes, The Greater Inclination, The Touchstone, The Hermit and the Wild Woman, Ethan Frome, The Custom of the Country, The Fruit of the Tree, The House of Mirth, Tales of Men and Ghosts, The Valley of Decision, The Reef.*

J2   *An Edith Wharton Treasury.*
          Edited and with an introduction by Arthur Hobson Quinn. New York: Appleton-Century-Crofts, 1950.
          Contains *The Age of Innocence, The Old Maid,* "After Holbein," "A Bottle of Perrier," "The Lady's Maid's Bell," "Roman Fever," "The Other Two," *Madame de Treymes,* "Xingu," "Autres Temps ... ," "Bunner Sisters." Warmly appreciative introduction covers many of the short stories and novels, defining Wharton as our chief social satirist whose skill lay "in making her characters dominate the situations, which yet in their turn illuminate both the past and the future of her

characters." Notes most of her great moments are dominated by her heroines, her women better drawn than her men. Praises style.

J3   *The Selected Works of Edith Wharton.*
Three volumes. London: John Lehmann, 1953-1954.
The House of Mirth, The Age of Innocence, The Custom of the Country.

J4   *Centennial Edition.*
Four Volumes. New York; Appleton-Century-Crofts, 1962.
The Age of Innocence, The Children, Hudson River Bracketed, The Gods Arrive.

J5   *The Edith Wharton Reader.*
Edited and introduced by Louis Auchincloss. New York: Scribner's, 1965.
Contains: "Little Girl" from chapter III of *A Backward Glance,* "The Pelican," "The Rembrandt," Book I of *The House of Mirth,* "The Eyes," *Ethan Frome,* "Bunner Sisters," "With the Tide," Book I of *The Age of Innocence, False Dawn, The Old Maid,* "A Bottle of Perrier," "Pomegranate Seed," "Henry James" from Chapter VIII of *A Backward Glance.* Introduction argues that when she wrote about the New York upper classes she was America's first-ranking novelist of manners. Praises her observant eye, the perfection of her ghost stories, but contends that after WWI she "allowed herself to become a crank" in assuming the role of censor of modern morals.

J6   *The Constable Edith Wharton.*
Four volumes. London: Constable, 1965-1966.
Contains: *Ethan Frome, Summer, The Custom of the Country, The House of Mirth, The Age of Innocence.*

J7   *Madame de Treymes and Others.*
New York: Scribner's, 1970.

Contains: *The Touchstone, Sanctuary, Madame de Treymes,* "Bunner Sisters."

J8   *The Edith Wharton Omnibus.*
        Introduction by Gore Vidal. New York: Scribner's, 1978. Contains: *The Age of Innocence, Ethan Frome, False Dawn, The Old Maid, The Spark, New Year's Day.* Introduction appeared previously in slightly different form as "Of Writers and Class: In Praise of Edith Wharton." *Atlantic* 241 (February 1978): 64-67. Argues Wharton has been denied her rightful place in American literature because of her sex, class and residence in France. Maintains, despite her reputation as a stuffy *grande dame,* she was always direct and honest about sexual relationships. Speculates that, with the decline in prejudice against women writers: "They look to be exactly what they are: giants, equals, the tutelary and benign gods of our American literature."

J9   *Madame de Treymes and Others: Four Short Novels.* Introduction by Marilyn French. London: Virago, 1984. Introduction contains feminist commentary on *The Touchstone, Sanctuary, Madame de Treymes* and "Bunner Sisters," which comprise the volume. Terms the collection "a coherent whole, a set of studies, each probing more deeply than the preceding one into self-sacrifice." Contends Wharton believed that gender-based natures were conferred at birth and yet "offers ironic commentary on sex-roles and on men's perception of women."

J10   *Wharton: Novels.*
        Ed. R.W.B. Lewis. New York: Library of America, 1986. Contains: *The House of Mirth, The Reef, The Custom of the Country, The Age of Innocence.*

J11   *The Works of Edith Wharton.*
        Introduction by Ruth Lake Tepper. New York: Avenel Books, 1987.

Contains: *Ethan Frome, The House of Mirth*, B5.
Important as an available text of *Tales of Men and
Ghosts*. Introduction offers biographical insights into the
works included, and comments on anti-Semitism of
Rosedale's characterization. Concludes Wharton was "a
liberated woman, attaining [the status of one of
America's most famous and popular authors] against
great odds."

J12   *Ethan Frome and Other Short Fiction.*
        Introduction by Mary Gordon. New York: Bantam,
        1987.
        Contains *Ethan Frome, The Touchstone,* "The Last
        Asset," "Xingu," and "The Other Two."   Insightful
        introduction offers critical commentary on each of the
        stories included. Contends EW's view is tragic, and her
        heart is with the sensitive, "the impetuous, the sexually
        responsive" but her reason convinced her the individual
        must be sacrificed for the good of the whole. Cites the
        powerful language of *Ethan Frome* and the beautiful
        sentences of the short stories--the foundation of
        Wharton's formal genius. Maintains she writes at an
        aristocratic remove, yet she is never cold, for her
        sympathy is with "the innocents who are shredded in the
        teeth of the machinery of the world."

J13   *Madame de Treymes and Three Novellas.*
        New York: Collier Books, 1987. Introduction by Susan
        Mary Alsop.
        Contains: *Touchstone, Sanctuary, Madame de Treymes*
        and *Bunner Sisters*. Introductory biographical sketch
        recounts meeting Wharton in Paris in 1934. Impressions
        were of a rather dowdy old lady, gossiping about the
        past. Terms the theme of *Madame de Treymes* family
        ties. Notes Wharton dissects the French society with the
        same Balzacian flair as she did New York society
        earlier.

J14   *The Complete Works of Edith Wharton.*
        26 Volumes. Ed. Yoshie Itabashi and Miyoko Sasaki.
        Kyoto: Rinsen, 1989.
        [In Japanese.] Complete works of EW including poetry,
        translations, novels, novellas, short stories, nonfiction,
        and works edited by EW. Also includes uncollected
        reviews and articles. This is the only existing published
        collection of this scope.

Chapter 2

Bibliographies

This chapter lists bibliographical studies of Edith Wharton's work, alphabetized by compiler. The only complete descriptive bibliographical study of the primary material is contained in the invaluable Garrison dissertation, K7, revised and expanded for the Pittsburgh bibliographical series, scheduled to appear in 1990.

K1   Bendixen, Alfred. "A Guide to Wharton Criticism, 1974-1983." *Edith Wharton Newsletter* 2.2 (Fall 1985): 1-8.
       Updates the Springer bibliography (K14) with annotated entries drawn from books, literary surveys, journals, newspapers, dissertations 1974-1983. Different years are compiled by different scholars, and therefore the extent of the coverage varies in each section. Entries and annotations are reliable.

K2   Bendixen, Alfred. "Recent Wharton Studies: A Bibliographic Essay." *Edith Wharton Newsletter* 3.2 (Fall 1986): 5.
       Covers Wharton scholarship 1984-1985. Notes Wharton scholarship was of excellent quality during those

years. Cites articles covering biography, EW's place in the American literary tradition, James, EW's relationship to other women writers, EW's intellectual heritage, the neglected fiction and the supernatural tales. Discusses feminist criticism. Lists areas that need further exploration.

K3   Bendixen, Alfred. "Wharton Studies, 1986-1987: A Bibliographic Essay." *Edith Wharton Newsletter* 5.1 (Spring 1988): 5.

Covers Wharton criticism 1986-1987 with note that it "rarely breaks new ground" and focuses on "a relatively small number of Wharton's works and a handful of issues." Cites feminist criticism as well as articles complaining of the limitations of feminist criticism, essays on EW's relationship to other writers and literary traditions, current approaches to James and EW. Laments the neglect of the short stories, the nonfiction and less famous novels and novellas.

K4   Brenni, Vito J. *Edith Wharton: A Bibliography.* Morgantown: West Virginia University Library, 1966.

The Brenni bibliography is not as reliable in terms of accuracy and completeness as the Springer (K14), and should be relied upon with some caution. Ninety-nine pages long, it contains a list of novels and dates of their before-publication serialization, a list of short stories and an incomplete listing of their magazine appearances prior to collection, list of poetry collections and individual poems with their journal publication data, miscellaneous works, translations of Edith Wharton's writings, book reviews (unannotated), biographical and critical writings about Edith Wharton (largely unannotated), list of theses and dissertations (sporadically annotated), list of bibliographies, obituaries and portraits and an index. Introduction by James W. Skelton.

K5   Crane, Joan St.C. "Rare or Seldom-Seen Dust Jackets of American First Editions V111 and 1X." *The Serif* 9.3 (1972): 45-47 and 9.2 (1972): 36-37.

Bibliographical data describing dust jackets of first editions of *The Decoration of Houses* (1897) *HofM* (1905), *The Hermit and the Wild Woman* (1908), and *EF* (1911). Second article details dust jackets of first editions of *CC* (1913), *Summer* (1917), *AofI* (1920) and *Glimpses of the Moon* (1922).

K6   Davis, Lavinia Riker. *A Bibliography of the Writings of Edith Wharton*. Portland, Maine: Southworth Press, 1933.

     Divided into five sections: 1) full collations of the first American editions; 2) uncollected essays, poems and stories in magazines; 3) articles, reviews, appreciations appearing in American and European magazines; 4) contributions to books, including prefaces, translations, etc.; 5) comment on Wharton's work appearing in essays and books by others.

K7   Garrison, Stephen Michael. "A Descriptive Bibliography of Edith Wharton." Ph.D. dissertation. South Carolina, 1982.

     For abstract see DAI 43 (1982), 1971A. Styled on lines of Pittsburgh Series in Bibliography. Important primary descriptive bibliography with descriptions of her 52 titles, tracing publication history through American and European editions. Lists collections of Wharton's writings, contributions to books, pamphlets, magazines and newspapers, and works she edited. Preface explains how data may be used to trace cultural trends and book trade practices of her time. [This valuable dissertation has been revised for the Pittsburgh Series in Bibliography and will be available in 1990.]

K8   Johnson, Merle, and Frederick M. Hopkins. "American First Editions ... Edith Wharton." *Publishers' Weekly* 102 (10 March 1923): 796.

     Checklist of her publications to date, noting mistaken quotation from Burial Service instead of Wedding Service as distinguishing mark of *AofI*. [See R12.46]

K9   Melish, Lawson McClung. *A Bibliography of the Collected Writings of Edith Wharton*. New York: Brick Row Book Shop, 1927.

Lists first editions by publication dates, ending with *Here and Beyond* in 1926.

K10   Monteiro, George. "Addenda to the Bibliographies of Boyle, Conrad, DeForest, Eliot, Ford, Hemingway, Huxley, Wharton and Woolf." *PBSA: Papers of the Bibliographical Society of America* 74 (1980): 153-55.

Adds review of *A Backward Glance* by Aldo Sorani to the Springer bibliography. See V86.

K11   Plante, Patricia. "The Critical Reception of Edith Wharton's Fiction in America and England with an Annotated Enumerative Bibliography of Wharton Criticism from 1900 to 1961." Ph.D. dissertation. Boston University, 1962.

Important discussion of the critical reception, still valuable, with annotations of reviews and articles. Not as exhaustive as Springer [See K14], but does contain material Springer lacks.

K12   Schriber, Mary Suzanne. "A Checklist of French Commentary on Edith Wharton 1906-1937." *American Literary Realism 1870-1910* 13 (1980): 61-68.

Valuable checklist of articles on Wharton in French periodicals during her lifetime accompanies bibliographic essay on French criticism of Wharton. See Q72.

K13   Sklepowich, Edward A. "Review of Dissertations." *American Literary Realism 1870-1910* 8 (1975): 331-40.

Overview of Wharton dissertations, with commentary on each, noting the conspicuous neglect of her position as a woman writer from a privileged class. Categorizes dissertations [reference in parenthesis to number in that category] as: bibliographical studies (2); those dealing with: novel of manners (3), ghost stories (1), themes of love and romance (3), emotional liberation (1), women (2), psychology (2), family (2), wealth (2), Wharton as social novelist (2), WWI (1), decline in her reputation (3), morality (4), literary theory (1), short fiction (1), style (1), imagery (1).

K14　Springer, Marlene. *Edith Wharton and Kate Chopin: A Reference Guide.* Boston: G.K. Hall, 1976.

Covers secondary bibliographical material 1897-1973. Organized by year, citing both books and periodical commentary. Covers reviews extensively. Carefully annotated. The Springer has been the backbone of Wharton scholarship since its appearance--reliable, exhaustive.

K15　Springer, Marlene, and Joan Gilson. "Edith Wharton: A Reference Guide Updated." *Resources for American Literary Study* 14.1-2 (Spring and Autumn 1984): 85-111.

Updates the original Springer bibliography (K14) 1973-1983, with some selections from 1984. Arranged chronologically by year. Annotated books, articles, and dissertations with unannotated foreign titles.

K16　Tuttleton, James W. "Edith Wharton: An Essay in Bibliography." *Resources for American Literary Study* 3 (1973): 163-202. Supplemented and reworked for *American Women Writers: Bibliographical Essays* edited by Maurice Duke, Jackson R. Bryer, M. Thomas Inge. Westport, Connecticut: Greenwood, 1983.

Tuttleton's bibliographic essays are thorough, scholarly, well-organized, coherently written, and cover primary as well as secondary material. They serve as the soundest available introduction to Wharton scholarship and a useful overview of scholarship (with the supplement) through the late 1970s.

K17　Zilversmit, Annette. "Appendix Bibliographical Index." *College Literature* Edith Wharton Issue (Fall 1987): 305-309.

Selective, annotated bibliography of important Wharton criticism appended to the Edith Wharton Issue.

Chapter 3

Biography

Major biographical material can be found in three places in this bibliography. This chapter contains pertinent biographical material from newspapers, memoirs, surveys and articles that is not primarily related to literary influences. A small, selected sample of reviews of the major biographies is also included as well as present reaction to the Lewis biography (N17) and the *Letters* (H1). Scholarship addressed to literary influences, including all of the material related to Edith Wharton's relationship with Henry James (except that pertaining to his family) is in Chapter 5. Book-length biographical studies are in Chapter 6, which includes the major biographies, N17, N20, N22, and N28. Essentially biographical Fitzgerald material is included here. Biographical references in contemporary studies, surveys and general articles are noted throughout. For important autobiographical materials see E9, H1, I.3, and I.5.

L1   Allen, Gay Wilson. *William James. A Biography.* New York: Viking, 1967.

       Mentions in passing Henry James's 1905 Lenox visit and William James's May 7, 1910, visit to Wharton in Paris.

L2   Andrews, Wayne. "The World of Edith Wharton: Fragment
         of a Biography in Progress." Introduction to *The Best Short
         Stories of Edith Wharton*. New York: Scribner's, 1958.
                Outdated because of Fullerton material in the Lewis
         biography (N17) in 1975, but fascinating because he
         includes, at this early date before the Yale papers were
         opened, excerpts from the Love Diary (I.5). Mentions:
         *VofD, MmeT, EF, Reef, CC, Marne, French Ways and Their
         Meaning*.

L3   Anonymous. "Edith Wharton." *New York Times*, 13 August
         1937, 16.
                Obituary remarks "[s]he should have been greater,
         but ... she will not rank among the giants." Only *EF* is
         termed perfection. Notes her as both cosmopolitan and
         social historian, but argues she will be remembered for
         writing of "the things that twist the hearts and minds of
         men and women." Cites: *HofM, AofI*.

L4   Anonymous. "Edith Wharton." *Time* 30 (23 August 1937):
         53.
                Obituary with thumbnail biography notes her "famed
         New England tragedy, *Ethan Frome*" and the Pulitzer for
         Age of Innocence.

L5   Anonymous. "Edith Wharton, 75, Is Dead in France." *New
         York Times*, 13 August 1937, 17.
                Obituary with extensive recapitulation of her life and
         honors, noting her reputation rested upon her achievement
         as a chronicler of Fifth Avenue, and the "great love story,"
         Ethan Frome. Mentions that critics say lack of real people
         was her greatest flaw. Cites: *AofI, HofM*.

L6   Anonymous. Obituary. *Commonweal* 26 (27 August 1937):
         412.
                Obituary praises *HofM, CC* and *EF* as being almost
         unmatched in contemporary letters. Of her later work,
         AofI is noted. Only objects to the lack of a religious,
         rooted morality as a flaw in all her fiction.

L7   Anonymous. Obituary. *Newsweek* 10 (21 August 1937): 5.
       Obituary mentions her aristocratic heritage, her
defiance of family to become a writer, and her "boast" that
"she never drew a character from real life." Notes most
critics call *EF* her best. Also cites *AofI*.

L8   Anonymous. "Our Family Album." *Ladies Home Journal* 44
       (November 1927): 38.
       Chatty notes accompany "Atrophy." Laments Lily Bart
is forgotten despite her universality.

L9   Anonymous. "Our Most Distinguished Ambassador to
       Europe." *Vanity Fair* 28 (March 1927): 60.
       Photo EW in garden at Hyeres carries long caption
praising her art, studies of both Americans and foreigners,
social criticism, *Ethan Frome*, warwork.

L10   Anonymous. "The Sharp Eye of Edith Wharton." *Apollo*
       103 (Jan 1976): 2-12.
       Discusses EW as pioneer "tastemaker" in decorative,
gardening arts and traces her taste in art, painting and
sculpture in her nonfiction and her use of art in fiction.
She emerges as an independent thinker in an article that
ranges widely over the place of art in her life. [Tintner
gives author as Denys Sutton. See R15.25.] Cites: *The
Valley of Decision*, *The Decoration of Houses*, *Italian Villas
and Their Gardens*, *Italian Backgrounds*, *Motor-Flight
Through France*, *In Morocco*, *AofI*, *CC*, *GofM*, *Summer*.

L11   Anonymous. "Wharton Will Is Filed." *New York Times*,
       29 August 1937, sec.1, 4.
       Details Wharton will leaving over $10,000 in NY
holdings and property. Names French charities as
beneficiaries, Mrs. Elisina Tyler to administer disposal of
estate.

L12   Anonymous. "What Really Happened at the Pavillon
       Colombe." *Fitzgerald Newsletter* 7 (Fall 1959): 1-2.
       Gives Theodore Chanler's version of the story of
lunch with Fitzgerald at the Pavillon Colombe which

differs from other accounts. [See L36, L84, L85, L115, L116]

L13   Auchincloss, Louis. "Correspondence." *Edith Wharton Newsletter* 1.2 (Fall 1984): 6.
        Spirited defence of Lubbock in answer to Katherine Joslin-Jeske's comments on *Portrait of EW*. [See L60, L61]

L14   Auchincloss, Louis. "Edith Wharton and Her Letters." *Hofstra Review* 2 (Winter 1967): 1-7.
        Biographical information accompanies excerpts from Auchincloss's collection of EW letters. Discusses her sometimes difficult personality. Mentions *M'sR*.

L15   Balsan, Consuelo Vanderbilt. *The Glitter and the Gold* London: Heinemann, 1953.
        Photo--EW at Blenheim, 1904. Contains NY heiress's personal impressions of EW from houseparties as precise, tailored, lacking spontaneity, seeming to dislike women, Teddy Wharton her equerry.

L16   Barnes, Eric W. *The Man Who Lived Twice*. New York: Scribner's, 1956.
        Biography of Edward Sheldon recounting EW's long friendship, noting their mutual love of tales of terror and horror.

L17   Bedford, Sybille. *Aldous Huxley. A Biography*. New York: Knopf/Harper & Row, 1974.
        Two passing references to Wharton and two brief anecdotes: a Huxley picnic where she exhibited her "iron discipline," and a visit to the Huxleys when Aldous patted her behind.

L18   Bell, Millicent. "Lady into Author: Edith Wharton and the House of Scribner." *American Quarterly* 9 (Fall 1957): 295-315.
        Traces Wharton's relationship with Scribner's, the editors, Brownell and Burlingame, the move to Appleton, the history of the unfinished *Literature*--through excerpts

from her correspondence with the firm. Mentions: *HM, FT, CC, Summer, SatF, WF, EF.* [See M6]

L19   Benstock, Shari. *Women of the Left Bank, Paris, 1900-1940.* Austin: University of Texas Press, 1986.
        Account of Wharton in Parisian salon society. Much stems from the Lewis biography, *A Backward Glance* and *French Ways and Their Meaning.* The thrust of the Wharton material is that she was *not* a part of what is commonly thought of as the "Left Bank expatriate community." Material on the place of homosexuals and lesbians in Parisian society of the time, with note that Wharton avoided overtly unconventional people. Long speculation in the conditional tense on what *would* have happened had she met Pound. Note unique street map locating American expatriates. [See N17]

L20   Berenson, Bernard. *Rumor and Reflection.* New York: Simon and Schuster, 1952.
        Berenson's wartime diary, 1941-44, has three very brief comments on Wharton and Hyeres. Short reference to degenerates of *Summer* in connection with Steinbeck's *Tortilla Flat.*

L21   Berenson, Bernard. *Sketch for a Self-Portrait.* New York: Pantheon, 1949.
        See pages 24-25. Briefly details Berenson's initial hostile meeting with EW, and their subsequent great friendship.

L22   Bourget, Paul. *Outre-Mer: Impressions of America.* London: 1895.
        See pages 93-94. In *Edith Wharton: A Biography* Lewis contends the portrait of the American intellectual tomboy here with the mind of a "thinking machine" is modelled on Edith Wharton. [See N17]

L23   Brooke, Pamela. "The Essence of a Life." *Humanities* (May 1977): 4-7.

Commentary on Lewis's painstaking research in the preparation of *Edith Wharton: A Biography*. [See N17]

L24　　Brooks, Van Wyck, and Otto Bettman. *Our Literary Heritage*. New York: Dutton, 1956.
Illustrated survey, discusses EW under "New York High Society." Contends she was best in recreating atmosphere of Old New York.

L25　　Brown, Ashley. "Homage to Percy Lubbock." *Southern Review* 15 (January 1979): 22-33.
Short, biographical essay on Lubbock contains a few paragraphs on Wharton, noting their relationship was "more complicated than either was willing to admit." Notes his unquestioned admiration for her art, his antipathy to Berry, Wharton's hostility to Sybil.

L26　　Burlingame, Roger. *Of Making Many Books*. New York: Scribner's, 1946.
Centenary history of Scribner's focuses on relationships with its authors. Mention of EW as war correspondent, French gratitude, her early complaints about lack of advertising, search for titles, her worries about structure of *The House of Mirth*. Cites: *Greater Inclination*, *Fruit of the Tree*.

L27　　Carroll, Loren. "Edith Wharton in Profile." *New York Herald Tribune*, 16 November 1936, Paris edition, p.6.
Notes this as her first interview. EW mentioned surprise that now she is spoken of in terms of "violets and old lace" when once she was considered revolutionary. Names *CC*, *Summer*, *Children*, *HRB*, and *GA* as her favorites. Objected to "radical" new novelists.

L28　　Chanler, Margaret Terry. *Autumn in the Valley*. Boston: Little Brown, 1936.
Memoirs of her long friendship with EW: Wharton's friendships with James and Roosevelt, their Aegean cruise, EW's war work.

L29   Chanler, Margaret Terry. *Roman Spring: Memoirs*. Boston: Little, Brown, 1934.

Briefly recounts EW's lack of interest when they first met in Newport, and adds that later EW enriched her life.

L30   Chanler, Margaret Terry. "Winters in Paris." *Atlantic Monthly* 158 (October 1936): 473-80.

Chapter from *Autumn in the Valley* discusses Wharton circle in Paris and James.

L31   Clark, Kenneth. *Another Part of the Woods*. London: John Murray, 1974.

Lord Clark's memoirs contain a touching character sketch of the elderly Edith Wharton with all her many contradictions--haughty, warm, difficult, generous.

L32   Clark, Kenneth. "A Full-Length Portrait." *Times Literary Supplement* (London), 19 December 1975, 1502-03.

Review of R.W.B. Lewis's biography ranges widely over EW's life and relationships. Lord Clark knew her in later life, and his descriptions of Lubbock, Lapsley, Berry, James, Fullerton and Edward Wharton are invaluable. Praises readability and inclusiveness of the biography. [See N17, N20]

L33   Codman, Florence. *The Clever Young Boston Architect*. Augusta, Maine: 1970.

Privately printed bio-appreciation of the architect, Ogden Codman, who collaborated with Wharton on *The Decoration of Houses*. Fascinating, if biased account of Wharton's relationship with Codman who stated he did all the work on their book and she "merely polished off the forms of sentences." Contains title page of *Decoration of Houses*. Maintains the book was successful because of the "authors' knowledge and self-confidence which gave assurance to the aspirations of the nouveaux riche." When Wharton collapsed from the heat at his house in 1937 he found it a "bore" because to have a foreigner die in one's house in France, as he explained, "is an extremely bothersome matter of official red tape."

L34   Colquitt, Clare. "Unpacking Her Treasures: Edith Whar-
          ton's 'Mysterious Correspondence' with Morton Fullerton."
          Library Chronicle of the University of Texas New Series No.
          31 (1985): 73-107.
              Sensitive and detailed discussion of the affair as
          revealed through the previously unknown letters. Charts
          Wharton's early holding back, her growing self-confidence
          in "passionate forms of expressions," her sense of what she
          lacked as a woman, her struggles with Fullerton's inconsis-
          tency, her attempts to make him honestly admit that he
          had tired of her, and her persistent efforts to build and
          maintain an intellectual camaraderie that would outlast
          their intimacy. Discusses *The Reef*, Wharton's belief that
          Fullerton could be a far better writer than he was, and her
          acute criticism of his work. Offers extensive quotes from
          the letters; relies heavily on material in R.W.B. Lewis's
          biography and Wolff's *A Feast of Words*. [See N17, N28]

L35   Connolly, Cyril. *Previous Convictions: Selected Writings of
          a Decade*. New York: Harper and Row, 1963.
              Brief comparison of Turnbull-Mizener versions of
          Fitzgerald lunch at Pavillon Colombe, favoring Turnbull.
          [See L12, L84, L85, L115, L116]

L36   Connolly, Cyril, and Jerome Zerbe. *Les Pavillons*. London:
          Hamish Hamilton Ltd., 1962.
              See pages 62-67 and Introduction. History of Pavillon
          Colombe with photographs, in a pictorial guide to French
          pavillons. Notes objections to EW's perfectionism, but
          defends her as one who settled in France to escape
          nineteenth-century family belongings.

L37   Edel, Leon. *Bloomsbury, A House of Lions*. Philadelphia:
          Lippincott, 1979.
              Merely mentions that Desmond McCarthy imagined
          himself "projected ... into the world of [the] grande dame
          of American letters" when he reviewed Percy Lubbock's
          "conversation piece about Edith Wharton."

L38 Edel, Leon. "Henry James, Edith Wharton and Newport."
Newport: Redwood Library and Newport Atheneum,
1966.

Pamphlet available from Newport Library contains
Edel's address documenting references to Newport in
James and Wharton fiction and letters. Differentiates
Newport of Wharton and James, comments on their
relationship, recounts his visits to the 70-year-old EW at
Pavillon Colombe.

L39 Edel, Leon. *Literary Biography*. Canada: University of
Toronto, 1957.

Compares Lubbock's *Portrait* to Geoffrey Scott's study
of Zélide as the portrait style of biography, essentially
"two-dimensional" with a "constant focusing on the central
figure." [See N20]

L40 Edel, Leon. "Walter Berry and the Novelists: Proust,
James, and Edith Wharton." *Nineteenth Century Literature*
38.4 (March 1984): 514-528.

Argues Berry's association with the three novelists
grew less from his "faculty for friendship" than his need to
associate with those who had greatness and imagination.
Berry offered Wharton authority through identification
with him, and "sanctioned" her life as an artist. Edel
surveys Berry's fierce anti-German sentiments; Proust's
flattery and love of Berry; Percy Lubbock's portrait of him;
Wharton's role in his funeral arrangements; and discusses
his own attempts to gain information about this little-
known figure, which included meetings with Wharton.

L41 Edel, Leon. "Wharton, Edith Newbold Jones." In *Dictionary of American Biography* 11 Part II, Supplement II. New
York, 1958.

Defines Wharton as the historian of Old New York.
Distinguishes Wharton from James in his psychological
probing of the international theme, while she "remained
close to the actual data she found...." Dated, but influential
assessment before the Yale papers were opened.

L42   Edel, Leon. *Writing Lives: Principia Biographica*. New
        York: Norton, 1984.
            Reprint of discussion of portrait style of biography
        from *Literary Biography*. Notes opening of Wharton Yale
        archives aided him with 127 James letters. [See L39]

L43   Edmiston, Susan, and Linda D. Cirino. *Literary New York:
        A History and Guide*. Boston: Houghton-Mifflin, 1976.
            Wharton mentioned often in this pictorial history of
        writers who lived in, and wrote about, New York City.
        Gives locations of Wharton's various homes in the city,
        with references to the residences in *The Age of Innocence*.

L44   Ellmann, Mary. "Manners, Morals and Mrs. Wharton."
        Sewanee Review 84 (1976): 528-32.
            Reviews R.W.B. Lewis's biography and Gary
        Lindberg's *EW and the Novel of Manners*. Terms Lewis
        lacking in perceptive, detailed literary criticism, but
        believable, thorough, honest and valuable. Finds Lindberg
        serious, intelligent and thorough but "extremely difficult to
        read."

L45   Fedorko, Kathy. "Storming the Chateau at Hyères." *Edith
        Wharton Newsletter* 4.2 (Fall 1987): 7.
            Personal account of 1987 visit to EW's home on the
        Riviera, Chateau Ste. Claire at Hyères.

L46   Fife, Hilda. "Letters from Edith Wharton to Vernon Lee."
        Colby Library Quarterly Ser. 3 (February 1953): 139-44.
            Two EW letters with commentary. The 1903 letter
        offers to set up a lecture tour for Lee in America and
        comments on the "exquisite" play *Ariadne in Mantua* with
        the suggestion that narrative (not dramatic) form would
        enhance Lee's brilliant descriptions. The 1907 note of
        condolence on her brother's death also recounts her
        solicitations for funds for Villa Borghese and her eager-
        ness to write an article on Lee's *Studies in the Eighteenth
        Century in Italy* (1880).

L47   Fitch, Noel Riley. *Sylvia Beach and the Lost Generation.* New York: Norton, 1983.

One paragraph comment mentions Wharton struggling through *Ulysses* and her comment to Berenson that it was pornographic, unformed, unimportant "drivel." Contends Wharton lived extravagantly, apart from the avant-garde world, and that only a few like Gide or Valery associated with both circles.

L48   Flanner, Janet. *Paris Was Yesterday.* New York: Viking, 1972.

Very unflattering, emphasizing Wharton's background, homes, social life, and persona over her writing. Argues she was cold, over-organized, always an outsider, ignoring the senses--moving with "unerring failure between two careers--that of a great woman of the world and a great woman novelist." Contends that, overly influenced by James, she achieved her literary height in their friendship.

L49   Fleischman, Doris. "Women in Business." *Ladies Home Journal* 47 (March 1930): 24.

One brief mention of EW in this practical guide for a young lady choosing a career.

L50   Flynn, Dale. "My Edith Wharton Pilgrimage." *Edith Wharton Newsletter* 4.2 (Fall 1987): 6.

Charming personal account of 1980's visits to EW's homes Pavillon Colombe and Chateau Ste. Claire and EW's grave.

L51   Ford, Hugh. *Published in Paris: A Literary Chronicle of Paris* in the 1920's and 1930's. New York: Collier/MacMillan, 1988.

Brief account of Berry's bequeathing his library to Harry Crosby except for what Wharton wanted, of Wharton's wishing almost all of it, and Crosby's opposition. She eventually received about 500 volumes, and Crosby retained the invaluable remainder.

L52   French, Mrs. Daniel Chester. *Memoirs of a Sculptor's Wife.*
        Boston: Houghton Mifflin, 1929.
             Unindexed. Passim and pp. 205-206. Notes in
        particular Wharton's gardens in Lenox which were
        "perfectly and artistically done, by development of the
        natural beauty of the landscape rather than by
        enforcement of preconceived ideas."

L53   Friedl, Herwig. "Edith Wharton: Von Nutzen und Nachteil
        einer Biographie fur die Literaturkritik." *Archiv fur das
        Studium der Neuren Sprachen und Literaturen.* Heidelberg:
        214 (1977): 82-88.
             In German. Review of Lewis's biography (N17).

L54   Garland, Hamlin. *Afternoon Neighbors: Further Excerpts
        from a Literary Log.* New York: Macmillan, 1934.
             Chapter "Edith Wharton's Home." Account of his visit
        Sunday, July 27, 1924, gives brief excerpts of their
        conversation covering WWI and changing literary scene.
        Notes she seemed confident, secure--glad her work was
        still in demand.

L55   Gide, André. *The Journals of André Gide.* Volume II. 1914-
        1927. Translated and annotated by Justin O'Brien. New
        York: Knopf, 1951.
             Passing references to meeting and writing Wharton in
        1915 and 1916 with account of incident when waiting for
        Wharton to leave the room before discussing "sexual
        perversion" in his novel.

L56   Gribben, Alan. "The Heart *Is* Insatiable: A Selection from
        Edith Wharton's Letters to Morton Fullerton." *Library
        Chronicle of the University of Texas* New Series No. 31
        (1985): 7-18.
             Surveys 26 letters with brief biography of Fullerton,
        sketching the genesis of the affair, Wharton's initial
        reluctance and fear of exposure, the dynamics of
        Fullerton's typical pattern of involvement with women
        (passionate onslaught and subsequent "long sad decline" of
        ardor), and Wharton's ultimate, heartbreaking inability to

rekindle the affair by moving Fullerton through her writing.

L57   Hadley, Rollin Van N. *The Letters of Bernard Berenson and Isabella Stewart Gardner.* Boston: Northeastern University Press, 1987.

        1887-1924. Includes correspondence by Mary Berenson. References to Wharton throughout. Berenson calls her Della Robbia "find" "crude, hideous, local work." Editor notes Wharton's daily attendance on Berenson after Mary's breakdown and Berenson's appreciation of *The House of Mirth.* See Mary Berenson's comments on Edward Wharton's illness, p.499.

L58   Hassal, Christopher Vernon. *A Biography of Edward Marsh.* New York: Harcourt, Brace, 1959.

        Mentions Rupert Brooke's liking Wharton, a humorous story she told Brooke, and her scolding Marsh for recommending *Sons and Lovers*: "Bungled work."

L59   Holzer, Harold. "Edith Wharton's First Real Home: Remembering Life and Work at the Mount." *American History Illustrated* 17 (September 1982): 10-15.

        Details history of the Mount, offering extensive descriptions of rooms and grounds and biographical details of Wharton's relationship to her home, with notes on the present reconstructive effort.

L60   Joslin-Jeske, Katherine. "Correspondence." *Edith Wharton Newsletter* 1.2 (Fall 1984): 6.

        Response to Auchincloss's defense of Lubbock. [See L13, L61]

L61   Joslin-Jeske, Katherine. "What Lubbock Didn't Say." *Edith Wharton Newsletter* 1.1 (Spring 1984): 2-4.

        Based on a study of Wharton's letters and Percy Lubbock's notes for his *Portrait of Edith Wharton,* contends that the book is biased and in some senses vindictive, excluding comments on her warmth and overly emphasizing her difficult personality. [See L13, L60]

L62   Kaplan, Amy. "Edith Wharton's Profession of Authorship."
        ELH 53.2 (Summer 1986): 433-457. Revised reprint in *The
        Social Construction of American Realism.* Chicago: The
        University of Chicago Press, 1988.
             Examines Wharton's apprenticeship, citing *The
        Decoration of Houses*, "The Pelican," *The Touchstone, Fast
        and Loose*, "April Showers," "The Expiation," "Copy,"
        "Bunner Sisters," *The House of Mirth* and her 1902 essay
        on George Eliot in the *Bookman.* Analyzes her struggle
        to escape a suffocating domesticity, the stereotypes of both
        female domestic writers and society novelists, charges of
        voyeurism, and the trap of artist or novel turned into yet
        another commodity. Sets forth the various problems facing
        a woman writer seeking to enter the marketplace as a
        professional and retain both her artistic integrity and
        private identity.

L63   Karl, Frederick. "Three Conrad Letters in the Edith
        Wharton Papers." *Yale University Library Gazette* 44 (1970):
        148-51.
             First part of article concerns slight (6 letters) James-
        Conrad correspondence. Second part has 24 July 1915
        James letter to Conrad soliciting contribution to *Book of
        the Homeless*, and two letters to EW--24 Dec 1912 gives
        his reservations about a French translation of *The Secret
        Sharer* and 1 Oct 1917 praises *Summer* but in his usual
        phrasing to other authors.

L64   Kazin, Alfred. "New York from Melville to Mailer." In
        *Literature and the Urban Experience: Essays on the City and
        Literature.* Edited by Michael C. Jaye and Ann Chalmers
        Watts. New Brunswick, New Jersey: Rutgers University
        Press, 1981.
             Collection of essays is from the Conference on
        Literature and the Urban Experience at Rutgers in
        Newark, April 17-19, 1980. A few passing comments on
        Wharton, noting she fled the "sterile upper class life of
        New York."

L65   Knollenberg, Bernard. "Edith Wharton's Papers." *Times Literary Supplement* (London), 20 May 1939, 298.

        Knollenberg, Yale librarian, notes in letter to the editor that Yale is recipient of EW's manuscripts, papers and letters which will be available for study in 1968. Requests letters in private hands.

L66   LaFarge, John, S.J. "The Troubled Soul of Edith Wharton." *America* 58 (13 Nov 1937): 138-39.

        LaFarge knew EW as a child and wonders why she did not become a Catholic with her war work and her furthering of French charities. Maintains she would have converted except for her social world which, because of its materialistic basis, was antagonistic to spirituality, but he contends that her soul was troubled because she was at odds with that world.

L67   Laguardia, Eric. "Edith Wharton on Critics and Criticism." *Modern Language Notes* 73 (December 1958): 587-89.

        Quotes EW letter 22 Oct 1922 to Zona Gale, expressing pleasure that younger writers respected her, and noting exasperation that her reviewers first objected she could not construct a novel, yet now say she is too structured. Short analysis of critical attitudes to EW follows letter.

L68   L'Enfant, Julie. "Edith Wharton: Room with a View." *Southern Review* 12 (1976): 398-406.

        Concerns Lewis biography (N17). Feels Lewis overturns two errant assumptions readers and critics took from Lubbock: 1) EW was superficial as an artist, 2) Walter Berry "was somehow the evil genius who created this false sureness in her." Finds new private details illuminate many aspects of her fiction. Cites: "Fullness of Life," *ABG*, *WofF*, *VofD*, "Eyes," *AofI*, *EF*, "Terminus," *Reef*, *GofM*, "Roman Fever," *Children*, *M'sR*.

L69   Lennartz, Franz. "Edith Wharton." In *Auslandische Dichter und Schriftstellar unserer Zeit*. Stuttgart: Kroner, 1955.

Biographical overview in German from a dictionary of modern authors. Terms her writing the highlight of the realistic society genre. Inaccurate in saying she won two Pulitzers. Mentions Michaud called her the Paul Bourget of Fifth Avenue. Contends that although she laid bare the weaknesses of the aristocratic society, she remained its prisoner. Finds this tie to the dying aristocracy what gives her work its tragic tone.

L70   Lewis, Nancy. "Living With the Angel of Devastation." Speech. The Saturday Morning Club, New Haven, n.d.
        R.W.B. Lewis's wife and co-editor of the *Letters* recounts their experiences while he was researching his biography (N17). Charming account of meeting Lord Clark and Philomène, and her own evolving sense of Edith Wharton. [See H1.]

L71   Lewis, R.W.B. "Edith Wharton: The Beckoning Quarry." *American Heritage* 26 (1975): 53-56.
        Professor Lewis describes his quest for EW while writing her biography. Mentions misconceptions he had had, apocryphal anecdotes he traced down, his discovery of the Fullerton material, and the finding of the Beatrice Palmato fragment.

L71.1   Lewis, R.W.B. "Letter to the Editor." London *Times Literary Supplement*, February 17-23, 1989, p.165.
        Lewis answers charges by Mainwaring (L75) and Pitlick (L91) that his 1975 biography (N17) contains serious errors. Argues that "Mainwaring's wordy charges and sweeping rhetoric have mostly to do with wrong street addresses and proper names in Paris" which have "no bearing on the portrait of Wharton." Maintains that Pitlick is wrong, that EW did have a nervous breakdown "and a serious one," but he does not ascribe her creativity to her illness.

L72   Lewis, Rosa. *The Queen of Cooks--and Some Kings. (The Story of Rosa Lewis)*. Recorded by Mary Lawton. New York: Boni & Liveright, 1925.

See page 176. Rosa Lewis owned the Cavendish Hotel in London where Edith Wharton stayed, and here in her memoirs she maintains she always had "the very best Americans"--Wharton among them. She comments that outwardly Wharton was shy, retiring and cold: "I think she's never really been unlocked, that most of her emotions have gone into her books."

L73 Lodge, Henry Cabot. *The Storm Has Many Eyes*. New York: Norton, 1973.

Brief, fond recollection of Wharton (a family friend) as awe-inspiring to adults, but affectionate and kind to children. Praises her helping his recently widowed mother settle in Paris in 1912. Cursory references to Berry, Gaillard Lapsley, William Gerhardi.

L74 Lynes, Russell. "Edith Wharton's Summer Cottage." *Architectural Digest* 40 (April 1983): 44-46.

Discusses the restoration of the Mount, Wharton's home at Lenox, Massachusetts. Notes it was her preaching against Victorian clutter "put into practice." Praises the restoration: Wharton "might step through the door to the terrace at any moment to smile her approval."

L75 Mainwaring, Marion. "The Shock of Non-recognition." *Times Literary Supplement*, December 16-22, 1988, p. 1394.

The Paris researcher for Lewis's biography claims that the biography is factually incorrect as to the nature of Fullerton's employment with the *Times*, his Paris address, his divorce decree and his wife and daughter, the identity of Henrietta Mirecourt, and the circumstances of Wharton's composition of "Terminus." Also discusses errors in the spelling of French names in the biography and the *Letters*. Contends that Lewis "lavishly praised" her research but "distorted or neglected much of the material." Contends Lewis's "carelessness is extraordinary." Also cites errors in the *Letters*. [See N17, H1, L91, Q83. For Lewis's rebuttal see N71.1.]

L75.1   Mainwaring, Marion. "Feminists and Edith Wharton." The
         New Criterion 7.10 (June 1989): 85-86.
                 Letter to the editor answers Tuttleton (Q83) and
         explains the personal difficulties that kept her from raising
         her objections to the Lewis biography (N17) sooner.
         Refers to her research on the biography as "mangled" by
         Lewis. [See L71.1, L75.]

L76   Marbury, Elizabeth. *My Crystal Ball*. London: Hurst and
         Blackett, 1924.
                 Brief reference praising *The Age of Innocence*'s
         accurate depiction of its era, Wharton's indisputable taste,
         literary style, talent and hard work. Marbury's companion,
         Elsie de Wolfe, wrote a book influenced by *The Decoration
         of Houses*: See Coles, xxxix, note 4. [See V96]

L77   Mariano, Nicky. *Forty Years with Berenson*. New York:
         Knopf, 1966.
                 Kenneth Clark contends in his introduction that the
         EW material is authentic, valuable for literary historians.
         Contains account of the Berensons' and Mariano's
         friendship with EW, a sometimes difficult companion, but
         warmly beloved once intimacy was established. Furnishes
         material on EW as hostess with friends.

L78   Marra, Umberto. *Conversations with Berenson*. Translated,
         Florence Hammond. Boston: Houghton-Mifflin, 1965.
         Translation of *Colloqui con Berenson*. Milan: Garzanti,
         1963.
                 A few comments on Wharton, including Berenson's
         contention that her "invincible timidity with new people"
         made her very difficult when she met them.

L79   Matthiessen, F.O. *The James Family*. New York: Alfred A.
         Knopf, 1947.
                 Passing references to EW as disciple of James, noting
         length of their friendship. Same material covered
         extensively elsewhere. [See M6]

L80   Maugham, W. Somerset. "Give Me a Murder." *Saturday Evening Post* 213 (28 Dec 1940): 27.
Recounts his one meeting with EW. [See L81].

L81   Maugham, W. Somerset. *The Vagrant Mood*. London: Heinemann, 1952.
Unindexed. See p. 237. Calls her novels "costume pieces." Describes meeting EW. Although she "said nothing but the right thing about the right person" he found her "devoid of frailty" and not his "cup of tea." [See L80]

L82   Meral, Jean. "Edith Wharton, Dorothy Canfield, John Dos Passos et la présence Américaine dans le Paris de la Grande Guerre." *Caliban* 19 (1982): 73-82.
In French. Discusses presentation of the American colony in Paris during WWI in the fiction of Wharton, Canfield and Dos Passos. Finds Wharton, the aristocrat, irritated by the newly arriving Americans, but Canfield sympathetic. Discusses sexuality and sexual liberation. Argues Wharton refused to see the evolution of America and France, and the unreality of her heroes--sons she never had. Cites: *SatF, Marne*.

L83   Miller, Karl. "Edith Wharton's Secret." *New York Review of Books* 23 (Feb 1978): 10-15.
Review of Cynthia Griffin Wolff's *A Feast of Words* traces romantic elements in EW, the double motif and flight and stealing imagery. Takes issue with several of Wolff's conclusions, particularly regarding Undine Spragg and Charity Royall. Objects to the jargon-nature of Wolff's approach, and contends that Wolff's own feelings run high here. Cites: *CC, Summer, AofI, ABG, EF*, "Eyes," "Triumph of Night," "Beatrice Palmato." [See N28]

L84   Mizener, Arthur. *The Far Side of Paradise*. Boston: Houghton Mifflin, 1951.
EW material pp. 154, 170, 183-184. Recounts Fitzgerald's bursting in on her at Scribner's, Gilbert Seldes's review that points to EW (from James) as

influence for scenic structure of *The Great Gatsby*, and incident at Pavillon Colombe when Fitzgerald was drunk and (to shock EW) told company he and Zelda spent two weeks in a bordello. [See L12, L36, L85, L115, L116]

L85   Mizener, Arthur. "Scott Fitzgerald and Edith Wharton." *Times Literary Supplement* (London), 7 July 1966, 595.

Letter to editor refutes Turnbull's version of Fitzgerald's visit to EW. Quotes letter from Roderick Coupe to Cyril Connolly which affirms Mizener's version and states he had his information from Esther Chanler who (he insists, not Theodore Chanler) accompanied Fitzgerald. Speculates that Fitzgerald was part of the inspiration for Vance Weston. [See L12, L36, L84, L115, L116]

L86   Nevius, Blake. "Edith Wharton." *Lexikon der Weltliteratur im 20. Jahrhundert*. Vol. II. Freiburg: Herder, 1961.

In German. Biographical information in a dictionary of twentieth-century authors.

L87   Oehlschlaeger, Fritz H. "Hamlin Garland and the Pulitzer Prize Controversy of 1921." *American Literature* 51 (November 1979): 409-414.

Argues Garland actually undercut *Main Street* as the Pulitzer Prize novel of 1920, as his note that "It would be in a way a tribute to the magnificent work Mrs. Wharton has done to vote the prize to her," was influential in the choice of *The Age of Innocence* which he found lacked originality and emotion but possessed dignity and technical merit.

L88   Origo, Iris. "The Home-Coming." *New Statesman and Nation* 53 (16 Feb 1957): 199-200.

Sybil Cutting's daughter was one of house party where EW stayed after she received her doctorate at Yale. She remembered EW from Europe, but notes that evening EW was not interested in intellectual conversation, but only wanted to reminisce.

L89   Origo, Iris. *Images and Shadows: Part of a Life.* New York: Harcourt Brace Jovanovich, 1971.

    Autobiography by Sybil Cutting's daughter contains a few references to EW as friend of the family. Anecdote here that EW said to her husband it was just as well they had no children after overhearing a child practicing the piano.

L90   Phelps, William L. *Autobiography with Letters* New York: Oxford, 1939.

    Several references to EW including an account of lunch at the Pavillon Colombe August 13, 1928, and her letter acknowledging his on *A Backward Glance.*

L91   Pitlick, Mary. "Edith Wharton." *Times Literary Supplement,* December 30, 1988, p. 1443.

    Letter to the editor from one of Lewis's researchers for his biography argues "a crucial event in the American segments of both Lewis books [the biography and the *Letters*], the two-year breakdown suffered by Edith Wharton in the 1890s, did not take place." Contends there are 6,000 Wharton letters, not 4,000, as the Lewises assert. Claims that Wharton is misrepresented in both the biography and the *Letters*, and that "The conjuring of phantom facts ... suggests a passive ... acceptance, if not entire comprehension, of materials that have 'come into view', and ... a dearth of active curiosity: a failure to go out and see if there might not be something else." [See N17, H1, L75, L75.1, Q83. For Lewis's rebuttal see N71.1.]

L92   Plante, Patricia R. "Edith Wharton and the Invading Goths." *Midcontinent American Studies Journal* 5 (Fall 1964): 18-23.

    Explains EW's intellectual vision of WWI as the war threatening beauty and order and taste, maintaining that taste in EW's work is equated with morality. Draws parallels between her love of France and her love of conservative Old New York which also guarded good taste from invaders. Cites: *SatF, Marne, ABG.*

L93   Poirer, Suzanne. "The Weir Mitchell Rest Cure: Doctors and Patients." *Women's Studies* 10.1 (1983): 15-40.

Discusses the controversial Weir Mitchell rest cure and its effects on Jane Addams, Charlotte Perkins Gilman,Virginia Woolf, William Dean Howells's daughter, and EW. Mentions the irony that Mitchell is supposed to have encouraged EW to write, but contends he would not have proposed the life independent from her husband her writing opened.

L94   Powers, Lyall H. "Correspondence." *Edith Wharton Newsletter* 5.1 (Spring 1988): 9.

Adds notes to three articles appearing in Fall, 1987, *Newsletter*: 1) Joan Templeton's--adding the Pavillon Colombe was originally residence of *two* Italian mistresses, and 2) Alan Price's and Dale Flynn's, who both mention Wharton's rue de Varenne residence but as no. 53 and no. 58. Powers explains EW lived both places. [See L50, L95, L114]

L95   Price, Alan. "Tracking Wharton in Paris." *Edith Wharton Newsletter* 4.2 (Fall 1987): 3.

Personal account of 1980's search for EW's residences at 53 rue de Varenne and the Pavillon Colombe at St. Brice.

L96   Prokosch, Frederic. *Voices: A Memoir*. London: Faber and Faber Ltd., 1983.

In a discussion with a friend on resident artists in Paris during their first trip there, author "cautiously" adds Wharton's name, thinking: "Edith Wharton lived in Paris but was nowadays regarded as a member of a stale, dusty oligarchy. Still, I remembered *Ethan Frome* as a ruthless little masterpiece, and I secretly preferred the Whartonian alabaster to the Steinian granite or the Joycean porphyry."

L97   Repplier, Agnes. "Edith Wharton." *Commonweal* 29 (25 November 1938): 125-26.

Obituary praises Wharton's artistry, style and detail. Mentions particularly the ghost stories, *Children* and *EF*, contending "The Descent of Man" and "The Other Two" equal the best French models. Also cites: *Buc.*

L98   Roberts, Morley. "Meetings with Some Men of Letters." *Queen's Quarterly* 39 (February 1932): 62-80.

Primarily concerns Meredith and James with brief reference to EW meeting Meredith.

L99   Samuels, Ernest. *Bernard Berenson: The Making of a Legend.* Cambridge, Mass.: The Belknap Press of Harvard University, 1987.

Extensive, sporadic mention of the warmth of their long friendship, detailed in correspondence (only one-line notes), and the frequent visits between Hyères and I Tatti. Interesting sidelight that Mary Berenson, after a visit to Pavillon Colombe, thought the company all Fascists, p. 334.

L100   Samuels, Ernest. *Henry Adams: The Major Phase.* Cambridge, Mass.: The Belknap Press of Harvard University, 1964.

Henry Adams, American historian, scholar and man of letters, recalls Wharton in Paris looking as "fragile as a dandelion seed" but possessing much knowledge about the literary, artistic life of the city. Contends her salon was a Paris center of his set--"an unmatched world of refined elegance."

L101   Sasaki, Miyoko. "E. Wharton no Kyozo to Jitsuzo: Lewis Kyoju no Shinhyoden." Tokyo. *Eigo Seinen.* (*The Rising Generation*), 121 (1976): 588-89.

Review of the Lewis biography [N17].

L102   Scherman, David E. *Literary America.* New York: Dodd, Mead, 1952.

Short biography mentions her three principles as "culture, class and morality." Photos of Land's End and Courthouse Hill in Lenox where Ethan Frome supposedly coasted.

L103   Schorer, Mark. *Sinclair Lewis*. New York: McGraw-Hill, 1961.

Commentary throughout details their meetings and correspondence, focusing on Lewis's admiration for Wharton, hers for him--with brief analysis of their similarities--particularly in terms of names and attitudes toward America. Recounts 1920 Pulitzer Prize controversy and reactions to Lewis's Nobel Prize.

L104   Scott-James, R.A. "Edith Wharton." *London Mercury* 36 (September 1937): 417.

Obituary terms her strengths were her culture, cleverness, intellectual agility--which also imposed limitations. Mentions *EF* as her best. Contends she was Jamesian with more common sense and a style of her own.

L105   Secrest, Meryle. *Being Bernard Berenson*. New York: Holt, Rinehart and Winston, 1979.

Passing references throughout. Notes that Berenson assumed the anti-Semitism of James, Wharton and Henry Adams. Also speculates that Berenson's early friendliness for Wharton was motivated by her social position. Contends Berenson stood in awe of her insights and was also delighted by her jokes--the coarser, the better.

L106   Simpson, Colin. *Artful Partners: Bernard Berenson and Joseph Duveen*. New York: Macmillan, 1986.

Only mention of Wharton is of her lobbying to obtain Berenson a sinecure at the U.S. Army headquarters in Paris during WWI.

L107   Sloane, Florence Adele. *Maverick in Mauve*. New York: Doubleday, 1983.

Auchincloss's wife's grandmother's diary covers years 1892-1896 and illuminates EW's world, particularly *The House of Mirth*. Commentary by Auchincloss.

L108   Smith, Logan Pearsall. "Slices of Cake." *New Statesman and Nation* NS 25 (5 June 1943): 367-68.

Reminiscences of James, recalling his becoming a British citizen, his reaction to the war, and his meeting Santayana. Mentions EW in connection with Paris intellectual life.

L109 Smith, Logan Pearsall. *Unforgotten Years*. London: Constable, 1938.

See Chapter 10, "The Expatriates." Smith was Berenson's brother-in-law and he recounts Aegean cruise with EW. Mentions Berenson's initial dislike of EW, followed by great admiration. Discusses her hauteur as defense against shyness, her love of conversation, ribaldry and laughter.

L110 Spurling, Hilary. "They Do It All the Time." *New Statesman*, 31 October 1975, 545-46.

Review: R.W.B. Lewis's *Edith Wharton: A Biography*. Notes the new sexual material with conclusion that here Wharton has a persuasive, discerning advocate who will help reverse old sexist, class prejudices.

L111 Stanfill, Francesca. "A Visit to the Mount." *New York Magazine* 23 May 1988, 25.

Recounts visit to the restored Mount in Lenox, Massachusetts.

L112 Strachey, Barbara, and Jayne Samuels. *Mary Berenson: A Self Portrait from her Letters and Diaries*. London: Victor Gallancz, 1983.

Sporadic references to Wharton in Mary Berenson's letters. Mentions their mutual "tempered New Englandism" and Wharton's goodness as a friend. Interesting material on Edward Wharton, after a visit to Paris, that describes him in classically manic-depressive terms.

L113 Swann, C.S.B. "Edith Wharton." *Delta* No. 57 (1977): 30-34.

Review of Cynthia Griffin Wolff's *A Feast of Words* discusses problems of EW's unevenness and questions premises of psychological criticism in general. [See N28]

L114   Templeton, Joan. "France Honors Wharton." *Edith Wharton Newsletter* 4.2 (Fall 1987): 4.

Account of the September 6, 1987, day-long colloquium honoring EW organized by M. Fosse at St. Brice with American scholars Edel, Bell, Powers, Dwight and French admirers such as M. Artin, Wharton's physician and Madame Hery--historian of St. Brice (who spoke of EW's gardens).

L115   Turnbull, Andrew. *Scott Fitzgerald*. New York: Scribner's, 1962.

Turnbull's version of the Great Bordello Controversy, i.e., what happened when Fitzgerald had lunch with Wharton at the Pavillon Colombe. This account furnished by Theodore Chanler, who was present, places Fitzgerald in a sympathetic light trying to break the ice and Wharton ill at ease and hiding behind the facade of a haughty aristocratic New Yorker, although Chanler admits Fitzgerald had a few "bracers" on the drive out. [See L12, L36, L84, L85, L115]

L116   Turnbull, Andrew. "Scott Fitzgerald and Edith Wharton." *Times Literary Supplement* (London), 29 September 1966, 899.

In letter to editor, Turnbull rebuts Mizener's account of the Fitzgerald visit to EW in some detail, arguing that his version came from Margaret Winthrop Chanler's son, Theodore. Quotes Chanler's letter to him after he sent Mizener's version from *The Far Side of Paradise*. In Chanler's version, Fitzgerald is fawning and flattering, Wharton, shy and ill at ease, and the bordello comment is supposedly part of a rough joke to break the ice. [For cross references see L115.]

L117   Tuttleton, James W. "Edith Wharton, High Priestess of Reason." *The Personalist* (Pacific Philosophical Quarterly) 47 (July 1966): 382-98.

Argues that EW, as some have suggested, was not leaning to conversion to Catholicism. Cites evidence of her early reading, her rejection of intuition as opposed to reason, her insistence on man's place in society as paramount to his identity, her pragmatic outlook, her basic philosophy of "courageous resignation." Cites: *ABG, VofD, EF, HofM, New Year's Day, SatF, Motor-Flight through France, FofT, AofI.*

L118   Tuttleton, James W. "Life-Lover." *Commentary* 86.3 (September 1988): 65-68.
      Review of R.W.B. and Nancy Lewis's *Letters of Edith Wharton*. Notes the letters bury the frigid Grande Dame image, offer new insights into the Fullerton affair, illuminate her attitude toward America and her move to France, trace the formation of her literary principles and critical judgment and disclose her political views. [See H1]

L119   Tuttleton, James W. "The President and the Lady: Edith Wharton and Theodore Roosevelt." *Bulletin of the New York Public Library* 69 (January 1965): 49-57. [Note: Since Spring, 1978, *Bulletin of Research in Humanities*.]
      Gives three reasons for Newland Archer's entering politics and the reference to Roosevelt in *Age of Innocence*: 1) "to reflect a transition in the opinion of conservative New Yorkers about involvement" in politics; 2) to further characterize Archer; 3) to offer Roosevelt as the "perfect antithesis" to Archer and his passive world. Discusses EW's friendship with Roosevelt, draws parallels between their lives, and includes "With the Tide"--written by EW on Roosevelt's death.

L120   Tyler, William R. "Personal Memories of Edith Wharton." *Proceedings of the Massachusetts Historical Society* 85 (1973): 91-104.
      Read at the 1972 meeting at the Club of Odd Volumes, Boston, and later (May 1973) at the Society meeting. Details his relationship from childhood with EW. Contains his letter to Lubbock praising *Portrait of Edith Wharton*, Lubbock's reply, and notes his (Tyler's) negative reevaluation of Lubbock's book in later life. Many warm reminiscences of EW and quotes from her letters to him

until her death serve to refute Lubbock's negative characterization.

L121   Updike, Daniel Berkeley. "Notes on the Press and Its Work." In *Updike: American Printer and His Merrymount Press*. New York: The American Institute of Graphic Arts, 1947.

Generously applauds Wharton as a valuable friend of Merrymount Press who stipulated that Updike should print *The Greater Inclination* for Scribner's and thus set up the fortunate Scribner connection. Mentions printing: *Touchstone, CI, VofD, Sanctuary, MdeT*. Includes title pages from *The Greater Inclination* and *Sanctuary*.

L122   Vanderbilt, Kermit. *Charles Eliot Norton: Apostle of Culture in a Democracy*. Cambridge: Harvard, 1959.

Two brief mentions of his help guiding EW's career and reference to his injunction (in light of *Valley of Decision*) to avoid illicit passion as subject.

L123   Weber, Katharine. "R.W.B. Lewis." *Publishers Weekly*, 24 June 1988, 90-91.

Interview with R.W.B. and Nancy Lewis that concerns their collaboration on *The Letters of Edith Wharton*. To Professor Lewis, the revelation of the letters was "not of any *event*, but ... what a disgraceful, thoughtless, selfish pig Fullerton was." [See H1.]

L124   Wilson, Edmund. *The Crack-Up*. New York: New Directions, 1945.

See "Introduction." Reprints EW's letter 1925 on *Gatsby* with her praise and the complaint that he did not include more of Gatsby's background.

L125   Wilson, Edmund. "Edith Wharton: A Memoir by an English Friend." *New Yorker* 23 (4 Oct 1947): 101-04. Rpt. *Classics and Commercials: A Literary Chronicle of the Forties*. New York: Farrar, Straus, 1950.

Discussion of problems of Lubbock's *Portrait of EW*. Cites Lubbock's failure to understand EW as an American, the concrete details of her life that are not considered, Lubbock's attitude toward EW's men, his personal animosity toward Berry. [See N20; in N14]

L126 Wilson, Vincent. *The Book of Distinguished American Women*. Brookeville, Maryland: American History Research Associates, 1983.

Contains page-length biographies of fifty distinguished, native-born American women. Wharton's notes influence of James, similarities to Proust and Thackeray. Aimed at high-school readers.

L127 Wolff, Cynthia Griffin. "The Women in My Life." *Massachusetts Review* 24.2 (Summer 1983): 438-452.

Discusses how she came to write *Feast of Words* and retells her relationship with EW. Recounts finding of the Palmato fragment at the Beinecke, friendship with R.W.B. Lewis. [See N17, N28]

L128 Wolff, Geoffrey. *Black Sun*. The Brief Transit and Violent Eclipse of Harry Crosby. New York: Random House, 1976.

Quotes *A Backward Glance* on Wharton's debt to Walter Berry (Harry Crosby's cousin) as editor and literary mentor--which role Berry also played in Crosby's life. Claims she wanted to marry Berry. Describes Wharton's role in "comic opera scenes" after Berry's death, involving his ashes and the extremely valuable library he willed to Wharton and Crosby.

L129 Zilversmit, Annette. "Feminists and Edith Wharton." *The New Criterion* 7.10 (June 1989): 83-85.

Letter to the editor in response to Tuttleton's charges that feminists have "taken over" Wharton scholarship from a former President of the Edith Wharton Society. Notes male interest in Wharton scholarship and the variety of feminist approaches. [For Tuttleton's original article see Q83.] Argues that Tuttleton speaks from an "ultra-reactionary platform."

Chapter 4

Literary Relationships

The majority of the studies in this chapter deal with Edith Wharton's relationship with Henry James. There is necessarily some overlapping with Chapter 3 (Biography) in terms of other literary relationships, particularly with Fitzgerald. Fitzgerald biographical material is in Chapter 3 and scholarship focusing on Wharton as a literary influence on Fitzgerald is here. Many of the book-length studies (See Chapter 9) include important studies of literary relationships also. Refer to the Subject Index for all material on any particular author.

M1 Ammons, Elizabeth. "New Literary History: Edith Wharton and Jessie Redmon Fauset." *College Literature* 14.3 Edith Wharton Issue (1987): 207-218.

  Argues that the Black Harlem Renaissance author, Jessie Fauset, "stands as one of Edith Wharton's most important peers and inheritors." Maintains the new literary history sheds light on traditional critical categorizing, that there are significant similarities between Wharton and Fauset (particularly class as it affected their work) and significant differences that emphasize the racism of white literary criticism which assumes as universal issues and perspectives that are often actually characteristic of white women--e.g., the question of the break with a negative mother against whom the daughters rightly rebel.

M2   Anderson, Hilton. "A Whartonian Woman in *Dodsworth*." *Sinclair Lewis Newsletter* 1 (Spring 1969): 5-6.

Notes Lewis's admiration for Wharton and her probable influence on Edith Cartwright in *Dodsworth*. Also mentions Fanny deMalrive, Anna Leath and Rose Sellars as possible other influences, admired by Lewis and, like Wharton, American women estranged from their husbands, American in spite of their years abroad, ideal in manners, morals and social position and all in love with American men.

M3   Atkinson, Brooks. "A Peek Beneath the Immaculate Surfaces of Henry James and Edith Wharton." *New York Times*, 20 April 1965, 36.

Occasioned by the publication of Millicent Bell's *Edith Wharton and Henry James*. Maintains that from a modern perspective their "circumscribed sphere of life seems absurd, and their personal failures seem petty and droll." Nevertheless, notes that each had a personal hell and in the deepest sense, in spite of their genteel development, they were underprivileged people. [See M6]

M4   Bell, Millicent. "The Eagle and the Worm." *London Magazine* 6 (July 1966): 5-46.

Material here appears in Bell's *Edith Wharton and Henry James*. Letters from James to Wharton, Berry, Lapsley, Sturgis, Mary Cadwallader Jones, Sally Norton and quotations from the Love Diary--mistakenly attributed to her relationship with Berry. Details Wharton's relationship with James, his comic and serious view of her and her life, and the disintegration of her marriage. James emerges as sympathetic, but also at times satirical, and at others, a sober questioner of her values. Cites: *EF, Reef*. [See M6]

M5   Bell, Millicent. "Edith Wharton and Henry James: The Literary Relation." *PMLA* 74 (December 1959): 619-37.

Traces early critical pronouncements that she was Jamesian. Contends with *HofM* in 1905 she emerged as a definite individual. Argues that although Wharton was attracted by James's *kind* of story--involving subtleties of moral responsibility and the artistic life--*treatment* is significantly different: Wharton short story is based on situation, Jamesian, on the character of the reflector. Unlike James, Wharton has talent for the definition of social types, is a satirist as an end, not a means, has sociological concern for forces of environment, anticipating naturalism, and employs the chronicle novel. In short, difference lies in her outward, his inward, gaze. Argues only in *Reef* are both method and intention Jamesian. Many carefully chosen parallels and contrasts. Discusses: *M'sR*, *AofI*, *EF*, *Reef*, *CC*, *MdeT*, *FofT*, *Greater Inclination*, *VofD*, *HofM*, *Touchstone*, "Pretext," "Moving Finger," "Muse's Tragedy," "Portrait." For full treatment see M6.

M6   Bell, Millicent. *Edith Wharton and Henry James: The Story of Their Friendship*. New York: Braziller, 1965.

Valuable study of friendship and literary influences. Two parts: History of the friendship as available through unpublished letters and other manuscript sources. Mistakes Berry for Fullerton. Second Part assesses the influences of James--similarities and differences. Concludes: Wharton's "ethical impulse ... always bears reference to a particular time and place." In James, there is "an inexpungable attachment to transcendent values...." James's primary concern, Bell contends, is not as sociological as Wharton's. Appendix: "Lady Into Author: Edith Wharton and the House of Scribner." Strives to cover all aspects of the literary influence: form, subject, theories of fiction. [See L18, M4, M5]

M7   Berthold, Michael Coulson. "The Idea of 'Too Late' in James's 'The Beast in the Jungle.'" *Henry James Review* 4 (1983): 128-139.

Cites, within a discussion of the idea of "too late" in
James's *The Beast in the Jungle*, Wharton's use of the
theme in *The House of Mirth* and *The Age of Innocence*,
noting similarities in Marcher, Selden and Archer.
However, argues that Wharton works with a clearer sense
of inevitability than James with his open-endedness.

M8   Bewley, Marius. *The Eccentric Design*. London: Chatto and
        Windus, 1959.
              Brief mention of Wharton in discussion of James's
        "Crapy Cornelia" maintains she knew the new moneyed
        New York as opposed to the old social New York better
        than he did and terms *CC* superb.

M9   Blackall, Jean Frantz. "Henry and Edith: 'The Velvet
        Glove' as an 'In' Joke." *Henry James Review* 7.1 (Fall
        1985): 21-25.
              Maintains that reading James's "The Velvet Glove"
        with attention to the title, as well as other titles within
        the work, yields a sense of a "more intimate ... open"
        response to Wharton's fiction than Adeline Tintner's
        "courtly joking" or Leon Edel's theory of explicit parody.
        Cautions James's viewpoint should not be assumed to be
        Berridge's in the story. [See M20, M21, M48]

M10   Blom, T.E. "Anita Loos and Sexual Economics: Gentlemen
        Prefer Blondes." *Canadian Review of American Studies* 7.1
        (Spring 1976): 39-47.
              Describes Wharton's letter of January 1926 in praise
        of *Gentlemen Prefer Blondes* to Frank Crowninshield and
        Wharton's protest, when Loos argued that she had
        overpraised the book as the Great American Novel, that
        she meant every word.

M11   Brownell, W.C. "Henry James." *Atlantic Monthly* 95 (April
        1905): 494-519. Rpt. *Modern Prose Masters* (New York:
        1909) and "Modern Student's Library" Edition of *American
        Prose Masters* (New York: 1923).
              Brownell, Wharton's editor at Scribner's, here takes up
        the problems of the later James, stemming from his

theoretical bias, detachment and particular type of realism. Wharton supposedly agreed with Brownell's reservations.

M12   Cady, Edwin H. *The Realist at War: The Mature Years of William Dean Howells*. New York: Syracuse University Press, 1958.

In second half of biography of Howells, sporadic Wharton commentary--her contention that *A Modern Instance* was forerunner of *Main Street* and *Babbitt* and her complaint about his "Incurable moral timidity." Also notes his praise of Wharton in *Harper's* as "a star of literary conscience and artistic ideal, pure, clear, serene." Cites: *BkofH*. [See O40]

M13   Coard, Robert L. "Edith Wharton's Influence on Sinclair Lewis." *Modern Fiction Studies* 31 (Autumn 1985): 511-527.

Succinct, comprehensive, excellent study of Lewis's debt to Wharton. Notes that it is with "Wharton's Balzackian side and its sustained descriptions of society rather than with her analytical, highly selective Jamesian side that Lewis identifies." Draws parallels between several Lewis novels and short stories and *The Custom of the Country, Summer, Ethan Frome, The House of Mirth, The Age of Innocence, The Reef*, "Bunner Sisters," "Xingu," "The Pelican," "The Legend," and also Wharton herself. Concentrates on parallels between *Main Street* and *Summer*.

M14   Cooke, Delmar G. *William Dean Howells, A Critical Study*. New York: Dutton, 1922. Rpt. 1967.

Wharton only briefly mentioned as a contrast to Howells's style, with her superior artistry, as in description of dawning of spring in Italy. Contends she can make the reader a direct spectator better than either Howells or James. *Italian Backgrounds*.

M15   Cowley, Malcolm. *Exile's Return*. New York: Norton, 1934.

Unindexed, p.8. Only mention of Wharton comes in Cowley's objection to Fitzgerald's contention that the older generation could never understand those born at the turn of the century. Cowley argues Wharton probably understood Fitzgerald better than he understood her.

M16   Duggan, Margaret M. "Edith Wharton's Gatsby Letter." *Fitzgerald-Hemingway Annual* 1972: 85-87.
        Reprints EW's letter on *The Great Gatsby* with comment on first meeting with Fitzgerald at Scribner's when he threw himself at her feet. Notes Edmund Wilson's reprint of letter in *The Crack-Up* and his footnote that erroneously corrects Wharton's "Hildeshiem" to Hildeseim--although that name is actually Wolfshiem in *Gatsby*. [See L124]

M17   Dupee, Frederick W. *Henry James*. New York: Sloane, 1951.
        Briefly mentions Wharton's visits to Lamb House and her memories of James in *A Backward Glance*.

M18   Dupree, Ellen Phillips. "Wharton, Lewis and the Nobel Prize Address." *American Literature* 56.2 (May 1984): 262-270.
        Stems from Wharton's letter to Sinclair Lewis, naming *The Man Who Knew Coolidge* his best novel. Notes warm early relationship with the Lewises that had cooled by the time of Lewis's Nobel Prize. Recounts Wharton's criticism of Lewis's derogatory remarks about William Dean Howells in his Nobel Prize address.

M19   Edel, Leon, and Gordon N. Ray. *Henry James and H.G. Wells*. Urbana: University of Illinois, 1958.
        A few references to Wharton, mentioning social visits and inclusion of James's London *Times* article "The Younger Generation" which has a discussion of *CC*. [See M35]

M20   Edel, Leon. *Henry James: A Life*. New York: Harper and Row, 1985.
        This one-volume revision and condensation of Edel's five-volume life of James contains Wharton material in the

other volumes, condensed, and interesting revision that names Wharton as one of the inspirations for the negative view of the rich in "Crapy Cornelia." [See M21, M22, M23]

M21   Edel, Leon. *Henry James: The Master: 1901-1916.* Philadelphia: Lippincott, 1972.

Full and insightful account of Wharton's relationship with James, describing her visits to Lamb House, James's knowledge of her affair with Fullerton, his visits to her at Lenox and in Paris, his satire of her in "The Velvet Glove," her attempts to raise funds for his seventieth birthday gift, their motor trips, their circle of friends. Edel concludes that James preserved a certain detachment, and that he admired her as he did other assertive women, but had a tendency to become rather passive under her dominating presence and had reservations about her manner of life, although his warm friendship in her time of troubles with the increasingly unstable Teddy and during the affair with Fullerton was deeply genuine. Traces the development of the relationship, and James's growing affection. Also discusses Berry's place in her life. Valuable material on Fullerton throughout the volume, and thoughtful analysis of James's response to Wharton's work. Mentions: *The Custom of the Country, Ethan Frome, The Fruit of the Tree, The House of Mirth, A Motor-Flight Through France, Summer, The Reef.*

M22   Edel, Leon. *Henry James: The Middle Years: 1882-1895.* Philadelphia: Lippincott, 1962.

Wharton mentioned only in connection with Vernon Lee and Morton Fullerton, although volume is interesting for material on James's beginning friendship with Fullerton.

M23   Edel, Leon. *Henry James: The Treacherous Years: 1895-1901.* Philadelphia: Lippincott, 1969.

Wharton mentioned as wishing James good luck with *Guy Domville*--which Minnie Bourget told him. Most valuable for material on Fullerton.

M24   Firkins, Oscar W. *William Dean Howells, A Study.* New
        York: Russell and Russell, 1963.
            Passing references to Wharton throughout, all brief
        and used to illustrate an aspect of Howells--e.g., he was
        unable to transcend his customary material as Wharton
        does in *EF*.

M25   Gelfant, Blanche H. "Beyond Nihilism: The Fiction of
        George P. Elliott." *The Hollins Critic* 5 (December 1968):
        8-12.
            One brief mention of Wharton in this essay on
        George P. Elliott mentions that Wharton, like Elliott and
        James, deals in considerable detail with architecture, seeing
        a house as it projects an individual's social class, personal
        taste and moral sensibility.

M26   Hanley, Lynne T. "The Eagle and the Hen: Edith Wharton
        and Henry James." *Research Studies* 49.3 (September 1981):
        143-153.
            Analyzes difference in theory and technique between
        James and Wharton. Contends that, though Wharton
        learned much craft from James, she was "suspicious of the
        master's preoccupation with theory, aesthetic control, and
        detachment from life." Argues their greatest difference lies
        in "their sense of their relation to their subject; the
        woman interacts, records, and receives, the man
        commands, dictates and constructs." Contends James's
        highest value is composition; Wharton's, verisimilitude.
        Cites: *CC*, *Buc*, *ABG*, *WofF*.

M27   Hays, Peter L. "Edith Wharton and F. Scott Fitzgerald."
        Edith Wharton Newsletter 3.1 (Spring 1986): 2.
            Argues Fitzgerald learned technique, use of symbolism
        and "sharp, concise imagery" in part from Wharton.
        Discusses *Ethan Frome*'s influence on his early story, "The
        Cut Glass Bowl" (1919).

M28   Hoffman, Frederick J. "Points of Moral Reference: A
        Comparative Study of Edith Wharton and F. Scott

Fitzgerald." English Institute Essays. Edited by Alan S. Downer. New York: Columbia University Press, 1950.

Contends Wharton always desires order--and that she kept a fixed point of moral reference--the values of Old New York before the Civil War. Her view of order is associated with the question of taste. Fitzgerald, on the other hand, after the disintegration of cultural values after WWI, was left in a void--searching for form and order and morally ineffective. Cites: *HofM, CC*.

M29   Hyde, H. Montgomery. *Henry James at Home*. New York: Farrar, Straus and Giroux, 1969. Expanded to book-length from speech of the same name delivered March 23, 1972, published in *Transactions [alternate title: Essays by Divers Hands]*, Royal Society of Literature of the United Kingdom, 38 (1975): 58-77.

Extensively quotes *A Backward Glance* on James's "pride that apes humility" as a host, his servants, Wharton's visits to Lamb house and their sometimes "absurd" motor tours in England. Discussion of their friendship portrays her somewhat unsympathetically. Claims Wharton saw herself as James's disciple and had an affair with Walter Berry, whom she wanted to marry.

M30   James, Henry. *The Letters of Henry James*. Edited by Leon Edel. Cambridge, Massachusetts: Belknap Press of Harvard University, 1987. Volumes III, 1883-1895 and IV, 1895-1916.

Volume III: Mention only in notes and a reference to her in Bourget letter (1895). However, contains interesting letters to Fullerton. Vol IV: Introduction contains valuable analysis of the Wharton-James relationship, noting "James's literary inventions and techniques were of secondary interest to her. She was always a conventional writer and interested above all in the story she had to tell." Maintains that James felt "mingled admiration with hesitation before her driving energies and the cleverness of her novels and stories." Also contends Wharton knew James's ambivalence toward her. Memorable material from Edel's own meetings with Wharton and Fullerton.

Contains 177 letters from James to Wharton from 1904-1915. Lists owners of letters. Appendix "Edith Wharton's Subsidy of *The Ivory Tower*." Well-indexed. Note James's comments on "The Line of Least Resistance," *Valley of Decision, Crucial Instances, The Touchstone,* "The Moving Finger," *Ethan Frome, The Reef, The House of Mirth,* and *The Fruit of the Tree.* Also see Wharton material in letters to Sturgis, Fullerton and Lapsley. [See M20, M21, M22, M23]

M31   James, Henry. *Henry James, Selected Letters.* Edited by Leon Edel. Cambridge: Belknap Press of Harvard University, 1987.

Introduction discusses James's friendship with Wharton and Fullerton; James was Wharton's confidante in the affair with Fullerton that both liberated and shamed her. In response to Fullerton's "sensuousness and romanticism," Wharton *and* James importuned him for more attention. Fascinating comparison of Wharton/Fullerton/James to Madame de Vionnet/Chad/Strether in *The Ambassadors.* Includes new letters from James to Fullerton, a letter to Howard Sturgis about Wharton's marital troubles. Five letters to Wharton discuss James' 1905 American tour, her marriage and affair, Fullerton's being blackmailed, Proust, James's horror over approach of WWI.

M32   James, Henry. *The Letters of Henry James.* 2 Volumes. Edited by Percy Lubbock. London: Macmillan, 1920. Rpt. N14.

See index Vol. II for complete Wharton material. The famous letter of December 4, 1912, on *The Reef* is here in which James terms it the finest thing she has done and calls it Racinian. Here, too, is comment she lacks a country of her own. [See M30, M31, M34]

M33   James, Henry. *Letters of Henry James to Walter Berry.* Edited by Harry and Caresse Crosby. Paris: Black Sun Press, 1928.

Letters of 1905-1908 and 1911 contain frequent references to the "Lady of Lenox" and the "Angel of

Devastation"--with James's marvel at her way of life. Available Columbia University Rare Books.

M34   James, Henry. *The Selected Letters of Henry James.* Edited by Leon Edel. New York: Farrar, Straus and Cudahy, 1955.
        Letter to Wharton from London December 1, 1914, sent by Walter Berry--talks of Berry's account of the "transcendent high pitch of Berlin." Mentions staying with her to Robert Norton in 1914 letter.

M35   James, Henry. "The Younger Generation." *Times Literary Supplement*, 2 April 1914, 157-158. Rpt. *Notes on Novelists, With Some Other Notes.* New York: Scribner's, 1914. Also in Leon Edel and Gordon N. Ray. *Henry James and H.G. Wells.* Urbana: University of Illinois Press, 1958.
        James's discussion of *The Custom of the Country* which notes Wharton as applying the principle of selectivity and intention--as against those who merely document--and as being almost "scientifically satiric" in the novel. He finds that a "dry light" gathers in the novel, the essence of which is a "particular fine asperity" with "the masculine conclusion tending so to crown the feminine observation."

M36   Lawson, Richard H. "Gesellschaft als Verbindungselement zwischen den Seldwyla-Novellen Gottfried Kellers und den Romanen Edith Whartons." Festschrift. 1971.
        ["Society as the Connecting Element Between the Seldwyla Novels of Gottfried Keller and the Books of Edith Wharton."] In German. Contends Wharton's Preface to the English translation of "A Village Romeo and Juliet" demonstrates an understanding of Keller and his time. Traces Keller's influence on *Summer* and *The Age of Innocence.* Concludes that Wharton saw in Keller a model and an author with whom she shared nearly identical social and literary attitudes.[See N16]

M37   Lawson, Richard H. "Thematic Similarities in Edith Wharton and Thomas Mann." *Twentieth Century Literature* 23 (1977): 289-98.

Analyzes parallel themes in the work of Thomas Mann
and Wharton 1900-1913. Notes the basic theme in both
was "the decline and disintegration of that ancestral *haut-
bourgeois* society ... together with the effects of that
disintegration on its descendants." Discusses parallels in
use of the *Bildungsroman*, irony, characterization, narrative
technique and philosophical orientation as well as their
significant differences. Cites: *HofM, FofT, CC, Reef.* [See
N16]

M38   Leach, Nancy R. "Edith Wharton's Interest in Walt
        Whitman." *Yale University Library Gazette* 33 (Oct 1958):
        63-66.
            Notes EW's admiration for Whitman, apparent from
        the manuscript of *Literature* and her notes outlining a
        book-length study of the poet. Speculates that in Whitman
        EW found "the clearest exponent of her yearning for
        release from the stifling conventions surrounding her life
        as a woman and artist in America."

M39   Lewis, Grace Hegger. *With Love From Gracie: Sinclair
        Lewis, 1912-1925.* New York: Harcourt, 1955.
            Personal, anecdotal approach to life of Sinclair Lewis
        by his first wife. Notes meeting Wharton at Pavillon
        Colombe where conversation turned on "much delicate
        dissecting of the technique of writing," that she warned
        him against the use of slang, that EW said Lewis, in *Main
        Street*, taught her of a Midwest she knew nothing about.

M40   Millgate, Michael. "Scott Fitzgerald as Social Novelist:
        Statement and Technique in *The Great Gatsby*." *Modern
        Language Review* 57 (July 1962): 335-39.
            Notes Wharton's influence on *The Great Gatsby*.
        Quotes her criticism of the book (Lack of Gatsby's
        background) and argues she used this technique in
        presenting Elmer Moffatt in *CC*. Mentions other parallels
        between the two books and similar social subject matter,
        characters and attitude toward the American class system
        dominated by money. Also cites: *FofT*.

M41   Puknat, E.M. "American Literary Encounters with Rilke." *Monatshefte* (University of Wisconsin) 60.3 (Fall 1968): 245-256.

Notes Wharton as one of the earliest American authors to admire Rilke who, to her, represented part of the flowering of European civilization which was shattered by WWI.

M42   Rothwell, Kenneth S. "From Society to Babbittry: Lewis's Debt to Edith Wharton." *Journal of Central Mississippi Valley American Studies Association* 1 (Spring 1960): 32-37. N.B.: Journal retitled as *Midcontinent American Studies Journal*, again retitled *American Studies*.

Compares *Babbitt* and *The Age of Innocence* in plot, theme and character. Contends that Lewis's respect for Wharton added a dimension to *Babbitt* that "may guarantee the survival of its forlorn hero long after the bulk of his creator's works have been forgotten."

M43   Rouse, Blair. *Ellen Glasgow*. New York: Twayne, 1962.

A few references to Wharton with comment that she was far superior in portraying New York because Glasgow only knew it as a visitor.

M44   Seldes, Gilbert. "Spring Flight." *Dial* 79 (August 1925): 162-64.

Briefly alludes to Wharton as influencing the scenic structure of *The Great Gatsby*, a method derived from James.

M44.1   Seymour, Miranda. *A Ring of Conspirators: Henry James and his Literary Circle: 1895-1915*. Boston: Houghton Mifflin, 1989.

Chapter includes entertaining overview of Henry James's relationship with EW, set in the context of the mostly American circle of Howard Sturgis and his friends at Queen's Acre. Praises Sturgis as an ideal host, funny and a perfect "intellectual sparring-partner." Includes James's devastating criticism of Sturgis's *Belchamber*. Discusses James's and EW's

shared sense of humor and the "malice, envy and
irritation" in their friendship, including their comments
on each other's work. Contrasts their careers and calls
EW a social satirist, James, a psychologist. Says HJ
misrepresented EW as The Angel of Devastation and
The Mount as "oppressively rich" when he deeply
enjoyed her hospitality and the use of her cars. Sketch
of the Fullerton affair seems to ignore Wharton's
letters to Fullerton. Shows EW turning to Berry after
the affair, in part as indefatigable travelling
companion. Heavily draws from *A Backward Glance*
and Lewis's biography (N17).

M45   Sharp, Sr. M. Corona. *The Confidante in Henry James*.
Notre Dame: University of Notre Dame Press, 1963.
Defines Wharton as a maternal friend of James.
Argues that her conversation offered him "the sustaining
firmness which had so characterized his mother." Discusses
Wharton along with other women in his life in light of his
own bachelorhood.

M46   Tintner, Adeline R. "Fiction Is the Best Revenge: Portraits
of Henry James by Four Women Writers." *Turn of the
Century Women* 2.2 (Winter 1985): 42-49.
Contends Vernon Lee (Violet Paget), Mrs. Humphrey
Ward, Olive Garnett and Wharton took revenge on James
"by making him a character in their stories and thereby
under their control." Wharton section is shortest, restating
the case of her earlier article [See T35], noting Wharton's
portraits of James in "The Hermit and the Wild Woman,"
"Ogrin the Hermit," "The Eyes," and "Writing A War
Story."

M47   Tintner, Adeline R. "Jamesian Structures in *The Age of
Innocence* and Related Stories." *Twentieth Century
Literature* 26 (1980): 332-47.
Examination of the Jamesian influence on *The Age of
Innocence* and *Old New York*, arguing that this was a
period in her life when Wharton was deeply involved in
thinking about James and planning for the publication of

his letters. Also cites: "Writing A War Story" and "The Eyes."

M48   Tintner, Adeline R. "James's Mock Epic: 'The Velvet Glove' Edith Wharton and Other Late Tales." *Modern Fiction Studies* 17 (1971-72): 483-99.

    Argues James's short story, "The Velvet Glove" is a "mock-epic with a meticulously worked out classical mythology understructuring the imagery, language, and characterization, all mounted to launch an elaborate literary joke"--on Wharton. Using references from James's letters and life, builds the case that Wharton is both Artemis and the Scribbling Princess, Amy Evans. Also suggests Wharton as inspiration for aspects of "Crapy Cornelia," The Bench of Desolation," and "A Round of Visits."

M49   Tintner, Adeline. "The Metamorphoses of Edith Wharton in Henry James's *The Finer Grain*." *Twentieth Century Literature* 21 (1975): 355-79.

    Proposes that the stories of James's *The Finer Grain* "are the fictional analogues of the complex ... feelings that characterized" his friendship with Wharton. Careful readings of the separate stories support the thesis. Concludes with an interpretation of "The Eyes" seeing James as Culwin. *Reef, FofT, HofM*, "Cup of Cold Water," "Mission of Jane," "Lamp of Psyche," "Introducers."

M50   Tintner, Adeline. "Wharton and James: Some Literary Give and Take." *Edith Wharton Newsletter* 3.1 (Spring 1986): 3.

    Insightful speculation about the influence of James's work on Wharton, and vice versa. Cites examples from *Crucial Instances* and *Touchstone*--James's "The Birthplace" influenced by "Angel at the Grave"--"The Recovery" indebted to "The Tree of Knowledge"--Wharton's "Copy" reminiscent of "Broken Wings"--and parallels existing between "Moving Finger" and two James stories: "The Special Type" and "The Tone of Time." Notes *Touchstone* contains dialogue similar to "A Given Case" and itself perhaps was the inspiration for the last pages of *The Wings of the Dove.*

M51   Tuttleton, James W. "Henry James and Edith Wharton: Fiction as the House of Fame." *Midcontinent American Studies Journal* 7 (Spring 1966): 25-36.

      Discusses Virginia Woolf's criticism of the Balzacian mode of characterization, and details Wharton's use and defense of it with the observation that novelists like Wharton and James believed that "the material properties of existence not merely express, but also, in a special sense, 'constitute' character." Examples drawn from *CC, HofM* and *Buc.*

M52   Tuttleton, James W. "Louis Auchincloss: The Image of Lost Elegance and Virtue." *American Literature* 43 (January 1972): 616-32.

      Passing references to Wharton in a general appreciation of Auchincloss as a relevant novelist in the tradition of the novel of manners. Most of what is said about Wharton contrasts the possibilities of the novel of manners set in New York in her more class-conscious society with the novel of contemporary upper-class life. Cites: *ONY.*

M53   Warren, Joyce W. *The American Narcissus: Individualism and Women in Nineteenth Century American Fiction.* New Brunswick, New Jersey: Rutgers University Press, 1984.

      Wharton mentioned in connection with James. Notes his sympathy on her divorce, terms her one of his closest friends, proving the point that James respected women as individuals like himself.

Chapter 5

Book-length Studies and Essay Collections

This chapter includes all book-length studies and essay collections devoted to Edith Wharton, except M6, which covers Edith Wharton's relationship with Henry James; R7.13, which pertains exclusively to Ethan Frome; and R15.16, which deals with *Old New York*.

N1   Ammons, Elizabeth. *Edith Wharton's Argument with America*. Athens: University of Georgia Press, 1980.
       Excellent, definitive, seminal feminist study which details Wharton's argument with patriarchal society. Examines the issue of the child-woman, the economic foundations of patriarchy, and Wharton's eventual mysticism in her concept of the maternal principle which grew out of her war experiences. Traces mythic and fairy tale patterns throughout her work. Should be consulted as the basis for later feminist analyses. Discusses all of the major fiction, "Bunner Sisters," "Beatrice Palmato," "The Valley of Childish Things."

N2   Auchincloss, Louis. *Edith Wharton*. Minneapolis: University of Minnesota Press, 1961. University of Minnesota

Pamphlets on American Writers Series, No. 12. Rpt. *Seven Modern American Novelists*. Edited by William Van O'Connor.

[See Q5]

N3   Auchincloss, Louis. *Edith Wharton: A Woman in Her Time*. New York: Viking, 1971.

Illustrated, well-written biography.

N4   Baril, James Ronald. *Vision as Metaphorical Perception in the Fiction of Edith Wharton*. Colorado: University of Colorado Press, 1969.

Published dissertation. Applies Robert Heilman's four-part division of the activity of seeing--act of seeing; object seen; condition of seeing and means for seeing--to *The House of Mirth*, *The Custom of the Country*, *Ethan Frome* and *The Age of Innocence*. Studies patterns of imagery that are repeated from work to work and interconnected thematically.

N5   Bloom, Harold. *Edith Wharton*. New York: Chelsea House, 1986.

Essay collection contains: "A Writer of Short Stories," by R.W.B. Lewis; "Undine" by Richard Lawson [N16]; "Fairy-tale Love and *The Reef*" by Elizabeth Ammons [R8.9]; "*Hudson River Bracketed* and *The Gods Arrive*" by Margaret B. McDowell [N22]; "*Ethan Frome*: This Vision of His Story" from *A Feast of Words* by Cynthia Griffin Wolff [N28]; "Edith Wharton and the Ghost Story" by Allan Gardner Smith [T34]; "Purity and Power in *The Age of Innocence*" by Judith Fryer [R12.39]; "The Divided Conflict of Edith Wharton's *Summer*" by Carol Wershoven [R10.27]; "Debasing Exchange: Edith Wharton's *The House of Mirth*" by Wai-chee Dimock [R4.50]; "The Death of the Lady (Novelist): Wharton's *House of Mirth*" by Elaine Showalter [R4.92]. Includes bibliography. Bloom's introduction concerns *The Custom of the Country* as Edith Wharton's portrait, in Undine, of her antithetical self and *Ethan Frome* as stemming from the American romantic tradition of Hawthorne and Melville.

N6   Bretschneider, Margaret Ann. *Edith Wharton: Patterns of Rejection and Denial*. Case Western Reserve University, 1969.

Published dissertation examines as the basic psychological pattern underlying Wharton's novels characters who are initially rejected, or feel that they are, who then engage in self-defeating behavior which ultimately leads to further rejection. Traces character patterns of the reluctant hero and the unloved woman.

N7   Brown, Edward K. *Edith Wharton: Etudes Critiques*. Paris: Librarie Droz, 1935.

In French. Brown's book is his thesis presented at the University of Paris. It has never been translated into English, but see his articles in English for his positions. He covers the short stories, novellas and novels, the international theme, similarities with Henry James, Sinclair Lewis, Ellen Glasgow, Washington Irving, Jane Austen, George Eliot, Thackeray, Balzac, Bourget, Tolstoy. Covers the novel of situation, character and manners, theories of the novel, style, New York society in her work, France in her work, her poetry, travel writings, her reputation, influence, and contribution to the American novel. [In N14]

N8   Coolidge, Olivia. *Edith Wharton 1862-1937*. New York: Scribner's, 1964.

Well-written young people's biography.

N9   Cross, Wilbur. *Edith Wharton*. New York: Appleton, 1926.

Pamphlet. Appreciative overview mentions meeting Wharton when she received her honorary doctorate at Yale. Examines Wharton as an artist, drawing comparisons with George Eliot, James, Hawthorne and Thackeray. Notes her differences from the chaotic moderns like Joyce. Comments *The House of Mirth* struck him as a tragic situation with unrealistic character and incident, overly determined by the author. Also cites: *ONY*, "The Other Two," "The Long Run," *EF*, *Summer*, *AofI*, *GofM*, *M'sR*,

"The Seed of the Faith," "Velvet Earpads," "Bewitched," "The Young Gentlemen."

N10   Fryer, Judith. *Felicitous Space: The Imaginative Structures of Edith Wharton and Willa Cather.* Chapel Hill: University of North Carolina Press, 1986.

Feminist inquiry into the relationship between space and the female imagination at the beginning of modern America. Loosely organized in terms of meditations, ranges widely with material drawn from history, literature, environmental psychology, sociology, anthropology, geography, philosophy, architecture and the arts, exploring Wharton as a woman defined by space and the restrictions of her time and place as those considerations affect her fiction. Defines Wharton as "a true Renaissance woman" who "provides an appropriate index to the period." Finds that her books *The Decoration of Houses* and *Italian Villas and Their Gardens* as well as her novels "comprise a great lode of information about human enclosures and human interactions." Detailed readings of *The House of Mirth, The Custom of the Country, The Age of Innocence, Ethan Frome, Summer* and *A Backward Glance.* [See V97, Q26, R12.39]

N11   Gerould, Katharine Fullerton. *Edith Wharton: A Critical Study.* New York: Appleton, n.d. [probably 1922]

Available Beinecke Yale. Written by Morton Fullerton's former fiancee who was raised as his sister and later herself became a writer. Twelve-page pamphlet refutes argument Wharton merely imitated James, gives brief biographical data, defends Wharton's choice of cultured protagonists and emphasizes her passionate preoccupation with her own country and the technical proficiency that makes her a great storyteller and very popular. Cites: *HofM, EF, GofM.*

N12   Gimbel, Wendy. *Orphancy and Survival.* Landmark Dissertations in Women's Studies, edited by Annette Baxter. New York: Praeger, 1984.

Feminist study of the ways the heroines of *The House of Mirth, Ethan Frome* and *Summer* shrink from experience and Ellen Olenska in *The Age of Innocence* attains maturity in light of Wharton's own quest for emotional independence. Studies particularly the metaphor of the house.

N13   Griffith, Grace Kellogg. *The Two Lives of Edith Wharton: The Woman and Her Work*. New York: Appleton-Century, 1965.
       Popularized biography outdated by Lewis and Woolf, but interesting for descriptions of her life and society--somewhat overly dramatized. [See N17, N28]

N14   Howe, Irving. *Edith Wharton: A Collection of Critical Essays*. *Twentieth Century Views*. Englewood Cliffs, New Jersey: Prentice-Hall, 1962.
       Contents: "Introduction: The Achievement of Edith Wharton" by Irving Howe [Q40]; "Justice to Edith Wharton" by Edmund Wilson [O91]; "Edith Wharton and Her New Yorks" by Louis Auchincloss [Q4]; "The Novels of Edith Wharton" by Percy Lubbock [O49]; "Edith Wharton" by E.K. Brown [N7]; "Henry James's Heiress: The Importance of Edith Wharton" by Q.D. Leavis [O45]; "Edith Wharton" by Alfred Kazin; "Edith Wharton: The Art of the Novel" by E.K. Brown [N7]; "*The House of Mirth* Revisited" by Diana Trilling [R4.98]; "A Reading of *The House of Mirth*" by Irving Howe [R4.29]; "On *Ethan Frome*" by Blake Nevius [R7.13]; "The Morality of Inertia" by Lionel Trilling [R7.54]; "On *The Reef*: A Letter" by Henry James; "Our Literary Aristocrat" by Vernon L. Parrington [R12.14]; "What Edith Wharton Saw in Innocence" by Louis O. Coxe [R12.34]; "On *The Age of Innocence*" by Blake Nevius; "Edith Wharton: A Memoir by an English Friend" by Edmund Wilson [L125]. Contains bibliography of Wharton's major writings and selected secondary bibliography.

N15   Lawson, Richard H. *Edith Wharton*. New York: Ungar, 1977.
       A short, general survey--part of the Modern Literature Monographs. Analyzes *The House of Mirth*, *Ethan Frome*,

The Reef, The Age of Innocence and *The Custom of the Country*. Biographical overview without the anachronistic impression of work published before the Fullerton material was available. Bibliography.

N16   Lawson, Richard H. *Edith Wharton and German Literature*. Bonn: Bouvier Verlag Herbert Grundmann, 1974.

Defines the two chief denominators of the German influence in Wharton's work as the "fairy-tale-medieval camp" and the "social camp" with the exception of Nietzsche to whom she responded "on a primarily emotional basis." English edition available. Contains bibliography and index. Discusses various sources for the Undine myth, the Bildungsroman, Goethe, Nietzsche, the influence of Sudermann and Gottfried Keller. Discusses the major novels and "The Blond Beast." [See M36, M37, R6.10, R10.24, T16, W7]

N17   Lewis, R.W.B. *Edith Wharton: A Biography*. New York: Harper and Row, 1975. Rpt. New York: Fromm, 1985.

The definitive biography published after the opening of the Yale archives. Important, compellingly written, extremely well-researched text. Won the Pulitzer Prize. Invaluable for information on Wharton's childhood, literary and social friendships, travels, homes, the place of each separate work in her life, her relationships with her various publishers, Henry James, Walter Berry, Morton Fullerton, her marriage, her war work, her residence in France. Published the "Beatrice Palmato" fragment for the first time. Contains appendices on the question of her paternity, Fullerton, and the "Beatrice Palmato" fragment. Contains long annotated bibliography, locations of major collections, detailed list of sources to consult for background information. Well indexed.

N18   Lindberg, Gary H. *Edith Wharton and the Novel of Manners*. Charlottesville, Virginia: University Press of Virginia, 1975.

Studies Wharton as a novelist of manners, concentrating on *The House of Mirth, The Custom of the*

Country and *The Age of Innocence*. Defines Wharton as a novelist "primarily interested in the meaning and effect of society" with a "peculiar genius" for "defining the traditions, duties, and social assumptions that impede the individual." Argues that "her inability to imagine the free self has serious consequences to her characterization."

N19   Lovett, Robert Morss. *Edith Wharton*. New York: Robert M. McBride, 1925.

    Lovett's book became a rallying point over the years, strongly attacked by those who favored Wharton and influential in the assessments of her detractors. He characterized her as defined by "Culture, class, morality" and of an old-fashioned Victorianism, devoted to Jamesian technique and his fidelity to moral values, absorbed in the "mechanical operations of class" and bound by the upper-class perspective. Lovett contended that she "remains for us among the voices whispering the last enchantments of the Victorian age" out of touch with the modern literary vision.

N20   Lubbock, Percy. *Portrait of Edith Wharton*. New York: Appleton-Century-Crofts, 1947.

    Gaillard Lapsley asked Percy Lubbock to write this book after Edith Wharton's death. It contains memoirs solicited from people who knew her as well as Lubbock's prefatory and transitional material. Condemns Berry. Has become highly controversial and seen as snide and at times vindictive, with an emphasis on the "grande dame" rather than the writer--whom he seems to dismiss. See references to Lubbock in Subject Index for commentaries.

N21   Lyde, Marilyn Jones. *Edith Wharton: Convention and Morality in the Work of a Novelist*. Norman: University of Oklahoma Press, 1959.

    Attempts to resolve the seeming contradictions in Wharton's art between a moral conservatism and sympathy for individual rebellion against convention through an analysis of Wharton's complex view of the relationship between morality and convention, involving her belief that beauty was an important aspect of morality and that individual circumstances always have a bearing on morality. Also discusses the role of wealth and the concept of tragedy in her vision and work and her aesthetic theory, attitudes toward religion and the influence of Darwin, Pascal, Hamilton and Coppée on the development of her thought. From "The Relation of Convention and Morality in the Work of Edith Wharton." Ph.D. dissertation. Chicago, 1957. For abstract see DAI X1957.

N22   McDowell, Margaret B. *Edith Wharton*. Twayne Series. Boston: G.K. Hall, 1976.

A measured, balanced analysis of Wharton and her work, written with grace and clarity. Particularly valuable for the attention given to the neglected fiction and the short stories. Argues that the work after 1920, so often dismissed, deserves renewed consideration. Contends that Wharton was a moralist as well as a writer of manners and a profound psychologist who could evoke the metaphysical and symbolic dimension of the experiences she dramatizes. Valuable also for the interpretation of Walter Berry's meaning and influence. Discusses: *The House of Mirth, The Fruit of the Tree, Madame de Treymes, Ethan Frome, Summer,* "Bunner Sisters," *The Custom of the Country, The Age of Innocence, A Son at the Front, Twilight Sleep, The Children, Hudson River Bracketed, The Gods Arrive, The Buccaneers.* Annotated bibliography of criticism.

N23   Nevius, Blake. *Edith Wharton: A Study of Her Fiction.* Berkeley: University of California, 1953. Sections rpt. *Twentieth Century Views* and Scribner Research Anthology.

The first major reassessment of Wharton after her death. Argues she has been neglected because of the modern "man with dinner pail" mentality. Contends she deserves attention because she chronicles a major aspect of social history--"the dramatic conflict between the ideals of the old mercantile and the new industrial societies." Next to James, she is America's most successful novelist of manners, and she develops two great themes. First, the trapped sensibility of the large, generous nature chained to a meaner nature. Second, the nature and limits of individual responsibility--what allowance of freedom the trapped sensibility can have without threatening the social structure. Chapter on *The Valley of Decision*, extended discussion of *The Fruit of the Tree,* *The Reef, Ethan Frome, The Custom of the Country, Summer, The Age of Innocence.* Index and bibliography.

N24   Quinn, Arthur Hobson. *Edith Wharton.* New York: Appleton-Century, 1938.
       Warmly appreciative 12-page publishers' publicity pamphlet written for Appleton on the publication of *The Buccaneers*. Ranges widely over her work, with emphasis that her major theme is "men and women whose moral or emotional reactions were determined by their social relations." Cites: *ABG*, "Bunner Sisters," *AofI, HofM,* "Roman Fever," *MdeT, EF, VofD, Buc,* dramatizations.

N25   Rahi, G.S. *Edith Wharton: A Study of Her Ethos and Art.* Amritsar: Guru Nanak Dev. UP, 1983.
       Studies Wharton's work in terms of the influence of her class and her "complex and ambivalent attitude towards [its] ethos" with emphasis on *The House of Mirth, The Reef, The Custom of the Country, The Age of Innocence, Ethan Frome* and *Summer*. Individual chapters cover the conflict between Old New York and the invading nouveaux riche, the place of women, convention versus individual freedom, wealth, style and technique. Employs theories of Thorstein Veblen in *Theories of the Leisure Class*.

N25.1   Sasaki, Miyoko. *Frisson and Reason: The World of Edith Wharton.* Tokyo: Kenkyūsha, 1976.
        * Not seen.

N26   Walton, Geoffrey. *Edith Wharton: A Critical Interpretation.* Rutherford: Fairleigh Dickinson University Press, 1970. Revised, 1982.

As an English critic, Walton draws interesting comparisons and contrasts with English novelists in his discussion of the major novels and nonfiction--particularly Jane Austen and George Eliot. His revision utilizes the new material from the opening of the Yale papers. Sees Wharton as a developing artist. Takes up the question of the James influence and the problems of the later work with insightful analyses. Considers *The House of Mirth, The Custom of the Country, Ethan Frome, Summer, Twilight Sleep*, and *The Buccaneers* her best and writes valuable critiques of each one as well as thoughtful commentary on *The Fruit of the Tree, The Children*, "Bunner Sisters" and the early novels and travel books. Concludes that she made a "distinctively upper-class contribution to literature" and stands for "cultural and social continuity and the maintenance, but also the constant readaptation of tradition." Bibliography.

N27   Wershoven, Carol. *The Female Intruder in the Novels of Edith Wharton*. Rutherford: Fairleigh Dickinson University Press, 1982.

Insightful study of the female intruder, "the woman who is in some way outside her society" in Wharton's fiction. Defines her functions as: 1) forcing a member of society to reexamine his world; 2) contrasting with other female characters to demonstrate their entrapment; 3) often teaching the male character about alternative ways to live; 4) serving as a reproach to the false values of society; 5) forcing the reader to judge society in terms of the intruder; 6) embodying positive values of the author. Discusses intruder figures in *The Touchstone, The Valley of Decision, The House of Mirth, The Custom of the Country, The Fruit of the Tree, The Age of Innocence, The Reef, The Children, Twilight Sleep, Hudson River Bracketed, The Gods Arrive, The Buccaneers* and "New Year's Day." Refutes the argument that Wharton lacks positive values and is anachronistic. Ph.D. dissertation. University of Florida, 1979. For abstract see DAI, 41, 675A.

N28   Wolff, Cynthia Griffin. *A Feast of Words: The Triumph of Edith Wharton*. New York: Oxford, 1977.

Major psychological biography which studies Wharton's fiction in terms of her own conflicts and growth. Uses Erikson's model of human development. Point of departure is that she was heavily influenced by maternal rejection, nurtured strong, deeply repressed feelings for her father and, from her emotionally starved upbringing, suffered serious sexual problems that were partially resolved through her mid-life affair with Morton Fullerton, and eventually overcome through her writing. Valuable analysis of the image of woman in Wharton's society and her struggles to escape social expectations and mold her own individuality. These various personal complexes and the difficulties of women in her society are examined in light of the ways they affect the fiction. Beautifully written with valuable footnotes and an appendix on the dating of the Beatrice Palmato fragment. Cites all the novels, most of the short stories and much important manuscript material. Insightful new readings of: *The Age of Innocence, The Buccaneers, The Children, The Custom of the Country, Ethan Frome, The House of Mirth, The Mother's Recompense, Old New York, The Reef, Summer, The Valley of Decision*.

Chapter 6

Contemporary Criticism (1897-1938)

This chapter includes references to Edith Wharton in surveys, books, and articles throughout her lifetime, as well as the year after her death, with two important exceptions. Reviews are listed under the work to which they refer and material that focuses on a particular work is included with studies of that work. For reviews of individual novels, see Chapter 9; of the short story collections, Chapter 10; of the poetry, Chapter 12; of the nonfiction volumes, Chapter 13.

O1   Anonymous. "Edith Wharton in 1905." *Bookman* 75 (October 1932): 577.

       Reprint of picture from April, 1905, issue carries comment that reviewers of *The House of Mirth* found "simply the impression of poignant tragedy" without explicit morality or preaching, but reviewers of her recent books, particularly, *The Gods Arrive*, feel that she overemphasizes "messages, morals, and criticisms of life."

O2   Anonymous. "Edith Wharton: Two Conflicting Estimates of Her Art." *Current Opinion* 58 (April 1915): 272.

       Articulates two sides of the EW controversy: 1) the warm praise of James and Lubbock for her range and intelligence and 2) Robert Herrick's contention that she writes "too consciously well" and that, beyond Lily Bart, "little of importance remains." Argues *Ethan Frome* shows her real power which is not as a social historian but in the depiction of universal spiritual conflicts. [See O35, O49]

O3   Anonymous. "Mrs. Wharton's Nativity." *Munsey's Magazine* 25 (June 1901): 435-436.
       Calls EW most distinguished of the New York authors, and notes she has a broad European cultural background, that she, though rich, does not write for a "social coronet" and her stories are not distinctively of New York. Mentions objections to her male characters, speculating the fault may actually lie in her subjects, not characterization.

O4   Anonymous. "The Twelve Greatest Women in America." *Literary Digest* 74 (8 July 1922): 36.
       Notes that in response to a query to the National League of Women Voters several periodicals have issued lists of the twelve greatest American women. On every serious list EW and Carrie Chapman Catt appeared. Mentions all women on list are childless.

O5   Beach, Joseph Warren. *The Twentieth Century Novel: Studies in Technique.* New York: Century, 1932.
       Within the context of the well-made novel, discusses "overwhelming trend" in EW "towards the restricted point of view." Cites expert dialogue. Analyzes *AofI* particularly, finding its unity and compactness stem from Archer's point of view. Observes that, although everything is rendered through his consciousness "nothing is made" of it, thus he is "one of the palest and least individualized [of] characters" and "hardly more than a device for projecting a situation and characters made more real than himself." However, there is "much less weight of the subjective to make the story drag." Contrasts EW and James. Cites: *AofI, VofD, HofM, FofT, CC, MdeT, EF, Summer, Children, SatF.*

O6   Beard, Charles, and Mary Beard. *The Rise of American Civilization.* New York: Macmillan, 1927.

       Brief, two-sentence mention in chapter, "The Machine Age." Places EW as a writer of that era with Old New York trying to ward off invaders and "Captains of Industry expressing benevolence in welfare work." Cites atmosphere of fatality as in *EF*.

O7   Blankenship, Russell. *American Literature as an Expression of the American Mind.* New York: Holt, 1931.

       In chapter "The Rise of Realism," EW cited as producing work more in the American mainstream than James, although he influenced her. Defines her major theme as individual versus convention. Notes similarities to Sinclair Lewis. Terms EW an aristocratic intellectual, a high-bred realist. Praises *EF*, *ONY* and calls EW one of the finest living craftsmen. Cites: *HM, CC.*

O8   Boas, Ralph, and Katherine Burton. *Social Backgrounds of American Literature.* Boston: Little, Brown, 1933.

       Discusses *CC* and *EF*, the former in terms of the society depicted with the chief interest stated as EW's position as an insider, the latter, as a tragedy of the "monotonous, hard compulsions of the poor" which theorists maintained could not be the basis of tragedy.

O9   Bolton, Sarah Knowles. *Famous American Authors.* Revised by William A. Fahey. New York: Crowell, 1954. [Note various editions. Bolton's work first appeared in 1887, was revised in 1938.]

       Biographical data, now dated, tracing highlights of EW's life. Includes popular appraisals of *EF*. Cites her realism, style, characterization and plot. Mentions: *HM, AofI.*

O10   Boynton, Percy. "American Authors of Today: Edith Wharton." *English Journal* 12 (January 1923): 24-32. Rpt. *Some Contemporary Americans.* Chicago: University of Chicago, 1924.

Brief biographical note. Discusses EW in terms of the international theme. Contends she writes of society in terms of the social code and the domination of strong over weak, but outside society she invokes fate. Finds her intellectual rather than emotional, her work characterized by "keenness, brilliancy ... cleverness." Cites: *AofI, CC, EF.*

O11   Boynton, Percy H. *A History of American Literature.* Boston: Ginn, 1919.
       Brief, 2-page discussion of EW focuses on her "pictures of the American woman which for harshness of uncharity are difficult to parallel." Feels "Wharton formula" is that "none of her women really triumphs." Argues there is really no national type of woman. Cites: *HM, CC.*

O12   Boynton, Percy H. *Literature and American Life: For Students of American Literature.* Boston: Ginn, 1936.
       Discusses Wharton briefly under heading Personality and Fate in Fiction, finding that personality as fate is her theme rather than social criticism. Maintains her characters are dominated by a social code stronger than the law, and the reader's attitude becomes "compassionate amusement." Cites: *CC, AofI.*

O13   Brodin, Pierre. *Le Roman Regionaliste Américain.* Paris: G.P. Maisonneuve, 1937.
       In French. Pamphlet has two short references to EW. First, mentions her Puritanism, particularly in *Ethan Frome,* and her demonstration of the inflexibility of Puritan philosophy. Second, defines her as an aristocratic novelist who knows society well and paints it with realism and a nuance of bitterness.

O14   Brooks, Van Wyck. *Letters and Leadership.* New York: Huebsch, 1918.
       Unindexed. See page 10. Reference to Wharton argues Wharton's "intellectuality positively freezes the fingers." Argues people detached from life do not grow.

O15 Brown, Edward K. "Edith Wharton." In *The Art of the Novel from 1700 to the Present Time*. Edited by Pelham Edgar. New York: Macmillan, 1933.

Short biography and bibliography. Concentrates on craft, noting Jamesian influence, citing similarities to George Eliot--contending Wharton transcends limitations of her sex as did Eliot with her realistic first-person male narrators, but Wharton was liberated from necessity of double plot and authorial intrusions. Analyzes point of view in Wharton, use of dialogue. Praises *EF* as her most enduring work. Mentions her desire, like Theodore Roosevelt, to stir a sense of social responsibility among aristocrats. Terms Turgenev her "true analogue" with "the same kind of intelligence, addressing itself in the same kind of medium, to the same kind of task." Cites: *EF*, *Reef*, *Summer*, *HofM*, *TS*.

O16 Brown, Edward K. "Edith Wharton." *Etudes Anglaises* II (January-March 1938): 16-26.

Important analysis of Wharton immediately after her death because it emphasizes the points--her expatriation, the international theme in her writing, the importance of taste in her morality, her conscious artistry, her narrow field, deficiencies of characterization--that emerge from much of the body of contemporary criticism. Contends she will be read for her interest in technique, her social observation, and the "temper of her mind." Cites: *ABG*, *HofM*, *MdeT*, *ONY*, *HRB*, *M'sR*, *Reef*, *Summer*, *FofT*, *AofI*, *SatF*, *Crucial Instances*, *FF*, *CC*, *GA*, *EF*, *The Greater Inclination*, *The Hermit and the Wild Woman*, "Bunner Sisters." [See N7, O15, V76]

O17 Bruns, Friedrick. *Die amerikanische Dichtung der Gegenwort*. ["American Writing of the Present."] Leipzig & Berlin: Verlag und Druck von B.G. Teubner, 1930.

In German. Surveys contemporary American writing. Describes Wharton as the most famous pupil of James, but argues Wharton is closer to reality. Synopsis and commentary: *The House of Mirth*, *The Fruit of the Tree*,

The Reef, The Age of Innocence, Ethan Frome, and *The Custom of the Country.*

O18   Burdett, Osbert. "Contemporary American Authors, I: Edith Wharton." *London Mercury* 13 (25 November 1925): 13. Rpt. *Contemporary American Authors.* Edited by J.C. Squire. New York: Holt, 1928.
          Discusses EW as an American novelist whose primary subject is "plutocratic world of New York." Defines her purpose as bringing the rapidly shifting panorama of the American social experience into focus. Praises her accuracy of observation and form. Terms her influenced by Old World models. Cites: *HM, CC, EF, AofI.*

O19   Canby, Henry Seidel. "Edith Wharton." *Saturday Review of Literature* 16 (21 August 1937): 6-7.
          Discusses changes in American fiction which has become sociological so that great craftsmen seem old-fashioned. Wharton, he contends, like Glasgow and Cather, belongs to the tradition that emphasizes "the results of powerful evolutionary forces working upon groups, classes, and individuals rather than the forces themselves." Maintains *HofM, AofI* and *EF* establish her claim to fame. Defines her theme as the New York aristocracy, or attempt to create one. Finds her "less subtle, less original, less rhetorical" than James, with less power. Complains magazine serialization accounted for the "competent mediocrity" of many of her stories.

O20   Clark, Emily. *[See Balch, Emily Tapscott Clark] Innocence Abroad.* New York: Knopf, 1931.
          Pages 62-63. Briefly compares Wharton and Glasgow, finding them alike in urbanity, irony, and upper-class background, yet terms Glasgow compassionate while Wharton regards her "puppets ... heartlessly."

O21   Cleaton, Irene, and Allen Cleaton. "Edith Wharton." *Books and Battles: American Literature 1920-1930.* Boston: Houghton-Mifflin, 1937.

Brief commentary calls Wharton, Cather and Glasgow the "feminine wing of American literature," with Wharton missing greatness (except in *EF*) and always revealing her admiration for James.

O22   Collins, Joseph. *Taking the Literary Pulse: Psychological Studies of Life and Letters.* New York: Doran, 1924.

Unindexed, see pp. 48-55. In informal, breezy manner Collins judges that Wharton can create human beings, but cannot always bring them to life. Her characters have more "head than heart" and lack "red blood." However, maintains she is the best chronicler of the manners and customs of her time. Defines her as an intellectual realist. Cites: *FofT, SatF, HofM, AofI.*

O23   Cooper, Frederic Taber. *Some American Story Tellers.* New York: Holt, Rinehart and Winston, 1911.

Short bibliography of critical estimates and separate reviews. An expansion of his *Bookman* material. Cites her "rare mental subtlety," the "unusual breadth of culture," her "wide cosmopolite sympathies," yet her rather "rigid prejudice of social caste." Finds her viewpoint narrow, but her thought, deep and that she deals with victims of fate. She surpasses any other living woman writer at exposing the "sordidness and cowardice of human souls in all their nudity." [See his articles in *Bookman* under pen name Calvin Winter.] Cites: *VofD, HofM, MdeT, Descent of Man, FofT,* "Muse's Tragedy," "Pelican," "Other Two," "Daunt Diana," "Letters," "Journey."

O24   Cross, Wilbur L. "Edith Wharton." *Bookman* 63 (August 1926): 641-46. Abridged rpt. "Great Novelist of the American Scene." *World Review* 8 (20 May 1929): 234.

Mentions meeting Wharton at the degree ceremonies at Yale. Gives an appreciative, chronological overview of her work with the contention that "Art is the path" that leads to her novels. Discusses James with the note that without his influence she "would never have gone so far into psychological refinement," yet she has never had his "obscure complexities of style and manner." Argues she is not modern in the sense of Joyce and Bennett, rather, selective and artistic. Cites: "Other Two," "Long Run."

O25   Dickinson, Thomas H. "Edith Wharton." *The Making of American Literature.* New York: Appleton, 1932.
        Discusses Wharton under the "Pre-War Era" and the Realistic Period, briefly noting major work. Contends she is derivative rather than an original genius, her work representing both the deliberate, analytical formulas of the late nineteenth century and the dissolution of the old orders and moral codes with a characteristic tone of "fate and transience."

O26   Dwight, H.G. "Edith Wharton." *Putnam's Monthly* 3 (February 1908): 590-96.
        Overview of Wharton's work to date. Argues she should not be judged as a woman writer because in significance and workmanship her thirteen books are far superior to the majority of contemporary writing. Particularly praises *HofM* with Lily Bart's great credibility. Contends she alone among American writers faces the fact that sorrow often outweighs joy, good is mingled with evil and difficult questions are worth asking. Takes issue with Carpenter who complained she "defeminized and denationalized" herself, maintaining that is a compliment to Wharton. Cites: *VofD, MdeT, HofM, FofT.* [See V18]

O27   Flanner, Janet. "Dearest Edith." *New Yorker* 5 (2 March 1929): 26-28. Expanded slightly for *An American in Paris.* New York: Simon and Schuster, 1940.
        Somewhat snide overview of Wharton's career, family, expatriation and social life, equating her with Newland Archer. Calls her novels "Historical report[s] on a manner of living and thinking, often enough (for she is a moralist) bad." Characterizes her as the first to "utilize the breakup of the American mold ... the last to understand it." Terms Lily Bart a drug addict. Concludes her "real excellencies (known to her friends) are never marketed." For a posthumous, slightly extended appraisal, see *An American in Paris.* Cites: *HofM, FofT, EF, Children, AofI.*

O28   Follett, Helen T., and Wilson Follett. *Some Modern Novelists*. New York: Henry Hall, 1918.

Wharton chapter discusses her masculine quality, determining sexlessness a more appropriate term, but argues her chief allegiance is to the "scientific spirit of modern realism." Also terms her cosmopolitan. Notes that, like James, she saw that the very short story was a vehicle for a more unified, focused, selective, climactic novel. Cites: *EF, Summer, VofD, HofM, FofT, CC*.

O29   Follett, Wilson. "What Edith Wharton Did--And Might Have Done." *New York Times Book Review*, 5 September 1937, 2.

Ranges widely over Wharton's career, noting surprise at the volume of her work. Contends she seemed to change directions abruptly several times, and that her once acclaimed social chronicles are now but curiosities whereas *The Valley of Decision* and *EF* are enduring. *Cites: HofM, GofM*.

O30   Gilbertson, Catherine. "Mrs. Wharton: 'The Agate Lamp Within Thy Hand.'" *Century* 119 (Autumn 1929): 112-19.

Vigorous defence of Wharton argues her ideals of "reasonableness, clarity, orderliness and the aristocratic tone and temper" are not peculiarly Victorian but universal and that critics have not appreciated her restraint, form, perfection of technique and intelligence. In the machine age she has put emphasis where it should be, on individuals. Detailed analysis of *The Reef* as her most perfect work follows. Cites: *Summer, Children, VofD, TS, AofI, EF, HofM, M'sR, Reef, CC*.

O31   Green, Paul, and Elizabeth L. Green. "Edith Wharton." *Contemporary American Literature*. Chapel Hill: University of North Carolina Press, 1927.

Book presents course outlines for study of fourteen outstanding contemporary writers. Cites Wharton as link to the past who continues in her brilliant, dignified style the tradition of Howells and James, yet is modern in her realistic portrayal of the individual in conflict with society. Short bibliography. Cites: *AofI.*

O32   Hartwick, Harry. *The Foreground of American Fiction.* New York: American, 1934.
       Calls Wharton a dated Jamesian traditionalist, untouched by the modern world, uninformed of the vital contemporary issue of class relationships, whose thematic emphasis on punishments for breaking social conventions has no modern relevance.

O33   Hatcher, Harlan. *Creating the Modern American Novel.* New York: Farrar and Rinehart, 1935.
       Contends Wharton's novels are distinguished above other problem novels by their realistic portrait of society and psychological analysis. Argues she wrote about a specialized group with painstaking art and her first principle was selectivity. Therefore, though sometimes lacking vitality, her work has grace and finish. *Cites: HofM, CC.*

O34   Hawthorne, Hildegarde. *Women and Other Women: Essays in Wisdom.* New York: Duffield, 1908.
       Maintains Wharton is inspired by intellect, not emotions. Argues her women are drawn with an extraordinary lack of sympathy and leave the reader unmoved. Complains *FofT* is lifeless. Contends: "Breeding is ... a luxury of hers, a cult, and one is subconsciously and yet constantly aware of her behind the book, seated in a graceful and composed attitude."

O35   Herrick, Robert. "Mrs. Wharton's World." *New Republic* 2 (13 February 1915): 40-42
       Objects that, except for Lily Bart, Wharton has done little "toward painting in our national canvas," principally because, coming from the French tradition, she writes "perhaps too consciously well." Complains she tends to be unrealistic, her stories are "almost manless" while the women are too thin, and there is little contrast with her nice people "pallid ghosts." Maintains *EF* is truly powerful,

and in this type of universal spiritual conflict--not as social historian--she is strongest. *Cites: CC, FofT.*

O36   Heydrick, Benjamin A. "As We See Ourselves: The Novel." *Chautauquan* 64 (September 1911): 25-40; (October 1911): 165-84.

Portrait of Wharton and Wenzell's drawing of Lily Bart. Two-part article attempts to formulate a definition of the American and American society from descriptions in realistic fiction. Wharton cited as giving the fullest description of the "society column" set in New York. Quotes from her work illustrate descriptions of society and mansions in *HofM* and workers' homes in *FofT.*

O37   Hicks, Granville. *The Great Tradition.* New York: Macmillan, 1933.

Discusses Wharton in terms of the problems of the "middle generation" which faced an unstable economic and social situation. Argues she chose to "portray the delicate and subtle kinds of conflict that can develop only in an organized social group." However, her inability to make a final break with good society eventually resulted in a loss of her sense of moral values--for she had taken a critical attitude toward it from the first--and therefore she became lost in "romantic trivialities."

O38   Hind, C. Lewis. *Authors and I.* New York: John Lane, 1921.

Former editor of *Academy* reminisces about Wharton, remembering a conversation with an Intelligent Woman who said "I was brought up on her" and "There are lots of Lilys about." Notes his pleasure in Wharton except for excessive culture of the travel books and states readers must be content with ladies and gentlemen, not men and women. Calls *EF* her best.

O39   Honey, John L. "Edith Wharton." *The Story of Our Literature.* New York: Scribner's, 1923.

Incomplete primary; high-school text.

O40   Howells, William Dean. "Editor's Easy Chair." *Harper's Monthly Magazine*, December 1900, 153-158.

    Howells's first Easy Chair essay deplores the popularity of the historical novel and the "imbecility" in modern fiction, but maintains that "against a night as cheerless for the friend of serious fiction as any that ever was there has risen in the name of Mrs. Edith Wharton a star of literary conscience and artistic ideal, pure, clear, serene."

O41   Kaltenbacher, Therese. *Frauenfragen im Amerikanische Frauenroman.* Kallmunz: Michael Lassleben, 1936.

    * Not seen.

O42   Knight, Grant C. "The Literature of Realism: Edith Wharton." *American Literature and Culture.* New York: Ray Long and Richard R. Smith, 1932.

    Emphasizes Wharton's style, intelligence, subtlety, irony, cosmopolitanism and art. Cites: *ONY, AofI, GofM, HRB, HofM, M'sR.*

O43   Knight, Grant C. *The Novel in English.* New York: Richard B. Smith, 1931.

    Notes debt to James, with comment that "what in James it [the public] saw through a glass darkly in her it saw face to face." Praises *EF* as an American classic. Contends her preoccupation with social parasites--who are not characteristically American--alienates readers and will harm her reputation. Calls her "non-friendly" to her characters, particularly women. Contends style makes her the foremost living American writer, but argues her fame will pale next to Dreiser's because she is narrower. Cites: *VofD, HofM, FofT, EF, CC, AofI, GofM, M'sR, ONY, Children, HRB.*

O44   Lawrence, Margaret. *The School of Femininity.* New York: Frederick A. Stokes, 1936.

    Places Wharton in category of helpmeet woman--romantic, self-effacing--whose primary interest is relationship with a man, whose sympathies lie with men. Cites: *AofI*.

O45   Leavis, Q.D. "Henry James's Heiress: The Importance of Edith Wharton." *Scrutiny* 7 (December 1938): 261-76. Rpt. N14.

Argues Wharton is not a great novelist like Austen or Eliot because she lacks positives and has no foundation to work on--rejecting both her inherited mode of living and the society she grew up into. Cites *CC* as her masterpiece. Calls her "an extraordinarily acute and far-sighted social critic" of value to anyone interested in the cultural basis of society. [In N14]

O46   Leisy, Ernest Erwin. *American Literature: An Interpretive Survey*. New York: Crowell, 1929.

Two-page comment places Wharton within the tradition of the novel of manners and mentions her concept of fate, irony toward both social climber and the smart set, craftsmanship, psychological insight and diction.

O47   Lewisohn, Ludwig. *Expression in America*. New York: Harper, 1932.

Calls her works "perishable" for her "heart and instincts" are with her social class although her intelligence transcended it. Cites: *HofM*, *CC; Sanctuary*, *EF*, "After Holbein."

O48   Loggins, Vernon. "Edith Wharton." *I Hear America*. New York: Crowell, 1937.

In chapter titled "Manners," Wharton section ranges widely over her career, praising her as a "serious, readable" writer of manners. Synopses of *HofM*, *EF* (greatest achievement) and *AofI*. Mentions dramatizations of *HofM*, *AofI*, *The Old Maid*, and *EF*. Concludes she "caught just in time a vanishing phase of American life."

O49   Lubbock, Percy. "The Novels of Edith Wharton." *Quarterly Review* 222 (January 1915): 182-201. Rpt. N14 and *Living Age* 284 (6 March 1915): 604-616.

Published in 1914, Lubbock's article discusses the early stories, *HofM, CC, EF,* and *The Reef.* He speaks of her "critical intelligence," the "blade of analysis," the "incessantly inquisitive criticism." Praises imagery, particularly in *The Reef.* Notes lack of philosophy of life, criticizes detachment as detracting from immersion. Terms leading qualities her "swiftness and acuteness." [In N14, R7.13]

O50   McCole, C. John. "Some Notes on Edith Wharton." *Catholic World* 146 (January 1938): 425-31.

Balanced assessment after her death, noting weaknesses--principally she was "written out" fifteen years before she stopped writing, she emphasized social sanctions over moral, wrenched coincidences, melodrama, unrealistic, wealthy, isolated characters. Strengths termed creation of atmosphere, phrasing, irony, satire, humor and technique. *Cites: HRB, NY'sD, EF, ONY, FD, MdeT, Touchstone, Spark, AofI, M'sR, Children, HofM, VofD, WofF,* "Xingu," "The Other Two," "The Lady's Maid's Bell."

O51   Marble, Annie R. "Edith Wharton." *A Study of the Modern Novel British and American Since 1900.* New York: Appleton, 1928.

Appreciative overview of Wharton as writer who was mature from the first and takes sophisticated society people as her most convincing types. Critical commentary on Wharton's sustained vigor and moral irony in *The Children.* Bibliography.

O52   Masson, Thomas T. "Ten Houses for Ten Authors." American *Country Life* 45 (April 1924): 35-41.

Author designs imaginary houses for ten American authors--Wharton's a stately manor, "a combination of Italian Renaissance with solid Georgian and mosaic incrustations"--severe but not cheerless, with technical excellence and no childish prattle or loud laughter.

O53   Michaud, Régis. *The American Novel To-Day: A Social and Psychological Study.* (Translation of *Le Roman*

Américain d'Aujourdhui. Paris: Boivin, 1926.) Boston: Little, Brown, 1928.

Volume grew out of his lectures at the Sorbonne. Discusses James, Wharton and Howells as greatest American writers since Hawthorne who continued the novel of intrigue, character and manners. Praises Wharton's craftsmanship, calling the society novel her speciality. Notes her objectivity and maintains she contributed a great deal to American social criticism, and throws light on American sexual problems. Cites: *Summer, EF, CC, AofI, HofM.*

O54   Michaud, Régis. "Le Roman américain: Mme. E. Wharton." *Revue du Mois* 8 (10 December 1909): 673-685.

Terms Wharton the Bourget of Fifth Avenue, and contends historians of the future will turn to her to understand the American type. Defines Wharton as objective and realistic, but warns the reader that it is dangerous to judge the entire society from her books. Finds her gentlemen amazing with their gauche, stiff, authoritarian ways and the women more subtle and refined. Interesting analysis of American psychology from a French perspective. Takes issue with her disparagement of the French stable family life in *Madame de Treymes.* Discusses: *The House of Mirth, The Fruit of the Tree, The Valley of Decision* and *Madame de Treymes.*

O55   Michaud, Régis. *Mystiques and Réalistes Anglo-Saxon d'Emerson à Bernard Shaw.* Paris: A. Colin, 1918.

In French. Praises Wharton as an observer and a stylist in the Jamesian tradition, calling her best in short stories. Summarizes *The House of Mirth* and *The Fruit of the Tree.* Contrasts French novel with American in terms of *The Reef* with its American Puritanism which requires the characters to suffer. Also argues woman is more important to man in Europe, whereas in America the man's life centers in his office. Terms her characters tragic and decorative people who do not live, but improvise.

O56   Millett, Fred B. *Contemporary American Authors*. New
        York: Harcourt Brace Jovanovich, 1922 and 1940.
                Defines Wharton as genteel realist of Jamesian
        tradition. Praises classic *EF*, maintaining after 1914 her
        artistry showed no development. Terms her strengths lay
        in design and composition, clarity, dignity, good manners
        and elegance, but she was limited by her personality and
        experience. Biographical sketch and bibliography. Also
        cites: *HRB*.

O57   Morley, Christopher. "Granules From an Hour Glass."
        Saturday Review of Literature 10 (2 June 1934): 727. Rpt.
        Streamlines. New York: Doubleday, Doran, 1936.
                Unindexed. See "The Distinguished Thing," p. 280.
        Praises *A Backward Glance*, especially memoirs of James,
        and applauds Wharton for overcoming obstacles of her
        birth and class "with extraordinary patience and courage"
        to become a writer.

O58   Oberholtzer, Ellis P. "Mrs. Wharton's Place in American
        Letters." *Book News Monthly* 26 (November 1907): 175-
        178.
                Praises Wharton as satirist, contending that, except for
        HofM, she excels in the short story rather than the novel.
        Positive comments on all fiction to date, with particular
        commendation that she has stayed in America and proved
        the value of American material, unlike James and Marion
        Crawford. Cites: *HofM*, *Touchstone*, *MdeT*, *VofD*.

O59   Overton, Grant M. *American Nights Entertainment*. New
        York: Appleton, 1923. Rpt. *Authors of the Day*. New York:
        George H. Doran, 1924.
                Chapter: "Edith Wharton and the Time Spirit." Argues
        Wharton's fame rests on *AofI* and *EF*--different
        superficially and alike as tales of America and frustration
        in which "background is responsible for the actors
        themselves as well as the play." Biographical information
        concludes two traditions bound her: Old New York and
        the literary tradition of France. Ends with dialogue
        between Edith Wharton and the Time Spirit. She says: "If

in those years of writing we achieve art once or twice, we are among the rare, fortunate ones."

O60   Overton, Grant M. *Cargoes for Crusoes*. New York: Appleton, 1924.

Contends Wharton's best work grew out of experiences before she was twenty. Her pictures of Old New York, except for *EF*, therefore have the most vitality. Summarizes *Old New York* stories. Also cites: *AofI*.

O61   Parrington, Vernon L. *Main Currents in American Thought*. New York: Harcourt Brace and World, 1927. See also *The Beginnings of Critical Realism in America: 1860-1920*. Harcourt, Brace and World, 1930.

Wharton mention lies mainly in his Addenda, although there are passing references throughout. His incomplete notes focus on her as a "temperamental aristocrat" of the Genteel Tradition. Contends she was one of the few who didn't move in 1903-1917 in a frontal attack on the new plutocracy--such as London and Sinclair. Cites: *HofM*, *EF*, *CC*, *AofI*, *ONY*. See his review of *The Age of Innocence* for a complete statement of his assessment.[See N14, R12.14]

O62   Pattee, Fred L. *The New American Literature 1890-1930*. New York: Century, 1930.

Chapter on "The Feminine Novel" discusses Wharton as representing the cultivated, aristocratic viewpoint, her atmosphere French rather than English or American. Contends, like James, she is an intellectual concerned with form, manners, art and her function is to diagnose diseases of civilization. Argues she lacks soul to be great, fails because she defines life in terms of the artificial, not nature.

O63   "Pendennis." "The Thinking Heart: An Impression of Mrs. Wharton at Close Range." *Book News Monthly* 26 (November 1907): 171-73.

From an interview at lunch at Lenox. Concludes she "keeps an intellectual grip" on impulses of the heart.

Praises Lily Bart and remarks on the "sting of autumn" in her themes. Text of poem "Mould and Vase" is here.

O64   Phelps, William Lyon. "The Advance of the English Novel, X." *Bookman* 43 (July 1916): 515-24. Rpt. *The Advance of the English Novel.* New York: Dodd Mead, 1916.

Lengthy analysis of contemporary American writers. He acknowledges Wharton is considered the best, but disagrees. Terms *EF* her only masterpiece, yet finds the suicide attempt unrealistic. Objects *HofM* requires "No unusual intelligence" to write or read. Finds *CC* exaggerated. Calls her a "good hater" and wishes her humor and sympathy were as developed as "hate, disgust and irony." Notes lack of spiritual. Cites: *VofD*, *Reef*, *MdeT*, *FofT*.

O65   Phelps, William Lyon. "An Appreciation of Edith Wharton." *Delineator*, 120 (February 1932): 7.

Occasioned by publication of *The Gods Arrive* in the *Delineator*. Serves as an introduction to Wharton as well as a warm appreciation, noting her Yale degree, her purity from purpose in her best work, her American characters and subjects--calling her a patrician of art who is "our foremost living American novelist." Notes her attention to selection in a novel, her realism. Does not regard *The House of Mirth* as one of her best, preferring *Ethan Frome*, *The Reef*, *The Age of Innocence*, *The Children* and *Hudson River Bracketed*.

O66   Phelps, William Lyon. *Twentieth Century American Novels.* Chicago: American Library Association, 1927.

In this book Phelps offers brief discussions of major novels for readers interested in a course covering "representative fiction of our own time and country." Argues Wharton stands at the head of contemporary writers--*EF* already a classic, *AofI* extraordinarily beautiful and not marred by satire of *CC* and *TS*.

O67   Pollard, Percival. *Their Day in Court.* New York: Neale, 1909.

      Highly critical of Wharton as merely imitating James, arguing "Jacobite English about Jacobite subjects is all she cares to engage in. Hers, indeed, is the most abnormal case we know of one artist being wedded to the art of another." Contends that only women with masculine minds can serve as social historians.

O68   Quinn, Arthur Hobson. *American Fiction: An Historical and Critical Survey.* New York: Appleton-Century, 1936.

      Short bibliography. Very favorable assessment calling her the supreme artist in modern American fiction. Maintains she belongs to no group or movement, has assimilated French and Italian culture but remained essentially American in choice of material and artistic point of view. Contends with *HofM* she became "our chief social satirist." Claims she dominates her contemporaries because her characters dominate situations. Feels her women are better than her men and notes variety of feminine types. Surveys almost all her work.

O69   Roberts, R. Ellis. "Edith Wharton." *Bookman* (London) 64 (September 1923): 262-64.

      Warmly appreciative. Calls Wharton the most important American novelist after James's death. Praises her artistry, contrasting her satire of Americans with younger, cruder writers like Sinclair Lewis. Lauds her treatment of American women, studies of simpler people in *EF* and *Summer*, gifts as story-teller. Also cites: *CC*, *GofM*.

O70   Roz, Firmin. *Les Américains Vus par leurs romanciers.* Monaco: Société de Conferences, 24 January, 1927.

      In French. Pamphlet places author of *The House of Mirth* as the premier American author of the day. Argues Wharton's incontestable authority paints a piercing tableau that penetrates the vanity and emptiness of New York life. Maintains the character and conduct of Lily Bart are determined by her social milieu.

O71   Russell, Frances Theresa. "Edith Wharton's Use of
       Imagery." *English Journal* 21 (June 1932): 452-461.

       Analyzes Wharton's imagery, classing her as a
       humanist whose metaphors are most often drawn from
       human "implements and activities" and used to illuminate
       individuals, society, and humanity in general. Concludes
       her imagery is sometimes trite, occasionally repetitive,
       rarely shrill, frequently witty and often original, apt and
       ingenious. Cites: *HofM*, *Children*, *M'sR*, *Marne*, *VofD*,
       "Eyes," "Pelican."

O72   Russell, Frances Theresa. "Melodramatic Mrs. Wharton."
       Sewanee Review 40 (October-December 1932): 425-437.

       Discusses background and theory of melodrama,
       arguing it has a bad name because of sensationalism
       (defined strictly as appealing to the senses), which is
       undeserved. Contends with her preference for the
       extraordinary and the marvelous, strict selection, reliance
       on coincidence, use of supernatural, character subordinate
       to plot, ornate social background, strong language of the
       war period, emphatic beliefs, dynamic style and satiric
       substance is melodramatic but supplies the human craving
       for thrills--the "vivid and vibrant." Cites: *Crucial Instances*,
       Sanctuary, *FofT*, *Reef*, *Children*, *CC*, *GofM*, *EF*, *HRB*,
       "Pelican," "Muse's Tragedy," "Her Son."

O73   Schyberg, Frederik L. *Moderne Amerikansk Litteratur 1900-
       1930*. Copenhagen: Gyldendal, 1930.
       *Not seen.

O74   Sedgwick, Henry D. *The New American Type and Other
       Essays*. Boston: Houghton-Mifflin, 1908.

       Chapter "Mrs. Wharton" discusses adjective "clever" as
       applied to her first stories. Terms her an American woman
       of energy and nervousness. Finds the mastery of
       composition in Lily Bart is the great achievement of *HofM*
       in spite of deficiencies. Concludes term "brilliancy" applies
       to her. Cites: "Dilettante," *Sanctuary*, *Touchstone*, *VofD*,
       IV&G, *Italian Backgrounds*, *HofM*, *FofT*.

O75   Sedgwick, Henry D. "The Novels of Mrs. Wharton."
       Atlantic Monthly 98 (August 1906): 217-28.
           Evaluates Wharton's career so far. Discusses the
       cleverness of her short stories, epigrammatic style,
       characteristics of the American woman writer, use and
       mastery of episodes, culture--particularly in *VofD*--
       popularity of *HofM* and the achievement of Lily Bart,
       objecting that she departs from realism and determinism
       in favor of satire and--in Lily Bart--romantic effects. Looks
       forward   to   her   more   important   novels   to
       come. "Dilettante," *Sanctuary*, *Touchstone*, *VofD*, *IV&G*,
       Italian Backgrounds, *HofM*.

O76   Sencourt, Robert. "Edith Wharton." *Cornhill Magazine* 157
       (June 1938): 721-36.
           Biographical material. Argues much of her best work
       came in the last twelve years of her life: *Twelve Poems*,
       Certain People, *Human Nature*, and *A Backward Glance*.
       Praises *EF* and contends she had what Dante called "'the
       habit of art': a developed dexterity which answered to a
       refined instinct for beauty." Contends her finest work
       appears in *The Mortal Lease*. Praises *Vesalius in Zante*
       and *Margaret of Cortona*, *The Tryst*. Cites: *BkofH*, *In
       Morocco*.

O77   Sherman, Stuart Pratt. *Life and Letters*. 2 Vols. Eds. Jacob
       Zeitlin and Homer E. Woodbridge. New York: Farrar and
       Rinehart, 1929.
           See Volume 2. Contains an unindexed 1925 letter to
       Glasgow (693), commenting on Wharton, also includes his
       changing view of Wharton in that he once held her art in
       lower esteem, but he protests the type of restricted
       sociological criteria Lovett uses to judge her. For his
       spirited defense of Wharton, see his review of *The
       Mother's Recompense*. [See R16.20]

O78   Sholl, Anna McClure. "The Work of Edith Wharton."
       Gunton's Magazine 25 (November 1903): 426-32.

Defines Wharton's style as, like James's, artificial, but contends she overcomes his limitations. Maintains she will be read for her beautiful style. Notes she is not judgmental and that her intellect overbalances her heart. High praise for her short stories, particularly "The Pelican" and "The Muse's Tragedy." Also cites: *VofD*.

O79   Stalnaker, John M., and Fred Eggan. "American Novelists Ranked; A Psychological Study." *English Journal* 18 (April 1929): 295-307.

Gives table of critical responses to a request to rank 72 contemporary American novelists on the basis of general literary merit. Wharton and Cather were ranked at the top, Cather first. Essay discusses critical criteria and details various responses. Wharton ranked in group 1 by 16 critics, group 2 by 10, and group 3 by 4.

O80   Stocking, Elizabeth L. "Edith Wharton's Heroines." *Americana* 5 (January 1910): 80-87.

Calls Wharton typically American. Cites her clever, brilliant, epigrammatic style, pessimism, tendency to emphasize the weaknesses and foibles and sins of women. Likes *Touchstone* best because the heroine is strong and noble with a regenerative influence on her husband. *FofT, HofM, Touchstone, H&WW*.

O81   Taylor, Walter F. *A History of American Letters*. Boston: American Book Company, 1936.

This history of American letters addressed to undergraduates contains bibliographical and biographical material. Defines Wharton as an intelligent, observant craftsman who dealt with the American aristocracy, a transitional figure between Howells and Lawrence and Shaw, particularly in dealing with sexuality, who was deficient in sympathy and too readily accepted the assumption that illicit sex is the staple of fiction. Cites: *HofM, EF, CC, AofI*.

O82   Teincey, M. de. "Les Romanciers Américains." *Correspondant* 254 (10 January, 1914): 161-167.

In French. Notes Wharton's pessimism in what is essentially a long synopsis of *The Fruit of the Tree* which has, it is argued, the same power, movement and sincerity as the acclaimed *House of Mirth*. Calls Wharton one of the great novelists of our era, and asserts no one has brought more color, emotion and movement to the picture of modern American society.

O83 Trueblood, Charles D. "Edith Wharton." *Dial* 68 (January 1920): 80-91.

Analyzes the cleverness of Wharton's characters as a social, modulated, intellectual quality. Discusses the place of women in Wharton as equal to men and her basic conservatism. Cites: *HofM, FofT, EF, CC, VofD, Reef, Summer*.

O84 Tutweiler, Julia R. "Edith Wharton in New York City." *Women Authors of Our Day in Their Homes: Personal Descriptions and Interviews*. Edited by Francis W. Halset. New York: James Pott, 1903.

Notes Wharton's distinction and the cult growing up around her. Discusses Jamesian influence and her own more direct handling of motive. Praises her knowledge of Italy, but contends her characters are "studies" rather than real people and mentions those who condemn her as lacking warmth and too literary. *Greater Inclination, Crucial Instances, VofD, Touchstone*, "Mrs. Manstey's View."

O85 Underwood, John C. *Literature and Insurgency: Ten Studies in Racial Evolution*. New York: Mitchell Kennerley, 1914.

Chapter: "Culture and Edith Wharton." Essays were written to stimulate interest in American literature. Terms Wharton an academic artist and argues she has furthered the cause of literary art in America, but the "lasting impression...is that she cares comparatively little for anything but the impression she is trying to produce," and that "brilliancy" is the best term applied to her with her patrician qualities. Cites: *Artemis to Actaeon, Sanctuary, EF, MdeT, VofD, HofM, FofT, Reef*, "Quicksand," "Dilettante," "Pelican."

O86   Van Doren, Carl, and Mark Van Doren. *American and British Literature Since 1890.* New York: Century, 1925.

Three-page overview terms Wharton a "delight to sophisticated minds." Notes her satire and irony, her theme portraying the individual at odds with a compact community. Praises *EF* as "universal tragedy." Also cites: *HofM, AofI, ONY,* "The Spark."

O87   Van Doren, Carl. "Contemporary American Novelists." *Nation* 112 (12 January 1921): 40-41. Rpt. *Contemporary American Novelists 1900-1920.* New York: Macmillan, 1922.

Contends Wharton's power lies in illustrating the force of a compact community on an individual. Notes her irony, objectivity, arguing though that she does assign to decorum unrealistic power and thus her fated lives are in part an illusion for artistic effect. Cites: *HofM, CC, AofI, EF, Summer.*

O88   Willcox, Louise Collier. "The Content of the Modern Novel." *North American Review* 182 (June 1906): 919-29.

Analysis of the deficiencies of the modern novel, concluding the novel "has had its day and must cease." Selects Wharton's *HofM* and Glasgow's *The Wheel of Life* as the two best novels of the year. Contrasts the two in that Glasgow's is more forcefully insightful and Wharton's is carefully selected, fatally truthful and stylistically beautiful.

O89   Willcox, Louise Collier. "Edith Wharton." *Outlook* 81 (25 November 1905): 19-24.

Evaluates Wharton's achievement, defining her as in vision like deMaupassant, in style, like James. Notes her distinction from the first, gives pertinent biographical material, praises *Touchstone*, but thinks *VofD* loses vitality in being taken from scholarship and terms *HofM* a work which establishes her reputation in English literature. Applauds her realism. Cites: *Crucial Instances*, "Portrait," "Mrs. Manstey's View," *Greater Inclination*, "Muse's Tragedy," "Coward," "Pelican."

O90   Wilson, Edmund. "The All-Star Literary Vaudeville." *New Republic* 47 (30 June 1926): 158-63. Rpt. *The Shores of Light: A Literary Chronicle of the Twenties and Thirties.* New York: Farrar, Straus and Young, 1952.

Terms Wharton, by craftsmanship and culture, of an earlier tradition, and by critical point of view contemporary. Argues she differs from James as a bitter social satirist and that she was one of the first to write with indignation against American values at the end of the century.

O91   Wilson, Edmund. "Justice to Edith Wharton." *New Republic* 95 (29 June 1938): 209-13. Rpt. *The Wound and the Bow.* Boston: Houghton-Mifflin, 1941. Also rpt. in *Criticism: The Foundations of Modern Literary Judgment.* Edited by Mark Schorer et. al. New York: Harcourt Brace, 1948. Italian rpt. "Giustizia per Edith Wharton." *Paragone* Anno 2, Numero 22 (October 1951): 15-26. Also in Howe, N14.

Often cited as the essay that renewed interest in Wharton immediately after her death. Emphasizes her achievements from 1905-1917. Discusses major novels, arguing "for a period of fifteen years or more she produced work of considerable interest both for its realism and its intensity."

O92   Winter, Calvin. [Pen name of Frederick Taber Cooper.] "Edith Wharton." *Bookman* 33 (May 1911): 302-309. Expanded for *Some American Story Tellers.* See O23.

Analysis of Wharton's fiction covers short stories and novels. Notes subtlety, culture, wide cosmopolitan sympathies, rigid principles of social caste, choice of artists and academics as subjects. Praises her understanding of human nature and motive. Notes determinism in her stories: characters destroyed by a tragic misunderstanding or the demands of a social tradition. Cites: *VofD, FofT, HofM, MdeT, Greater Inclination, Descent of Man,* "Journey," "Pelican," "Other Two."

Chapter 7

Surveys 1939-1987

This chapter includes mentions of Edith Wharton in literary surveys from 1939 through 1987, with a few major additions after that date. Surveys during her lifetime are covered in Chapter 6. Survey studies that focus on one work are listed under that work and can be found in the Works Index.

P1   Ballorain, Rollande. "From Childhood to Womanhood (or from Fusion to Fragmentation): A Study of the Growing Up Process in 20th Century American Women's Fiction." *Revue Française d'Etudes Américaines* 6.2 (1981): 97-112. Not seen. Cited in Bendixen. [See K1]

P2   Berthoff, Warner. *The Ferment of American Realism: American Literature 1884-1919*. New York: Free Press, 1965.

       Passing mention of Wharton throughout. Extended commentary in chapter "Novels and Novelists: Humorists and Moralists: The Heirs of Howells and James." Terms Wharton the "most accomplished novelist" of her generation. Notes her artistic thoroughness, pessimism, and the unrealistic manipulation of character. Cites: *AofI*, "Bunner Sisters," *VofD*, *HofM*, *Reef*, *EF*, *Summer*, *FofT*, *CC*, *MdeT*, *Sanctuary*, *ABG*, "Angel at the Grave."

P3   Brooks, Cleanth, R.W.B. Lewis, and Robert Penn Warren.
          American Literature--The Makers and the Making. New
          York: St. Martin's, 1973.
                Volume II. Includes "The Other Two" and "The Eyes"
          and "A Portrait of Henry James" from *A Backward Glance.*
          Brief list of Further Readings. Wharton discussed in
          chapter "The New Consciousness" (1861-1914). Biographical
          material, discussion of major novels, *CC* designated her
          best. Places Wharton as an artistic realist, arguing she is
          indebted to James principally only for sense of form and
          craft. Contends her power arises "from her settled belief
          that moral commitment was absolute ... to violate it ... was
          to endanger the whole fabric of society....The pathos in her
          work arises from her parallel conviction that society was
          all there was." Places Wharton in terms of James, Howells,
          Dreiser, Lewis and Fitzgerald, with mention (in New
          England discussion) of importance of the condition of
          woman in late nineteenth-century America. Cites: *VD,
          HofM, EF, AofI, Buc, ABG, Greater Inclination.*

P4   Brooks, Van Wyck. *The Confident Years: 1885-1915.* New
          York: Dutton, 1952.
                Cites her greatest gifts as the power of creating
          atmosphere all over the world and the pictorial phrase,
          but contends her mind was shaped by Europe, the only
          type of male she seemed to know was the dilettante, she
          seemed to write for English readers, she was too deeply
          involved with her upper-class world, her vision was
          immature, and she only came into her own when she
          relived Old New York, not when she defended it. Cites:
          VofD, HofM, CC, AofI.

P5   Canby, Henry Seidel. "Fiction Sums Up A Century." In
          Literary History of the United States. Edited by Robert E.
          Spiller et al. Vol. II. Rev. 1960. New York: Macmillan,
          1948.
                Volume II. Categorizes Wharton as having roots in
          the nineteenth century. Argues Stendhal-like she writes
          "studies of significant manners in a group where worth as
          human beings had little relevance to the importance of

their behavior as individuals observably conditioned by a uniform environment." Contends her satire has the authenticity of the insider; she did not learn technique from the subtler, more natural James, but artistry; she is a master of the short story, was one of the last regionalists, and will be remembered "as the memorialist of a dying aristocracy," although her effect on technical standards of popular fiction was great. Cites: *HofM*, *AofI*, *Old Maid*, *EF*, *HRB*.

P6   Chase, Richard. *The American Novel and Its Traditions*. Garden City, New York: Doubleday, 1957.

      Defines Wharton as novelist of manners who (except for James) are second or third rate. However, among those are also Fitzgerald, Howells and Sinclair Lewis. *AofI* mentioned as an example of how "aberrations and distortions" in social conduct will lead to expulsion from society.

P7   Cooperman, Stanley. *World War I and the American Novel*. Baltimore: Johns Hopkins University Press, 1967.

      Scattered references condemn "Miss Wharton" for her provincial and sentimental treatment of World War I. Argues she repeats "atrocity-inflated" Allied propaganda and "every political and military cliche." Contends *The Marne* and *A Son at the Front* are unreal because of American attitudes "towards the glories of war" which pictured pure, God-fearing American boys liberating the world.

P8   Cournos, John, and Sybil Norton. "Edith Wharton." *Famous American Novelists*. New York: Dodd, Mead, 1952.

      Young people's series has brief comment mentioning Wharton as a social historian in New York and Newport, as an influence on Fitzgerald and Marquand, as in decline after 1920. Compares her with Sinclair Lewis as reporter, artist, reformer.

P9   Cunliffe, Marcus. *The Literature of the United States*. London: Penguin, 1954.

Classes Wharton with the expatriates. Says she and James "deal with the tension between the individual and the social framework," but Wharton sees society as collapsing. Maintains her leading characters have grudges they cannot resolve, and she has a "sharp eye for social absurdities, and compassion for the victims of social change," but, like Dreiser, she rarely does more than harrow the reader. She is "most people's Henry James" with "similar preconceptions and similar themes, manoeuvred more briskly and superficially." See discussion of *HRB*.

P10   Elles, Harold M., et al. "Edith Wharton." *College Book of American Literature.* New York: American Book, 1939-40 and 1965.
       Volume II undergraduate text with short biographical introduction and appended bibliography. Reprints "The Other Two." Terms *AofI* her best.

P11   Fetterley, Judith. *The Resisting Reader: A Feminist Approach to American Fiction.* Bloomington: Indiana University Press, 1978.
       Unindexed. Brief mention in introduction, p. xii, that Wharton is the exception (along with Dickinson) to the male image of American literature.

P12   Freemantle, Anne. "Edith Wharton: Values and Vulgarity." In *Fifty Years of the American Novel: A Christian Appraisal,* edited by H.C. Gardiner, S.J., 15-32. New York: Scribner's, 1951.
       Viewing Wharton from a Christian perspective, contends her characters are involved in moral situations because character does determine fate in her work, yet it is tragic that her own recognition of the supernatural basis of life was so uncertain. Wharton termed the greatest American woman writer; however, "she had no message; she had nothing, even, that she very desperately wanted to say, but she quite desperately wanted to tell."

P13   French, Marilyn. *Beyond Power.* New York: Summit, 1985.

Feminist. Brief mention of James and Wharton as two who wrote tellingly of the separation of the sexes in America and contrasted this with European society's fostering of social intercourse.

P14   Gelfant, Blanche Housman. *The American City Novel.* Norman: University of Oklahoma Press, 1954.

Argues that "the twentieth-century American city novel has developed as a generic literary form." Discusses *HofM, CC, AofI*. Concludes "Wharton's insight into the workings of the destructive element in New York society ... makes her novels unique in city fiction."

P15   Gelfant, Blanche Housman. *Women Writing in America: Voices in Collage.* Edited by Susan Merrill Squier. Hanover, New Hampshire: University Press of New England, 1984.

Passing feminist comments on Wharton, notably that critics with their "persistent imputations cast upon the origins of Wharton's art," for example, Edmund Wilson and Cynthia Griffin Woolf, are "ungenerous and peculiar." Notes the cruelty of fate in her fiction. Cites *HofM, EF.* [See N28, O91]

P16   Gilbert, Sandra M., and Susan Gubar. "Forward Into the Past." In *Historical Studies in Literary Criticism*, 240-265. Edited by Jerome J. McGann. Madison: University of Wisconsin Press, 1985.

One direct reference to Wharton as one of the women artists who "analyze the relationship between male history and newly visible female origins [and] ... perceive themselves as ... free to adopt the powers of paternal and/or maternal traditions" in an investigation of the conflicts involved for women writers in defining their affiliation with women writers of the past whom they need, admire and also fear and compete with as an alternative to the male-dominated literary heritage.

P17   Gilbert, Sandra M., and Susan Gubar. *No Man's Land: The Place of the Woman Writer in the Twentieth Century.*

Volume 1: *The War of the Words*. New Haven: Yale University Press, 1988. Volume 2: *Sexchanges*. New Haven: Yale University Press, 1989.

Vol 1: In a feminist overview of modern literature in England and America, Wharton is cited several times: *The Touchstone* mentioned as offering an image of a female writer "empowered by her talent to transcend what is supposedly for women the insurmountable pain of unrequited love;" "Angel at the Grave" as example of daughter's seduction and betrayal by the male tradition. Also cites: *EF*. Vol. 2: Chapter "Angel of Devastation: Edith Wharton on the Arts of the Enslaved." This important feminist analysis contends that "EW was neither in theory nor in practice a feminist, [however] her major fictions, taken together, constitute perhaps the most searching--and searing--feminist analysis of the construction of 'femininity' produced by any novelist in this century." Traces in Wharton's work the Veblenesque process by which women are socialized into "sex parasites," through a horrific technique of feminization. Argues EW's work, marked by "despair and desire," shifts the burden of the "unsayable" to outside the ordinary world into the decoration of houses (and their naming), her erotica, letters, the love diary, and, particularly, the ghost story. Lengthy reading of *HofM*. Also cites: *DofH*, *CC*, *AofI*, *ABG*, *Summer*, *EF*, "The Valley of Childish Things," "Kerfol," "Miss Mary Pask," "Mr. Jones," "Pomegranate Seed," *Touchstone*, "Mortal Lease," and "Beatrice Palmato."

P18   Gilbert, Sandra. "Tradition and the Female Talent." In *Literary History: Theory and Practice*. Edited by Herbert L. Sussman. *Proceedings of the Northeastern University Center for Literary Studies* 2 (1984): 1-27.

Feminist. Brief reference to Wharton in the context of male writers who were troubled by the competition of "too good" female contemporaries. Contends: "A kind of scribbling sibling rivalry is almost established between pairs like James and Wharton....And in almost every case the male half of the pair devises a variety of strategies for defusing his anxiety about the threat represented by his female counterpart...."

P19   Haliegger, Alfred. *Gender, Fantasy and Realism in American Literature*. New York: Columbia University Press, 1982.

Passim.

P20   Heiney, Donald. "Edith Wharton." In *Recent American Literature*. Great Neck, New York: Barron's Educational Series, 1958.

Chapter titled "The First American Realists 1880-1914." Textbook-style analysis classes Wharton as a "psychological realist," noting she is erroneously called a "society novelist." Brief biography followed by synopsis and discussion of major novels--*EF, HofM, CC, AofI*.

P21   Hoffman, Frederick J. *The Modern Novel in America 1900-1950*. Chicago: Henry Regnery, 1951.

Terms Wharton writer most sympathetic to James. Finds their greatest affinity lies in their concern over a "precisely formulated moral evaluation of their subjects" as distinguished from social, political or economic concerns. Notes her greater flexibility in point of view, a "contrived maternal assistance often given her characters. Terms the theme of her major novels the "moral decline of an older New York" under attack by modern forces. Maintains after 1920 her work declines, at times having a magazine slickness. Cites: *WofF, Reef, CC, HofM, AofI*.

P22   Hoffman, Frederick J. *The Twenties*. New York: Viking, 1955.

Discusses Wharton's attitude toward WWI, her seeing it--as did Cather and Caulfield--from cultural standpoint as "an education in ultimate responsibility": art and religion versus vulgarity and militarism. Terms *SatF* "wishfully false." Also notes the unreality of her treatment of the Midwest. Selected, annotated bibliography. Paragraph biography of Wharton. Also cites: *HRB*.

P23   Horton, Rod W., and Herbert W. Edwards. *Backgrounds of American Literary Thought*. New York: Appleton-Century-Crofts, 1952.

Names *AofI* and *ABG* under sources for chapter on the Genteel Tradition titled "Gentility and Revolt" in which several of Wharton's comments on that era are cited.

P24   Howard, Leon. "Edith Wharton." In *Literature and the American Tradition*. Garden City, New York: Doubleday, 1960.

In chapter titled "Society and the Individual." Overview mentions Jamesian influence, contending she lacked "his capacity for belief in the reality of freedom." Notes the pessimism in her sophisticated world view.

P25   Howard, Maureen. *Seven American Women Writers of the Twentieth Century: An Introduction*. Minneapolis: University of Minnesota Press, 1977.

Passing mention in chapter on Glasgow, with similarities noted. Also brief biography and critical mention. Editor notes Edith Wharton is discussed at length in *Seven Modern American Novelists: An Introduction*. [See Q5]

P26   Howard, Maureen. *Women, the Arts and the 1920's in Paris and New York*. Eds. Kenneth W. Wheeler and Virginia Lee Lussier. New Brunswick: Transaction Books, 1982.

In chapter titled "City of Words." Discusses the ways Wharton, Gertrude Stein, Edna St. Vincent Millay, Marianne Moore and Willa Cather, each conscious of place, transcended the usual ideas we have about the Paris and New York of expatriate writing. Terms *AofI* Wharton's final acceptance of her American heritage.

P27   Kazin, Alfred. *On Native Grounds*. New York: Harcourt, Brace and Co., 1942. Revised from "The Lady and the Tiger: Edith Wharton and Theodore Dreiser." *Virginia Quarterly Review* 17 (Winter 1941): 101-19. Rpt. N14.

Argues EW accepted much about her society--its gentility and conventions. Contends she became a writer not in revolt, but from boredom, and that she began without curiosity, or the sense of art and craftsmanship of James, and specialized in tales of victimization, unable to transcend her own personal experience. Thus, he claims she never became a great artist because she did not tell the full story of the rise of the nouveaux riche, unlike Dreiser who stumbled into naturalism by exploding the Genteel Tradition to become "one of the great folk artists."

P28   Kimbel, Ellen. *The American Short Story 1900-1945: A Critical History*. Edited by Philip Stevick. Boston: Twayne, 1984.

     In chapter "The American Short Story: 1900-1920." Contends Wharton was the first to record the female's plight in American culture, and she added to James this feminine experience. Praises "The Eyes," "Souls Belated," "The Other Two" and "Autres Temps ...."

P29   Knight, Grant C. *The Strenuous Age in American Literature*. Chapel Hill: University of North Carolina Press, 1954.

     Discusses literature in terms of social history, 1900-1910. Terms *VofD* superior to other historical fiction of the period; calls Lily Bart as "touching" a figure as the period has, although Wharton is "aloof and dispassionate and judicial." Praises *HofM* for unifying art and experience, but finds *FofT* a contrived failure. Also cites: *Sanctuary, MdeT*.

P30   Kunitz, Stanley J., and Haycroft, Howard. *Twentieth Century Authors*. New York: Wilson, 1942.

     Brief, encyclopedia-style reference in a biographical dictionary of modern literature.

P31   Lewis, R.W.B. *The American Adam*. Chicago: University of Chicago Press, 1955.

     Brief mention of Wharton's objection to Fitzgerald that he had not filled in Gatsby's background. Lewis defends Fitzgerald, arguing that Gatsby's lack of background is thematically important.

P31.1   McDowell, Margaret B. "Edith Wharton." *Dictionary of Literary Biography*. Vol. 4, American Writers in Paris, 1920-1939. Edited by Karen Lane Rood. Detroit: A Bruccoli Clark Book, 1980. 408-413.

Brief, concise biographical entry focuses on EW's life in France and literary treatment of French culture. Mentions her war work, her personal relationships with both French and English intellectual society during her expatriation and offers valuable insight into EW's shyness which was generally perceived as haughtiness. Recognizes her affiliation with the socially rebellious authors of the twenties such as Sinclair Lewis, F.S. Fitzgerald and Anita Loos. Emphasizes that though EW was deeply immersed in social, literary and intellectual networks she was, at no time, a part of Stein's salon in Paris or Bloomsbury in London. Reads *Madame de Treymes* and *The Reef*, both set in France, as Jamesian. Also includes short, select primary and secondary bibliography.

P32   Mailer, Norman. *Cannibals and Christians*. New York: Dial, 1966.

Unindexed. See pp. 98-101 and Chapter 6, "The Argument Reinvigorated." Discusses war in American letters between the Genteel Tradition and naturalism, EW and Dreiser being examples of the split. Argues Wharton's descendant is Truman Capote and feels now the true novel of manners has been watered down to the documentary and satire. Concludes that literature failed to define American life and thus the work fell to television and movies. Cites: *HofM*.

P33   Martin, Jay. *Harvests of Change*. Englewood Cliffs, New Jersey: Prentice-Hall, 1967.

In chapter titled "The Visible and Invisible Cities" critic defines Wharton's version of the novel of estrangement and notes her two types of naturalistic novel. In one, the self aspires against the stifling forces of environment and in the other, the "things" of society encumber and trap the self. Contends in *ABG* she found an affirming strategy to solve the problem of isolation by imagining an "ancient invisible city" with a place for her. Cites: *EF*, *Summer*, *HofM*, *CC*, *AofI*, "Bunner Sisters."

P34   Maxwell, D.E.S. *American Fiction: The Intellectual Background*. London: Routledge and Kegan Paul, 1963.
      Chapter "Edith Wharton and the Realists" covers *HofM*, *CC*, *AofI*. Finds in Wharton's realism a more balanced view of the virtues and vices of Old New York than other critics have. Defines her realism as not merely of manners, but also in terms of a "profounder" meaning, "grasping and conveying the core of beliefs, assumptions, precepts, which lay behind the outward forms of manners and behavior."

P35   Millgate, Michael. *American Social Fiction: James to Cozzens*. New York: Barnes and Noble, 1964.
      Chapter "Edith Wharton" attempts to place Wharton within the context of the American social novel. Terms her businessmen plausible and argues she deals effectively with the business world. Cites her distinction as social novelist, like Fitzgerald, as her ability to create within the novel's world a scale of values that includes the businessman, and, instead of becoming a demi-god or a villain, he can be viewed critically, yet with a sense of proportion. [See Q55] Cites: *ABG*, *HofM*, *FofT*, *CC*.

P36   Milne, Gordon. *The Sense of Society: A History of the American Novel of Manners*. Rutherford, New Jersey: Fairleigh Dickinson University Press, 1977.
      Study combines a historical survey of the American novel of manners with emphasis on the major practitioners: James, Howells, Wharton, Glasgow, Marquand and Auchincloss. Chapter on Wharton concludes she saw morals in manners and is the link between James and Howells. Notes tone, setting, diction, precisely outlined characters, patterns of imagery, the selection and balance contributing to form, satire.

Discusses "amalgamation of aristocracy and plutocracy."
Extensive coverage of *The Age of Innocence*, *The Mother's
Recompense*, *The House of Mirth*, *The Custom of the
Country*, *The Buccaneers*.

P37   Monroe, N. Elizabeth. *The Novel and Society*. Chapel Hill:
        University of North Carolina Press, 1941.
            Chapter "Moral Situation in Edith Wharton" argues
        Wharton had the gift of tragedy, but was limited by her
        subject matter to a concentration only on negative values.
        Traces obscurities in her work arising both from confused
        moral values and material unsuited to tragedy. Praises her
        technical gifts highly. Cites: *HofM*, *Reef*, *CC*, *EF*, *Summer*,
        Old Maid, *M'sR*, *Children*, *FofT*, *AofI*, *GofM*, *HRB*, *GA*,
        Buc, "Atrophy."

P38   Morgan, H. Wayne. *Writers in Transition: Seven Americans*.
        New York: Hill and Wang, 1963.
            Discusses conflict between new Western wealth and
        the old Eastern establishment as Wharton presents it.
        Contends in EW's work this transfer of power is
        broadened and becomes a great cultural and intellectual
        conflict, and that she is a classicist with a profoundly
        conservative view of humanity. Notes that she is
        considered dated, and will only be revived if people realize
        she was actually dealing with eternal questions.

P39   Morris, Lloyd R. *Postscript to Yesterday; the Last Fifty
        Years*. New York: Random House, 1947.
            Attempts to sketch "the principal social changes that
        took place in American life between 1896 and 1946."
        Wharton is discussed in terms of the concept of the "Lady"
        and her society--its attitude to her literary career and her
        treatment of it. Bibliography.

P40   Mussell, Kay. *Fantasy and Reconciliation: Contemporary
        Formulas of Women's Romance Fiction*. Westport,
        Connecticut: Greenwood Press, 1984.
            Study of contemporary women's romance fiction.
        Concludes Wharton drew on romance conventions but her

constructs transcended and commented on them. Terms *The House of Mirth* an example of "novels in which socially approved models lead to disaster."

P41   O'Connor, William Van. "The Novel Of Experience." *Critique* 1 (Winter 1956): 37-44.
      Defines the Jamesian novel of experience in which an innocent protagonist must come to terms with a difficult reality as a line in twentieth-century American literature. Notes that in Wharton's use of this form, the essential quality is "the ironic pleasure to be found in defeat and in compromise." Briefly cites *FofT*, *EF*, *AofI* and "The Reckoning" and points out her interest in the compromises of marriage.

P42   Rodgers, Audrey T. "Images of Women: A Female Perspective." *College Literature* 6 (Winter 1979): 41-56.
      Traces images of women in twentieth century literature--from Wharton to Adrienne Rich, noting the movement from "an objective tone; veiled and detached" often distanced from the female characters to the modern subjective view in which writer and character merge. Analyzes Wharton's heroines who fail because they are regarding social versus individual claims. Cites: *AofI*, *HofM*, *EF*, *Old Maid*.

P43   Schriber, Mary Suzanne. *Gender and the Writer's Imagination: From Cooper to Wharton.* Lexington, Kentucky: University Press of Kentucky, 1987.
      Chapter. Argues Wharton challenged the current cultural ideology concerning the intellectual and sexual nature of woman, raising invisible, unimaginable and frightening issues in terms of the culturally powerful gender expectations. Important readings of the neglected *Hudson River Bracketed*, *The Gods Arrive* and *Twilight Sleep*. Concludes that although her conscious mind "did not break free entirely from her culture's ideology of woman" her imagination did. Also analyzes: *HofM*, *Touchstone*, *Reef*, *CC*.

P44   Showalter, Elaine. *The New Feminist Criticism: Essays on Women, Literature and Theory.* New York: Pantheon Books, 1985.
        Passim.

P45   Simon, Jean. *Le Roman Américain au XX siècle.* Paris: Boivin, 1950.
        In French. Chapter defines Wharton as Jamesian only in the analysis of refined people and the relationships between Europeans and Americans. Otherwise, she is a student of Bourget as much as James. Summarizes *House of Mirth* and *Age of Innocence.* Notes her satire, her excellence within a limited genre. Concludes that both she and James are essentially isolated, uninfluenced by really American literature which revolved around Howells and those who followed Dreiser. Cites: *IV&G, EF, ONY, WofF.*

P46   Snell, George D. *Shapers of American Fiction 1798-1947.* New York: Dutton, 1947.
        Discusses Wharton under "The James Influence." Terms her world rather superficial and heartless. But praises her as the woman writer who encouraged other American women to write honestly from personal experience and observation. Cites: *HofM, EF, CC, AofI.*

P47   Spiller, Robert E. *The Cycle of American Literature.* New York: Macmillan, 1955.
        Volume grew out of Spiller's experience working on the *Literary History of the United States.* Mentions Wharton briefly in conjunction with writers who, in the late nineteenth and early twentieth centuries, owed much to the older, native tradition of psychological fiction of Hawthorne and Poe in that they did not seem to feel "that the basic structure of American social ethics was threatened." They wrote of the "problem of an individual whose personal values were challenged by social change, but who would survive or fall according to his own ethical courage."

P48   Straumann, Heinrich. *American Literature in the Twentieth Century*. New York: Hutchinson's University Library, 1951.
        Places Wharton among the determinists, but not the naturalists. Finds her "chiefly concerned with the overpowering effect of social and tribal conventions on the individual. Notes she is distinguished from naturalists by choice of subject material (upper class) and the reticence of James and Howells. Cites: *HofM, EF, AofI*.

P49   Taylor, Walter F. *The Story of American Letters*. Chicago, Henry Regnery, 1956. Revision of *A History of American Letters*. [O81]
        Discusses Wharton in chapter, "The Humanist and Conservative Tradition--Fiction." Notes Jamesian influence, her emphasis on construction and the well-made novel, and her central theme of the individual in conflict with society. Terms her short stories--with sometimes too extreme situations and sentimentality--of less consistently fine quality than the novels. Defines her limitations of class, narrowness, illicit sex as a staple, and lack of a broad human sympathy, balanced by her keen, intelligent observation, artistry and imaginative power. Cites: *HofM, EF, AofI*.

P50   Terrier, Michel. *Individu et Société dans le Roman Américain de 1900 à 1940*. Paris: Didier, 1973.
        In French. Passim. Notes Edenic myth, the fatally tragic role played by morals and the decline of the aristocracy. Terms Wharton, along with Dreiser, London, Fitzgerald and Wolfe the poets of "le monde enchanté."

P51   Thorp, Willard. *American Writing in the Twentieth Century*. Cambridge: Harvard University Press, 1960.
        Contends Wharton's writing fell off after *GofM*, but her earlier novels are mirrors of their age and should hold a permanent literary place. Contends her metier is the problem novel. Argues she is a master of satire, born from both her disdain and admiration for New York society. One of her greatest assets is thought to be her love of detail and use of it. Concludes in her best work "her

judgment of life was capable of resolving" the moral dilemmas of her characters which places her above other problem novelists. Cites: *VofD*, *AofI*, *HofM*, *CC*, *EF*, *GofM*, *Reef*. Bibliography.

P52   Tuttleton, James W. "'Combat in the Erogenous Zone':
          Women in the American Novel between the Two World
          Wars." In *What Manner of Woman*. Edited by Marlene
          Springer. New York: New York University Press, 1977.
          271-296.
          Mentions Wharton in introductory remarks to an essay
          concerned with the response to various types of women in
          the fiction of Fitzgerald, Hemingway and Faulkner. Takes
          The Age of Innocence as a point of departure with its
          negative portrait of the emotionally and sexually
          infantilized May Welland--product of the earlier Genteel
          Tradition--arguing in its conclusion the novel forecasts the
          sexual liberation of the twentieth century.

P52.1   Tuttleton, James W. "Edith Wharton." *Dictionary of
          Literary Biography*. Vol. 12, *American Realists and
          Naturalists*. Edited by Donald Pizer and Earl N. Herbert.
          Detroit: A Bruccoli Clark Book, 1982. 433-450.
          Critical evaluation of EW's work focuses on her
          technique and theory of fiction. Sees EW's literary merit
          in "the clarity of her social vision, the particular angle of
          that vision ..., and her subtle mastery of the techniques of
          fiction." Offers significant commentary on *VofD*, *CC*, *AofI*,
          Madame de Treymes and *HofM* which author sees as
          marred by "weaknesses of style and plotting and a strain
          of sentimentality ...." Sees impact of both Edith and Teddy
          Wharton's breakdowns in the ghost stories. Contends *AofI*
          marked the end of her best work. Offers valuable insights
          into her later work, particularly *HRB* and *GA* for their
          penetration into the novelist's art and technique. This
          essay is, in itself, an important bibliographic source.
          Includes select primary and secondary bibliography, photos
          of title pages of *HofM*, *EF*, *AofI*, *M'sR*, and EW's
          notebook.

P53   Tuttleton, James W. *The Novel of Manners in America.* Chapel Hill: University of North Carolina Press, 1972.

Chapter on Wharton titled "Edith Wharton: Social Historian of Old New York" cites Wharton as a major link between the generation of Howells and James and that of Lewis and Fitzgerald. Notes she emphasizes tradition and continuity and takes as her subject "the self in full engagement with the social world." Cites: *French Ways and Their Meaning, Reef, HofM, CC, AofI, GofM, ONY, M'sR, TS, Children, HRB, GA, Buc,* "Autres Temps ... ," "Duration." Note references to Wharton throughout book. [K16, L117, L118, L119, M51, M52, P52, Q81, Q82, Q83, Q84, R8.15, X77]

P54   Van Doren, Carl. *The American Novel 1789-1939.* New York: Macmillan, 1940.

Survey of major works with slight critical commentary on *HofM, CC, AofI, EF.* Notes EW's ironical intelligence, the clash of community standards with passion, defines Lily Bart as "Aristotelian hero." Contends she conveys a sense of people living so closely that "no one ... may vary from the customary path without breaking a pattern or inviting a disaster." Notes the antiquarian flavor of her work--but maintains she had a "sharper intelligence" than James, and therefore her irony is lasting in illuminating still crucial situations. Cites: *HofM, CC, AofI, EF.*

P55   Wagenknecht, Edward. *Cavalcade of the American Novel.* New York: Holt, Rinehart and Winston, 1952.

Chapter on Wharton, "Edith Wharton: Social Background and Ethical Dilemma" briefly analyzes her novels. Defines her subject as "social and ethical problems among cultivated people, mostly Americans, at home and abroad." Calls her psychological, with debts to the French, Bourget and James. Defends her against charges that she was a society novelist and cold, arguing that she was closer to determinism than James. Also refutes Wilson's theory that she wrote out of the pain of her marriage. Cites: *GA, HRB, Buc, VofD, Marne, SatF, EF,* "Bunner Sisters," *HofM,*

FofT, Reef, CC, AofI, ONY, GofM, M'sR, TS, Children, Touchstone, Sanctuary, MdeT.

P56   Wasserstrom, William. *Heiress of All Ages: Sex and Sentiment in the Genteel Tradition.* Minneapolis: University of Minnesota Press, 1959.

Brief comments contend Wharton exposed American materialism by imitating James, but was less humane and "only a slightly better amateur than Fuller or Herrick." Notes her severe opinion of American women and, like James, her belief in the benign influence of Europe and sexual experience on innocent Americans. Cites: "The Last Asset," *CC, AofI.*

P57   Whicher, George F. "Lingering Urbanity." *The Literature of the American People: An Historical and Critical Survey.* Ed. Arthur Hobson Quinn. New York: Appleton, 1951.

Maintains Wharton was more aesthetically satisfying to the cultivated reader through her craftsmanship and style than any other writer of the century. Praises her artistry, calling *EF* one of the few great tragic novels in English. Compares Wharton to Anne Douglas Sedgwick, both of whom were liberated rather than controlled by James. However, notes that Wharton's emphasis on conventions is dated, and she may endure for works like "Bunner Sisters" that stress timeless values. Also cites: *Old Maid, AofI, HofM.*

P58   Wilson, Edmund. *The Thirties: From Notebooks and Diaries of the Period.* Edited with an introduction by Leon Edel. London: Macmillan, 1980.

Two mentions: one, of reading *A Backward Glance,* and two, discussing with Phil Littell (Winter 1937-1938) why Percy Lubbock doesn't read Wharton.

P59   Wilson, Edmund. *The Twenties: From Notebooks and Diaries of the Period.* Edited by Leon Edel. New York: Farrar, Straus and Giroux, 1975.

Brief, passing references. Notes Elinor Wylie's husband told Elinor to have nothing to do with Walter Berry because he had syphilis. *Age of Innocence* appears on a list of books of the twenties which tell "what a terrible place America is."

P60 Winters, Yvor. *Maule's Curse.* In *In Defense of Reason.* Denver: Alan Swallow, n.d. [1947] N.B. *Maule's Curse* originally published New York: New Directions, 1938.

Passing references to Wharton with summation she is best in *Bunner Sisters, False Dawn,* and *The Valley of Decision* (a nearly perfect example of the art of exposition and historical summary). But except for these and *The Age of Innocence* (which with Jamesian art surpasses James) and *The Custom of the Country,* she is "mediocre when she is not worse." See Wharton references in chapter "Primitivism and Decadence" also.

P61 Wolff, Cynthia Griffin. "Edith Wharton." *Dictionary of Literary Biography.* Vol. 19, *American Novelists 1910-1945.* Edited by James J. Martine. Detroit: A Bruccoli Clark Book, 1981. 126-142.

Biographic overview of EW's life recognizes her best work done before 1922. Includes survey of critical appraisals which only aided the decline of her literary reputation. Cites Lubbock as responsible for evaluation of EW as a talented imitator of James. Maintains EW's work, which held the societal constrictions of Old New York in a tense balance with that society's moral strength, has its thematic roots in "the emotional and social dilemmas of her own life...." Includes readings of *HofM, EF, Reef* ["weakest" of the major works], *CC* ["one of her two or three best novels"], *Summer, AofI.* Sees Goethe as greatest influence on EW. Notes the decline in the later work, but states "an incomparable understanding of complex psychological motivation and perhaps the keenest satiric capacity in American fiction" as reasons for a permanently reclaimed literary reputation. Includes primary and secondary bibiliography and a copy of a corrected typescript of *AofI.*

Chapter 8

General Discussions of Edith Wharton
in Articles and Books
1939-1987

Chapter lists critical discussions of Edith Wharton in articles and books, 1939-1987. For contemporary studies, see Chapter 6. For survey material after 1938 see Chapter 7. For material related to one particular work check individual listings and Works Index.

Q1 Anderson, Hilton. "Edith Wharton and the Vulgar American." *The Southern Quarterly* 7 (October 1968): 17-22.

   Discusses Wharton's Americans in Europe, who were usually vulgar types and not the genteel cosmopolitans of her own circle. Maintains that she only shows a deep understanding and sympathy for "sensitive, aristocratic American women" in Europe with problems in some way like her own. Cites: *GofM, MdeT, CC, Marne, GA, Buc.*

Q2 Anderson, Hilton. "Edith Wharton as Fictional Heroine." *South Atlantic Quarterly* 69 (Winter 1970): 118-23.

   Finds Fanny de Malrive, Anna Leath and Rose Sellars "present pictures of her concept of the ideal American woman in Europe." Focuses on EW's frustrating marriage and love for Walter Berry. Terms Nan St. George Wharton's last ideal, and traces correspondences between these heroines and her own situation. Cites: *Marne, MdeT, Reef, Children, Buc.*

Q3   Anonymous. "The Age of Edith." *Newsweek* 59 (29 January 1962): 82

Occasioned by editions of *The Age of Innocence, Hudson River Bracketed, The Gods Arrive* on Wharton's centenary. Praises Wharton as "superb social historian" with psychological depth. Anticipates opening of her papers at Yale will reveal much about the mysteries of her life.

Q4   Auchincloss, Louis. "Edith Wharton and Her New Yorks." *Partisan Review* 18 (July-August 1951): 411-19. Rpt. N14 and *Reflections of a Jacobite.* Boston: Houghton Mifflin, 1961.

Maintains that Wharton was at her best and uniquely qualified as an interpreter of aspects of New York life in the period of *HofM* and *CC* and should have kept to that era rather than moved to contemporary life, for she was an excellent analyst of the paralysis that attends business failure and the coarseness that attends success. Also cites: *AofI.*

Q5   Auchincloss, Louis. *Pioneers and Caretakers.* Minneapolis: University of Minnesota Press, 1961. Wharton chapter revised reprint of his pamphlet in the University of Minnesota Series on American Writers. Also reprinted in *Seven Modern American Novelists* [Q5]. Edited by William Van O'Connor. Minneapolis: University of Minnesota Press, 1964. pp. 11-45.

Covers Wharton's life and all of her work. Somewhat dated because of the lack of the Fullerton material, but valuable as an introduction to her major themes and subjects. Argues her conservatism eventually enchained her, but that her value and reputation will rest on her two great novels of manners: *The House of Mirth* and *The Age of Innocence.* Serves as an almost perfect, balanced example of evaluations of Wharton before the Yale papers were opened and feminist criticism.

Q6   Avendaño, Olga De Valdivia. "Edith Wharton." *Andean Quarterly* (Summer 1943-44): 8-21, 39-58; (Spring 1944): 65-84; (Fall 1944): 28-46; (Winter 1944): 56-73; (Christmas, 1944): 66-86.

Mentions all novels and most novellas and significant short stories. Mentions all Wharton sources to date except (notably) Lubbock. Scholarly, important for its time. Of note is attention to the later work and contention Wharton is overlooked because of sex. Chapters cover: the history of the question of Wharton scholarship (notably the Jamesian influence); Wharton's theory, technique and style; major moral problems covered in the fiction; psychological problems such as cosmopolitanism and aestheticism; Wharton's philosophy of life; her world--themes and characters--her limitations.

Q7   Baxter, Annette K. "Caste and Class: Howells' Boston and Wharton's New York." *Midwest Quarterly* 4 (Summer 1963): 353-61.

Defines differences in character between Howells's Boston and Wharton's New York 1865-1915. Finds Bostonians more self-sufficient, lacking "the panoramic quality and variegated structure of New York" and its "formal appendages, the arbiter and the professional confidante." Terms, according to these novelists, that "breadth and mobility" characterize New York; "compactness and repose," Boston. Cites: *CC, HofM, AofI*.

Q8   Bellringer, Alan W. "Edith Wharton's Use of France." *The Yearbook of English Studies* 15 (1985): 109-124.

Argues Wharton showed "great skill in handling the Franco-American subject" in her neglected work. Praises her "coherent and informed study of Gallic temperament and principles." Notes French influence in *The Decoration of Houses, Ethan Frome, The Marne, A Son at the Front*, but relies on *French Ways and Their Meaning* as a demonstration of her admiration for French mores and manners examined at length in *The Reef, Custom of the Country, Madame de Treymes* and "The Last Asset." Notes her understanding of France can be traced to W.C. Brownell's *French Traits* (1889).

Q9   Blackall, Jean Frantz. "Edith Wharton's Art of Ellipsis." *Journal of Narrative Technique* 17 (Spring 1987): 145-162.
       Discusses, with carefully documented examples, Wharton's use of ellipsis, particularly as it "elucidate[s] the dynamics of subtly crafted texts and clarif[ies] our understanding of the relationship she sought to cultivate between author and reader." Cites: *EF*, "Refugees," "Mission of Jane," "Confession," "Coward," "After Holbein," "Joy in the House," "Expiation," "Journey," "All Souls,'" "Xingu," "Muse's Tragedy."

Q10   Bloom, Lillian D. "On Daring to Look Back With Wharton and Cather." *Novel: A Forum on Fiction* 10 (1977): 167-78.
       Discusses Wharton and Cather in light of Lindberg's *Edith Wharton and the Novel of Manners* and Stouck's *Willa Cather's Imagination*. Analyzes reasons for the decline of interest in their work, with a plea for renewed appreciation. Finds Cather more "biographically elusive" than Wharton after the Lewis biography. Wishes Lindberg had chosen *The Reef* for close analysis, but calls his book "Cogently reasoned and unpretentious."[See N18]

Q11   Blum, Virginia L. "Edith Wharton's Erotic Other World." *Literature and Psychology* 33 (1987): 12-29.
       Freudian explication traces the vampire woman image and the bisection of the feminine into the angel/whore dichotomy, typical of Wharton's men, in "Miss Mary Pask," "Bewitched," "Pomegranate Seed," *Summer, Ethan Frome, The Age of Innocence* and *The House of Mirth*.

Q12   Brooks, Van Wyck. *The Dream of Arcadia: American Artists and Writers in Italy 1760-1915*. New York: Dutton, 1958.

Chapter on Wharton called "The Collectors." Feels she "evoked most vividly the old static feudal order." Mentions *False Dawn* in connection with Ruskin. Intermittent references to Wharton's love, of Italy and use of the country in her work. Cites: *IV&G, Italian Backgrounds, VofD,* "Venetian Night's Entertainment," "Duchess at Prayer," "Angel at the Grave."

Q13 Burgess, Anthony. "Austere in Whalebone." *Spectator* 215 (3 December 1965): 745.

Comments on Constable's reissuing of *CC, EF* and *Summer.* Maintains Wharton is a lesser artist than James because she is too much the "cold planner" with contrived effects; she has a fierce intelligence with no "intuitive daemon." Terms the utter pessimism of *EF* "too bad to be true."

Q14 Canby, Henry Seidel. "Great Talk." *Saturday Review of Literature* 30 (25 October 1947): 17-18.

Reviews Lubbock's *Portrait of Edith Wharton* as not a biography, not a literary critique, but "a portrait of a noble character and personality." Contends the importance of the book lies in the "great talk" it suggests which flourishes in a perfected culture. Praises Wharton as a fine American mind and craftsman, who kept to the highest standards and still won popularity. [See N20]

Q15 Chapman, Hester W.L. "Books in General." *New Statesman and Nation* NS 29 (20 January 1945): 43.

General overview of Wharton's background and fiction with the conclusion that she was not a genius, but an extremely competent professional novelist whose characters are doll-like and who will be remembered for the "outmoded qualities of self-effacement and a sense of form." Contends she played Mrs. Thrale to James's Dr. Johnson. Cites: *CC, EF, Summer,* "Bunner Sisters," *AofI.*

Q16 Coard, Robert L. "Names in the Fiction of Edith Wharton." *Names* 13 (March 1965): 1-10.

Traces origins of titles, names of characters, and fictional works within the text. Finds her titles reveal her seriousness, irony and interest in science, literature and interior decoration. Points out the satire in many of her names and similarities with naming in Sinclair Lewis. Cites: *VofD, HofM, ABG, M'sR, Crucial Instances, Descent of Man, HRB, CC, EF, AofI,* "Full Circle," "Debt," "Angel at the Grave."

Q17   Cohn, Jan. "The House of Fiction: Domestic Architecture in Howells and Edith Wharton." *Texas Studies in Literature and Language* 15 (1973): 537-49.

Discusses problems the genteel realists faced in their use of houses as symbols, and the cultural myth in America of the moral man in the moral house. Illustrates argument using confusions apparent in *The Rise of Silas Lapham, HofM* and *HRB.* Contends that reconciliation of success and virtue was a central problem in realistic fiction. Both the log cabin myth and the mansion are part of the culture, and thus "one ought to strive for wealth and its material manifestations, yet one should be rewarded for avoiding the materialistic struggle" that reward being a house "in its double role of mansion and log cabin."

Q18   Cuddy, Lois A. "Triangles of Defeat and Liberation: The Quest for Power in Edith Wharton's Fiction." *Perspectives on Contemporary Literature* 8 (1982): 18-26.

Examines the triangular relationships in *HofM, EF,* and *AofI,* and traces an evolution in male-female relationships parallel to Wharton's own growth and changing perceptions. Notes that the female is dominated by males in the earliest work, and the male by females in the last. Also notes the errors of perception in the protagonists, who assume their self-determination at the beginning of the novels, and are shown to actually be manipulated in another triangular pattern. Provides chart of the triangular structures.

Q19   Dessner, Lawrence J. "Edith Wharton and the Problem of Form." *Ball State University Forum* 24 (1983): 54-63.

Contends Wharton failed to find an appropriate form, a technical problem, with moral implications because of "an incipient moral solipsism...." Emphasizes retrospective ironies (e.g., the end embedded in the beginning) better suited to the short story that fail in the novel and Jamesian central intelligences with insufficient moral character. Cites: *ONY, CC, HofM, Reef, AofI, HRB.*

Q20   Dooley, R.B. "A Footnote to Edith Wharton." *American Literature* 26 (March 1954): 78-85.

Gives evidence for prototypes for Julius Beaufort in August Belmont, Mrs. Lemuel Struthers in Mrs. Paran Stevens and Mrs. Manson Mingott in Wharton's great-aunt Mrs. Mary Mason Jones. Contends that "certain actual persons had sufficiently captured her imagination to be set down almost as they were."

Q21   French, Marilyn. "Muzzled Women." *College Literature* Edith Wharton Issue 14.3 (1987): 219-229.

Examines the problem that women's fiction "has not reflected the fullness of life some women writers themselves achieved" and that women writers grant their heroines "fewer choices and greater constriction than they themselves experienced." Discusses Cather, George Sand, George Eliot, Virginia Woolf as well as Wharton. Cites: *Reef, Summer, GA.*

Q22   Friedl, Bettina. "Frauen in der Literatur." In *Einfuhrung in die Amerikanische Literaturegeschrichte.* Edited by Jakob Kollhöfer. Heidelberg: Deutsche-Amerikanshes Institut, 1979.

* Not seen.

Q23   Friedl, Herwig. "Problemgeschichtliche Uberlegungen zum Stellenwert der Kunst in Amerikanischen Kunstlererzahlungen." *Anglia* 97 (1979): 153-167.

["Thoughts on the Problems of Taking a Stand on the Art of American Storytelling."] In German. Article concerns the relationship of the artist to society, and examines James's, Poe's and Wharton's response to the problems of the conflicts between art and reality. Argues that the hero-artist concept of James saw the artist as the embodiment of all that is true and sensitive and his withdrawal from society thus becomes a measure of its delusions. Cites Wharton as James's pupil, but contends she was unable to solve the dilemma of the artist as readily as James. Argues that, for Wharton, communication between artist and society can occur only in the realm of status symbols and market value; thus, the artist stands alone. Finds her position reaches its climax in "The Daunt Diana."

Q24   Friedman, Henry J., M.D. "The Masochistic Character in the Work of Edith Wharton." *Seminars in Psychiatry* 5.3 (August 1973): 313-329.

A practicing analyst, Friedman contends that an unconscious sense of guilt arising from repressed anger causes masochistic reactions in many of Wharton's characters. Traces the subtle masochism evident in Wharton's own relationships--before the Fullerton material was available, however. Concentrates on *EF*, *AofI*, *CC*, *Reef*, *HofM*.

Q25   Friedman, Norman. "Point of View in Fiction: The Development of a Critical Concept." *Publications of the Modern Language Association* 70 (December 1955): 1160-84.

Covers background of point of view emerging as an important artistic technique. Discusses Wharton's *Writing of Fiction* on importance of point of view and James's Prefaces. Terms her work the most significant after Lubbock's *Craft of Fiction* and Beach's *The Method of Henry James*.

Q26   Fryer, Judith. "Women and Space: The Flowering of Desire." *Prospects* 9 (1984): 187-230.

Brief discussion of Wharton's *The Decoration of Houses* and "The Valley of Childish Things" in the context of a wide-ranging meditation on public and private space and the female imagination. Weaves together Gilman's *Herland*, Chopin's *The Awakening*, architects Frank Lloyd Wright and Louis Sullivan, the Women's Building at the 1893 Columbian Exposition, women's 19th century writing on housing and the home. Appears as Prologue and Chapter I of the author's *Felicitous Space: of Edith Wharton and Willa Cather*. [See N10]

Q27   Gibson, Mary Ellis. "Edith Wharton and the Ethnography of Old New York." *Studies in American Fiction* 13 (Spring 1985): 57-69.

Study of Wharton's ethnographic and anthropological language and metaphor in *The House of Mirth*, *The Custom of the Country* and *The Age of Innocence* in the context of recent anthropological theory. Employs Mary Douglas's analysis of natural symbols and of pollution and taboo to analyze Wharton's understanding of social symbolism, her ambivalence toward social change and the complexities of her treatment of New York society. Cites Douglas's *Natural Symbols: Explorations in Cosmology* (1973) and *Purity and Danger: An Analysis of Concepts of Pollution and Taboo* (1966).

Q28   Goodwyn, Janet. "One More Boundary to Cross for the Friend of Henry James." *Guardian*, 6 July 1983, p. 10.

Written on the occasion of the Virago reprints. Appreciative evaluation notes Wharton "crossed boundaries and forged links between the popular and the academic. But the hybrid nature of her work is partly responsible for the general neglect into which she has fallen." Maintains the important thing for Wharton is that her women "risk themselves, be prepared to suffer pain in order to attain and demonstrate the rewards of independence, of maturity."

Q29   Grant, Robert. "Edith Wharton." *Commemorative Tributes of the American Academy of Arts and Letters 1905-1941*. New York: The Academy, 1942.

　　　　Tribute from Wharton's personal friend ranges widely over her life and work, emphasizing her culture, the perfection of her style, and the "fastidious reticence" which refused to violate the canons of artistic truth, "the hue and cry of democracy to the contrary, notwithstanding."

Q30   Gray, J. *On Second Thought*. Minneapolis: University of Minnesota Press, 1946.

　　　　Discusses Wharton, John Marquand and Struthers Burt as satirists, arguing they are all really under the spell of the worlds they satirize. Feels her art deteriorated after *AofI*. Says she had great gifts and was influential but had more sly insight than profound moral conviction. Feels *EF* was her best and if she had developed that aspect of her art she wouldn't be known as a brilliant social satirist, but "one of the really great, instead of a successful and influential craftsman whose inspiration steadily diminished."

Q31   Greenwood, Joan Voss. "The Implications of Marital Status in Edith Wharton's Short Stories and *Nouvelles*." *Kobe College Studies* 5 (February 1959): 9-28.

　　　　Categorizes marital status in Wharton's shorter work, using a wide range of brief examples. Concludes that the suffering, the small number of reasonably happy marriages, the many unsuccessful loves and the number of bachelors makes a pessimistic impression. Speculates this attitude may have arisen from her own unfulfilling marriage.

Q32   Greenwood, Joan Voss. "The Importance of Milieu in Edith Wharton's Short Stories and *Nouvelles*." *Kobe College Studies* 5 (October 1958): 1-28.

　　　　Examines variety of milieu Wharton used, listing settings in New York, France, Italy, England and New England. Contends details of milieu are not extraneous but a contribution to structure and theme.

Q33   Greenwood, Joan Voss. "The Nature and Results of Conflict in Edith Wharton's Short Stories and *Nouvelles*." *Kobe College Studies* 6 (June 1959): 1-27.

Analyzes types of conflicts in Wharton's short stories and *nouvelles* using a wide range of brief examples. Categorizes conflicts as those arising from the individual versus society, egotism, self-sacrifice (often ironically self-destructive), and the powers of convention--noting these forces operate in the strongest ghost stories as well, and that sometimes the main concern of the story is not conflict, but rather the revelation of character, situation or a group of facts.

Q34   Hamblen, Abigail Ann. "Edith Wharton's New England." *New England Quarterly* 38 (June 1965): 239-44.

Critical of Wharton's attitude toward New England in *EF* and *Summer*, contending it is detached, and Wharton "views this particular culture as if it were in a laboratory." Argues Wharton was too rich and led too cosmopolitan a life to come close to her subject. Cites: *ABG*.

Q35   Hardwick, Elizabeth. "Mrs. Wharton in New York." *The New York Review of Books* 34, nos. 21 and 22 (21 January 1988): 28-34.

Ranges widely over Wharton's career with discussion of her restricted focus in terms of New York City. Synopsis and critical discussion of *HofM, Reef, M'sR, CC, AofI, ONY*. Wharton emerges as an aristocratic, bestselling writer of manners--narrow in focus and given to coincidences, viewed now with "landmark affection." Cites: *EF*, "Bunner Sisters," "Beatrice Palmato."

Q36   Harvey, John. "Contrasting Worlds: A Study in the Novels of Edith Wharton." *Etudes Anglaises* 7 (April 1954): 190-98.

Discusses effect of France on Wharton's fiction, maintaining her life there gave her necessary perspective. Argues she cannot be dismissed as James's pupil because she learned much of her craft from the French nineteenth-century novelists--Stendahl and Balzac, for example.

Contends *M'sR* and *FofT* fail because of weaknesses of Bourget.

Q37   Hatch, Ronald B. "Edith Wharton: A Forward Glance." In *The Twenties*. Edited by Barbara Smith Lemeunier. Aix-en-Provence: University de Provence, 1982.

Contends that in such works as *HofM*, *EF*, and *AofI* lies one of the first explorations of modern themes, particularly, "the effects of an alienating society on consciousness and moral values," and thus she made possible the "modernism" of the twenties in such writers as Fitzgerald, Virginia Woolf and Hemingway.

Q38   Hays, Peter L. "Bearding the Lily: Wharton's Masks." *American Notes and Queries* 18.5 (January 1980): 75-76.

Traces sources of names in *AofI*, *EF* and *HofM*, concluding that Wharton's names imply multiple meanings.

Q39   Herron, Ima H. *The Small Town in American Literature*. Durham, North Carolina: Duke University, 1939.

Argues in *EF* and *Summer* Wharton demonstrates her familiarity with the aspect, dialect and mental and moral attitudes of rural New Englanders and in the former gives a "masterly interpretation of the strict New England code." She rejects idealistic views of New England and depicts her characters bound by forces beyond their power to control or defy.

Q40   Howe, Irving. "The Achievement of Edith Wharton." *Encounter* 19 (July 1962): 45-52. Slightly revised as introduction to *N14*. Also rpt. in *A World More Attractive: A View of Modern Literature and Politics*. New York: Horizon, 1963.

Overview of problems facing EW's critics: the Jamesian debt, range and restriction of her work, changes in society she had to deal with, her personal vision with its European sense of fatality. Howe contends: "Where she failed was in giving imaginative embodiment to the human will seeking to resist defeat or move beyond it." Counts *HofM*, *CC* and *AofI* her best.

Q41   Jessup, Josephine Laurie. *The Faith of Our Feminists: A Study in the Novels of Edith Wharton, Ellen Glasgow, Willa Cather.* New York: Richard B. Smith, 1950.

Argues that in Wharton woman always rises above man except in "Bunner Sisters." Yet contends that this feminism "inspired no great literary portraits" of women. Bibliography. Cites: *HofM, CC, TS, Children, M'sR, ONY, AofI, FofT, MdeT, VofD, HRB, GA, GofM, Marne, SatF, EF, Summer, Reef, Buc.*

Q42   Joslin, Katherine. "Edith Wharton at 125." *College Literature* Edith Wharton Issue 14.3 (1987): 193-206.

Based on her keynote address at the Edith Wharton Conference in Lenox, Massachusetts, June 1987. Article presents attitudes of critics toward Wharton, focusing on charges of pessimism, Wharton as a naturalist and novelist of manners, misogynist attitudes, feminist reevaluations, and concluding that Wharton is emerging as a major writer in the mainstream of American literature.

Q43   Koprince, Susan. "Edith Wharton's Hotels." *Massachusetts Studies in English* 10.1 (Spring 1985): 12-23.

Analyzes Wharton's distaste for hotels and their use as setting in her fiction as "the antithesis" of the ideal home. Cites: *CC, HofM, Reef, M'sR,* "Souls Belated."

Q44   Krenn, Sister Heliena. "The American Identity in the 'Novel of Manners.'" *FuJen Studies* 10 (1977): 41-57. See: *Literature and Linguistics,* FuJen University, Taipei, Taiwan. Available Library of Congress.

Analysis of the international theme--principally in Twain, Hawthorne's *The Marble Faun,* Howells's *A Foregone Conclusion,* James's *The Europeans, Portrait of a Lady, The American, Daisy Miller,* and, much less centrally, Wharton's *HofM* and *CC.* Wharton discussed in terms of the Europeanized lady in her own country--e.g., Lily Bart, and the hardworking American fathers, contrasted with leisured Europeans. Bibliography.

Q45   Küster, Dieter. *Das Frankreichbild im Werk Edith Whartons*.
       Mainzer Studien zur Amerikanstik Band I. Frankfurt:
       Bern, Herbert Lang, 1972.
           [*The Image of France in Edith Wharton's Work*.] In
       German with table of contents and abstract in both
       English and German. Description, interpretation and
       evaluation of the image of France from Wharton's early
       poem "Chartres" (1893) to her autobiography. Traces
       characteristics of France in Wharton, contrasts with
       America, France in WWI, theme, form, and style in
       relation to France and the meaning of France
       biographically. Discusses: "Chartres," "The Lamp of
       Psyche," *VofD*, *HofM*, *MdeT*, "The Last Asset," "Les
       Metteurs en Scene," *Reef*, *CC*, "Kerfol," "Coming Home,"
       Marne, "In Provence," *AofI*, *SatF*, "Miss Mary Pask" *GA*,
       Motor-Flight Through France, *Fighting France*, *French Ways
       and Their Meaning*, *WofF*, *ABG*.

Q46   La Belle, Jenijoy. *Herself Beheld*. Ithaca: Cornell, 1988.
           Thought-provoking study of the relationship between
       women and mirrors in literature finds that, in the French
       tradition, Wharton's women accept that their selves and
       their lives are decided in large measure by what they look
       like in the mirror." Discusses: *The House of Mirth*, *The
       Reef*, *The Custom of the Country*, *The Mother's Recompense*
       and *Summer*.

Q47   Lerman, Leo. "The Golden Era of Edith Wharton." *New
       York Times Book Review*, 27 August 1950, p.1.
           Occasioned by the publication of *An Edith Wharton
       Treasury* edited by Arthur Hobson Quinn [J2]. Discusses
       her influence on Fitzgerald, her similarity to Sinclair
       Lewis, and her importance in the twenties, and contends
       her decline in popularity stems from both the intervening
       Depression and herself (the bestselling Grande Dame.)
       Also argues that before 1920 she wrote out of pain,
       rebellion and rage at the society of her youth, but after
       that she wrote "drivel" probably from habit. Regrets that
       Quinn did not include *EF*. Cites: *HofM*, *AofI*, "Bunner
       Sisters."

Q48   Lynskey, Winifred. "The Heroes of Edith Wharton."
        University of Toronto Quarterly 23 (July 1954): 354-61.
            Argues that Wharton's heroes are not modeled on
        Walter Berry, but are a sentimental projection of herself
        and her own struggles to overcome the constrictions of her
        background, and that the women who inspire them are a
        projection of Walter Berry. Cites: *AofI*, *HofM*, *CC*, *HRB*,
        Old Maid.

Q49   McDowell, Margaret B. "Viewing the Custom of Her
        Country: Edith Wharton's Feminism." *Contemporary
        Literature* 15 (1974): 521-38. [Note: Formerly *Wisconsin
        Studies in Contemporary Literature*.]
            Excellent, feminist reading of Wharton through
        analysis of her critical reception and fiction, demonstrating
        her feminist criticism of man in American society through
        analysis of her weak males and her courageous women.
        Maintains Wharton's feminism is cumulative and implicit
        rather than explicit, yet clearly evident as she poses
        questions about women and the roles which society expects
        them to play. Also notes the changes in Wharton's view
        of women over the years. Cites: *FofT*, *Reef*, *AofI*, *HofM*,
        HRB, *GA*, *French Ways and Their Meaning*, *TS*, *In
        Morocco*, *CC*, "Quicksand," "Lamp of Psyche," "Letters."

Q50   McGinty, Sarah M. "Houses and Interiors as Characters in
        Edith Wharton's Novels." *Nineteenth Century* 5 (Spring
        1979): 48.
            Focuses on *The House of Mirth* and *The Age of
        Innocence* in a discussion of Wharton's use of architecture
        and interiors as integral parts of her characterization,
        plotting, structure and theme. Analyzes the structure of
        The House of Mirth as corresponding to the various houses
        through which Lily travels, and the more sophisticated use
        of domestic detail in *The Age of Innocence* to develop a
        number of themes. Argues in the latter novel it emerges
        as almost a character in itself, "a force working ... through
        the story." Illustrated with pertinent photographs.

Q51   Mcmanis, Jo A. "Edith Wharton's Hymns to Respectability." *The Southern Review* 7 (1971): 986-93.

Analyzes recurring self-sacrifice in Wharton's characters in light of her essay on George Eliot which contended Eliot's works are a "hymn to respectability" as a compensation for her own unconventional life. Maintains because of the association with Walter Berry the case is exactly the same with Wharton, who "serves her penance through her characters. She makes them conform where she did not." Cites: *AofI*, *EF*, "Bunner Sisters," *FofT*, *MdeT*, *CC*, *Reef*, *Children*, "Angel at the Grave."

Q52   Malcolm, Janet. "The Woman Who Hated Women." *New York Times Book Review*, 16 November 1986, pp.11-12.

Occasioned by reprints of *HofM*, *Reef*, *CC* and *AofI*. Maintains Wharton's works are "pervaded by a deep pessimism and an equally profound misogyny." Concludes her strongest work, with its "stylization and abstraction" moves away from nineteenth-century realism toward "the self-reflexive literary experimentation" of the twentieth century.

Q53   Miller, James E., Jr. *Quests Surd and Absurd*. Chicago: University of Chicago Press, 1968.

Argues Wharton's singular strength lies in the creation of the social world. Contends that from the modern perspective, the problem with Wharton and Cather is that they do not fit easily into any established movement or period. We might term the years 1900-1920 the Age of Wharton and Cather. Similarities between the two include the search for values and the American, feminine sensibility.

Q54   Miller, Karl. *Doubles*. New York: Oxford, 1985.

Work deals with the concept of duality, seeking "to demonstrate a continuity that proceeds from the Romantic period to the present." Chapter titled "Edith Wharton's Secret" examines the "dynamic metaphor of the second self" in her life and art, particularly in terms of patterns of flight from conventional restrictions and use of the concept of theft--stemming from her sense of leading two lives: in the philistine world of practical reality and the "esoteric, exotic, erotic" realm of the true self. Traces these metaphoric patterns in *Summer, CC, HofM, AofI, EF* and "Beatrice Palmato."

Q55   Millgate, Michael. "The Novelist and the Businessman: Henry James, Edith Wharton, Frank Norris." *Studi Americani* 5 (1959): 161-89. Also in *American Social Fiction: James to Cozzens*. New York: Barnes and Noble, 1964.

Chapter "Edith Wharton." Discusses, with particular reference to *HofM, FofT,* and *CC,* Wharton's understanding of the relationship between business and social success. Places Wharton in the context of the American social novel; contends her businessmen are plausible and she deals effectively with business world.

Q56   Nevius, Blake. "Edith Wharton Today." *Pacific Spectator* 5 (Spring 1951): 233-41.

Explains why her reputation has waned and lists reasons why she is enduringly important. Maintains the triumph of proletarian literature, accusations she was a snob, paucity of biographical data, supposed narrowness of social outlook and the chilling rationality of her temperament make readers doubt she was genuinely sympathetic and led to her decline. Contends she deserves attention because she illuminates a major aspect of social history, is second only to James as novelist of manners, and she overcomes her narrow subject matter through her two great themes: 1) a greater personality trapped by a lesser; and 2) definition of the limits of responsibility of the individual and effects of rebellion on the social structure. Argues her great importance as a spokesman for Western culture. [See N23] Cites: *ABG, CC.*

Q57   Okada, Akiko. "Edith Wharton." *America Bangaku no Jiko Keisei: 20 seiki America Bungaku I.* Edited by Toshihiko Ogata. Kyoto: Yamagachi, 1981, iii.
       * Not seen.

Q58   Olin-Ammentorp, Julie. "Edith Wharton's Challenge to
        Feminist Criticism." *Studies in American Fiction* 16.2
        (Autumn 1988): 237-244.
           Argues that Wharton was not an "inherent feminist"
        and that feminist criticism does not recognize "that the
        social structures of Wharton's world cause as much male
        waste as female" and both deserve our sympathy.
        Reassesses Gus Trenor, George Dorset and especially
        Selden in *The House of Mirth*, pointing out a double
        standard in judgments of Selden and Lily.

Q59   Ozick, Cynthia. "Justice (Again) to Edith Wharton."
        Commentary, October 1976, 48-57.
           Extensive analysis of Wharton by an accomplished
        essayist and short story writer. Discusses Lewis as the
        biographer of her public life, the substitutions Wharton
        seemed to make--e.g., servants for family, dogs for
        children--and feminist neglect of her contending that
        Wilson [O91] and Kazin [P27], who find the impetus of
        her writing in personal pain, are misguided in that
        Wharton did everything to keep pain at a distance,
        including putting away her insane husband. Finds the most
        telling incident in Lewis's [N17] book to be Wharton's
        rage that her hotel bed was not placed correctly for her
        morning writing. Concludes that her writing was the only
        unprofound part of her life. Contends she had one subject,
        society, was not a genius like James but a "canny realist"
        who has influenced popular fiction. Cites: *AofI*, *HofM*, *EF*.

Q60   Perng, Ching-Hsi. "Reappraising Edith Wharton." *Americai
        Studi* (Taipei) 8 (March 1978): 81-118.
           * Not seen.

Q61   Phelps, Donald. "Edith Wharton and the Invisible." *Prose*
        7 (1973): 227-45.
           Analyzes the reality of what is seen as the common
        denominator of her realism, and yet contends the most
        hypnotic of her powers is to suggest what is *missing*--"the
        void of time, the weight of wasted years, aborted energies."

Discusses *HofM* and *CC* as her "diptych"--which exhibit her range, and, in the former, the weight of the invisible--what is missed--is eloquently stated, although the ending is too dramatically weighted for the prevalent rhythm of classical comedy. Analyzes rhythm and form as they relate to her vision. Also cites: *False Dawn*, *Old Maid*, "Bunner Sisters."

Q62   Phillips, Dewi Zephaniah. *Through a Darkening Glass: Philosophy, Literature and Cultural Change.* Notre Dame, Indiana: University of Notre Dame Press, 1982. First published in *Philosophy and the Arts*, Royal Institute Lectures 6 (1971-72), edited by G. Vesey. New York: Macmillan, 1973.

Chapter title: "Allegiance and Change in Morality--A Study in Contrasts." Argues against the idea that there can be general moral principles governing ethical behavior universal to all reasonable people. Maintains the point can be proved through a study of Wharton's novels and the moral ideas which enter into the relationships she depicts. Concentrates on *The Age of Innocence*, refuting critics who see Archer as weak and his and Ellen Olenska's lives as meaningless. Concludes that modern moralists tend to oversimplify and that novels--with their dramatization of complexities--can correct this tendency.

Q63   Plante, Patricia R. "Edith Wharton: A Prophet Without Due Honor." *Midwest Review*, 1962, 16-22.

Explains Wharton's decline through examination of the values and techniques of her society novels. Contends that modern readers are put off by the seemingly superficial facade of her work, see her aligned with the old aristocracy, and are influenced by her reputation as cold and snobbish. Terms taste the foundation of Wharton's morality. Argues naturalism and Freud led to her decline because she affirms individual responsibility. Also mentions problem that she is considered a minor James and that her heroes are intellectuals. Cites: *HofM*, *AofI*, *CC*.

Q64   Richards, Diane R. "Psychoanalyzing Wharton." "Letters." *New York Times Book Review*, December 14, 1986, p. 37.

Letter to the editor refuting the Janet Malcolm charge that Wharton was a misogynist. [See Q52]

Q65   Rubin, Larry. "Aspects of Naturalism in Four Novels by Edith Wharton." *Twentieth Century Literature* 2 (January 1957): 182-92.

Traces aspects of naturalism in *HofM*, *FofT*, *CC* and *AofI*. Finds Dreiser and Wharton alike: "The fact that Mrs. Wharton's characters are trapped in gilded drawing-rooms, whereas Dreiser's are often imprisoned in the slums, is of minor significance in an over-all appraisal. The pathetic figures in her books are molded, cornered and crushed by impersonal forces beyond their control."

Q66   Sanna, Vittoria. "I Romanzi Edith Wharton e la Narrativa Jamesiana." *Studi Americani* 10 (1964): 229-91.

[In Italian.] Lengthy study of EW in terms of Jamesian narrative.

Q67   Sasaki, Miyoko. "Between Appearance and Substance: A Study of Edith Wharton." *Studies of American Literature.* American Literature Society of Japan No.11 (1975): 30-47.

Discusses sense of horror in Wharton that stems from the abysmal depths beneath the appearance of things, speculating this attitude comes from her personal experience. Biographical data, however, from Wayne Andrews, before the Lewis biography. Also considers the function of children in Wharton. Cites: *EF*, *AofI*, "Bewitched," "Quicksand," "Mission of Jane," "Last Asset." [L2, N17]

Q68   Sasaki, Miyoko. "Edith Wharton and New England." *Tsuda Review* No. 18 (November, 1973): 41-68.

[In English.] * Not seen.

Q69   Sasaki, Miyoko. "The Lamp of Psyche." Tsuda Review No. 19 (1974): 19-47.

[In English.] * Not seen.

Q70   Saunders, Catherine E. *Writing the Margins: Edith Wharton,*
        Ellen Glasgow, and the Literary Tradition of the Ruined
        Woman. Cambridge: Harvard University Press, 1987.
            Argues because they themselves couldn't fit "into a
        narrow conception of women's role," Wharton and
        Glasgow were drawn to using "fallen," marginal women in
        their fiction. Contends Glasgow wanted to expand literary
        tradition to depict women realistically, while Wharton put
        herself in the mainstream "as she saw it" and used
        literature to attack society's ills and the social code under
        which she suffered. Compares *Summer* to *Barren Ground,*
        and *Old New York* with *They Stooped to Folly,* starting
        with a discussion of *A Backward Glance* and Wharton's
        isolation as a creative, intelligent child.

Q71   Schriber, Mary Suzanne. "Convention in the Fiction of
        Edith Wharton." *Studies in American Fiction.* 11.2 (Autumn
        1983): 189-201. Rpt. in *American Fiction 1914 to 1945.*
        Edited by Harold Bloom. New York: Chelsea House
        Publishers, 1986.
            Feminist. Insightful, well-written analysis of the
        treatment of convention in Wharton's fiction and its
        connection to the cultural idea of woman. Argues that
        Wharton demonstrates the consequences, individually and
        socially, of limiting women to marriage; she shows that
        convention tends to distort perceptions, and exposes the
        ways expectations of women are subject to manipulation
        by both sexes. Concludes that in Wharton's fiction
        convention, while shown as useful and necessary at times,
        restricts human possibilities. Notes that Wharton's fiction
        suggests that individuals must be alert to the power of
        conventions lest they become a substitute for life itself.
        HofM, CC, TS, Touchstone, AofI, "Fullness of Life," "Joy
        in the House."

Q72   Schriber, Mary Suzanne. "Edith Wharton and the French
        Critics 1906-1937." *American Literary Realism 1870-1910* 13
        (1980): 61-68. [See K12]
            Contains bibliography of French criticism 1906-1937.
        Traces Wharton's critical reception in France. Finds it

focused on four aspects of her work: "its revelations of
the American soul, its sympathy for France, its formal and
technical virtuosity, and its echoes of the French literary
tradition." Finds French criticism falls into pre- and post-
WWI evaluations: the quality shifted "from energetic
enthusiasm to warmth and loyalty." Cites: *HofM, AofI,
Reef, M'sR, WofF, Fighting France, French Ways and Their
Meaning, SatF, MdeT, Motor-Flight through France, EF,
Touchstone, Human Nature, Summer, VofD, ONY, ABG.*

Q73   Sears, Donald A. "Journalism Makes the Style." *Journalism
       Quarterly* 47 (Autumn 1970): 504-09.
            Argues writers with a journalistic background--here,
       Stephen Crane, Dreiser, Hemingway, John Hersey--have a
       tendency toward "the elimination of semantic noise,
       characterized by compressed syntax, clear and active word
       choice, and concrete, objective detail." James, Wharton,
       Thomas Wolfe and Truman Capote are the control group.
       Includes tables of analysis.

Q74   Spacks, Patricia Mayer. *The Female Imagination.* New
       York: Knopf, 1975.
            Feminist discussion of the female imagination in
       Wharton as both providing hope for individual salvation
       and producing irreconcilable conflicts with society. Reads
       Buccaneers as comment on James's *Portrait of a Lady* from
       female viewpoint. Discusses: *M'sR, AofI, HofM.*

Q75   Spacks, Patricia Mayer. *Gossip.* New York: Knopf, 1985,
       173-181.
            Discussion of *The House of Mirth* with references to
       The Age of Innocence and *The Custom of the Country.*
       Argues "Wharton's New York novels treat [symbolically
       female] gossip as a social force and link it with the
       [symbolically male] operations of finance." Finds that in
       The House of Mirth, which is unusually explicit in
       examining "the operations of a money-dominated
       society ... endless restless talk about human behavior
       establishes and limits possibility."

Q76   Stein, Allen F. *After the Vows Were Spoken: Marriage in American Literary Realism.* Columbus: Ohio State University Press, 1984.

       Three chapters on Wharton cover her three visions of marriage: "The Marriage of Entrapment," "Marriage in an Imperfect Society" and "Moral Growth and Marriage." Extensive study of marriage in Wharton covers the major novels and short stories. Concludes that, although marriage is often bleak and fails to live up to romantic illusions in Wharton's work, she definitely advocates marital commitment as a necessary part of social stability and a vehicle, under favorable circumstances, for moral growth. Cites: *M'sR, EF, HofM, FofT, CC, TS, HRB, Summer, GA, ONY, Old Maid,* "Fullness of Life," "Lamp of Psyche," "Souls Belated," "Line of Least Resistance," "Quicksand," "Joy in the House," "Reckoning," "Pretext," "Atrophy," "Mission of Jane," "Other Two," "Letters," "Last Asset."

Q77   Stouck, David. "Women Writers in the Mainstream: A Review Essay." *Texas Studies in Literature and Language* 20 (1978): 660-70.

       Discusses revival of interest in three women writers: Cather, Stein and Wharton. Wharton section cites an end to the view she is a minor James and the modern recognition: "She wrote about the problems of women raised in a society which regarded women as beautiful objects exclusively, and she wrote about individuals oppressed by the conventions of that society represented and endorsed by James." Praises Lewis biography [N17] and Wolff's *A Feast of Words* [N28] for giving a new vision both of Wharton's passionate sexuality and her psychological development.

Q78   Swan, Michael. "The Early Edith Wharton." *Times Literary Supplement* (London), 20 March 1953, 177-78. Rpt. *A Small Part of Time.* London: Jonathan Cape, 1957.

       Occasioned by the reissue of *HofM* and *AofI.* Ranges widely over Wharton's career, speculating that her early work stems from the conflicts of her marriage and love for Walter Berry. Cites: *VofD*, "Muse's Tragedy," *CC*, *EF*.

Q79   Tintner, Adeline R. "Mothers, Daughters and Incest in the Late Novels of Edith Wharton." In *The Lost Tradition: Mothers and Daughters in Literature.* Edited by Cathy N. Davidson and E.M. Broner. New York: Ungar, 1980.

Discusses strained relationships between the mothers and daughters in the later novels, which emerges as a struggle for the father. Terms these mother-daughter roles the most dramatic as well as touching representation of the twentieth-century change in the family. Considers *SatF*, *Old Maid*, *M'sR*, *TS*, "Beatrice Palmato." Notes parallels with Grace Aguilar's work and James's *The Chaperon*.

Q80   Tintner, Adeline R. "Mothers vs. Daughters in the Fiction of Edith Wharton and Henry James." *Bookman's Weekly*, June 6, 1983, 4324.

Tintner offers two reasons that, in the stories of Wharton's which deal seriously with the mother-daughter relationship, the mother is bad and affects her daughter malevolently: 1) Wharton hated her own mother and had incestuous feelings for her father; 2) she was influenced by James, in whose fiction bad mothers greatly predominate and the daughters are either also bad or victims. Cites: *Old Maid*, *M'sR*, *TS*, "Mrs. Manstey's View," "Friends," "April Showers," "Misson of Jane," "Line of Least Resistance," "Roman Fever," "Autres Temps...," "Les Metteurs en Scène," "Beatrice Palmato." [Q79]

Q81   Tuttleton, James W. "Edith Wharton: The Archeological Motive." *The Yale Review* 61 (1972): 562-74.

Discusses the effect of scientific theories of evolutionary development on Wharton's thought, particularly her respect for tradition and continuity and her impulse, in her later years, to reconstruct the social world of her youth and the traditions of Old New York. Traces in her fiction the theme of rapid social change which, without a respect for continuity, can do great damage. Cites: *HofM*, *HRB*, *GA*, *AofI*, *CC*, *Buc*, *French*

Ways and Their Meaning, ABG, VofD, "The Great American Novel," "A Little Girl's New York."

Q82   Tuttleton, James W. "Edith Wharton: Form and the Epistemology of Artistic Creation." *Criticism* 10 (Fall 1968): 334-351.

Traces similarities in Vance Weston's development as an artist and Wharton's own, particularly in respect to the principle of continuity and the search for an appropriate form. Concludes, "Mrs. Wharton's defensive feelings about the form of fiction produced in her critical attitudes far too rigid for general application." Feels that, expressed through Vance's experience, Mrs. Wharton's "developing conception of the artistic process" came from Coleridge, Goethe, Whitman, and an essentially "romantic epistemology." *HRB, GA, WofF, ABG.*

Q83   Tuttleton, James W. "The Feminist Takeover of Edith Wharton." *The New Criterion* (March 1989): 1-9.

Takes issue with Marion Mainwaring's charges of Lewis's biographical inaccuracies [N17], calling her essay "embittered" and "mean-spirited and condescending" and "utterly muddled." Also argues that Mary Pitlick's contention that EW had no nervous breakdown between 1894 and 1896 disregards Lewis's abundant documentary evidence and his "admittedly speculative and cautious account of her illness." Contends that the claim that Edith Wharton was neglected before the feminist movement in the early 1970's ignores "the massive bibliography of Wharton studies before the 1970s." Notes that critics on the Left disparaged her, but sees the problem now in that "there appears to be a new battle developing for control of Wharton criticism--for power to reshape the dominant view of the woman and her work, of which the attack on R.W.B. Lewis's scholarship seems ... the first really direct ... salvo." Maintains EW's fiction does not support a feminist ideology of women's victimization in a patriarchal culture. Discusses: *French Ways and Their Meaning, The Valley of Decision, The Age of Innocence.* [See L75, L91. For Lewis's rebuttal see L71.1. For

Mainwaring's answer to Tuttleton see L75.1; for Zilversmit's, see L129.]

Q84   Tuttleton, James W. "Leisure, Wealth and Luxury: Edith Wharton's Old New York." *Midwest Quarterly* 7 (Summer 1966): 337-52.

Analysis of the role of wealth in Wharton's novel of manners, particularly *HofM*, *CC*, *GofM*. Notes that, unlike other novelists of manners, she could write as an insider of Old New York aristocracy, and traces her criticism of the invading nouveau riche, 1870-1925, which effected social transition in New York. Cites: *AofI*, *ABG*, *HRB*.

Q85   Wegelin, Christof. "Edith Wharton and the Twilight of the International Novel." *Southern Review* 5 (Spring 1969): 398-418.

Contends Wharton's international novels offer a short course in the development of the genre, beginning in the pre-war years of the international "boom." Traces the international novel throughout Wharton's career. Points out two main differences between Wharton and James: She focused on social circumstances rather than the inner life and was affected by WWI and the radical change in relations between America and Europe. Cites: "Roman Fever," *ABG*, *MdeT*, *Reef*, *CC*, *GofM*, *Marne*, *SatF*, *French Ways and Their Meaning*, *TS*, *Children*, *GA*, *AofI*, *Buc*.

Q86   Wegelin, Christof. "The Rise of the International Novel." *Publications of the Modern Language Association* 77 (June 1962): 305-10.

Answers Cargill's article calling *The American* by James the first international novel. (*PMLA* 73, September 1958: 418-425.) Argues "though the genre came into its own under James and Edith Wharton, they did not create it *ex nihilo*. It had a history, and its evolution was tied closely to the evolution of the social relations between the New World and the Old." Cites: *CC*. [See Q85]

Q87   Widmer, Eleanor. "Edith Wharton: The Nostalgia for Innocence." In *The Twenties: Fiction, Poetry and Drama*.

Edited by Warren French. Festschrift. Deland, Florida: Everett/Edwards, 1975. 27-38.

Maintains Wharton was unable to deal with the modern world after WWI, and that though she apparently repudiated Old New York and its equation of "conformity to its rules with personal fulfillment" she nevertheless could not break with it. Cites: *AofI, HofM, CC.*

Q88 Witham, W. Tosker. "Edith Wharton." *Panorama of American Literature.* New York: Daye, 1947.

High school text with comment that "her simpler style and more apparent irony make her more popular than James could hope to be."

Q89 Wolff, Cynthia Griffin. "Edith Wharton and the 'Visionary Imagination'." *Frontiers: Journal of Women Studies* 2.2 (1977): 24-30.

Analysis of Wharton's struggles with her own intense visionary imagination. Covers her childhood "making up" of stories, through her retreat 'from and fear of the powerful emotions released in her visions and her condemnation of a society built up on visions and illusions and demands that women be beautiful objects to her final coming to terms with her creative power as she became a professional novelist and found the rewards her career brought in terms of making her personal reality fulfilling. Cites: *HofM, EF, CC, AofI.* [See N28]

Q90 Worby, Diana Zacharia. "The Ambiguity of Edith Wharton's 'Lurking Feminism.'" *Mid-Hudson Language Studies* 5 (1982): 81-90.

Cites Wharton's "ambiguous attitude toward women," involving unsympathetic treatment of wronged women (sometimes arising from subtle authorial identification with male observers), yet her denunciation of the double sexual standard, and her very consideration of the "woman problem." Makes a few questionable biographical generalizations, such as the lack of any sustained friendship with a woman. Cites: *Reef, HofM, CC.*

Chapter 9

Novels

Chapter lists reviews, books, introductions, dissertations and articles principally concerned with one novel. Also see critical analyses of separate novels in book-length works in Chapter 5. Novels are cited chronologically and criticism is organized into four sections, where applicable: (1) Reviews; (2) Book-length studies; (3) Introductions, Forewords, Afterwords; (4) Articles, books and dissertations. Anonymous reviews are alphabetized by name of journal or newspaper.

The Touchstone--Reviews

[English edition of *The Touchstone* was titled *A Gift From the Grave*.]

R1.1   Anonymous. Review of A Gift From the Grave.
         Athenaeum (London) No. 3799 (18 August 1900): 210.
                 Contends this "clever" and "delicately told tale," like those of many other American writers, is "almost too polished," lacking the grace of "perfect simplicity and plain language."

R1.2   Anonymous. "Recent American Fiction." *Atlantic Monthly* 86 (September 1900): 418-19.
            Praises Wharton's earlier work and her psychological analysis. Contends the story here suggested by publication of the Browning love letters. Admires her as a psychologist. Warns that, although she has learned much from Henry James, she now "would do well to rise from her deferential attitude" because "[b]etter things than he can inspire are ... within the scope of her still widening possibilities."

R1.3   Anonymous. Review of *A Gift From the Grave*. *Bookman* (London) 18 (September 1900): 189.
            Paragraph praises Wharton for doing "the work to which she is called" in writing fiction, claiming this is better than most of what comes from America with its sound, vigorous characterization and lack of sentimentality and only an occasional hint of "Meredithese." Mentions Murray's title change.

R1.4   Payne, William Morton. "Recent Fiction." *Dial* 29 (1 September 1900): 126.
            Calls this not a true novel, yet nevertheless a valuable psychological study. Argues that although the subject repels and the hero is unsympathetic, the distinctive style is fascinating.

R1.5   Peck, Harry Thurston. "*The Touchstone*." *Bookman* 11 (June 1900): 319-23.
            Praises *The Greater Inclination*, her debut, for artistic feeling and profound insight, and finds *The Touchstone*, "not quite a novel" but fascinating with its intelligence, powerful analysis, and style. Cites her excellent epigrams, but finds Alexa Glennard unconvincing and inconsistent, and Glennard too much "the product of a feminine imagination."

R1.6   Sherman, Ellen Burns. "Two Novels of the Psycho-Realistic School." *Book Buyer* 20 (May 1900): 320-22.

Praises the "delicate psychic overtones of her feeling and fancy" and the psychological insight that eschews stock phrasing. Finds a Greek catharsis in her pathos.

The Touchstone--Articles

R1.7   Raphael, Lev. "Haunted by Shame: Edith Wharton's *The Touchstone.*" *The Journal of Evolutionary Psychology* 9.3-4 (August 1988): 287-296.

Major new reading of *The Touchstone* in light of Silvan Tomkins's Affect Theory, particularly in relation to the affect of shame as a touchstone for Wharton's work and in terms of the subtle interweaving of Glennard's "public" humiliation and Aubyn's own private shame at being unloved made triumphantly public after her death.

The Valley of Decision--Reviews

R2.1   Anonymous. Review of *The Valley of Decision.* *Athenaeum* (London) No. 3894 (14 June 1902): 748-49.

Argues that although congested, heavy and labored in manner, the novel shows "considerable thought and careful observation."

R2.2   Anonymous. "The Columbian Reading Union." *Catholic World* 75 (June 1902): 422-23.

Includes a reprint of the April 20, 1902, *Chicago Chronicles* attack on the book as a "malign influence ... upon the aspirations of American women for university privileges." Argues that here higher education is alienated from religious and moral control. In fact, terms novel "the subtlest assault ever invented in English literature against the Catholic Church." Notes Italy was the first to open university doors to women, but in the case of Fulvia, education did not lead to moral or spiritual growth because she led an immoral life.

R2.3   Anonymous. Review of *The Valley of Decision*. *Outlook* 71 (24 May 1902): 209.
          Calls this a careful study of a period and a temperament of deep and unusual interest, yet finds it lacks drama and does not deal with the "master passions."

R2.4   Boynton, H.W. "Books New and Old." *Atlantic Monthly* 89 (May 1902): 710-11.
          Terms this "the first novel of a writer of matured power." Contends, however, that Wharton is intellectually, rather than passionately, "sympathetic with life," interested more in art than audience, and the crisis of Odo Valsecca's life occurs on an intellectual, moral plane. Maintains the novel does retain a direct human interest as we follow and grow attached to the young Duke.

R2.5   Cooper, Frederic Taber. "Mrs. Wharton's *The Valley of Decision*." *Bookman* 15 (April 1902): 173-75.
          Maintains Wharton has taken on a difficult task in so sweeping a subject, creating a moving panorama of latter eighteenth-century Italy, in a book less a novel than a historical study. Lists faults as the lack of the concrete, tedious passages of aesthetics and philosophy, unmoving characterization and uninteresting plotting. Cites strengths as the human interest of brief, crucial moments and her "intuition in analyzing complex emotion."

R2.6   Gorren, Alice. "Mrs. Wharton's Philosophical Romance." *Critic* 40 (June 1902): 541-43.
          Praises Wharton's mastery of her material and finds the book to be a nearly perfect historical study, yet, as fiction, argues it needs to be "a little more wrong." Maintains it is not a novel in the modern sense because the novel is now conceived in terms of

a long short story emphasizing not reflection but condensation. Discusses the historical background of the novel and terms the eighteenth century in Italy "not a great" one.

R2.7   Hall, Gertrude. "One of the Unconquerable Army." *Book Buyer* 24 (April 1902): 196-98.
        Praises the book's "pageant of life" and Wharton's ease handling eighteenth-century Italy, but feels that the events, however shocking in themselves, are remote in this artistic medium, and it is the inner life of Odo Valsecca that has the most reality.

R2.8   Mabie, Hamilton W. "Mr. Mabie's Literary Talks." *Ladies' Home Journal* 19 (May 1902): 17.
        Short, positive review notes Wharton's "passion for giving her work the touch of perfection." Cites novel as her longest, strongest work to date.

R2.9   Mather, Frank Jewett, Jr. "Literature." *Forum* 34 (July 1902): 78-79.
        Praises the book's scholarship and the beauty of individual scenes, but finds the characters mere symbols, factors in her historical demonstration, all speaking in the distinguished literary tone of *Crucial Instances*.

The Valley of Decision--Criticism

R2.10   Brooks, Van Wyck. *Howells: His Life and World.* New York: Dutton, 1959.
        Brooks recounts that in a letter to Charles Eliot Norton, Howells mentioned copying Norton's praise of *VofD* in a note to Wharton and her pleasure with it. However, he admits he did not read the book because he was afraid to find Stendahl as he found Henry James in her stories. Howells says, "She is a great creature, and I wish she used her own voice solely."

R2.11   Fabris, Grube Alberta. "Edith Wharton's Italian
          Background." *Rivista di Studi Anglo-Americani* 3.4-5
          (1984-1985): 133-144.
               Treats the Italian influences on Edith Wharton's
          work, arguing that *The Valley of Decision*, particularly
          for the treatment of Odo's conflicts and the picture of
          eighteenth-century Italy, and *Italian Villas and Their
          Gardens* and *Italian Backgrounds* are unjustly neglected.
          Notes also Italian influences and settings in: *The
          Decoration of Houses, False Dawn, The Glimpses of the
          Moon, The Children,* "Roman Fever."

R2.12   Lee, Vernon. *Studies of the Eighteenth Century in Italy.*
          London: T. Fisher, 1907. Second Edition.
               Short comment in her Preface to the second
          edition that the Italian eighteenth century was far more
          prosperous, orderly and respectable than Wharton's
          "learned and finely romantic" *The Valley of Decision*
          suggests.

R2.13   Murphy, John J. "Edith Wharton's Italian Triptych: *The
          Valley of Decision.*" *Xavier University Studies* IV (1965):
          85-94.
               Demonstrates that the background is symbolically
          dramatized in the foreground, and "the novel suggests
          a painting." Argues that the women of the foreground:
          1) the Duchess Maria Clemenina who represents the
          established order, the nobility and the Church;   2)
          Fulvia Vivaldi, the symbol of Liberty and new forces;
          3) the woman of the deprived masses--a composite of
          Mirandalina of Chioggia, a popular actress, and
          Momola, a diseased foundling, make up a symbolic
          three-paneled painting (triptych) of the background.

R2.14   Norton, Charles Eliot. *Letters of Charles Eliot Norton
          With Biographical Comment by His Daughter Sara Norton
          and M. A. De Wolfe Howe.* Vol. II. Boston: Houghton-
          Mifflin, 1913.
               Contains letter to S. G. Ward March, 1902, on
          The Valley of Decision, which praises the novel as a

"wonderfully complete and vivid picture of the Italy of the period" although the characters "are not convincingly alive." Norton contends the book "places Mrs. Wharton among the few foremost of the writers in English to-day." Also contains a sonnet "High Pasture" commemorating Norton's eightieth birthday, Nov. 16, 1907.

Sanctuary--Reviews

R3.1   Anonymous. Review of *Sanctuary*. *Athenaeum* (London), No. 3971 (5 December 1903), p. 750.
         Finds the story familiar, but "invested with unwonted interest and grace" by Wharton's original treatment. Argues that although the setting is New York, "there is a remarkable absence of those peculiarities of thought and speech which prejudice some English readers against a book."

R3.2   Anonymous. "Edith Wharton's New Novel." *Independent*, 55 (10 December 1903), 2933-35.
         Criticizes Wharton's Kate Orme as unrealistic, not having the kind of "tender, stupid womanly sanity" of "normal women [whose] very obtuseness is a healing power." Finds the book typical of women writers with "a beautiful, tender sentimentality peculiar to women ... writers, mothers or missionaries."

R3.3   Anonymous. "*Sanctuary*--The Strength and Weakness of Edith Wharton's Latest Book." *Munsey's Magazine*, 31 (May 1904), 282.
         Judges the book a study in psychology, not a novel. Maintains she has deft characterization, but the plot is weak, with Kate Orme's reason for marrying almost absurd. Calls Wharton's lessening degree of humor regrettable.

R3.4   Anonymous. Review of *Sanctuary*. *Nation* 77 (24 December 1903), 508.

Notes the "quasi-scientific treatment of ... a
fantastic notion" in the first part, but finds the second
part realistic with much dramatic force. Maintains
Wharton is stronger in "dramatic narrative and
emotional scenes than in psychological analysis and
scientific adventure, where the temptation to say
something important leads her perilously near to
nonsense."

R3.5   Cooper, Frederic Taber. "Local Colour and Some
            Recent Novels." *Bookman* 18 (December 1903), 410-11.
                Concludes that the heroine is not flesh-and-blood
            but a "highly sensitised [sic] conscience." Summarizes
            the plot, refrains from interpreting the symbolism
            because "there are so many different things ... she may
            have meant."

R3.6   Gorren, Aline. "The Influence of Personality." *Critic* 44
            (March 1904), 269-70.
                Criticizes the work, particularly the
            characterization, as improbable. Finds the moral
            struggle is of little interest and the ending is unequal in
            subtlety, truth or purity to the beginning.

R3.7   Payne, William Morton. "Recent Fiction." *Dial* 36 (16
            February 1904), 118-19.
                Contrasts *Sanctuary* with Ellen Glasgow's *The
            Deliverance*, terming Wharton's art "subtler and more
            delicate." Evaluates *Sanctuary* as a deeply moving work
            of art, a "masterpiece of conscientious workmanship."

                            Sanctuary--Articles

R3.8   Raphael, Lev. "Kate Orme's Struggles with Shame in
            Edith Wharton's *Sanctuary*." *Massachusetts Studies in
            English* 10.4 (Fall 1986): 229-236.
                Striking reevaluation. Uses Silvan Tomkins's
            Affect Theory, which sees innate affects as the primary
            motivators of behavior, to examine the crucial role of

shame in Kate's relationship with her father, husband, and son. Insightful new reading of Kate's puzzling decision to marry Denis.

The House of Mirth--Reviews

R4.1   Anonymous. Review of *The House of Mirth*. *Academy*, 69 (4 November 1905): 1155.
       Reviewer names *The House of Mirth* the best thing Wharton has done. Critic finds no attempt at plot; "the author's sympathetic delineation of her heroine's character, her acute analysis of a woman's mind" stands out as the book's major achievement.

R4.2   Anonymous. Review of *The House of Mirth*. *Athenaeum* (London), No. 4074 (25 November 1905), p. 718.
       Terms *The House of Mirth* "a pitiful story, told with restraint and insight and not a little subtlety." Praises characterization of Lily Bart, the depiction of her external circumstances and the delineation of "the mixed condition of her emotions and morals."

R4.3   Anonymous. "Recent Fiction and the Critics." Current Literature (1905): 689.
       Summarizes reviews from *The New York Evening Post*, *The New York Times*, *Collier's Weekly*, *The Argonaut*, and the Boston *Herald*, concluding the general verdict is that the novel is admirably crafted, penetrating and pitiless, with Lily Bart's characterization singled out for particular praise. Cites several epigrams.

R4.4   Anonymous. "Mrs. Wharton's Latest Novel." *Independent* 59 (20 July 1905): 150-51.
       Deplores the fatalism of modern fiction and its tendency to blame environment. Dismisses Wharton's "fine manner" as a fashion of the times, contending that what she says will not last because "it is simply the fashionable drawing of ephemeral types and ... sentiments."

R4.5   Anonymous. "A Review of the Important Books of the
            Year." *Independent* 59 (16 November 1905): 1151.
                  Emphasizes the warning in Wharton's portrayal
            of Lily Bart, objecting that readers respond more
            readily to hope than threats of damnation.

R4.6   Anonymous. "The Abode of the Fool's Heart." *Literary
            Digest* 31 (9 December 1905): 886.
                  Refers to praise of the novel in various
            periodicals. Praises psychological analysis of Lily Bart
            and finds her characterization surpasses that of George
            Eliot's Gwendolyn Harleth. Contends this is one of the
            strongest works of fiction to appear in this country for
            some time.

R4.7   Anonymous. "*The House of Mirth*, and Other Novels."
            Nation 81 (30 November 1905): 447-48.
                  Calls Lily Bart unsympathetic with "not a particle
            of genuine, fundamental good human feeling." Finds the
            view of society prejudiced, but not untruthful.
            However, argues that this material is "utterly unsuitable
            for conversion into literature" which demands "ideas,
            intellectual interests, sentiment, passion, humor, wit,
            tact, and grace."

R4.8   Anonymous. "A Notable Novel." *Outlook* 81 (21
            October 1905): 404-06.
                  Very positive review, praises Wharton's
            workmanship and feels that her apprenticeship is now
            over and *The House of Mirth* marks the transition "from
            the region of cultivated tastes and skill to that of free,
            direct, individual creation."

R4.9   Anonymous. "To Lily Bart." *Reader* 8 (July 1906): 181-
            84.
                  Drawing of Lily Bart. One of several "Letters to
            Heroines." Ironic tone. Satiric letter to Miss Bart
            answers detractors who say she was unkind to Gerty, a
            bad example for young people and not "good art"

because her life had neither "honest love" nor "common honor" and good art must have both.

R4.10 Anonymous. Review of *The House of Mirth*. *Saturday Review* (London), 101 (17 February 1906): 209-10.

Contends Lily Bart remains sympathetic and lovable although she is a masterly study of the modern American woman with her "coldly corrupt nature and unhealthy charm." Praises novel as a criticism of modern civilization which appeals to our "nobler illusions."

R4.11 Anonymous. Review of *The House of Mirth*. *Spectator* 95 (28 October 1905): 657.

Finds the novel an "illuminating picture of the quest for pleasure as carried on by rich and 'smart'" New Yorkers. States the story is logically constructed, and Lily Bart in the end "excites the liveliest compassion."

R4.12 Anonymous. "*The House of Mirth*." *Times Literary Supplement*, 1 December 1905, p. 421.

Terms this an exceptional book, Wharton's best, praising Wharton's technique, spirit of comedy, and realism, yet finds it not the very greatest fiction because Wharton lacks "the creative gift at its fullest" which would conceive and embody "something entirely new."

R4.13 Bentzon, Thérèse. "Le Monde où l'on s'amuse aux Etats-Unis." *Revue de Deux Mondes*, 1 November 1906, 200.

In French. Mentions Wharton's short stories and compares them to deMaupassant because of her lack of emotion. Synopsis of *The House of Mirth* ends with conclusion French have drawn the moral that the emancipation of young women through work is necessary because the work itself protects them from inspiring men's contempt. Argues *Madame de Treymes* is unrealistic but interesting in that it reveals what Americans think about the French, and wonders if

society in *The House of Mirth* is also unrealistic.
However, maintains the novels are "remarkably well
told." Also cites: *VofD*, *Greater Inclination*, *Crucial
Instances*, *Sanctuary*, *Touchstone*, *Descent of Man*.
[Also see R4.36]

R4.14   Boutell, Alice May. "A Burst of Enthusiasm." *Critic* 48
            (January 1906): 87-88.
                  In answer to Dunbar [See R4.16], Boutell argues
            that the novel's chief charm lies in "the sense that one
            is living life."   The characters, to her, are not
            unpleasant, and she felt "real intimacy" with Lily Bart.

R4.15   Davray, Henry. "Lettres Anglaises." *Mercure de France*
            75 (1908): 182.
                  In French. Praises Charles du Bos's translation,
            but calls the novel much too long, full of shallow
            intrigues, ridiculous pretensions and artificial, odious
            people in a complete picture of American high life.

R4.16   Dunbar, Olivia Howard. "A Group of Novels." *Critic*
            47 (December 1905): 509-10.
                  Praises the structure but feels novel does not
            attain the quality of Wharton's best short stories chiefly
            because it lacks contrast.   The characters are all too
            unpleasant and thus the novel is not a comprehensive
            interpretation of life, but a "fastidiously conducted
            literary raid."

R4.17   Ford, Mary K. "Two Studies in Luxury." *Critic* 48
            (March 1906): 249-50.
                  The House of Mirth is compared to Howard
            Sturgis's *Belchamber*. Critic feels that both books are
            realistic and extremely well-written, matchless as studies
            of contemporary manners.   Wharton is wittier, but
            Sturgis's novel is more skillfully constructed with the
            advantage of the London locale and therefore more
            interesting.

R4.18   Hale, E.E., Jr. "Mrs. Wharton's *The House of Mirth*."
         Bookman 22 (December 1905): 364-66.
             Praises Wharton's ability to make Lily Bart, who
         on the surface is all beauty and charm, sympathetic, and
         finds real humanity, not merely logic and analysis, in
         the book. Argues that those who criticize the novel as
         unrelievedly bleak must remember that from Lily Bart's
         point of view it would be, and that Wharton cannot
         present the whole world.

R4.19   Lionnet, Jean. "Les Livres." *Revue Hebdomadaire* 17 (10
         October 1908): 253-256.
             In French. Very favorable review calls *The House
         of Mirth* close to a masterpiece, and certainly the most
         virile book by a woman in recent years. Cites the
         dispassionate style, for a book about such an unhappy,
         unfortunate heroine. Praises Bourget's preface.

R4.20   MacArthur, James. "Books and Bookmen." *Harper's
         Weekly*, 49 (2 December 1905): 1750.
             Compares *The House of Mirth* and Tarkington's
         The Conquest of Canaan. Praises Wharton's book as
         great literary art and commends her as prophet who
         should not be criticized as depressing but appreciated
         for writing such a timely commentary on society. Finds
         the "ethical significance is inseparable from the human
         interest."

R4.21   Maury, Lucien. "Les Lettres: Mme. Edith Wharton."
         Revue Politique et Littéraire (Revue Bleue). 46 (3
         October 1908): 444-447.
             In French. Terms this both a psychological and
         social novel, subtle and perilous. Comments that the
         society depicted is no different from any worldly society,
         American men and women resembling others--
         aristocrats of the dollar. Notes the lack of famous
         Yankee energy in that the men are apoplectic, dull-
         witted, dyspeptic, with no original figures, no leaders.
         Calls this the "grayest collection of elegant gentlemen"
         of "distinguished banality." Praises style and unity.

R4.22   Meynell, Alice. "*The House of Mirth*." *Bookman*
             (London) 29 (December 1905): 130-31.
                      Finds some of Gwendolyn Harleth and Hedda
             Gabler in Lily Bart, but basically complains of the
             author's moral detachment, feeling it unfortunate that
             Wharton keeps her own counsel. Maintains that "the
             better part" which Selden offers is inconclusive. Prefers
             Touchstone in which morality was clearer.

R4.23   Moss, Mary. "Notes on New Novels." *Atlantic Monthly*
             97 (January 1906): 52-53.
                      Argues that despite the brilliant picture of
             society and Lily Bart's realism, the novel is somewhat
             shallow. Lily inspires interest and curiosity, yet the
             reader does not deeply care.

R4.24   Payne, William Morton. "Recent Fiction." *Dial* 40 (1
             January 1906): 15-16.
                      Although critic asserts Wharton's "coupling of
             psychological insight with the gift of expression is
             probably not surpassed by any other woman novelist of
             our time," he finds the novel lacks interest because of
             the shallow society depicted. Asks if it is worthwhile to
             describe Lily Bart's career at such length when she "had
             never any real relation to life."

                      The House of Mirth--Introductions

R4.25   Bourget, Paul. "Introduction." *The House of Mirth. [Chez
             les heureux du monde]* Translated by Charles Du Bos, i-
             xii. Paris: Plon, 1908.
                               * Not seen.

R4.26   Brookner, Anita. "Introduction." *The House of Mirth*.
             New York: Collier Books, 1987.
                      Terms *The House of Mirth* Wharton's "most
             substantial and sophisticated" and "most Jamesian"
             novel. Argues Wharton has a remarkable understanding

of Lily Bart, stemming from a "gigantic stretch of the creative imagination and a realistic grasp of what it means to fail in the social game."

R4.27   Davenport, Marcia. "Foreword." *The House of Mirth*. New York: Scribner's, 1951.

Finds *The House of Mirth* a timeless, penetrating analysis of human values. Calls Lily Bart "disturbingly real"--and "the creation of a wise and mature mind ... treated with a compassion which belies the observation that her creator was a difficult woman, arrogant and cold." Argues that a technical virtuosity like Wharton's "can realize itself only in the hands of a writer who has something to say and the creative gifts through which to say it."

R4.28   French, Marilyn. "Introduction." *The House of Mirth*. New York: Berkley, 1981.

Three-part introduction covers first, biographical material, second, an overview of EW's fiction, citing *Sanctuary*, *The Reef*, *EF*, *AofI*, *Summer*, *The Mother's Recompense*, *CC*, *The Children*. Overview is intelligent, feminist. Argues EW never exalted the old; women in her fiction are often shallow and chameleon-like because they see themselves only in other's eyes; maintains she is as revolutionary as Joyce and Lawrence for her analyses of female attitudes toward sex. Argues EW's female characters deal with the painful constriction of the inability to speak the truth, and that EW emphasizes the bleakness of lives so constricted. Contends her strongest characters are morally courageous women who take risks. Defines her genius as sociological and psychological. Reading of *The House of Mirth* emphasizes Lily's moral growth within an increasingly constrictive society; "[Lily's] fineness has been judged expendable in [her] culture." Contends "Hers [Lily's] has been a process of finding and becoming her 'real self,' knowing and acknowledging her feelings, her emotional and moral texture."

Maintains that Lily's finely realized and morally exquisite self dwarfs all around her.

R4.29   Howe, Irving. "Introduction." *The House of Mirth*. New York: Holt, Rinehart and Winston, 1962. Rpt. N14. Also reprinted in *Introducing the Great American Novel*. Edited by Anne Skillon. New York: Stonesong Press, 1988.

Analyzes structure, the social groups through which Lily descends, point of view, authorial voice and commentary. Contends Lily Bart's ordeal is still significant because "the problem of mediating between the expectations of a commercial society and the ideals of humane civilization is not exactly unknown to us." Criticizes the "grinding, unrelenting, impatient tone."

R4.30   Lewis, R.W.B. "Introduction." *The House of Mirth*. Boston: Houghton-Mifflin, 1963. Rpt. *Trials of the Word*. New Haven: Yale University Press, 1965. Also Gotham Library Edition, New York University Press, 1977.

Discusses the modes of Wharton-James-Fitzgerald novel of manners and the picaresque novel since WWII. Finds Jamesian influence primarily in verbal borrowings. Analyzes the structure--Book I as Jamesian and Book II as episodic, akin to the post-WW II novel with its "episodic ramblings of the morally ambiguous personality through an unstable and discordant world." Does not find Lily Bart tragic, but rather victim of her fatal weakness--the love of luxury.

R4.31   Lewis, R.W.B. "Introduction." *The House of Mirth*. New York: Bantam, 1984.

Lewis's updated introduction focuses on the theatricality of the deteriorating and immoral society Wharton depicts. Gives important background of the novel in analysis of unpublished work that led up to it. Argues that "Lily always knows the real from the histrionic, and she always hangs on to at least a portion of her real self." Notes the reassessments of the novel and that "In some inexplicable way it has become a masterpiece." [See R4.30]

R4.32　Mizener, Arthur. "Introduction." *The House of Mirth*. The Limited Editions Club, 1975.

　　　　Dated biographical data. Argues Lily's innocence makes her story a particularly American tragedy of manners, illustrating the impoverishing conflict between social materialism and American idealism.

R4.33　Wolff, Cynthia Griffin. "Introduction." *The House of Mirth*. New York: Viking, 1985.

　　　　Notes the uncertain focus: Is the subject social corruption or Lily Bart's personal tragedy? Gives a biographical overview of Wharton and discusses the problem of woman in the novel--woman as a maker or object of beauty. Sees Lily's death as farewell to the conviction that woman must be passive to be feminine. See her *A Feast of Words* [N28] for development of these ideas.

R4.34　Wyndham, Francis. "Introduction." *The House of Mirth*. London: Lehman, 1953.

　　　　* Not seen.

R4.35　Zabel, Morton. "Introduction." *The House of Mirth*. New York: Bantam, 1962.

　　　　* Not seen.

The House of Mirth--Criticism

R4.36　Anonymous. "A French View of Our Smart Set." *Putnam's Monthly* 1 (January 1907): 476-77.

　　　　Discusses Mme Blanc's (Th. Bentzon's) comments on *The House of Mirth* in *Revue des Deux Mondes* (R4.13). Critic comments, "We cannot wonder if Europe occasionally gives us a few digs, nor, with *The*

House of Mirth before us, can we indignantly repel her accusations." [See R4.13]

R4.37   Anonymous. "Idle Notes by an Idle Reader." *Critic* 48 (May 1906): 463-64.

Objects to the novel's "logical conclusion" in that "Lily's real standards of behavior entitle her to a safe conduct from Vanity Fair to some less brutalizing environment, and any fair-minded creator would have provided her with one."

R4.38   Barnett, Louise K. "American Novelists and The Portrait of Beatrice Cenci." *The New England Quarterly*, 53 (1980): 168-83.

Cites Hawthorne's *The Marble Faun* and Melville's *Pierre* as romantic uses of the portrait and legend and Wharton's quite different use of it as part of the decor in Aunt Peniston's and Kate Clephane's husband's homes--where first it is a symbol of Lily's imprisonment not only literally but within, in her "romantic vision of life and self" and then is a "mundane souvenir" in *The Mother's Recompense* symbolizing Kate's husband's lack of knowledge of its meaning and her own self-deception.

R4.39   Bauer, Dale Marie. *Feminist Dialogics: A Theory of Failed Community.* Albany: State University of New York Press, 1988.

Attempts to combine a feminist perspective with "modern/postmodern criticism," filtered through Bakhtin's work on dialogue and carnival, to demonstrate how women's voices are stifled in the community of dialogues. Chapters on *The Blithedale Romance, The Golden Bowl, The House of Mirth* and *The Awakening*. The structure of these texts is seen as an opposition between the defining male "surveillant gaze" and the female's "disruptive" voice. While Shakespeare's fool questions authority through the freedom of wisdom and wit, Bakhtin's "fools" do so through incomprehension. Thus, Lily Bart misinterprets her world as a sentimental fiction when it is really a battle for domination of her voice and body. Includes brief discussion of "Roman Fever." From a dissertation. University of California (Irvine), 1985. For abstract see DAI, 46, 3718A.

R4.40   Beaty, Robin. "Lilies That Fester: Sentimentality in *The House of Mirth*." *College Literature* 14.3 Edith Wharton Issue (1987): 263-75.

Discussion of the problems of the sentimental incidents and "noncommittal point of view" of *The House of Mirth's* conclusion. Contends these confuse the reader and reduce Lily's complexity as she becomes increasingly a sentimental heroine.

R4.41   Benoit, Raymond. "Wharton's *The House of Mirth*." *Explicator* 29 (March 1971), Item 59.

Notes that the discarded title, "A Moment's Ornament" is probably taken from Wordsworth's poem, "She Was a Phantom of Delight," and contends that that poem epitomizes both the content and the form of *The House of Mirth*, although "Lily can find the opposite qualities she richly possesses as the ideal person of the poem only parceled out singly in the added social sphere of the novel."

R4.42   Brazin, Nancy Topping. "The Destruction of Lily Bart: Capitalism, Christianity, and Male Chauvinism." *Denver Quarterly* 17.4 (Winter 1983): 97-108.

Sees Lily's destruction in terms of capitalist, Christian, and male chauvinist ethics. Argues that in such a money-centered, nonandrogynous society every choice available to Lily entails the compromise of self-respect. Discusses rose and lily symbolism, Perseus-Andromeda myth, criticizes Wharton's "sentimentalization of the domestic ideal, the working class, the early pieties, and death...." Feels *The House of Mirth* leaves us with sense of the need "to enter the struggle to create an androgynous society."

R4.43   Bristol, Marie. "Life Among the Ungentle Genteel: Edith Wharton's *The House of Mirth* Revisited." *Western Humanities Review* 16 (Autumn 1962): 371-74.

On the occasion of Scribner's issuing the paperback *The House of Mirth*, long out of print, the critic notes Wharton has been neglected because she is dismissed as a disciple of James; she is classified as "dated" and as a writer of the Genteel School. Praises Wharton's "clear, lucid" style, "credible characterization," highly structured but intriguing plot." Finds *The House of Mirth* not of the Genteel Tradition but a combination of James and Dreiser--the novel of manners with elements of naturalism which might be termed the "novel of dialectics."

R4.44   Cargas, Harry J. "Seeing, But Not Living: Two Characters From James and Wharton." *New Laurel Review* 1.2 (1972): 5-7.

Argues that *The House of Mirth* is "very much related" to *The Ambassadors*, particularly in the similarities between Lambert Strether and Lawrence Selden, especially in that both characters fail to make use of their freedom and fail to live.

R4.45   Castro, Ginette. "*The House of Mirth*: Chronique d'une femme et d'une société." In *Séminaires, 1980*. Edited by Jean Béranger, Jean Cazemajou, and Pierre Spriet. Talence: Pubs. de la Maison des Sciences de l'Homme d'Aquitaine, Université de Bordeaux, 1981.

* Not seen.

R4.46   Colinson, C. S. "*The Whirlpool* and *The House of Mirth*." *The Gissing Newsletter* (La Madeleine, France) 16 (1980), iv: 12-16.

Notes plot parallels between George Gissing's *The Whirlpool* and *The House of Mirth* but cites differences in character and development of the heroine. Argues Wharton emerges as the more professional, the more stylish and more assured of the two.

R4.47   Dahl, Curtis. "Edith Wharton's *The House of Mirth*": Sermon on a Text." *Modern Fiction Studies* (1975) 21: 572-76.

In *The House of Mirth* Wharton "preaches an explicit 'sermon' with surprising exactness" on Ecclesiastes, chapter 7, verses 1-12. But she undercuts the homiletic quality of (and therefore enriches) the novel with three elements: (1) Selden's character; (2) a thread of naturalistic determinism; (3) her own ambivalence about luxury and dislike of "dinginess." In effect, "Wharton does not really want Lily to be different."

R4.48   Davidson, Cathy N. "Kept Women in *The House of Mirth*." *Markham Review* 9 (1979):10-13.

Feminist discussion of Wharton's analysis of the hopeless plight of women in the novel. Analyzes the minor female characters as illustrative of the alternatives open to Lily Bart, most of which involve a compromise with personal integrity.

R4.49   De Abruña, Laura Niesen. "Wharton's *House of Mirth*." *Explicator* 44.3 (Spring 1986): 39-40.

Points out the meaning of Selden's reading of Jean de La Bruyère's *Les Caractères ou les Moeurs de ce Siècle* (1688), in that Selden is similar to Bruyère in temperament and background and is motivated by the French moralist to criticize society, but also becomes detached.

R4.50   Dimock, Wai-chee. "Debasing Exchange: Edith Wharton's *The House of Mirth*." *PMLA* 100 (October 1985): 783-792.

Well-known, often-cited modern commentary on the language of the marketplace in *The House of Mirth* which legitimates socioeconomic demands throughout the novel. Excellent analysis of the invisible, ubiquitous marketplace and the fluctuating rates of exchange (often quite arbitrary) when all social life rests on economic premises. [Rpt. in N5]

R4.51   Dixon, Roslyn. "Reflecting Vision in *The House of Mirth*." *Twentieth Century Literature* 33.2 (Summer 1987): 211-222.

Maintains Wharton's use of multiple points of view and her modernism--the lack of a moral center and the viewing of "the actual from every angle" in *The House of Mirth* connect her not with the "Great Tradition" but the modern French tradition leading to structuralism. Argues Wharton's novels can be read as "empirical studies of the workings of society, presented through contrasting angles of vision ... that amalgamate to form comprehensive, and unsentimental, sociological assessments."

R4.52   DuPlessis, Rachel Blau. *Writing Beyond the Ending: Narrative Strategies of Twentieth Century Women Writers*. Bloomington: Indiana University Press, 1985.

Notes two root metaphors of *The House of Mirth* are gambling and prostitution. Terms Lily "an ornamental object to be purchased." Finds Lily's death, like all her decisions, is an example of one option foreclosing another--all of which she's trying to keep open. Maintains death is sensual and "her bier resonates with both narcissism and the failed community...."

R4.53   Edwards, Oliver. "Lily Bart." *London Times*, 19 July 1956, p.13.

Critic has always been fascinated by *The House of Mirth* and Lily Bart. Calls the book "beautifully constructed, extremely well written, and finely controlled." Notes that Lily is "presented to us whole," and the fascination lies not in guessing about her, but observing her.

R4.54   Fetterley, Judith. "The Temptation to Be a Beautiful Object: Double Standard and Double Bind in *The*

House of Mirth." Studies in American Fiction 5 (1977):
199-211. Rpt. *Fiction by American Women: Recent Views.*
Edited with introduction by Winifred Farrant
Bevilacqua. Port Washington, New York: Associated
Faculty Press, 1983.

Feminist viewpoint that *The House of Mirth* is "a
powerful denunciation of patriarchal culture." Discusses
objectification of Lily's physical beauty leading to her
feelings of powerlessness and self-hatred. Criticizes
Wharton for not fully understanding the double binds
that face Lily and for "overtones of a romanticization
of female masochism."

R4.55   Foster, Shirley. "Freedom, Marriage and the Heroine in
Early Twentieth Century Women's Novels." In *Women's
Writing: A Challenge to Theory*, edited by Moira
Monteith, 154-174. New York: St. Martin's Press, 1986.

Analyzes attempts by women writers to express
their attitudes about the restrictions of women in
society through their writing in a study of Cather's *The
Song of the Lark*, Chopin's *The Awakening* and
Wharton's *The House of Mirth:* Notes determinism in
Wharton, a "dualistic" outlook because of her
ambivalence toward society, and a sentimentality that
blurs the novel's overall clarity.

R4.56   Franklin, C.L. "Women and Business." *Bookman* 24
(November 1906): 249-50.

Letter to Editor. Cites inconsistencies at the end
of the novel which illustrate Lily's complete ignorance
of business matters, suggesting that women may be
woefully ignorant of simple business transactions and
therefore vulnerable to a fate like Lily's.

R4.57   Friman, Anne. "Determinism and Point of View in *The
House of Mirth." Papers on Language and Literature*, II
(Spring 1966): 175-78.

Discusses problem of materialistic determinism in
The House of Mirth, "a philosophy inconsistent with
Edith Wharton's characteristic view of life." Feels that

seemingly deterministic passages are actually Lily's sometimes thinking in deterministic terms (although she does not act in accordance with these thoughts), rather than the narrator's pronouncements on Lily's character or circumstances. Thus, the problem is one of "stylistic ambiguity."

R4.58   Gargano, James W. "*The House of Mirth*: Social Futility and Faith." *American Literature* 44 (1972): 137-43.

Argues the "word" at the end of *The House of Mirth* is "faith" which, to Wharton, "is no generalized and temperamental optimism; it is, instead, an almost mystical assurance that only moral action can save the ever-threatened continuity of human existence." The last chapters of the novel are seen as affirmative, for, in them, Wharton reaches beyond social concerns to a "larger, perhaps ultimately philosophical vision."

R4.59   Gelfant, Blanche Housman. "Sister to Faust: The City's 'Hungry' Woman as Heroine." In *Women Writers and the City: Essays in Feminist Literary Criticism*. Edited by Susan Merrill Squire. Part III. North American Writers. Knoxville: University of Tennessee Press, 1984.

A one-sentence reference to Lily Bart, who "sees her doom etched in the incipient lines of her face," carries the comment that a heroine who values her intellect and herself can survive without beauty.

R4.60   Grumbach, Doris. "Reconsideration." *New Republic* 168 (21 April 1973): 29-30.

Reassessment of Lily Bart in light of feminist interest in her as a "textbook on feminism." Contends that Lily is cast in the heroic mold by Wharton and represents tragedy of the trapped woman since "civilization" and "society" assigned her to bondage.

R4.61   Gubar, Susan. "'The Blank Page' and the Issues of Female Creativity." *Critical Inquiry* 8 (Winter 1981). Rpt. in *Writing and Sexual Difference*. Edited by Elizabeth Abel. Chicago: 1982. Also Rpt. in *The New*

Feminist Criticism. Edited by Elaine Showalter. New York: Pantheon, 1985.

Taking as a point of departure Isak Dinesen's short story, "The Blank Page," Gubar explores the problems of the woman artist seeking identity beyond cultural stereotypes that define her as an object closely identified with her own body. Examines Lily Bart as an example of a woman transformed into an art object.

R4.62   Harap, Louis. *Creative Awakening: The Jewish Presence in Twentieth Century American Literature, 1900-1940s*. New York: Greenwood, 1987.

Page-long discussion of Rosedale in *The House of Mirth*. Maintains Wharton's "patrician" anti-Semitism consists of identifying Rosedale's negative character traits with his "race" and "blood." Contends "The reader is never ... allowed to forget that Rosedale is a Jew and therefore a strangely repugnant object ipso facto to be held in contempt." Also notes Wharton's delighted praise of Fitzgerald's Wolfsheim in *The Great Gatsby*. [See M16 and L124]

R4.63   Hierth, Harrison E. "The Class Novel." *CEA Critic* 27 (December 1964): 1, 3-4.

Discussion of the class novel traces similarities between *The House of Mirth* and John O'Hara's *Appointment in Samara*. Parallels are: each was class conscious and thought snobbish; both were aware of reality of class distinction; both recognize the effects of social stratification on individuals; both were sensitive and skillful in delineating the subtler gradations of social status and cognizant of the dangers of violating convention and both had a strong element of determinism.

R4.63.1 Kaplan, Amy. "Crowded Spaces in *The House of Mirth*." In *The Social Construction of American Realism*. Chicago: University of Chicago Press, 1988.

Chapter offers insightful discussion of the class structure in the novel--of the dependence of the elite upon the adulation of the masses and the growing influence of the media as the upper classes became increasingly objects of a spectator public which both "defines and threatens" them. Explores EW within the realistic tradition.

R4.64   Karcher, Carolyn L. "Male Vision and Female Revision in James's *Wings of the Dove* and Wharton's *House of Mirth*." *Women's Studies* 10.3 (1984): 227-244.
           Feminist. Follows Sandra Gilbert and Susan Gubar's model of "revisionary struggle" formulated in *The Madwoman in the Attic*. Argues in *The House of Mirth* Wharton took issue with Henry James's patriarchal mythology in *Wings of the Dove* in these ways: (1) replaced "Crookes tube" of James's later method with "a fully delineated social world governed by behavioral codes and value systems that rigidly circumscribe its inhabitants freedom"; (2) fused the "split images of women ... into a single figure whose aspirations and limitations derive from social causes"; (3) presented a woman's "experience of entrapment and asphyxiation through her own consciousness"; (4) exposed "the male observer/author's judgement as obtuse and self-serving"; (5) provided "glimpses of [alternatives] that point the way toward an eventual solution of their predicament in patriarchal society."

R4.65   Koprince, Susan. "The Meaning of Bellomont in *The House of Mirth*." *Edith Wharton Newsletter* 2.1 (Spring 1985): 1.
           Interprets Bellomont in *HofM* as an ironic literary allusion to Shakespeare's Belmont in *The Merchant of Venice*.

R4.66   Kronenberger, Louis. "Edith Wharton's New York: Two Period Pieces." *Michigan Quarterly Review*, 6 (Winter 1965): 3-13.
           Discusses *The Age of Innocence* and *The House of Mirth* as novels of the 1870's and 1880's, respectively, in terms of the great social change that occurred between

those eras. Praises her realistic depiction of society and its values while questioning characterization and plotting as not always credible.

R4.67   Langley, Martha R. "Botanical Language in Edith Wharton's *The House of Mirth*." *NMAL: Notes on Modern American Literature* 5 (1980): Item 3.

Defines the "principal thematic cluster" as botanical metaphors, particularly the imagery of flowers. Argues that botanical language reinforces the novel's naturalism and suggests the thematic development, e.g., Lily Bart like the orchid, lily and rose is "beautiful, graceful, delicate, admired, and, finally, ephemeral."

R4.68   Lidoff, Joan. "Another Sleeping Beauty: Narcissism in *The House of Mirth*." *American Quarterly* 32 (1980): 519-39. Rpt. *American Realism: New Essays.* Ed. Eric J. Sundquist. Baltimore: Johns Hopkins University Press, 1982.

Psychological study of Lily Bart defining her as a passive heroine with an emotional style of primary narcissism. Terms Wharton ambivalent toward Lily - both sympathetic and punitive, because of her own unresolved conflicts which lead her in her fiction to confound realism with romance. Contends Wharton was unable "to image woman's responsibility for herself" and she "makes a life of practical action within accepted limitations seem intolerably harsh." Discusses limitations of Wharton's fictive world.

R4.69   Link, Franz. "A Note on the Apparition of These Faces ... in *The House of Mirth* and 'In a Station of the Metro'." *Paideuma: a Journal Devoted to Ezra Pound Scholarship* 10.2 (Fall 1981): 327.

Suggests that Pound took the image of Lily Bart in Grand Central Station as part of the impetus for "In A Station of the Metro" in which he first formulated the theory of juxtaposition as a structural device in poetry.

R4.70   Loney, Glenn M. "Dramatizations of American Novels 1900-1917." Ph.D. dissertation. Stanford, 1954.

Purpose of study was to "ascertain in what ways and to what extent theatrical techniques and theatre audience tastes of the 1900-1917 period influenced the adaptation of best-selling American novels for the New York stage during that era." Found that in every case except *The House of Mirth* the dramatists "avoided a serious treatment." [See R4.71 and G4] For abstract see DAI 14 (1954), 1843.

R4.71   Loney, Glenn M. "Edith Wharton and *The House of Mirth*: The Novelist Writes for the Theater." *Modern Drama* 4 (September 1961), 152-63.

Recounts Wharton's unsuccessful, largely unwanted, experience in the theater, with a full history of the dramatization of *The House of Mirth* which she was duped into writing in collaboration with Clyde Fitch. Contains interesting material on the changes made in the play, e.g., Lily commits suicide in the millinery shop over Selden's rejection and Selden earlier rushes in and saves her from Trenor. [See G4]

R4.72   McIlvaine, Robert. "Edith Wharton's American Beauty Rose." *Journal of American Studies* (Norwich, England) 7 (1973): 183-85.

Discusses the rose imagery, suggesting it may stem from a speech by John D. Rockefeller, Jr., in 1902 which associates growth of a corporation with that of an American Beauty rose and promotes social Darwinism. Notes Rockefeller's famous analogy was employed as symbolism by Robert Herrick in *The Memoirs of an American Citizen.* Contends Wharton uses rose imagery to describe both Lily's showy society and her conspicuous beauty and social grace shaped by and for that society.

R4.73   Michaelson, Bruce R. "Edith Wharton's House Divided." *Studies in American Fiction* 12 (Autumn 1984): 199-215.

Analyzes dramatic conventions of the well-made play in *The House of Mirth* and the thematic use of drama in that the novel is "about drama, about play-acting ... and about the problem of understanding ... where the stage-world and the posturings of daily existence end and where the real world and the real self begin." Thus, argues the novel, with its complex evaluation of modern "reality," is "one of America's most genuinely ambitious modern novels."

R4.74   Miller, Carol. "'Natural Magic': Irony as Unifying Strategy in *The House of Mirth*." *South Central Review* 4.1 (Spring 1987): 82-91.
Defense of Wharton's irony as a strategy that unifies her work, develops her vision of alienation and creates bonds between writer and reader. *The House of Mirth* analyzed as example.

R4.75   Mirabella, Bella Maryanne. "Part I--Mute Rhetoric: Dance in Shakespeare and Marston. Part II--The Machine in the Garden: The Theme of Work in "*Tess of the D'Urbervilles*." Part III--Art and Imagination in Edith Wharton's *The House of Mirth*." Ph.D. dissertation. Rutgers, 1979.
Part III analyzes Wharton's beliefs about art in the context of *The House of Mirth*. For abstract see DAI, 40 (1980), 4056A.

R4.76   Montgomery, Judith H. "The American Galatea." *College English* 32 (1971): 890-99.
Feminist. Analyzes Hawthorne's Zenobia, James's Isabel Archer and Edith Wharton's Lily Bart as examples of the Pygmalion/Galatea archetype in American Literature. Terms Lily "the ultimate Galatea" for she is "literally fulfilling the Pygmalion myth, as an objet d'art in the ... tableaux." Contends the myth fuses two basic impulses in man: creation and possession. The myth, fusing aesthetic sensibility with will to power, incorporates a secondary theme--decoration of the

woman--"which comes to figure most importantly in its American development."

R4.77   O'Neal, Michael J. "Point of View and Narrative Technique in the Fiction of Edith Wharton." *Style* (Spring 1983): 270-89.

Excellent, illuminating analysis of Wharton's style includes discussion of "the role that rapid tonal shifts play in the interlacing of multiple points of view." Concentrates on *The House of Mirth*, defining the novel as "not as much about character as about how one's character is a fragile product of someone else's judgment," with this theme reflected in language presenting Lily and Selden's feelings and perceptions. Well-supported, striking study of Wharton's use of language both to characterize and to judge.

R4.78   Overton, Grant M. "*The House of Mirth*: Do You Remember It?" *Mentor World-Traveller* 22 (September 1930): 41.

Synopsis of plot with comment on the novel's enduring popularity and its timely significance because the major characters are also contemporary types.

R4.79   Panaro, Lydia Adriana. "Desperate Women: Murderers and Suicides in Nine Modern Novels." Ph.D. Dissertation. New York University, 1981.

Studies Italian, French, English and American novels. Argues *The House of Mirth* is one of nine novels chosen to illustrate "a lack of inner freedom which is related to the [heroine's] role as woman." The psychologically based hypothesis is: "the female is perceived by others and herself as inferior; this perception predisposes her toward dependency which is the basis of her destructive behavior, whether directed toward another or herself." For abstract see DAI 42.7 (1983), 3150A.

R4.80   Pearson, Carol. *The Female Hero in American and British Literature*. New York & London: R.R. Bowker, 1981.

Archetypal study of the female hero's journey to self-discovery. Finds that the theme of *The House of Mirth* is "the betrayal of the inner vision for the sake of convention." Defines the tragedy as "a direct result of the opposition between Lily Bart's spontaneous heroic nature and conventional society which sees her heroic spirit as immoral."

R4.81   Pickrel, Paul. "*Vanity Fair* in America: *The House of Mirth* and *Gone With the Wind*." *American Literature* 59.1 (March 1987): 37-57.

Notes Wharton's admiration for Thackeray and traces thematic, titular, name and structural parallels between *Vanity Fair* and *The House of Mirth*. However, contends she expresses attitudes more or less opposite, as if her novel were a reply to Thackeray (e.g., Wharton shows the pain of trying to live in society without money).

R4.82   Poirier, Richard. "Edith Wharton's *The House of Mirth*." In *The American Novel: From James Fenimore Cooper to William Faulkner*. New York: Basic Books, 1965. Expanded Rpt. in *A World Elsewhere: The Place of Style in American Literature*. New York: Oxford University Press, 1966. Originally designed as an Oral Presentation for Voice of America.

Annotation from *A World Elsewhere* version. Argues that Wharton and James are quite dissimilar, first, in her use of the chronicle-novel's simple, sequential ordering of events versus James's elaboration from all angles of a central situation, but more importantly, because Wharton's characters are "propelled mostly by environmental circumstances external to them." In Wharton, "environment becomes force, totally shaping personal relations while remaining unaffected by them." Discusses Wharton in relation to Austen, George Eliot and Dreiser.

R4.83   Potter, Rosemary. "The Mistakes of Lily in *The House of Mirth*." *Talus* 4 (1971): 89-93.

Defining this as a naturalistic novel, analyzes errors in judgment, mistakes in timing and the play of circumstances as they affect Lily Bart's destiny. Concludes that Lily's mistakes were "the mistakes of a noble creature ill-equipped to survive" in her shallow society.

R4.84   Price, Alan. "Lily Bart and Carrie Meeber: Cultural Sisters." *American Literary Realism: 1870-1910* 13 (1980): 238-45.

Finds similarities between Carrie and Lily because of their society--"social change and dislocation tell equally on Dreiser's small-town girls and Wharton's Fifth Avenue ladies." Notes both are part of an acquisitive culture; both think of themselves as "decorative objects." Wharton's treatment makes Lily more complex with the "warring factions within her own nature and a moral growth which ironically accompanies her social and physical defeat." [See X58]

R4.85   Pritchett, V.S. "Books in General." *New Statesman and Nation*, NS 45 (25 April 1953): 489-90.

Occasioned by reprints of *The House of Mirth* and *The Age of Innocence*. Discusses Wharton as a social critic, characterizing her as rather a mother-figure: "determined, pragmatic, critical and alarming," whose great power as a novelist lay in creating scenes and incidents. Notes that, in the end, she was in favor of submission. Focus is on *The House of Mirth*.

R4.86   Radden, Jennifer. "Defining Self-Deception." *Dialogue: Canadian Philosophical Review/Revue Canadienne de Philosophie 23.1* (March 1984): 103-20.

Employs Lily Bart's self-deceptions in *The House of Mirth* to argue that philosophical discussions of self-deception are necessarily general and can never explain specific motivational contexts and thus make the dynamics of self-deception clear in the way that literature can.

R4.87 Randall, John H. "Romeo and Juliet in the New World: A Study in James, Wharton, and Fitzgerald 'Fay ce que vouldras.'" *Costerus* 8 (1973): 109-76.

N.B.: Editorship lies within the Department of English, Virginia Polytechnic, Blacksburg, Virginia, although the journal is published in Amsterdam. Lengthy, insightful study of *The House of Mirth, Daisy Miller* and *The Great Gatsby* as American versions of the Romeo and Juliet story which concern the problem of freedom in America and are tales of romantic love with political overtones. Explains the three stories reveal strengths and weaknesses of the national character: the carelessness and waste, the conformity-- with *The House of Mirth* "a landmark in the history of the relations between the sexes in America," Lily Bart the archetypal "modern American woman crying aloud to be molded by somebody who understands and cares" and a superior species who should attract a superior male, yet is undone by "organized mediocrity." Maintains the stories all contain an evangelical fervor and the reader feels motivated to change society.

R4.88 Restuceia, Frances L. "The Name of the Lily: Edith Wharton's Feminism(s)." *Contemporary Literature* 28.2 (Summer 1987): 223-38.

Feminist. Reflects that *The House of Mirth* illustrates the tension in contemporary feminist theory: "the apparent incommensurability of a social, humanist feminism that advances a position ... and a more literary feminism that refuses definable positions for their masterliness, wishing to maintain perpetual openness and inaccessibility." Argues the novel demonstrates risks to women of being bred as decorative objects but also the unattractive nature of inflexibility.

R4.89 Rideout, Walter B. "Edith Wharton's *The House of Mirth*." In *Twelve Original Essays on Great American Novels*. Edited by Charles Shapiro. Detroit: Wayne State, 1958. 148-76.

Careful analysis of the structure of *The House of Mirth* with striking insight into Chapter I as containing the essence of the entire book.

R4.90   Rooke, Constance. "Beauty in Distress: *Daniel Deronda* and *The House of Mirth*." *Women and Literature* 4.2 (1976): 28-39.

Argues that *Daniel Deronda* was a significant influence on *The House of Mirth*. Contends "the parallels are so extensive that *The House of Mirth* might be thought simply derivative were it not for the important circumstance that Wharton was contending with a social as well as a literary model." Finds important similarities in a common concern with the perverse socialization of women, particularly as symbolized in the *tableaux vivant*.

R4.91   Sasaki, Miyoko. "A Grotesque Perspective in Edith Wharton's *The House of Mirth*." *Tsuda Review* No. 15 1970.

    * Not seen.

R4.92   Showalter, Elaine. "The Death of the Lady (Novelist): Wharton's *House of Mirth*." *Representations* 9 (Winter 1985): 133-49. Rpt. N5.

Interpretation of *The House of Mirth* as a pivotal novel growing out of the change from the homosocial women's literature of the nineteenth century to heterosexual modern fiction and redefinitions of gender behavior and relationships. Argues Lily's death is symbolic of Wharton's death as the lady novelist which led to her rebirth as an artist "who would create the language of feminine growth and mastery in her own work." Maintains the ending contains a vision of "a new world of female solidarity." Points out both male and female entrapment in the novel, and the necessity Wharton saw for the abandonment of the rigid role of the lady. [Rpt. in N5]

R4.93 Shulman, Robert R. "Divided Selves and the Market Society: Politics and Psychology in *The House of Mirth*." *Perspectives on Contemporary Literature* 11 (1985): 10-19.

Argues Wharton "exposes the loneliness and alienation inseparable from the market society at the most elevated ... levels of the American class system." Interprets Lily Bart as a "capitalist exploiting her own alienated self in exchange for goods sanctioned by the official custodians of society."

R4.94 Spangler, George M. "Suicide and Social Criticism: Durkheim, Dreiser, Wharton and London." *American Quarterly* 31 (1979): 496-516.

Summarizes Durkheim's *Suicide* (1897) and applies its theories to Dreiser, Wharton and London, in each of whom "self-destruction" is found to be "one of the salient facts and the apt symbol of social conditions in Western Europe and the United States" because of the fragmented industrial society. Contends these three writers use suicide for social criticism, as in the case of Lily Bart, a victim of a corrupt society, whose loneliness is emphasized more than her vanity or ambition. Notes in these three writers the social consciousness of Howells and the reduced human images of literary naturalism.

R4.95 Steele, Erskine. "Fiction and Social Ethics." *South Atlantic Quarterly*, V (July 1906): 254-63.

Review of Ellen Glasgow's *The World of Life* and Wharton's *The House of Mirth*. Finds both novels illustrate a contemporary "preoccupation" ... with "the ethical and moral point of view." Praises *The House of Mirth* unreservedly in that "it inculcates a striking moral lesson" yet never is "marred by the faintest tinge of didacticism." Mentions that in a letter to him Mrs. Wharton said that the book's thesis is to be found in the passage in which Lily "as she looked back ... saw that there had never been a time when she had had any real relation to life...."

R4.96   Stineback, David C. "The Whirling Surface of Existence:
         Edith Wharton's *The House of Mirth*." In *Shifting World:
         Social Change and Nostalgia in the American Novel.*
         Lewisburg, PA: Bucknell University Press, 1976.
             Discusses Lily Bart's nostalgia for Bellomont and
         her drive for security and personal distinction in terms
         of the constant flux of her changing society. Book is a
         study of rapid social change and nostalgia as antagonists
         and the conflicts that arise in American Literature from
         these forces.

R4.97   Tintner, Adeline R. "Two Novels of 'the Relatively
         Poor': *New Grub Street* and *The House of Mirth*."
         NMAL: Notes on Modern American Literature 6.2
         (Autumn 1982): Item 12.
             Suggests parallels between George Gissing's *New
         Grub Street* (1891) and *The House of Mirth*, particularly
         in use of the phrase "relative poverty"; also cites, among
         other parallels, the similar profusion of classical
         references, and the inability of the hero and heroine to
         do the right thing at the right time. Speculates that
         James encouraged EW to read Gissing.

R4.98   Trilling, Diana. "*The House of Mirth* Revisited." *Harper's
         Bazaar* 81 (December 1947): 126-27, 181-86. Reprints:
         N14; *American Scholar* 32 (Winter 1962-63): 113-28.
         Revised Reprint: *Claremont Essays*. New York:
         Harcourt Brace and World, 1964.
             Analysis of the novel in attempt to establish
         Wharton's importance to modern readers. Emphasizes
         the class and economic basis of the novel. Contends
         "*The House of Mirth* is ... one of the most telling
         indictments of a social system based on the chance
         distribution of wealth, and therefore of social privilege,
         that has ever been put on paper."

R4.99   Trilling, Diana. "The Liberated Heroine." *Times Literary
         Supplement* 13 (October 1978): 1163-67.

Very brief reference to Lily Bart in a catalogue of the older, spirited heroines who tried to "make a destiny" but more often than not failed because of society. Contrasts these women with the modern liberated heroine, in an attempt both to define the concept and to assess its literary and cultural influence.

R4.100   Velia, Michael W. "Technique and Theme in *The House of Mirth*." *Markham Review* 2.3 (1970): 17-20.
Defines Wharton's technique of characterization in *The House of Mirth* as "a constant shifting of illuminating incidents in which character is revealed," which reflects the theme in that the limitations of character in the incidents expose the limitations of the society. Thus, argues the episodic structure and the illuminating incidents reveal her emphasis on characters "trapped and defined by their situations and milieu."

R4.101   Waldstein, Charles. "Social Ideals." *North American Review* 132 (June 1906): 840-52.
Critic offers a lengthy discussion of tragedy, concluding that modern tragedy stems from character and the individualization of specific social groups as well. He finds that Lily Bart's story is a tragedy because she loses both her lover and her self-esteem and thus we feel sympathy for her. Much of the interest of modern tragedy, he feels, shifts to the environment. Mrs. Wharton's portrayal of the vulgar conventions of the "best society" illustrates the social problem when the standards of that society become influential.

R4.102   Waldstein, Charles. "Social Ideals--II." *North American Review* 183 (July 1906): 125-36.
In a continuation of his previous article, critic finds the characters in *The House of Mirth* have no ideals (unlike *Daniel Deronda*) and therefore it becomes a "tragic satire" rather than a true tragedy. James also writes tragic satire, but his women, with their passion, are very different from Wharton's. He gives a lengthy

analysis of the effect the worship of the worldly and loss of ideals and a sense of duty have on society. [See R4.101]

R4.103   Wershoven, Carol J. "*The Awakening* and *The House of Mirth*: Studies of Arrested Development." *American Literary Realism 1870-1910* 19.3 (Spring 1987): 27-41.
           Traces similarities between Kate Chopin's *The Awakening* and *The House of Mirth*. Discusses: patterns of conflict, grouping of characters, development of protagonists, imagery. Finds both heroines "break the chain of human growth before ... connection of self to others." Therefore, the "embryonic new self never develops fully to become the self in the world."

R4.104   Westbrook, Wayne W. "*The House of Mirth* and the Insurance Scandal of 1905." *American Notes and Queries* 14 (1976): 134-37.
           Suggests that the title *The House of Mirth* may have come from the headlines of the insurance scandal of 1905. The headquarters of a key figure in the scandal in Albany was dubbed by the press, "The House of Mirth." Also notes that the novel can be read as a consciously constructed allegory of Wall Street. [See R4.105]

R4.105   Westbrook, Wayne W. "Lily-Bartering on the New York Social Exchange in *The House of Mirth*." *Ball State University Forum* 20 (1979): 59-64.
           Extensive, detailed reading of the novel as a stock market allegory, in which Lily Bart is like a fluctuating commodity. Concludes that Lily Bart ascends morally as she descends socially, so she is more tragic than pathetic. [See R4.104]

R4.106   Westbrook, Wayne W. *Wall Street in the American Novel*. New York: New York University Press, 1980.
           Reprints his previously published material on Lily Bart as a fluctuating commodity in this analysis of the genteel novel of high finance as about

"microeconomics"--i.e., "individuals whose lives are influenced and determined by economic factors." Notes society is so heavily influenced by Wall Street in both *The House of Mirth* and *The Custom of the Country* they are "governed by the same principles, operated by the same codes, and subject to the same fluctuations." [See R4.104 and R4.105]

R4.107   Wolff, Cynthia G. "Lily Bart and the Beautiful Death." *American Literature* 46 (1974): 40.

Striking psychological analysis of Lily Bart's depersonalization and Selden's part in her destruction, with his collector's attitude toward her and his implicit demand that she fulfill both aesthetic and moral absolutes.   Contends that "[c]onsistent confusion between the ideal and the real as it is manifested by all the characters in the novel ... leads directly to the heart of the tragedy."   Excellent discussion of murals, portraiture and Art Nouveau and the attitudes toward women in these movements as they contributed to Lily's downfall and lack of sense of self except through the responses of others to her.   [See N28]

Madame de Treymes--Reviews

R5.1   Anonymous. Review of *Madame de Treymes. Academy* 72 (11 May 1907): 465-66.

Admires Wharton's wit and distinction, but criticizes the novel for typical rather than individualized characterization.   Praises the contrast between civilizations, but objects that the characters do not stand out clearly.

R5.2   Anonymous. Review of *Madame de Treymes. Athenaeum* (London) No. 4149 (4 May 1907): 535.

Notes resemblance to *The American*, but finds Madame de Treymes a subtler study than any of James's characters. Finds pleasure in Wharton's "sturdy faith in the superiority of the Anglo-Saxon and Protestant tradition."

R5.3   Anonymous. "Recent Fiction and the Critics." *Current Literature* 42 (June 1907): 693-94.

Summarizes reviews, emphasizing Wharton's cleverness and coldness, and the "apparent heartlessness that invariably accompanies the analytic temperament."

R5.4   Anonymous. "Literature." *Independent* 62 (27 June 1907): 1528.

Objects that Wharton's idea evaporated into Jamesian subtleties, and thus "it is merely a little pamphlet of elegant discriminations ... devoid of profitable content." Speculates that the story may be based on Anna Gould.

R5.5   Anonymous. "A Guide to the New Books." *Literary Digest* 34 (20 April 1907): 640.

Praises Wharton as an American for picturing "such an exotic phase of" life so brilliantly, but objects that it is too slight a volume to fulfill expectations raised by *The House of Mirth*.

R5.6   Anonymous. Review of *Madame de Treymes*. *Nation* 84 (4 April 1907): 313.

Determines it is Wharton's fate to depict characters in the light of circumstance rather than to use them to individualize the universal. However, reviewer at first wondered if Madame de Treymes would be a realistic Frenchwoman and ended thinking her a believable woman. Remarks that this is another one of Wharton's unfortunate women.

R5.7   Anonymous. "Comment on Current Books." *Outlook* 86 (1 June 1907): 255.

Finds the American and the French woman skillfully done, although the French ideal has been questioned "by so good an authority as Madame Blanc." [See R4.13]

R5.8   Anonymous. "A Review of the Season's Fiction: Various Localities." *Review of Reviews* 35 (June 1907): 764-65.
         Furnishes plot summary and comments that Wharton "casts a light on the French fashion which might well incline the cool, commercial Yankee to remain content with a prose and apple pie" type of domestic happiness.

R5.9   Anonymous. Review of *Madame de Treymes*. *Spectator* 98 (11 May 1907): 764.
         Brief review lauds Wharton's study of personality, concluding that the French family as a powerful institution "has never been better treated by a foreign pen."

R5.10   Atwood, Vernon. "The Hammock Novel, and Others." *Putnam's Monthly* 2 (August 1907): 616-17.
         Calls this an "absolutely flawless and satisfying piece of workmanship." Finds authorial objectivity perfect, Wharton taking neither side.

R5.11   Dunbar, Olivia Howard. "Madame de Treymes." *North American Review* 185 (17 May 1907): 218-21.
         Lengthy discussion of Wharton's characterization in general precedes praise for the appeal and realism of Mme. de Treymes, who is "largely characterized by eliminations and reserves." Mentions Wharton's debt to *The American*. Praises her structure and style which make her work superior to other magazine fiction, and to writers of greater sympathy and spontaneity.

R5.12   Hawthorne, Hildegarde. "Mrs. Wharton's Heroines." *New York Times Saturday Review*, 9 March 1907, p.137.
         Characterizes Wharton's women as "creatures of the intellect," small of soul, expressing "not excess but emptiness." Argues their acts leave the reader unmoved, and that, above all: "They do not want to lose caste." Contends Madame de Treymes is more American than French. Praises artistry.

R5.13   Moss, Mary. "Mrs. Wharton's 'Madame de Treymes'."
          Bookman 25 (May 1907): 303-04.
                    Estimates that Wharton in some ways surpasses
          James here in her treatment of the international
          situation with greater subtlety, for she shows the point
          at which the Faubourg miscalculates the American
          Code. Praises her skill in bringing the women to life.

R5.14   Smith, Harry James. "Some Recent Novels." *Atlantic
          Monthly* 100 (July 1907): 131-32.
                    Contrasts James and Wharton, concluding that
          what is lost in nuance and repleteness in Wharton is
          gained in focus, brilliancy and definition.   Mentions
          French criticism of the characterization of Madame de
          Treymes, but notes that she "*seems*" actual enough.
          Feels gratified that after *The House of Mirth* here is an
          American hero, "typical and worthy of respect."

                    The Fruit of the Tree--Reviews

R6.1   Anonymous. Review of *The Fruit of the Tree Athenaeum*
          (London): 4181 (14 December 1907): 718.
                    Finds the book's two themes are the owner-
          employee relationship and euthanasia, arguing the latter
          is treated with all the strength and artistic restraint
          which we expect from Wharton. The characters, except
          for the hero, are termed excellently studied and
          contrasted.

R6.2   Anonymous. "Recent Fiction and the Critics." *Current
          Literature* 43 (December 1907): 691-92.
                    Summarizes reviews in several journals with the
          conclusion that it will not be as popular as *The House
          of Mirth*. Notes that here are "the same cold precision,
          the same technical mastery, and the same lack of heart,

the same hardness, which have made her unique among feminine writers of fiction."

R6.3   Anonymous. Review of *The Fruit of the Tree*. *Independent* 63 (12 December 1907): 1436-37.

Praises Wharton's versatility in that she writes here of common American realities, avoiding a "dim affectedness of phrasing" which made some fear she would become simply a disciple of James. Notes the contrast of rich and poor in the novel, but concludes that is the spirit of the age and names the real subject to be euthanasia, finding the cheerful ending, with Justine restored to her family, absolutely false.

R6.4   Anonymous. Review of *The Fruit of the Tree*. *Literary Digest* 35 (14 December 1907): 920.

Cites the press controversy over the euthanasia question, but believes the reader will enjoy the skillful and artistic interpretation of life in spite of the theme and a certain unconscious condescension stemming from the author's tradition and training.

R6.5   Anonymous. "Current Fiction." *Nation* 85 (17 October 1907): 352-53.

Plot summary, with the conclusion that Wharton has interpreted American life with ease and precision.

R6.6   Anonymous. "Novels and Tales." *Outlook* 87 (23 November 1907): 621.

Notes the novel lacks humor and contrasts of characters, but finds its analysis penetrating, and contends it evades none of the issues it raises. However, argues that the sense of futility which surrounds Mrs. Wharton's people could often be cut at a stroke with a little vigor of will.

R6.7   Marsh, Edward Clark. "Mrs. Wharton's *The Fruit of the Tree*." *Bookman* 26 (November 1907): 273-75.

Terms Wharton frankly disdainful of traditional precepts here, and the multiple point of view a

weakness. Argues the marks of James are gone. Finds
the characters types; objects there is more reference to
literature than to life.

R6.8   Payne, William Morton. "Recent Fiction." *Dial* 43 (16
           November 1907): 317.
                     Discusses euthanasia, noting the sense of ethical
           responsibility always present in Wharton. Contends the
           reader will sympathize with the heroine, although
           Wharton does not take sides, but offers a concrete
           example for study.

The Fruit of the Tree--Introductions and Afterwords

R6.9   French, Marilyn. "Introduction." *The Fruit of the Tree*.
           London: Virago, 1984.
                     Excellent introduction argues the underlying unity
           of the book and contends the main theme is the
           interconnection between all of life. Terms Justine Brent
           the moral center of the book and a type of "New
           Woman" entirely new, not just in Wharton's work, but
           in the novel as a genre.

The Fruit of the Tree--Criticism

R6.10   Lawson, Richard H. "Hermann Sudermann and Edith
           Wharton." *Revue de Littérature Comparée* 61 (January-
           March 1967): 125-31.
                     Analyzes the influence of Sudermann, whose *Es
           Lebe das Leben* Wharton translated, on *The Fruit of the
           Tree* and *The House of Mirth*, emphasizing "a certain
           permeation [of Sudermann's social concerns] at a
           deep[er] level, especially in respect to matters
           sanctioned by her own highly-developed antipathies and
           class consciousness." [See N16]

R6.11   Stein, Allen F. "Wharton's Blithedale: A New Reading of *The Fruit of the Tree*." *American Literary Realism 1870-1910* 12 (1979): 330-37.

Feels critics who have called the novel unfocused have misunderstood it. Argues *The Fruit of the Tree* "is, in short, like Hawthorne's *Blithedale Romance*, a discomfiting, somber novel pointing up that significant social amelioration can never occur until human nature itself improves...." Traces the self-centeredness of the three main characters and judges that Justine is the only one who grows, thus "[t]he only improvement which both authors, then, see as a real possibility is that which occurs for one individual and perhaps those immediately about him when he overcomes his devotion to self."

R6.12   Woodbridge, Homer E. "Fruit of the Tree and Ibsen's *Rosmersholm*." *Nation* 85 (5 December 1907): 514.

This letter to the editor points out the similarity of the central situation in Ibsen's *Rosmersholm* and *The Fruit of the Tree*. The writer also notes other similarities to Ibsen (Lily Bart reminiscent of Hedda Gabler, for example).

Ethan Frome--Reviews

R7.1   Anonymous. Review of *Ethan Frome*. *Bookman* (London) 41 (January 1912): 216.

Concludes Wharton's art has never been shown to greater advantage than in this "beautiful, sad, but intensely human story, working out to its final conclusion with all the inevitability of a great Greek tragedy."

R7.2   Anonymous. "Recent Fiction and the Critics." *Current Literature* 52 (January 1912): 112-13.

In a survey of critical articles from *The Sun*, *Outlook*, the *New York Tribune* and the *Boston Herald* (all very brief), critic concludes by agreeing with the *Sun* that *Ethan Frome* is her greatest book. Also notes that she has moved beyond her worship of James and any similarity to an English writer here would be to Thomas Hardy.

R7.3   Anonymous. "Feminine Literature." *Independent* 71 (30 November 1911): 1204.

Brief review praises Wharton's power as an artist that makes the homely details of New England farm life as vital as her settings in fashionable New York.

R7.4   Anonymous. Review of *Ethan Frome*. *Nation* 93 (26 October 1911): 396-97.

Remarks that "we might have been reasonably content to rank her as the greatest pupil of a little master, were it not for the appearance of *Ethan Frome*." Praises the New England atmosphere and the realistic characterization. Calls it surprising that "the spectacle of so much pain can be made to yield so much beauty."

R7.5   Anonymous. "Three Lives in Supreme Torture." *New York Times Book Review*, 8 October 1911, p. 603.

Concentrates on Wharton's vision as that of the tragic poet, who does not show life as it is, "as the great novelists do," but rather "the reflex of life on the writer." Cites Wharton as sharing the "remorseless spirit" of the Greek tragic muse. Names this--if not a novel--an impressive tragedy, and concludes that Wharton is truly a dramatist passing as a novelist.

R7.6   Anonymous. "Half a Dozen Stories." *Outlook* 99 (21 October 1911): 405.

Cites the quality of artistic workmanship, the unity of insight, structural skill and style. However, hopes in subsequent fiction she "will bring her great talent to bear on normal people and situations."

R7.7   Anonymous. Review of *Ethan Frome*. *Saturday Review* (London) 112 (18 November 1911): 650.

Discusses *Ethan Frome* as a novel in that it encompasses the lives of a few characters, and as a short story with its length and unified mood. Although the writing is termed "singularly beautiful," the reviewer criticizes the ending as without purpose and feels that if Wharton had let the characters die, the book would rank high indeed and their defiance, though sad, would be uplifting. As it stands: "There are things too terrible in their failure to be told humanly from creature to creature." We cover our eyes, the reviewer claims, at this ending, and do not at the spectacle of great tragedy.

R7.8   Cooper, Frederic T. "Ethan Frome." *Bookman* 34 (November 1911): 312.

Argues it is hard to forgive the utter remorselessness here, contending the one justification for a work so flawless in technique and relentless in substance is art for art's sake.

R7.9   G., J. "Sous la neige." *Revue Critique Des Idées et des Livres* 18 (10 August 1912): 380-81.

In French. Cites the classical quality of Greek tragedy, terming the book stripped down from Lily Bart into essential elements.

R7.10   Maury, Lucien. "Une Romancière américaine: Mme. E. Wharton." *Revue Bleue* 2 (3 August 1912): 154-57.

In French. Terms this a strong book, commenting other authors would have written a poem of death, but the sense of life triumphs in the English language novel where pity and love of virtue are great.

R7.11   Rachilde, C. "Sous la neige, par Edith Wharton." *Mercure de France* 98 (1 July 1912): 123.

In French. Terms *Ethan Frome* a curious, intelligent novel whose intimate details remind one of Dickens's interiors. Objects it ends in a very childish failed suicide attempt that doesn't jibe with the "cerebral tranquility" of the two protagonists.

Ethan Frome--Books

R7.12   Bloom, Lynne G. *Ethan Frome: A Critical Commentary.* New York: American R.D.M. Corporation, 1964.
         * From Springer, K14.

R7.13   Nevius, Blake. *Edith Wharton's* Ethan Frome: *The Story With Sources and Commentary.* New York: Scribner's, 1968.
         Includes an Introduction [R7.19]; the text; Wharton's early version of the "Prologue"; the "Writing of *Ethan Frome*" from *Colophon* [F3.11], and "The Genesis of *Ethan Frome*" from *A Backward Glance* [E9]; on "Telling a short story" from *The Writing of Fiction* [E8]. Includes excerpts from Percy Lubbock's "Novels of Edith Wharton" [O49]; Sergeant's "Idealized New England" [R7.49]; Burdett's "Edith Wharton and George Eliot" from *Contemporary American Authors* [O18]; Bernard De Voto's Scribner introduction [R7.14]; Brennan's "Structure and Metaphor" [R7.28]; Trilling's "Morality of Inertia" [R7.54]; and Bernard's "Imagery and Symbolism" [R7.24]. Nevius includes discussion of themes and backgrounds.

Ethan Frome--Introductions and Afterwords

R7.14   DeVoto, Bernard. "Introduction." *Ethan Frome.* New York: Scribner's, 1938. Rpt. R7.13.
         Terms *Ethan Frome* a "remarkable example of literary skill triumphing over deficiencies of experience and sympathy." Contends value lies in the technical expertise, with the characters but unmoving "literary"

villagers within the literary conventions of New England.

R7.15   Fadiman, Clifton. "Introduction." *Ethan Frome*. Limited Editions Club, 1939.

Contends *Ethan Frome* is not a classic, as it is devoid of passion and profound understanding. However, argues it lives because Puritanism is still such a strong force in American life and the quality of inarticulateness is still found in many people who don't know how to say that they don't want to be isolated. Maintains most of the characters of Wharton and James are bloodless--a "waxwork collection of elegant ghosts, whispering their involved relative clauses to a healthily unlistening world."

R7.16   Glendinning, Victoria. "Introduction." *Ethan Frome and Summer*. London: Oxford University Press, 1982.

Bio-critical introduction concentrates on *Ethan Frome*. Calls the two novels "changelings" in which Wharton tried to capture Gothic realities of the Berkshires. Notes the observer-narrator of Jamesian detachment and sensibility and contends Wharton switches sexes: Zeena=Teddy and Ethan Frome=Edith Wharton. Cites incest theme of *Summer*. Says Lawyer Royall named after Tyler Royall. Concludes "Edith never really seriously rebelled against her social background."

R7.17   Kazin, Alfred. "Afterword." *Ethan Frome*. New York: Collier Books, 1987.

Notes the "irresistible necessity," the sense of frustration that hangs over her idea of love. Contends the painful starkness "derives in part from [her] extreme consciousness of class," and that, despite sympathy for the lovers, she is "an old-fashioned American ... the strictest of moralists."

R7.18   Munn, Helen. "Foreword." *Ethan Frome*. New York: Scribner's, 1960.

* Not seen.

R7.19   Nevius, Blake. "Introduction." *Ethan Frome*. In *Edith Wharton's* Ethan Frome: *The Story with Sources and Commentary*. New York: Scribner's, 1968.

Terms the love affair--written out of Edith Wharton's deepest personal experience--one of the most moving episodes in American fiction. Interprets the novel biographically--in light of Wharton's marriage and her love for Berry, noting the theme of the greater personality imprisoned by the lesser. [In R7.13]

R7.20   Wolff, Cynthia Griffin. "Introduction." *Ethan Frome*. New York: New American Library (Signet Classics): 1986.

Reiterates the thesis of her *A Feast of Words* that maternal rejection was the source of Wharton's vision and struggle, contending that the images of cold and starvation in *Ethan Frome*, so important biographically, are here rendered through the vision of the narrator and stem from a "lethal passivity" in the characters. Thus, Wharton, through her art, asserts command over the troubling conflicts of her early life. [See N28]

Ethan Frome--Criticism

R7.21   Ammons, Elizabeth. "Edith Wharton's *Ethan Frome* and the Question of Meaning." *Studies in American Fiction* 7 (1979): 127-40.

Insightful analysis of the "deliberately inverted" fairy tale pattern in *Ethan Frome*. Cites the realistic social criticism and the narrative frame which "dramatizes a particular, and deeply rooted, male fear of woman." Finds a "coherent moral pattern" of cultural criticism: The isolated woman can become the witch. [See N1]

R7.22   Aomi, Miyoko. "A Study of Edith Wharton: The Characteristics of *Ethan Frome*." *Collected Essays:*

Kyoritsu Women's Junior College No. 9 (December 1965): 102-16.

In Japanese. Available Cornell. Very general biographical data, based on Irving Howe [N14], Louis Auchincloss [N2] and Millicent Bell [M6], describing Wharton's life and *Ethan Frome*, emphasizing its simple plot and great strength. Addressed to a general Japanese audience as an introduction to Wharton.

R7.23　Becker, May Lamberton. "Read This One First." *Scholastic* 31 (16 October 1937): 20-E.

As a disciple of Henry James, "she was able to use his method more successfully than he himself." *Ethan Frome* is to be read first for her art at its finest and most delicate pitch of apparently effortless perfection." Notes French title "Sous la Neige" ["Under the Snow"] is better, more descriptive because of implication of "volcanic emotions that lie beneath the chilly surface of north character and what we used to call 'the New England conscience'."

R7.24　Bernard, Kenneth. "Imagery and Symbolism in *Ethan Frome.*" *College English* 22 (December 1961): 178-84.

Maintains Wharton solved the difficulty of inarticulate characters through imagery and symbolism. Discusses compatibility of setting and character, use of light and dark and sexual (particularly the pickle dish) symbolism. [In R7.13]

R7.25　Bewley, Marius. "Mrs. Wharton's Mask." *New York Review of Books*, 24 September 1964, p.7-9.

Written on the re-issue of *A Backward Glance*, *Summer* and *Old New York*. Quotes from Edmund Wilson's comments on questions left unanswered by Percy Lubbock's *Portrait of Edith Wharton* and Trilling's "The Morality of Inertia." Notes that *A Backward Glance* chronicles merely the public Mrs. Wharton and cites the need for a definitive biography once the Yale papers are opened. Compelling response to Trilling in the extended analysis of *Ethan Frome* and the speculations that it arose from Wharton's own situation. Terms *Summer*, with its seduction theme, dated and a bore. Contends naturalism in *Summer* works to her detriment. Contends "False Dawn" leaves a promising subject undeveloped and the other novellas seem to "dynamite" a social structure she is commonly assumed to celebrate.

R7.26   Bjorkman, Edwin A. "The Greater Edith Wharton." *Voices of Tomorrow: Critical Studies of the New Spirit in Literature*. New York: Mitchell Kennerley, 1913. 290-304.

Analysis of *Ethan Frome* in chapter "The Greater Edith Wharton." Terms the tragedy here social, not personal, in which the characters cease to be individuals, but represent "whole social strata." Contends that Wharton has passed from individual to social art with fate here logical rather than unkind. Criticizes implication that romantic love would have fulfilled Ethan, arguing that it is no answer for the problems of Starkfield.

R7.27   Blackall, Jean Frantz. "The Sledding Accident in Ethan Frome." *Studies in Short Fiction* 21 (Spring 1984): 145-46.

Argues Ethan's wanting to sit ahead of Mattie is neither regressive nor infantile, but rather indicates his love of nature and affirmation of the values of home and protectiveness. Corroborates argument with newspaper account of an actual sledding accident stemming from a young woman's insistence on steering.

R7.28   Brennan, Joseph X. "*Ethan Frome*: Structure and Metaphor." *Modern Fiction Studies* 3 (Winter 1961): 347-56.

Argues that the intricate structure of the novel demands an analysis of the very important place of the narrator who is "actually a writer in disguise with the technical skill of a professional novelist and the sensibility of a poet." Contends that Ethan's tragic love is "so thoroughly informed by the sensibility and imagination of its narrator that the story can be adequately analyzed only in terms of that relationship," and that the novel is best judged in terms of the narrator's mind rather than in terms of psychological realism, for the characters are more imagined than real. Discusses chief pattern of contrast as between indoors and outside. [In R7.13]

R7.29   Bruce, Charles. "Circularity: Theme and Structure in *Ethan Frome*." *Studies and Critiques* 1 (1966): 78-81.
         Demonstrates the use of circularity in both theme and structure in *Ethan Frome* to develop the theme of inescapable determinism.

R7.30   Deegan, Dorothy Y. *The Stereotype of the Single Woman in American Novels*. New York: Octagon, 1951.
         Work is a study of single women in the American novel to determine what stereotypes exist and to promote awareness of them and to increase options for women. Treats Mattie Silver in *Ethan Frome*, arguing that Mattie's tragedy results from her lack of economic independence and that Wharton condemns her behavior and metes out a long, poignant period of suffering. Briefly mentions *The House of Mirth* and *The Old Maid*.

R7.31   Eggenschwiler, David. "The Ordered Disorder of Ethan Frome." *Studies in the Novel* 9 (1977): 237-46.
         Takes up both Trilling's argument that *Ethan Frome*'s universe is cruelly incomprehensible, and Kenneth Bernard's that a weak Ethan causes his own tragedy. Feels that the novel is too complex for simple interpretations: "Wharton will have it both ways, showing that man does determine his life in a universe that is not chaotic, but also showing that his lot is hard, his choices difficult ... [which is] not a perversely ambiguous pattern, but a strictly classical one." Discusses inner conflict in Ethan between desire for

freedom and excitement and stability.   [See R7.24, R7.54]

R7.32   Franciosa, Massimo. "Piu e meno dei maestri." *La Fiera Letteraria* 8 (1 November 1953): 1-2.
In Italian. Discusses influence of James and Hawthorne on Wharton--with commentary on *Ethan Frome*. Notes James's technique of the observer narrator and the Hawthornian suspense in that the terrible situation is not clear until the very end.

R7.33   Hafley, James. "The Case Against *Ethan Frome*." *Fresco* 1 (1961): 194-201.
Argues that *Ethan Frome* is full of improbabilities and inconsistencies and traces many of these.   Main objection is that the book isn't fully artistically or morally imagined in that the events happen, without true organic relation, *to* Ethan Frome, denying the novel meaning.

R7.34   Happel, Richard V. "Notes and Footnotes." *The Berkshire Eagle*, 25 February 1976, p.20.
For account of the original sledding accident upon which Wharton based the novel, see *Berkshire Eagle*, 12 March 1904, p. 1.

R7.35   Hays, Peter S. "First and Last in Ethan Frome." *NMAL: Notes on Modern American Literature* 1 (1977): Item #15.
Argues that Ethan putting himself "chivalrously" first on the sled iconographically presents his basic conflict between desire and duty and the unwelcome outcome--that his body protects Mattie from death--is symbolic of what has happened all his life when he takes on responsibility.

R7.36   Hays, Peter. "Wharton's Splintered Realism." *Edith Wharton Newsletter* 2.1 (Spring 1985): 6.

Notes Wharton's minor misrepresentations of a male mind in *EF* and her mistake in having Ethan deliver logs, not boards, to Hale.

R7.37   Herron, Ima Honaker. *The Small Town in American Drama*. Dallas: Southern Methodist University Press, 1969.

Discusses circumstances surrounding Owen and Donald Davis's dramatization of *Ethan Frome* and then critiques the adaptation, praising its power.

R7.38   Hovey, R.B. "*Ethan Frome*: A Controversy about Modernizing It." *American Literary Realism* 19 (Fall 1986): 4-20.

Argues that such modern interpretations as those of Elizabeth Ammons and Cynthia Griffin Woolf oversimplify the painful moral questions Wharton raises. Contends Ammons "edges toward a tract for Women's Lib" and Woolf "narrows toward the thesis-ridden" while concentrating too much on the unreliable narrator. Maintains the essential realism of the text: Zeena's neurosis is the destructive force. [See R7.21, N1, N28, R7.55]

R7.39   Iyengoor, K. R. Srinivasa. "A Note on 'Ethan Frome'." *Literary Criterion* 5 (Winter 1962): 168-78.

Argues against Trilling that the characters do make reasoned choices. Notes the illuminating incident of the pickle dish and draws parallels with love triangle situations in Ford Madox Ford's *The Good Soldier* and Tagore's *The Garden*. Defines the theme as both the consequences of poverty and the problem of a possessive wife in a marriage triangle. [See R7.54]

R7.40   MacCallan, W. P. "The French Draft of *Ethan Frome*." *Yale University Library Gazette* 27 (July 1952): 38-47.

Contains the French draft of *Ethan Frome* with editorial comments, containing the summation that it has little interest in that "the style is bad, the descriptions seem dragged in, the character of Mattie lacks definition, and the ending is unsatisfactory." Notes the most important differences are the lack of the suicide attempt and the character of the narrator.

R7.41   Murad, Orlene. "Edith Wharton and *Ethan Frome*." *Modern Language Studies* 13 (Summer 1983): 90-103.

Argues the biographical tie between Edith Wharton and Ethan Frome explains inconsistencies in the novel and accounts for its great power: "She has ... pushed on to Ethan the gruelling life ... she herself would have had to live had she tried to fathom and relieve her husband's despair." Maintains the narrator, modelled on a Balzac-Browning concept of multiple approach which is actually soon abandoned, is "condescending, pallid, unconvincing."

R7.42   Nevius, Blake. "*Ethan Frome* and the Themes of Edith Wharton's Fiction." *New England Quarterly* 24 (June 1951):   197-207.

Discusses theme of her work, after 1907 particularly, as the "immersion of the larger in the smaller nature which is one of the mysteries of the moral life." Employs *Ethan Frome*, as he says, as a "peg" on which to hang his generalizations about her themes. Notes a second theme becomes the question of the moral obligation to those who have a legal claim on one's loyalty. [See N23]

R7.43   Puknat, E. M., and S.B. Puknat. "Edith Wharton and Gottfried Keller." *Comparative Literature* 21 (Summer 1969): 245-54.

Demonstrates numerous similarities between *Ethan Frome* and Keller's *A Village Romeo and Juliet*. Tracks external parallels as well as "specific modes of expression used in the internal development both of motifs and characters."

R7.44   Randall, David A., and John T. Winterich. "Wharton, Edith: *Ethan Frome*." *Publishers' Weekly* 138 (20 July 1940): 191-92.

Bibliographical data including circumstances of composition. Notes the English version was a fresh start since the copybook with the French exercise was misplaced.

R7.45   Ransom, John Crowe. "Characters and Character: A Note on Fiction." *American Review* 6 (January 1936): 271-88.

Uses *Ethan Frome*'s narrative technique--the creation of a consciousness somewhat like the author's to tell the story--as springboard for a discussion of narrative technique and the disappearance of the author in modern fiction. Concludes that Wharton was unsuccessful in rendering Ethan's mind because he was a character "whom her special qualifications do not permit her to illuminate." Concludes with a list of principles for choice and placement of the narrator.

R7.46   Rose, Alan Henry. "Such Depths of Sad Initiation: Edith Wharton and New England." *New England Quarterly* 50 (1977): 423-39.

In a discussion, primarily of *Ethan Frome* and *Summer*, critic demonstrates how the use of the New England setting of "cultural emptiness" freed Wharton's imagination "to range in a manner not duplicated in her cluttered urban world," and "[i]n these barren settings Wharton seems to have felt the full extent of the negative, the sense of the void ... fundamental to experience in America." Contends it is this "sense of void" which causes the lack of maturity and growth in her New England characters, particularly Ethan Frome and Charity Royall.

R7.47   Rusch, Frederick S. "Reality and the Puritan Mind: Jonathan Edwards and Ethan Frome." *Journal of Evolutionary Psychology* 4.3-4 (1983): 238-47.

Reading of *Ethan Frome* in light of the theory of moral decisions expressed in Jonathan Edwards' *Freedom of the Will*. Argues Ethan is not the purely determined naturalistic protagonist, but his decisions have been the products of moral causes, and therefore he is "a prisoner of moral necessity, not natural necessity." Concludes that "although her depiction of the strict consequences of Ethan's choice suggests hopelessness, the fact that Ethan could make those choices is cause for some celebration."

R7.48   Sagarin, Edward. "Ethan Frome: Atonement Endures Until Darkness Descends." In *Raskolnikov and Others: Literary Images of Crime, Punishment, Redemption and Atonement*. New York: St. Martin's, 1981.

In study undertaken to enrich the field of criminology, criminologist author reads *Ethan Frome* as a paradigmatic study of the nature and meaning of "guilt, responsibility, punishment and expiation." Sees the bitter message as "Suffer, without repentance, without hope, just suffer." Characters are punished for no crime, suffer without hope of alleviation, and can never complete their atonement. Extensive story synopsis leads to conclusion that, cheated of death, characters are doomed to live past the sundown that will put an end to suffering.

R7.49   Sergeant, Elizabeth S. "Idealized New England." *New Republic* 3 (8 May 1915): 20-21.

Argues against Herrick's contention that Ethan Frome is less conditioned by environment than Lily Bart. Maintains that, despite the *vraisemblance*, Wharton has not understood the New Englander and therefore the novel is but a literary representation of life. [See O35. In R7.13]

R7.50   Shintri, Sarojini B. "In Defense of Ethan Frome." In *Indian Studies in American Fiction*. Edited by M.D. Naik, S.K. Desai and S. Mohoshi-Punekar. Dharwar: Karnatak University; Delhi: Macmillan India, 1974.

Argues Trilling is unfair, and responds to his accusations that Wharton had merely literary intentions in *Ethan Frome*, by citing Ethan's moral crisis, his stature, and Edith Wharton's own constricted life and basic seriousness as a writer. Also praises her narrative structure here. [See R7.54]

R7.51   Shuman, R. Baird. "The Continued Popularity of Ethan Frome." *Revue des Langues Vivantes* (Belgium) 37 (1971): 257-63.

Focuses on the Freudian sexual symbolism that develops the theme of the conflict between Puritan community mores and the passion of Ethan and Mattie and helps to explain Zeena Frome's hypochondria and masochism. Notes the work's value in discussions both of technique and family relationships.

R7.52   Thomas, J.D. "Marginalia on *Ethan Frome*." *American Literature* 27 (November 1955): 405-09.

Criticizes choice of male narrator, arguing that Edith Wharton only knew society men and makes significant mistakes in characterization. Also finds problems of chronology and a more important one in Ethan's motivation for not requesting the loan from Mr. Hale, which critic sees as neither true "repentance" nor "yielding," but as Wharton's clever dodge--having Ethan's decision at first motivated by his sense of responsibilities to the Hales, not his wife.

R7.53   Thomas, J.D. "Three American Tragedies: Notes on the Responsibilities of Fiction." *The South Central Bulletin* 20 (Winter 1960): 11-15.

Discusses the problem of censorship in literature with the contention that, although there should be a free flow of ideas, the critic may comment on the ethical element in a work when the work invites a readjustment of the reader's values. Contends reader identification with Neil Kingsblood in *Kingsblood Royal* and Ethan Frome, give these characters a strong moral force. Argues in *An American Tragedy* one feels more sympathy than identification with Clyde Griffiths.

R7.54   Trilling, Lionel. "The Morality of Inertia." *Great Moral Dilemmas in Literature, Past and Present*. Edited by

Robert M. MacIver. New York: The Institute for
Religious and Social Studies, 1956. 37-46.

Trilling's famous indictment criticizes Edith
Wharton as "a woman in whom we cannot fail to see a
limitation of heart, and this limitation makes itself
manifest as a literary and moral deficiency in her work."
She indulges herself by what she contrives--she is ...
"merely literary." Thus, "*Ethan Frome* [is] ... a dead
book, the product of ... cold hard literary will."
Discusses tragedy and its morality and comes to the
conclusion that Wharton "by reason ... of [her]
deficiencies" states an idea of considerable importance,
i.e., "moral inertia, the *not* making of moral decisions,
constitutes a large part of the moral life of humanity."
[Rpts. in R7.13, N14]

R7.55   Wolff, Cynthia Griffin. "Cold Ethan and 'Hot Ethan'."
College Literature 14.3 Edith Wharton Issue (1987): 230-
45.

Readings of *Ethan Frome* and *Summer* in relation
to Wharton's life when she wrote them and the crises
of James's illness and dependences, her marriage, and
the affair with Fullerton. Traces problems of
dependency as explored in the two works, concluding
that *Summer*'s ending reveals Wharton's conviction that
freedom is never complete and joy must be
"accommodated to the demands of the real world." [See
N28]

R7.56   Young, Margaret. "Unit on Ethan Frome." *High Point*
45 (March 1963): 63-72.

Lesson-plan guide for high school teachers of
Ethan Frome. Includes reviews from *Herald Tribune*
and *New York Times* of 1960 television production.
Appended are a vocabulary list and regents-exam-type
questions.

The Reef--Reviews

R8.1   Anonymous. "Current Fiction." *Nation* 95 (12 December 1912): 564.
        Objects that the action hinges on "carefully arranged contretemps," making a paltry story. Discusses the type of "blind alley" theme in which all possible solutions are unsatisfactory, and finds Wharton "addicted" to it.

R8.2   Anonymous. Review of *The Reef. New York Sun*, 23 November 1912, p. 8.
        Praises the stylistic simplicity and the opening prelude particularly, along with the psychological study of Anna Leath, who is one type of American woman, only uncommon in that here, "she tries to see beyond herself." Objects, however, to the story as "bitter, disheartening" and "sordid," wishing Wharton to look on brighter, nobler aspects of life.

R8.3   Anonymous. "Uncharted." *Saturday Review* (London) 114 (21 December 1912): 773-74.
        Blames the coincidences for the lack of credibility. Praises the delightful prose, but finds no hint of Wharton's theory of tragedy. Objects to the abnormal circumstances which prevent truly serious consideration.

R8.4   Brock, H.I. "Edith Wharton." *New York Times Book Review*, 24 November 1912, p. 685.
        Objects to Wharton's fiction in general, terming her plots the "vivisection" of her characters as she "diabolically" arranges events against them. However, praises realistic, vivid characterization of Sophy Viner.

R8.5   Michaud, Régis. "Le Roman aux Etats-Unis." *Revue du Mois* 15 (10 July 1913): 106-9.

In French. Notes the fashion of Racine, the tragic description of tragic mistakes and things unrevealed. Concludes Darrow realizes that Sophy Viner is the one he will never forget. Compares this to the Puritan style of Hawthorne.

R8.6   Willcocks, M.P. "A Tragedy of Four." *Bookman* (London) 43 (January 1913): 224-25.

Names the subject as the contrast between apparent victory and actual defeat for Anna Leath lost "when laying her hand on substance she found but shadow." Finds the character study simple but the spiritual tragedy very subtle. Notes the theme of the different attitudes men and women have toward love affairs. Objects that the men are phantoms, and her characters live in a vacuum, but praises the realistic women. Concludes that the defects stem from the Jamesian school.

The Reef--Introductions and Afterwords

R8.7   Auchincloss, Louis. "Introduction." *The Reef.* New York: Scribner's, 1965.

Discusses the Jamesian aspects of the novel. Speculates Fraser Leath was drawn from Walter Berry. Analyzes our problems understanding Darrow's view of Sophy.

R8.8   French, Marilyn. "Introduction." *The Reef.* London: Virago, 1986.

Argues *The Reef* is a novel of sexuality as it is "conceived of, felt, experienced by different people." Maintains Sophy Viner is the center and passion is the core, the reef. Thus, terms the last chapter the key. Contends the book is not a polemic for sexual liberation or repression, but a "deep, subtle, complex analysis of the implications for a society of seeing sexuality as tainted."

The Reef--Criticism

R8.9   Ammons, Elizabeth. "Fairy-Tale Love and *The Reef*." *American Literature* 47 (1976): 615-28.

Interprets *The Reef* in terms of the fairy-tale patterns of Sleeping Beauty and Cinderella, arguing the novel "exposes deluded female fantasies about love and marriage: false romantic visions generated and perpetuated by limitations imposed on women--in Sophy's case, economic dependence; in Anna's sexual repression." [See N1]

R8.10   Collins, Alexandra. "The Art of Self-Perception in Virginia Woolf's *Mrs. Dalloway* and Edith Wharton's *The Reef*." *Atlantis* 7.2 (Spring 1982): 47-58.

Traces similarities between Virginia Woolf's *Mrs. Dalloway* and Wharton's *The Reef* in that both authors are obsessed with entrapment in social convention, the search for spiritual freedom, relationship between present and past and share the attitude that art and creativity offer the best hope for social reformation. Notes Clarissa and Anna Leath are alike as aristocratic women of intuition; however, *Mrs. Dalloway* ends on an optimistic note whereas *The Reef* ends with Anna torn between spiritual release and possessive sexuality. Contends both writers were fascinated by society's spectacle, yet feared social conformity. Both Anna Leath and Clarissa Dalloway illustrate frustrations of woman's search for identity.

R8.11   Gargano, James W. "Edith Wharton's *The Reef*: The Genteel Woman's Quest for Knowledge." *Novel: A Forum on Fiction* 10 (1976): 40-48.

Reading of *The Reef* as Mrs. Wharton's conservative and classicist objection to Darrow's and

Sophy's conduct as the "'romantic lie' which promotes the idea of personal indulgence against the interests of the humane order," *but* finds "the meaning of the novel ... in Anna's penetration of the darkness," self-discovery, and personal growth. Defends *The Reef* against charges that it is dated: "The strong subject of *The Reef* ... is Anna's second chance for a freer and more expansive life."   Feels Anna's "liberation" culminates in a clarifying "epiphany."

R8.12   Gooder, Jean. "Unlocking Edith Wharton." *Cambridge Quarterly* 15.1 (1986): 33-52.
           Occasioned by the Virago Press reissues of Wharton's out-of-print work. Concentrates on *The Reef*, arguing it illuminates Wharton's "inmost self" and her understanding of the power of instinct beneath the ordered social surface. Traces title to remark made about the dangers of George Sand, and Paul de Musset's *Lui et Elle*--a fictional version of his brother's affair with Sand. Short critical comment on: "Roman Fever," "Xingu," "Bunner Sisters," "Autres Temps ...," *The Old Maid*, *MdeT*, "The Other Two," "Souls Belated," *FofT*, *Motor-Flight*, *ABG*, *Children*.

R8.13   Maynard, Moira. "Moral Integrity in *The Reef*: Justice to Anna Leath." *College Literature* 14.3 (1987): 285-95.
           Argues that the theme of *The Reef* is Anna Leath's awakening to moral maturity through her efforts to face reality, no matter how painful, and that Sophy Viner is actually an evader of some of the unpleasant realities of life and not as sensitive to the effect on others of her actions and decisions as is Anna.

R8.14   Raphael, Lev. "Fighting the Burden of Shame: A New Reading of *The Reef*." *The Journal of Evolutionary Psychology* 10.2 and 3 (August 1989): 208-22.
           Interprets *The Reef* in light of Silvan Tomkins's Affect Theory, particularly in the context of the affect of shame. Argues shame destroys the relationship between Anna Leath and George Darrow, distorts

Anna's identity and makes her incapable of loving or feeling freely. Striking new analysis of Darrow's shame, which is examined as the cause of his affair with Sophy Viner.

R8.15 Tuttleton, James. "Mocking Fate: Romantic Idealism in Edith Wharton's *The Reef*." *Studies in the Novel* 19.4 (Winter 1987): 459-74.

Insightful new reading of *The Reef* in light of the Fullerton letters argues that Wharton's departure from her customary structure of the episodic novel of manners was caused not only by James's influence but by her own need to give a formal pattern to her own chaotic emotions during and after her affair with Fullerton. Maintains that the ideal of a transcendent love that Anna Leath holds to is similar to Wharton's own response to the promiscuous Fullerton and that feminists who insist on idealizing Sophy Viner's freedom don't clearly understand or appreciate Wharton's own adherence to the ideal of a love grounded in mutual values and commitment. Argues the "contemporaneity of *The Reef* ... inheres in the image of the emerging independent heroine, much like the Mrs. Wharton of 1910, who holds to a romantic ideal of love and emotional and sexual fulfillment that is unsullied by desecrating compromises." Important comments on *Ethan Frome*, "Terminus," *Eternal Passion in English Poetry*, *The Fruit of the Tree* and "The Love Diary."

The Custom of the Country--Reviews

R9.1 Anonymous. Review of *The Custom of the Country*. *Athenaeum* (London), No. 4490 (15 November 1913): 554.

Notes the absence of sentimentality and the stress laid on environment and upbringing which makes her heroine "natural and pathetic." Praises characterization of Undine as sympathetic because

Wharton creates understanding. Terms the novel a courageous study of Americans.

R9.2   Anonymous. Review of *The Custom of the Country*. *Bookman* (London) 45 (March 1914): 330.
                Defines custom of the title as rapid, multiple marriage. Praises her artistic restraint, the description of Mrs. Spragg's isolation and loneliness, and the characterization, as well as lack of overt moralizing. Calls the unity and penetration here superior to her other work.

R9.3   Anonymous. "Customs of Two Countries." *Independent* 76 (13 November 1913): 313.
                States the "brief point" is the contrast between the customs of newer America versus older France. Defines the custom of the title as the American man's contempt for women, relegating them to a life of luxury away from Wall Street where true masculine passion lies.

R9.4   Anonymous. "The Custom of the Country." *Nation* 96 (15 May 1913): 494.
                Seeks to cast historical light on the novel. Terming Undine, the spending woman, as a stock character in newer fiction, explains her as the outgrowth of the American pioneer experience in which women made many sacrifices. Reviewer argues that women are at last able to enjoy the amenities of life, but that men, less adaptable, still have the habit of money-making; thus, for men to earn and women to spend has become an American cultural pattern.

R9.5   Anonymous. "Mrs. Wharton's New Novel." *Nation-Athenaeum* (London) 14 (December 1913): 446, 448
                Mostly plot summary, with the comment that Wharton has "compounded a portrait of perhaps the most detestable type of girl America has yet sent us."

R9.6   Anonymous. "Critical Reviews of the Season's Latest
          Books." *New York Sun*, 18 October 1913, p. 8.
                  Objects that, in her satire, Wharton has forgotten
          her art, creating abstract types, an "ideal monster,"
          rather than real men and women.   However, it is
          interesting to see Wharton move from her sphere."

R9.7   Anonymous. "The Hundred Best Books of the Year."
          New York Times Book Review, 30 November 1913, p.
          664.
                  Praises book as an important satire on tendencies
          in modern society, and comments that she is
          particularly fitted to develop this comparison of the
          new "smart set" with the old social order.   Finds
          Undine more realistic than *Vanity Fair*'s Becky Sharp.

R9.8   Anonymous. "Five New Novels by Women." *Outlook* 105
          (15 November 1913): 571.
                  Terms the social study merciless and penetrating
          but just because Wharton knows her material.

R9.9   Anonymous. "Novels." *Saturday Review* (London) (22
          November 1913): 658-59.
                  Defines the title's custom as the divorce court,
          and the novel as a "scathing exposure of the scandals of
          divorce and of the mean standards of a certain section
          of American society.   Praises brilliance, and says it
          should be read as a parable."

R9.10   B., H.W. "Mrs. Wharton's Manner." *Nation* 97 (30
          October 1913): 404-05.
                  Traces Wharton's career up to this point and
          then makes a number of critical comments, finding
          Undine a caricature who does not hold interest through
          such a long book and the characters in general
          unsympathetic. Finally, he questions Wharton's growing
          inclination toward satire, terming it "a dubious sign in
          a writer who has passed a certain age." Complains that
          Wharton has never "found herself."   Years ago, he

asserts, she was among the best American writers, but not now.

R9.11   Colby, F.M. "The Book of the Month." *North American Review* 199 (February 1914): 294-99.
          Finds book's primary interest lies in the "social scene." Includes a long discussion of Undine as a familiar type of American wife in literature, citing examples. Praises Wharton's ability, in a word or two, to make a type vivid, and extinguish a pretension."

R9.12   Cooper, Frederic Taber. Review of *The Custom of the Country*. *Bookman* 38 (December 1913): 416-17.
          Praises the novel as one of Wharton's finest achievements with its "brilliantly cynical picture of feminine ruthlessness."

R9.13   Edgett, Edwin Francis. "Edith Wharton's New Novel: An Extremely Conventional Portrayal of the Social Climber." *Boston Evening Transcript*, 18 October 1913, Part 3, p. 8.
          Laments her departure from the realistic novel. Complains that the theme of the social climber, given no dignity here, is time-worn and time- "unhonored." Criticizes the "constant recourse to exaggeration" and the "writing to startle, to slander, to hyperbolize." Finds a confusion in point of view between Undine and the author's perceptions.

R9.14   F., L.M. "Mrs. Wharton's Novel." *New York Times Book Review*, 19 October 1913, p. 557.
          Defines custom of title as "system of limited, half-contemptuous indulgence of lavishing one's fortune upon one's womenfolk, but withholding one's confidence." Praises Undine's reality, and notes that although the theme of the utterly selfish woman is not new, still Wharton develops it particularly skillfully, delicately and ruthlessly.

The Custom of the Country--Introductions and Afterwords

R9.15 French, Marilyn. "Introduction." *The Custom of the Country*. New York: Berkley, 1981.
   * Not seen.

R9.16 Nevius, Blake. "Introduction." *The Custom of the Country*. New York: Scribner's, 1956.
   Notes the European influence on the panoramic social novel and sources for Undine both in the type of the selfish, luxury-loving American "new Woman" and Cissy Eccleston in Howard Sturgis's *Belchamber*. Argues that Undine became a powerful permanent symbol in our culture of "the spiritual waste which the subduing of a continent entailed."

R9.17 Wolff, Cynthia Griffin. "Introduction." *The Custom of the Country*. New York: Collier Books, 1987.
   Terms this the most ambitious of Wharton's works--her contribution to the American epic. Notes there is no "moral center" with which to contrast Undine. Explains Wharton draws on the literary tradition of myth, the business novel and Jacobean drama. Contends Wharton did not write about the social and economic revolution of the time, but the "shadow drama"--the social domain of women.

The Custom of the Country--Criticism

R9.18 Anonymous. "Topics of the Week." *New York Times Book Review*, 2 November 1913, p.596.
   Praises the economy and realism of Abner Spragg's portrait. Terms him responsible for the custom of the country and that makes possible the feminine egoism of an Undine as well as a "colossal impersonation of the paternal sentiment." A separate

note comments on Wharton's juxtaposition of two societies.

R9.19   Ammons, Elizabeth. "The Business of Marriage in Edith Wharton's *The Custom of the Country*." *Criticism* 16 (1974): 326-38.

Feminist criticism by Ammons is invariably thoughtful, scholarly and well written. Here, she takes up the critical argument that Wharton is conservative, contending that her real subject matter is woman, and that she "directs her social criticism--which is not conservative until after WWI--primarily against cultural attitudes which demean or inhibit women." Focus of article is the characterization of Undine Spragg, which Ammons argues is symbolic, and the institution of marriage in the leisure class which Ammons sees as the novel's object of attack. Contends that Undine is the "monstrously perfect result" of an exploitive economic system and that she is not admirable because "within marriage, there is for women no admirable way to accept or escape male proprietorship." [See N1]

R9.20   Cabell, James Branch. *Beyond Life*. New York: Robert M. McBride and Co. (1919). 262.

Criticizes the "vitalness" of *The Custom of the Country* as founded upon untruth because the characters are all a "rather nasty and very dull blackness."

R9.21   Candela, Joseph L., Jr. "The Domestic Orientation of American Novels, 1893-1913." *American Literary Realism* 13 (Spring 1980): 1-18.

Study of Stephen Crane's *Maggie*, Kate Chopin's *The Awakening*, Theodore Dreiser's *Sister Carrie*, Upton Sinclair's *The Jungle* and *The Custom of the Country* treats family-related themes, arguing they reflect the growing concern about the instability of the family in industrialized society. Defines *The Custom of the Country* as a problem novel exploring the causes and effects of divorce--the main point found in the characterization of Paul Marvell: Children pay the penalty.

R9.22   Caserio, Robert L. "Edith Wharton and the Fiction of Public Commentary." *Western Humanities Review* 40 (Autumn 1986): 189-208.

Studies *The Custom of the Country* in light of theories of realism, arguing that "aboriginal" critics equate realist novels with history and sociological or political commentary (e.g., Edmund Wilson, Lionel Trilling, Diana Trilling, Irving Howe and Alfred Kazin) and neglect the importance of Elmer Moffatt, upon whom this reading--utilizing the theories of Jameson, Arendt, Eco, Saussure and Bakhtin--concentrates. Bowen is analyzed also and identified as Henry James.

R9.23   Collins, Alexandra. "The Noyade of Marriage in Edith Wharton's *The Custom of the Country*." *English Studies in Canada* 9.2 (June 1983): 197-212.

Analysis of Ralph Marvell's character and the Undine myth in relation to his conflicts (social reality versus an ideal) within the context of the novel as a comprehensive view of marriage immediately prior to WWI.

R9.24   Huneker, James. "Three Disagreeable Girls." *Forum* 52 (November 1914): 765-76. Rpt. *Ivory Apes and Peacocks*. New York: Scribner's, 1915.

Discusses Ibsen's Hedda Gabler, George Moore's Mildred Lawson and Undine Spragg. Contends that Wharton is "glacially cruel" to American women of this type, but maintains they are realistic. Calls Undine the newest variation of Daisy Miller, and the "most disagreeable girl in newest fiction." Notes the "clear hard atmosphere of the book is tempered by a tragic and humorous irony." Maintains that these are not necessarily portraits of the New Woman, but that craving for novelty in characterization has changed the nature of the heroine.

R9.25   McHaney, Thomas L. "Fouqué's Undine and Edith
          Wharton's *Custom of the Country.*" *Revue de Littérature
          Comparée* (Tours-Cedex, France) 45 (1971): 180-86.
                    Suggests the nineteenth-century German romance
          by Friedrich, Baron de la Motte Fouqué, *Undine* (1811)
          is the source of Undine Spragg. Notes development of
          Undine Spragg, at first an object of ridicule, into truly
          a soulless creature, and contends that Ralph Marvell's
          death "removes the Undine from the novel, as if his
          imagination alone could sustain the image." Points up
          the contrast between Fouque's lovely heroine and
          materialistic Undine Spragg. [Also see N16]

R9.26   Morrow, Nancy. "Games and Conflict in Edith
          Wharton's *The Custom of the Country.*" *American
          Literary Realism* 17 (Spring 1984): 32-39.
                    Analyzes the structural and metaphoric aspects of
          the destructive social games in *The Custom of the
          Country.*

R9.27   Price, Alan. "Dreiser's Cowperwood and Wharton's
          Undine Spragg: A Match Made in Spencer's Heaven."
          The Markham Review 16 (Spring-Summer 1987): 37-39.
                    Finds similarities between Dreiser's Frank
          Cowperwood in *Sister Carrie* and Wharton's Undine
          Spragg in that both are the "fictional embodiments of
          the ideas of Herbert Spencer and other apologists for
          Social Darwinism." Concludes, however, that whereas
          Cowperwood's values "open the possibility of the
          triumph of the individual over fate," Wharton views
          Undine's blind self-interest as destructive of the social
          order. [See X58]

R9.28   Tintner, Adeline R. "Henry James's 'Julia Bride': A
          Source for Chapter Nine in Edith Wharton's *The
          Custom of the Country.*" *NMAL: Notes on Modern
          American Literature* 9.3 (1985): Item 16.
                    Notes the striking resemblance of Chapter IX in
          The Custom of the Country to Part III of James's "Julia
          Bride."

R9.29   Tintner, Adeline R. "A Source from *Roderick Hudson*
for the Title of *The Custom of the Country*." NMAL:
Notes on Modern American Literature 1 (1977): Item 34.
        Suggests that the title comes from James's
Roderick Hudson rather than from the Jacobean play of
that name by Fletcher and Massinger, as Cynthia
Griffin Wolff speculates. [See N28]

Summer--Reviews

R10.1   Anonymous. Review of *Summer. Athenaeum* (London)
No. 4623 (November 1917): 597.
        Terms this a thoroughly individual treatment of
an old theme, a masterpiece of refined, economical art.

R10.2   Anonymous. Review of *Summer. Catholic World* 106
(October 1917): 127-28.
        Objects to lack of universality that would excite
sympathy. Finds characters unreal, viewed with
detachment, making the story "artifice, not life."

R10.3   Anonymous. "Plots and People." *Nation* 105 (2 August
1917): 124-25.
        Finds novel falls short of *Ethan Frome* in tragic
force, but calls Royall and Charity realistic, although
the "young Lothario" and the coincidences which mar
the action's integrity are not.

R10.4   Anonymous. "Mrs. Wharton's Story of New England."
New York Times Book Review, 8 July 1917, p. 253.
        Terms this minor Wharton, with only a trace of
the compelling quality of *Ethan Frome*. Praises analysis
of Charity's emotions and the style.

R10.5   Anonymous. "The New Books." *Outlook* 116 (1 August
1917): 522.

Terms the book depressing, eliciting pity but dragging the reader "without much purpose through these fictional sorrows."

R10.6   Anonymous. "Novels Whose Scenes are Laid in New England." *Review of Reviews* 56 (September 1917): 333.

Terms this a sordid story with two-dimensional characters. However, argues that it is a faithful representation of pre-automobile, rural New England. Comments that she is so skilled in portraiture, "the sentences bite like the acids of the etcher."

R10.7   Anonymous. "Fiction in Brief." *Saturday Review* (London) 124 (3 November 1917): 352.

Defines this as a woman's story told by a woman artist in which Wharton has abandoned "hair-splitting subtlety which ... marred her work" for simplicity in the picture of a young woman's emotional awakening.

R10.8   Anonymous. Review of *Summer*. *Spectator* 119 (13 October 1917): 389.

Questions the realism of the characterization, objecting that Lawyer Royall and Charity are difficult to comprehend, but praises simplicity of plot and descriptive passages.

R10.9   Anonymous. "Mrs. Wharton's '*Summer*'." *Springfield Republican*, 5 August 1917, Magazine Section, p. 15.

Answers those who charge Wharton with coldness with the argument that she is always truthful and treats unsympathetic subjects unsympathetically. Notes appeal of Charity, and calls the novel brilliantly conceived, with tense passages and striking portrayals of passions, yet contends "its conception of New England character is that of a "literary," even a romantic, visitor.

R10.10   Anonymous. Review of *Summer*. *Times Literary Supplement*, 27 September 1917, p. 464.

Praises Charity's characterization, finding the novel matches, and even in some respects surpasses,

Ethan Frome. Compares her feeling for incident with Flaubert, and finds this quality best in *Summer.*

R10.11   Boynton, H.W. "Outstanding Novels of the Year." *Nation* 105 (29 November 1917): 600.

Brief mention terms *Summer* moving, "hovering between ... tragedy and squalor" but finally drawn back by the force of "saving goodness in human nature, to a foothold of safety and of real if wintry sunshine."

R10.12   Boynton, H.W. "Some Stories of the Month." *Bookman* 46 (September 1917): 93-94.

Notes that Wharton has come perilously near being the "idol of snobs," but here she interprets life in the elements. Also argues that those who accuse her of bitterness should note that the "whole effect" hangs upon recognition "of the power of simple human goodness ... to make life worth living."

R10.13   Edgett, Edwin Francis. "Edith Wharton's Tale of Thwarted Love." *Boston Evening Transcript*, 25 July 1917, Part 2, p. 6.

Strongly objects to the picture of New England life and people as totally unrealistic, to the story as sluggish and commonplace, with casually sketched characters.

R10.14   Gilman, Lawrence. "The Book of the Month: Mrs. Wharton Reverts to Shaw." *North American Review* 206 (August 1917): 304-07.

Commends Wharton for abandoning romantic sentimentalism and portraying women as Shaw recommended, not as the helpless prey of man. Applauds her "grave contempt for the sexual cliches of romance."

R10.15   H[ackett], F[rancis]. "Loading the Dice." *New Republic* 11 (14 July 1917): 311-12. Rpt. *Horizons, A Book of Criticism.* New York: Huebsch, 1918.

Maintains the falsity here stems from Wharton's propensity to dramatize frustration. The story, loaded with human tragedy, is handled too mechanistically to be realistic, and therefore is empty, suggesting "the failings of a person who is capable of going slumming among souls."

R10.16   Macy, John. "Edith Wharton." *Dial* 63 (30 August 1917): 161-62.

Defends Wharton against those who say all she can write about is upper-class New York. Describes her New Englanders as elemental victims of circumstance but finds great realism and no cold detachment in their portrayal. Describes the tragedies of *Ethan Frome* and *Summer* as not shattered love affairs but stunted lives.

R10.17   Mondadon, Louis de. "Edith Wharton: Plein Eté." *Etudes* 157 (October-December 1918): 378.

In French. Praises the capable pen of *Summer* as it describes the customs of an American village and cites the author's talent for analysis, but doesn't recommend the book for everybody because of the importance given to the game of passion and the nature of the facts revealed.

Summer--Introductions and Afterwords

R10.18   French, Marilyn. "Introduction." *Summer*. New York: Collier Books, 1987.

Insightful introduction in three parts: Part I: Notes the problems of gender that beset her reputation in a biographical overview; Part II: Critical exegesis of several works, and a thematic overview of Wharton. Notes main theme is her concern for "the emotional moral life especially in the area of sexuality." Contends "the profundity of her analyses of female attitudes toward sex has still not been recognized." Part II deals with *Summer*, her finest novel. Finds the horror of

Summer in responses to sexuality--abortionist, prostitution, enforced marriage: "What is ugly is the female body as commodity." Contends the cyclical pattern of nature saves the novel from a sense of despair.

R10.19   Wolff, Cynthia Griffin. "Introduction." *Summer*. New York: Harper and Row (Perennial Library Edition), 1979.

Reading of *Summer* as a new type of female *Bildungsroman*--dealing frankly with female sexuality. Discusses Wharton's own experience growing up culminating in her sexual awakening with Fullerton. [See N28]

Summer--Criticism

R10.20   Crowley, John W. "The Unmastered Streak: Feminist Themes in Wharton's *Summer.*" *American Literary Realism 1870-1910* 15.1 (Spring 1982): 86-96.

Finds *Summer* radically feminist, with its contempt for romantic cliches rooted in a paternalistic attitude toward women. Royall's "assumption that women are a form of property underlies all his actions regarding Charity, but he is never conscious of this assumption. Neither is Charity...." Feels the marriage signifies "her final entrapment in the dependent childish identity from which North Dormer permits her no escape."

R10.21   Gilbert, Sandra M. "Life's Empty Pack: Notes Toward a Literary Daughteronomy." *Critical Inquiry* 11.3 (March 1985): 355-84.

Feminist analysis juxtaposing George Eliot's *Silas Marner* and *Summer* ("a revisionary daughter-text") in a study of female sexuality in patriarchal society and father-daughter relationships. Myth imagery is cited with the recurring pattern of the death of the mother and the daughter symbolically wedded to the father--i.e., assuming her culturally prescribed role.

R10.22   Gupta, Linda Roberta. "Fathers and Daughters in Women's Novels." Ph.D. dissertation. The American University, 1983.
          For abstract see DAI, 44 (1983), 1783A. Covers the fiction of Jane Austen, Elizabeth Gaskell, Charlotte Bronte, Kate Chopin, Edith Wharton, Virginia Woolf, Elizabeth Bowen, Margaret Atwood, and Mary Gordon. Argues *Summer* is the story of a daughter's struggle for maturity and independence.

R10.23   Hammer, Andrea Gale. "Recitations of the Past: Identity in Novels by Edith Wharton, Ellen Glasgow, and Carson McCullers." Ph.D. dissertation. University of California (Davis): 1981.
          For abstract see DAI, 42 (1982), 5121A.

R10.24   Lawson, Richard H. "The Influence of Gottfried Keller on Edith Wharton." *Revue de Littérature Comparée* 42 (July-September 1968): 366-79.
          Wharton wrote *Summer* immediately after participating in the translating, editing, and publishing of an English version of Gottfried Keller's *Romeo und Julia auf dem Dorfe*. Lawson traces similarities between the two works, speculating that, although *Summer* is not an imitation of Keller, his work was probably on her mind when she wrote the novel. [See N16]

R10.25   Morante, Linda. "The Desolation of Charity Royall: Imagery in Edith Wharton's *Summer*." *Colby Library Quarterly* 18.4 (December 1982): 241-48.
          Argues that the wasteland imagery of *Summer* reinforces the themes of "isolation, deprivation, and entrapment of the self in a culturally destitute New England town" and that this "poetic fabric becomes the essential key to character analysis" and theme.

R10.26   Walker, Nancy A. "'Seduced and Abandoned':
          Convention and Reality in Edith Wharton's *Summer*."
          Studies in American Fiction 11.1 (Spring 1983): 107-14.
                  Contends that although Wharton chooses the
          classic seduced and abandoned theme, her
          characterizations are far more realistic than in usual
          treatments of the theme, and the novel develops into a
          study of the ambiguity of human relationships. Terms
          the major force in *Summer* "the realistic, unsentimental"
          Charity.

R10.27   Wershoven, Carol. "The Divided Conflict of Edith
          Wharton's *Summer*." *Colby Library Quarterly* 21.1
          (March 1985): 5-10.
                  Reading of *Summer* as the story of Royall and
          Charity who both "come to terms with their destructive
          illusions in order to lead adult lives." [See N27]

R10.28   White, Barbara A. "Edith Wharton's *Summer* and
          'Woman's Fiction.'" *Essays in Literature* 11 (Fall 1984):
          223-35.
                  See her *Growing Up Female* for analysis of
          Summer in terms of the conventions of women's fiction.
          [See R10.29]

R10.29   White, Barbara A. "On the Threshold: Edith Wharton's
          Summer." In *Growing up Female: Adolescent Girlhood in
          American Fiction*. Westport, CT: Greenwood Press,
          1985.
                  Discusses *Summer* as a transitional novel away
          from the sentimental adolescent romance convention.
          Contends that although the plot follows the
          conventional pattern, the "texture of the novel and the
          characterization of the heroine are dramatically
          opposed" to the nineteenth-century model. Notes
          Wharton opens Charity's inner life and ironically
          comments on a society which encourages her to remain
          a child even as she assumes an adult role.

The Marne--Reviews

R11.1   Anonymous. "Echoes and Shadows." *Nation* 108 (11
           January 1919): 56.
                   Concentrates on plot summary under the general
           topic of the eagerness of young Americans to fight in
           France. Comments that she shows many Americans
           fighting not for "France the pitied but for France the
           adored."

R11.2   Anonymous. "Mrs. Wharton's Story of the Marne." *New
           York Times*, 8 December 1918, Section 7, p. 1.
                   Praises the book as beautifully written, and
           maintains that, though short, it conveys "much, if not
           the whole, of the meaning of the Marne, both to
           France and to America."

R11.3   Anonymous. Review of *The Marne*. *Times Literary
           Supplement*, 19 December 1918, p. 642.
                   Praises the qualities of France Wharton is able
           to capture in a short tale. Defends the rescue as a
           "consumating symbol for her conviction of the
           immortality of the French spirit and the French
           civilization."

R11.4   Cooper, Frederic T. "A Clear-Cut Gem of War Fiction."
           Publishers' Weekly 94 (28 December 1918): 2033.
                   Defines this as "one of the very few clear-cut,
           pure-water, almost flawless gems of war fiction,"
           although speculating that some readers will object to its
           "stinging frankness."

R11.5   Edgett, Edwin Francis. "The Indomitable Spirit of
           America." *Boston Evening Transcript*, 21 December 1918,
           Part 3, p. 8.
                   Praises the book's reality, its economy and its
           subtle analysis of both the reaction of war upon people
           and the egotism of many Americans.

The Marne--Criticism

R11.6   Anderson, Hilton. "Two Expatriate Novels of World War I." *Publications of the Mississippi Philological Association* (1986): 34-39.
      Examination of *The Marne* and Owen Johnson's *Wasted Generation*.

R11.7   Raphael, Lev. "Saving Face/Saving France--Edith Wharton, Shame and *The Marne*." Forthcoming in *University of Mississippi Studies in English* n.s. 8 (1990).
      Argues that studying this long-neglected war novella through the perspective of Silvan Tomkins's Affect Theory reveals a powerfully accurate representation of the phenomenology of shame, with unconscious roots in Wharton's own family experiences. Contends that elucidating the previously ignored centrality of shame in this book yields new insight into EW's oeuvre, how she responded to WWI, what her war efforts meant to her (and what they could not achieve), and why she, a successful war worker, chose such a helpless protagonist.

The Age of Innocence--Reviews

R12.1   Anonymous. "Mrs. Wharton's Novel of Old New York." *Literary Digest* 68 (5 February 1921), p.52.
      Defines the keynote of Wharton as sophistication, and feels this may account for her "jaundiced" view of Old New York. Objects to many anachronisms, wooden characterization, portrait of society as dull and unintellectual.

R12.2   Anonymous. "The Innocence of New York." *Saturday Review* (London) 130 (4 December 1920), p.458.
      Comments that the unattractive society here is rendered so by laughter initiated by its ridiculous standards combined with admiration for its finer

elements. Classes novel as on a level with Wharton's best work from a literary standpoint, but as history objects to the anachronisms.

R12.3   Anonymous. Review of *The Age of Innocence*. *Spectator* 126 (8 January 1921), 55-56.

Praises the finished, complete realization of the New York social scene in the 1870's, as well as the characterizations, both major and minor. Objects to the ending, calling it unrealistic because Archer's curiosity would have driven him to see Ellen.

R12.4   Anonymous. "The Age of Innocence." *Times Literary Supplement*, 25 November 1920, p. 775.

With strong praise for the novel, reviewer speculates that Wharton thrust back to the seventies because the current world is so unstable. Dismisses the anachronisms as of little consequence because it all *seems* so true. Terms this one of her best.

R12.5   Bellesort, Andre. "Les littératures étrangères: le dernier roman de Edith Wharton." *Revue Bleue* 59 (20 August 1921): 524-28.

In French. First gives a Frenchman's view of American society--conventional, with people more afraid of scandal than death or sickness. In *Age of Innocence*, finds Ellen Olenska has "wept real tears." However, terms this New York more respectable than today when Newland would divorce and probably not be happier. Concludes: "It is as if the story has been told to me by a person with an ironic smile on her lips and sadness in her eyes."

R12.6   Canby, Henry S. "Our America." *New York Evening Post*, 6 November 1920, p. 3. Rpt. *Definitions*. New York: Harcourt Brace, 1922.

Argues that the novel's subject is America, the land of cherished illusions and hypocrisies, and that, though she chooses a restricted canvas to illustrate her points, they are as valid as a broader epic could have made them. He contends that she treats large themes by "highly personal symbols," but this does not make her narrowness either small or a defect.

R12.7 Danchin, F.C. "Revue annuelle: Le Roman anglais." *Revue Germanique* 13 (1922): 155-59.

In French. Praises Wharton as deserving her high reputation and the novel for the vivid description of complex feelings and excellent' picture of pseudo-aristocratic circles in America.

R12.8 Edgett, Edwin Francis. The Strange Case of Edith Wharton." *Boston Evening Transcript*, 23 October 1920, Part 4, p. 4.

Complains of the Zolaesque quality of this family chronicle with its lame conclusion and terms this not up to her earlier great novels but rather of an age "that demands yellow pages in its fiction."

R12.9 Hackett, Francis. "The Age of Innocence." *New Republic* 24 (17 November 1920): 301-02.

Calls this a book of perception, passion, reserve and truth, noting the "parching wit" with which she has made of "the best people" a "clear, composed, rounded work of art."

R12.10 L., M.R. "Shorter Notices." *Freeman* 2 (22 December 1920): 358.

A glowing, one-paragraph review concentrates on Wharton as an artist.

R12.11 Loving, Pierre. "When Old New York Was Young and Innocent." *New York Call*, 12 December 1920, p. 10.

Defines Wharton as a novelist of manners whose greatest gift is tact. Here, she is more satiric and critical of society than usual with yet a "restrained artistry capable of ... delicately balanced thought and emotion...." Contends that the novel has contemporary relevance in that America still engages in hypocrisy and has a tribal consciousness "no less rampant today" than in the seventies.

R12.12   M[ansfield], K[atherine]. "Family Portraits." *Athenaeum* (London), No. 4728 (10 December 1920): 810-11. Rpt. *Novels and Novelists*. New York: Knopf, 1930.

Finds the time and scene suit Wharton's talent well. Notes the skill and delicate workmanship. However, Mansfield strongly objects to the coldness, asking, "Does Mrs. Wharton expect us to grow warm in a gallery where the temperature is so sparklingly cool?" She entreats "a little wildness, a dark place or two in the soul."

R12.13   Mason, A.E.W. Review of *The Age of Innocence*. *Bookman* 52 (December 1920): 360-61.

Terms the book a triumph of form, not theme, which is thin and familiar. Praises the details of city life which make the novel arresting and vivid.

R12.14   Parrington, Vernon L. "Our Literary Aristocrat." *Pacific Review* 2 (June 1921): 157-60.

Notes her distinction and craftsmanship but objects that "it doesn't make the slightest difference whether one reads the book or not." Argues she wastes her skill on insignificant material. Contends she would have been a greater and richer artist if she "had lived less easily ... been forced to skimp and save and plan." Considers her aloof from America. [In N14]

R12.15   Perry, Katharine. "Were the Seventies Sinless?" *Publishers' Weekly* 98 (16 October 1920): 1195-96.

Praises the "almost metallic brilliance" which hypnotizes, as it did in *The House of Mirth*. Terms the plot "unobvious," delicately developed, with "a fine finale." Maintains she "has a more human touch, a more vivacious humor" than James.

R12.16   Phelps, William Lyon. "As Mrs. Wharton Sees Us." *New York Times Book Review*, 17 October 1920, p.1, 11.

Review ranges widely, if in generalities, over Wharton's career, speculating on influences, particularly noting James. At times subtly snide, he concludes that this is one of the best books of the twentieth century. Dismisses the anachronisms as flecks. Photo.

R12.17   Townsend, R.D. "Novels Not for a Day." *Outlook* 126 (8 December 1920): 653.

Praises the captivating picture of Old New York society which repays careful reading because of the careful thinking and writing. Speculates that this is the best fiction of the season.

R12.18   V[an] D[oren], C[arl]. "An Elder America." *Nation* 111 (3 November 1920): 510-11.

Terms this a "masterly achievement," noting that Wharton knows fashionable New York well in contrast to others who write about it. Defines her triumph as the description of "rites and surfaces and burdens as familiarly as if she loved them and as lucidly as if she hated them."

R12.19   Watson, Frederick. "The Assurance of Art." *Bookman* (London) 59 (January 1921): 170, 172.

Praises novel as a tribute to Wharton's artistic freedom, maintaining that "no other living author handles with such fine ease the changing but authentic portraiture of the social aspect." Luckily, she has "no religion to teach, no grievance to air, no political betrayal to reveal. Her subjects are people. She writes of the 1870's with such realism these people might live next door."

R12.20   Whiting, Lilian. "Novels on the Season's List." *Springfield Republican*, 5 December 1920, Magazine Section, p.9-A.

Traces Wharton's career, defining her as an artist, and contends that this novel presents aspects of the social panorama and ends ineffectually, revealing her art, "for the kind of people she has upon this stage have not soul enough to love, or to feel, or to think."

The Age of Innocence--Dramatic Adaptation--Reviews

R12.21   Anonymous. "When New York Was 'Innocent'." *Literary Digest* 99 (15 December 1928): 27.
           Quotes St. John Erskine of the *New York World*: "Mrs. Barnes has skillfully, almost uncannily, avoided the dangers which beset adapters." Quotes Littell of the *New York Evening Post* in praise of Arnold Korff's Beaufort, and notes praise for Katharine Cornell.

R12.22   Bellamy, Francis R. "The Theatre." *Outlook* 150 (26 December 1928): 1395.
           Praises Cornell. Terms the adaptation strained and slow. However, maintains that the thought-provoking play induces new ideas about the present generation which would view its problems in a completely different light.

R12.23   "Wyatt, Euphemia Van Rensselaer." "The Drama II. Plays of Some Importance." *Catholic World* 128 (February 1929): 590-91.
           Reviews *The Age of Innocence* at the Empire Theatre with most attention paid to the actors, particularly Cornell, who excites quick sympathy for Ellen Olenska, and the costumes. Mentions the audience's confusion over old social conventions portrayed.

R12.24   Young, Stark. "Two New Pieces." *New Republic* 57 (12 December 1928): 96-97.
           Finds the writing "impossible," lacking life, with "scenes [that] got almost nowhere." Praises Cornell, costumes and sets.

The Age of Innocence--
Introductions and Afterwords

R12.25   Auchincloss, Lewis. "Foreword." *The Age of Innocence.* New York: New American Library, 1962.

Argues that "New York was always in [EW's] mind," even though she was driven abroad by its philistinism. Contends her early satire of it culminates in Mrs. Peniston in *The House of Mirth.* After WWI's destruction of French society which had given her a home, finds her tone changed to the nostalgia of *The Age of Innocence* and *A Backward Glance.* Praises *The Age of Innocence*'s "richness of color and detail" and sees it as part of EW's "definite picture of that world." Summarizes plot with analysis of the book's satire.

R12.26   Lewis, R.W.B. "Introduction." *The Age of Innocence.* New York: Scribner's, 1968.

Details several historical sources for the characters. Notes the "retrospective self-confrontation" in *The Age of Innocence*, Wharton contemplating what she might have become in Newland Archer and what she did, in Ellen Olenska. Defines the central moral theme as the individual in conflict with society where, for Wharton, the most important values lie--"loyalty, decency, honesty, fidelity, and the adherence to moral commitment."

R12.27   Lively, Penelope. "Introduction." *The Age of Innocence.* London: Virago, 1988.

Maintains Wharton's strength was that "she was able to combine the encyclopedic knowledge of an insider with the accuracy and selective power of a fine novelist and the detachment of a highly intelligent social and historical observer." Calls this one of her finest works--"a rich and powerful description of a vanished world."

R12.28   Lowe, Orton. "Introduction." *The Age of Innocence.* New York: Appleton, 1932.

Divided into three sections: "On Reading Novels"; "*The Age of Innocence*"; "Edith Wharton." Maintains *The Age of Innocence* is a realistic novel which satirizes the artificial aristocratic life of the seventies; finds it structurally resembles a Victorian novel. Notes the simple plot and excellent though learned style and ironic tone, "for Mrs. Wharton was in revolt against the people and their behavior as set forth." Maintains she has no sympathy for rigidity either in Old New York or rural New England. Sometimes inaccurate brief biography.

The Age of Innocence--Criticism

R12.29   Ammons, Elizabeth. "Cool Diana and the Blood-Red Muse: Edith Wharton on Innocence and Art." *American Novelists Revisited: Essays in Feminist Criticism*. Edited by Fritz Fleischmann. Boston: G. K. Hall, 1982.

Feminist. Concentrates on *The Age of Innocence*, terming it a pivotal book for Wharton, marking the end of her major period and her Progressive Era fictions, and an expression, with its polarized portraits of the American girl and the woman artist, of Wharton's frustration as an American woman writer. Parallels Ellen Olenska and Wharton, who both failed to find a place in America. [See N1]

R12.30   Atkinson, Brooks. "Critic at Large." *New York Times*, 27 March 1962, p.34. Rpt. *Tuesdays and Fridays*. New York: Random House, 1963.

Written as comment on the centenary edition (Appleton) of four novels, but only comments on *The Age of Innocence*. Although contending that the novel in plot and social criticism has little interest today, argues that it is still absorbing.

R12.31 Bremer, Sidney H. "American Dreams and American Cities in Three Post-World War I Novels." *South Atlantic Quarterly* 79 (1980): 274-85.

Discusses *The Age of Innocence, The Great Gatsby* and *Miss Lonelyhearts* as evidence of the pessimism emerging from WWI. Maintains that "Wharton projects backward the sense of historical discontinuity that the war embedded in her consciousness, and she also brings post war skepticism to bear on old ideals, on the old embodiment of the dream of community." Thus, New York emerges "as fundamentally dehumanized in each novel."

R12.32 Candido, Joseph. "Edith Wharton's Final Alterations of *The Age of Innocence.*" *Studies in American Fiction* 6 (1978): 21-31.

Study of Wharton's final changes of the galleys of *The Age of Innocence* finds that her substantive changes usually involve deletions of words and phrases, particularly adjectives, descriptive phrases and references to concrete objects and places which reflect the tendency to "blur the sharp contours of reality" and to create her economics of style, incident and emotion showing her "love for nuance."

R12.33 Cartwright, Faith C.W. "The Age of Innocence by Edith Wharton: A Critical and Annotated Edition." Ph.D. dissertation. University of Nebraska (Lincoln), 1970.

Provides commentary on topical allusions, map of New York in early seventies, introduction with focus on novel of manners. For abstract see DAI, 32 (1971), p. 1466A.

R12.34 Coxe, Louis O. "What Edith Wharton Saw in Innocence." *New Republic* 132 (27 June 1955): 16-18. [Rpt. N14]

Analyzes *The Age of Innocence*, finding its contemporary relevance lies in "the lost life of feeling." Contends that Wharton argues that only if "America can evolve a society which feels deeply and say what it feels can it do more than shift from generation to generation, without a sense of the past, without depth."

R12.35   Davis, Linette. "Vulgarity and Red Blood in *The Age of Innocence*." *Journal of the Midwest Modern Language Association* 20.2 (Fall 1987): 1-8.
          Feminist reading of *The Age of Innocence*, arguing that here Wharton "lays bare the mechanisms of patriarchy hidden beneath the conventional love story." Emphasizes that the novel illustrates that "[a] woman can reveal her own subjectivity ... only at the cost of exclusion from the symbolic system."

R12.36   Doyle, Charles Clay. "Emblems of Innocence: Imagery Patterns in Wharton's *The Age of Innocence*." *Xavier University Studies* 10.ii (1971): 19-25.
          Traces the recurring floral motifs, and concludes the novel deals with a central paradox of the American Dream--America, the refuge of the oppressed, became the land of the unfree. However, notes the attitude that ultimately prevails in the novel is that America is paradise and the implicit conclusion is that "true innocence, happiness, and even freedom consist in cheerful obedience."

R12.37   Evans, Elizabeth. "Musical Allusions in *The Age of Innocence*." *Notes on Contemporary Literature* 4.3 (1974): 4-7.
          Discusses use of musical allusions to further expose or satirize characters. Notes the most significant is to Gounod's *Faust*, and the similarity that emerges is of a great hopeless passion.

R12.38   Finucci, Valeria. "A Woman on the Mind: Aspects of Monomaniacal Love." Ph.D. dissertation. University of Illinois (Urbana-Champaign), 1983.
          "Study is a comparative reading of three novels on sentimental education: Flaubert's *L'Education Sentimentale*, D'Annunzio's *Il Piacere*, and Wharton's

The Age of Innocence. It chronicles the love obsessions of three young men as they search for the female embodiment of the mother-sister-friend-lover image projected by their imaginations." For abstract see *DAI*, 44/06-A, p.1783.

R12.39 Fryer, Judith. "Purity and Power in *The Age of Innocence*." *American Literary Realism* 17 (1985): 153-68.

Incorporated into *Felicitous Space: The Imaginative Structures of Edith Wharton and Willa Cather*. [See N10]

R12.40 Gargano, James W. "The Age of Innocence: Art or Artifice?" *Research Studies of Washington State University* 38 (March 1970): 22-28.

Argues that the novel is not, as some contend, a masterpiece of form and style, but suffers from three crippling faults: (1) style ends in burlesquing the characters and action; (2) it fails to focus on its main theme, freedom; (3) the resolution - "righteous and insipid"--is unearned. Concludes the novel is a great contrivance.

R12.41 Gargano, James W. "Tableaux of Renunciation: Wharton's Use of *The Shaughran* in *The Age of Innocence*." *Studies in American Fiction* 15.1 (Spring 1987): 1-11.

Analyzes importance of Wharton's echoes of and variations on Dion Boucicault's play, *The Shaughran*, in *The House of Mirth* to establish the themes of restraint and renunciation; whereas Gounod's *Faust* is the theatrical counterpoint of Archer's "quest for unlicensed freedom."

R12.42 Hopkins, Viola. "The Ordering Style of *The Age of Innocence*." *American Literature* 30 (November 1958): 345-57.

Analysis of Wharton's style in *The Age of Innocence* with attention to syntax, diction, and imagery, arguing that her style is both distinctive and "effective

as an instrument for converging the complexities of the
cultural values embodied in her novels."

R12.43   Jacobson, Irving F. "Perception, Communication and
           Growth as Correlative Themes in Edith Wharton's *The
           Age of Innocence.*" *Agora* 2.2 (1973): 68-82.
               Analyzes the problem of innocence within the
           context of a discussion of contradictions and changes in
           American culture in Old New York through a
           discussion of its thematic importance in *The Age of
           Innocence.* Defines ways in which innocence, as a way
           of life, distorts perception, communication, and growth,
           and leads to boredom, loneliness, ignorance, evasion,
           and hypocrisy, although it does have positive qualities
           which are outweighed by the negative.

R12.44   Ishimoto, Kimi. "In Praise of *The Age of Innocence.*"
           Essays in Literature and Thought (*Bungei to shis-o*) No.
           25 (March 1963): 14-16. N.B. Note Japanese title for
           search.
               In Japanese. Written on Wharton's centenary,
           article provides dated overview of her life and career.
           Notes speculation that James was "more than a mere"
           friend. Cites *Ethan Frome* and *The Age of Innocence* as
           American classics and praises the latter highly for
           realism and the Jamesian intensity of Archer's
           consciousness.

R12.45   Kekes, John. "The Great Guide to Human Life."
           Philosophy and Literature 8 (October 1984): 236-49.
               Argues Ellen Olenska and Newland Archer
           actually do not make sacrifices because they have both
           defined themselves in terms of their society and from it
           "they have derived their deepest convictions."

R12.46   Lamar, Lillie B. "Edith Wharton and the Book of
           Common Prayer." *American Notes and Queries* 7
           (November 1968): 38-39.
               Notes that one of the distinguishing marks of the
           first edition of *The Age of Innocence* is a misquote of

the opening line of the marriage service, which seems to belie Wharton's statement in *A Backward Glance* that she was saturated in the Episcopalian Book of Common Prayer. The phrase Wharton used actually comes from "The Thanksgiving of Women After Childbirth."

R12.47 Lamar, Lillie B. "Edith Wharton's Foreknowledge in *The Age of Innocence*." *Texas Studies in Literature and Language* 8 (Fall 1966): 85-89.

Challenges Wharton's assumption in *A Backward Glance* that she knew all about her characters from their inception, tracing errors in genealogy in the first edition of *The Age of Innocence* in relation to the Mingotts.

R12.48 Mizener, Arthur. *Twelve Great American Novels*. New York: New American Library, 1967.

Cites the intelligence of *The Age of Innocence* and the careful balance achieved between the themes of the necessary values of a traditional, stable society and that of the cost to the individual involved in preserving them which can ironically undermine these same values and rob that society of life and significance. Analyzes the split in Edith Wharton between the "talented self-made individual" and the undeveloped, passionate self longing to be loved "in an impossible way."

R12.49 Moseley, Edwin M. "*The Age of Innocence*: Edith Wharton's Weak Faust." *College English* 21 (December 1959): 156-60.

Finds many classical allusions in the names and behavior of all three main characters but concentrates on the Faust imagery and finds that although Archer "has a Faustian thirst for knowledge; he reads all the new books on anthropology, which enable him to see his own society in its proper perspective of time ... there is no faculty for translating his relativistic attitudes into action.... Ellen is a half-mock version of Goethe's second heroine, Helen of Troy."

R12.50   Murphy, John J. "The Satiric Structure of Wharton's
          The Age of Innocence." *Markham Review* 2.3 (1970): 1-
          4.
                    Examination of the "perfectly controlled and
          balanced" structure of *The Age of Innocence* as a satiric
          reflection of the rigidity and conventionality of Archer
          who, by advising Ellen against divorce, has chosen the
          conventional life of his society and thus formed his own
          trap.

R12.51   Nathan, Rhoda. "Ward McAllister: Beau Nash of *The
          Age of Innocence.*" *College Literature* 14.3 Edith Wharton
          Issue (1987): 276-84.
                    Notes that Ward McAllister, author of *Society As
          I Have Found It*, was the basis for Sillerton Jackson and
          Lawrence Lefferts of *The Age of Innocence*, and that his
          book, with marginal notes in his hand, provides striking
          evidence that the novel is a "biographically derived
          social history of an era in which every character
          corresponds with people Wharton mingled with in her
          youth."

R12.52   Nialle, Brenda. "Prufrock in Brownstone: Edith
          Wharton's *The Age of Innocence.*" *Southern Review*
          (South Australia) 4 (1971): 203-14.
                    Argues that Wharton is not looking back with
          nostalgia, that the authorial judgment of society is
          severe and that it is a study of moral timidity and
          wasted possibilities. Points out echoes of "The Beast in
          the Jungle" and the death imagery surrounding Old
          New York. Also quotes her letter to Sinclair Lewis
          when she won the Pulitzer over *Main Street* and her
          despair that the committee felt she was uplifting
          American morals.

R12.53   Payerle, Margaret Jane. "'A Little Like Outlaws': The
          Metaphorical Use of Restricted Space in the Works of
          Certain American Women Realistic Writers." Ph.D.
          dissertation. Case Western Reserve, 1984.

Study of metaphorical use of restricted space in Chopin, Wharton, Freeman, Gilman and Glaspell. Discusses *The Age of Innocence*. For abstract see DAI, 45, 2876A.

R12.54   Price, Alan. "The Composition of Edith Wharton's *The Age of Innocence*." *Yale University Library Gazette* 55 (1980): 22-30.

Detailed analysis of the significant revisions of *The Age of Innocence* taken from Wharton's notebook, "Subjects and Notes, 1918-1923," with insightful commentary on the motivations for changes in the outline.

R12.55   Robinson, James A. "Psychological Determinism in *The Age of Innocence*." *Markham Review* 5 (1975): 1-5.

Discussion of cultural relativism and determinism as they condition Newland Archer's inner conflict in *The Age of Innocence*. Maintains the outcome is not pessimistic, for Archer cannot break away from his background without tearing himself apart psychologically, and "the rituals, conventions and beliefs" which have shaped him are affirmed.

R12.56   Saunders, Judith P. "Becoming the Mask: Edith Wharton's Ingenues." *Massachusetts Studies in English* 8.4 (1982): 33-39.

Contends a study of Wharton's ingenues--May Welland in *The Age of Innocence* and Delia and Charlotte Lovell in *The Old Maid*--reveals Wharton's conviction that cultural expectations of the unmarried girl mask the reality beneath and have a pernicious effect on women throughout their lives.

R12.57   Scheik, William J. "Cupid Without Bow and Arrow: *The Age of Innocence* and *The Golden Bough*. *Edith Wharton Newsletter* 2.1 (Spring 1985): 2.

Discusses Diana/Artemis imagery in *AofI*, in light of Frazer's *The Golden Bough*, and Wharton's ironic use of myth to emphasize the "enervating 'preserved'

immaturity of American culture during the 1890's
through the turn of the century."

R12.58   Strout, Cushing. "Complementary Portraits: James's Lady
and Wharton's Age." *The Hudson Review* 35.3 (Summer
1982): 405-15.
           Emphasizes throughout the complementary nature
of the two novels--for example, in that Wharton puts
the psychological in a social context, tells the male side
of the story more fully and sees the hero and heroine
to the end of their situation. Contends "the individuality
of each is preserved without losing sight of the hinges
that firmly connect them." Analyzes renunciation in
each work, and argues they have in common a respect
for its value as well as its cost, with the complementary,
but vital, difference that Wharton's experience of
privation stemmed from her marriage and James's from
his work.

R12.59   Stuchey, W.J. *The Pulitzer Prize Novels: A Critical
Backward Look.* Norman, Oklahoma: University of
Oklahoma Press, 1981.
           Contends awarding Pulitzer to *The Age of
Innocence* was one of the committee's best decisions
and calls it the best novel to receive the prize.

R12.60   Wagner, Linda W. "A Note on Wharton's Use of *Faust*."
Edith Wharton Newsletter 3.1 (Spring 1986): 1.
           Reading of Newland Archer as Faust and tracing
of Faust imagery throughout *The Age of Innocence* with
brief comment on Faustian allusions in *CC*.

R12.61   Wershoven, Carol. "America's Child Brides: The Price
of a Bad Bargain." In *Portraits of Marriage in Literature.*
Edited by Anne C. Hargrove and Maurine Magliocco.
Macomb, Illinois: *Essays in Literature*, 1984.
           Feminist. Comparative reading of three child
brides in American literature in Hawthorne, James and
Wharton, concluding that the child bride is symptomatic
of "an entire culture." Argues that *The Age of Innocence*

is not "a loving and nostalgic" look backward, but "a cutting examination of the infantile state of American life."

R12.62   Wolff, Cynthia Griffin. "*The Age of Innocence: Wharton's 'Portrait of a Gentleman.'*" *Southern Review* 12 (1976): 640-58.
Reading of *The Age of Innocence* as "Newland Archer's journey toward emotional integrity, maturity, and self-respect." Psychological analysis of his growth is based on Erikson's theory of human development. Incorporated into her *A Feast of Words*. [See N28]

The Glimpses of the Moon--Reviews

R13.1   Anonymous. "Star-Laden Skies and Great Orange Moons." Current Opinion, 73 (September 1922): 391-93.
Mostly synopsis with the conclusion that "the book as a whole, is a chronicle of pleasure-seeking and is curiously lacking in social conscience or religious feeling." Objects to the preoccupation with sexual themes and parasitic lives.

R13.2   Anonymous. "The Current of Opinion." *Current Opinion* 73 (September 1922): 304.
Unique afternote mentions that the volume is reviewed elsewhere in the issue but warns readers against buying it or reading it because "the kind of people written about are of no value to the world either in or out of the pages of fiction."

R13.3   Anonymous. "Can Social Parasites Reform?" *Literary Digest* 74 (23 September 1922): 53.
Mostly plot summary, with praise for the forceful presentation of "rich idlers who are a blot on their country," and the triumphant portrait of the Hickses. Judges this novel the best since *The House of Mirth*.

R13.4   Anonymous. "A Page of Fiction." *New Republic* 31 (23 August 1922): 365.

Satiric paragraph cites this as the classic American romance in which they love each other all through and end up together. Objects that Wharton has done less here than before.

R13.5   Anonymous. Review of *The Glimpses of the Moon*. *Spectator* 129 (16 September 1922): 373-75.

Concludes that the details of American divorce are realistic here and that rich, aimless Americans have never been more remorselessly analyzed. Calls the reader's sympathy for Nick and Susy a tribute to Wharton's skill.

R13.6   Anonymous. "A New Divorçons." *Times Literary Supplement*, 7 September 1922, p. 566.

Speculates that this will be considered minor Wharton, yet finds here her familiar distinctive style, humorous detachment and powers of characterizing the worldly. Notes that the ghost of James hovers here, yet Wharton has her own feminine point of view, simpler, more philosophical. Finds the ending unlikely, the minor characters more vivid than Susy and Nick who are too much "algebraic symbols."

R13.7   Boynton, H.W. "Mrs. Wharton on Character." *Independent* 109 (19 August 1922): 79-81.

Notes less ironic detachment and skepticism here, less Jamesian. Argues that "her present interpretation of character in action may be ... as realistic ... as any of our current imitations of an alien and negative realism."

R13.8   Broun, Heywood. "It Seems to Me." *New York World*, 27 July 1922, p. 13.

Finds novel disappointing. Doubts that wealth and stupidity are so frequently synonymous. Complains that Nick Lansing and the children are unrealistic.

R13.9   Canby, Henry Seidel. "Out of Vanity Fair." *New York Evening Post Literary Review*, 19 August 1922, p. 883.

Contends that book presents a moral problem in a year of photographic realism with a sharper, simpler theme than *The Age of Innocence* and a new tenderness. Argues she is now interested in the struggle out of Vanity Fair, for she, too, after the war, seeks to break away from society into a broader world. Susy is not the greatest, but the most appealing, of her heroines.

R13.10   Danchin, F.C. "Le Roman Américain." *Revue Germanique* 14 (1923): 193-95.

In French. Positive review discusses the consequences of divorce in the novel.

R13.11   Edgett, Edwin Francis. "Edith Wharton's Latest Novel." *Boston Evening Transcript*, 9 August 1922, Part 2, p. 6.

Strongly objects to this "commonplace recital of conventional events" as far from the Wharton of yesterday before the "preposterous *Summer*."

R13.12   Follett, Wilson. "The Atlantic's Bookshelf." *Atlantic Monthly* 130 (October 1922): 10.

Addresses the controversy surrounding the novel and decides that though it is imperfect, lacking the integrity and totality of a major work, the reader finds compassion in place of irony, and this new warmth will eventually be united with her art, producing her true masterpiece.

R13.13   Gerould, Katharine Fullerton. "Mrs. Wharton's New House of Mirth." *New York Times Book Review*, 23 July 1922, p. 1, 3.

Praises Wharton's masculine sense of structure and humor as well as the absence of sentimentality. Finds this better than *The Age of Innocence* and *The House of Mirth* because of the reality of the love relationship itself, even though Nick has the faults of her other Selden-like men.

R13.14   Gould, Gerald. "New Fiction." *Saturday Review*
           (London) 134 (2 September 1922): 355.
               Contends that American women writers produce
           novels "utterly different in kind" from English women,
           and wonders if this dissimilarity stems from the more
           rooted, ordered experience of the English. Argues
           Wharton has an incomplete understanding of English
           society. Finds real beauty in the book, and admires her
           hold on the simple human needs, but criticizes the
           occasional crudity of her satire.

R13.15   Hale, Ruth. "Two Lady Authors." *Bookman* 54
           (September 1922): 98-99.
               Refers to Kathleen Norris and Wharton. The novel
           is criticized sharply as an insincere puppet show with
           "absurdly impossible people." Hale finds the
           stereotyping inexcusable in Wharton, who can do better,
           and goes so far as to state baldly: "Edith Wharton has
           no business to be writing such trash."

R13.16   Levoy, Alice Sessums. Review of *The Glimpses of the
           Moon*. *The Double Dealer* 4 (September 1922): 157-58.
               Criticizes the novel as boring, "disjointed, badly put
           together," an "improbable jambalaya." Regrets that
           Wharton is an indifferent artist here, and hopes the
           metamorphosis is temporary.

R13.17   Middleton, Murry J. "Books, and Real Books." *Nation
           and Athenaeum* 32 (28 October 1922): 164-65.
               Finds this novel backs the excellence of her other
           work, and complains that although it has "all the
           trappings and the outward show of life," it does not
           live.

R13.18   P., S. "Edith Wharton's Latest." *Forum* 68 (October
           1922): 905-06.
               Argues the book lacks plausibility, and the main
           characters are less real than the minor. However, notes
           she can still "sit a dozen characters down to a dinner

and keep the conversation of all twelve going with remarkable realism," and she demonstrates increased skill in terms of fluency which makes the reader eager to turn the page.

R13.19   Randell, Wilfrid L. "Misunderstandings." *Bookman* (London) 62 (September 1922): 256.

Maintains this is better than either *The House of Mirth* or *The Reef.* Contends that Wharton can describe parasitic people better than any other author, yet keep interest partly through her clever style. Argues that immoral people may well be worth writing about as a source of ironic comment and emotional color through their ideas of morality.

R13.20   Rascoe, Burton. "An Entomologist of Society." *New York Tribune*, 23 July 1922, Section V, p. 5.

Objects to Wharton's detachment, contending that we are "likely to be as little concerned" with her characters, who never emerge as flesh and blood people, as she is. Argues that she is neither ironist nor satirist, both of which imply authorial commentary, but rather a superior reporter.

R13.21   Seldes, Gilbert. "The Altar of the Dead." *Dial* 73 (September 1922): 343-45.

Objects to a structural fault in the novel, in that Wharton fails to render Susy and Nick's past life together so that we have no basis for believing in their deep love. Maintains that they are merely Lily and Selden, and on this altar of her dead, Wharton sacrifices them.

R13.22   Townsend, R.D. "The Book Table." *Outlook* 122 (20 September 1922): 119.

Terms the writing restrained without appeals to emotionalism, and concludes that it sustains Wharton's position among the leaders in American fiction.

R13.23   Van Doren, Carl. "Unsuccessful Parasites." *Nation* 115
          (2 August 1922): 128.
          Finds the novel friendlier and more human than
          her other books, and explains that social parasites are
          a favorite Wharton theme. Notes that here are her
          customary touches of social caricature, but her children
          are not always convincing and the book is nearly
          farcical at the end.

R13.24   West, Rebecca. "Notes on Novels." *New Statesman* 19
          (2 September 1922): 588.
          Calls the book dead, stating it is well done, but it
          was not worth doing. Argues the problems stem, not
          from the development of the novel itself, but from Mrs.
          Wharton's own development. First, she was born in
          America at the wrong time, when the Jamesian method
          would influence her, and that method is unsuited to her
          environment. Second, the truth that novelty is a test of
          the authenticity of art was unfashionable when she
          began writing. Contends she wants to achieve the same
          beauty as James, to express the same wisdom, to write
          books exactly like his.

R13.25   Whiting, Lilian. "Mrs. Wharton Portrays Smart Life of
          Europe." *Springfield Republican*, 6 August 1922,
          Magazine Section, p.7-A.
          Discusses the theme of the novel as living
          genuinely, and contends that Wharton has "presented a
          vivid, graphic transcription of one phase of
          contemporary life." Gives source of the title as the
          poem "To A Mummy." Quotes advice on living from
          James's "Lesson of the Master" and Eliot's *Daniel
          Deronda*.

The Glimpses of the Moon--Criticism

R13.26   Hoffman, C.G. "Re-Echoes of the Jazz Age: Archetypal
          Women in the Novels of 1922." *Journal of Modern*

Literature 7 (February 1979): 62-86.

Study of representative novels of 1922 argues the common thematic pattern is "the archetypal role of woman as love goddess or mother imago," for, despite the superficial changes in the status of women, "the novelist of 1922 envisioned the world of social and economic action as belonging to men and the world of moral and psychological sensibility as belonging to women." Interprets *The Glimpses of the Moon* as Wharton's "unconscious parody of Lawrence's serious treatment" of the theme that men and women in love are different. Terms Susy and Nick traditional, conventional, middle-class.

A Son at the Front--Reviews

R14.1   Anonymous. Review of *A Son at the Front. Bookman* (London) 65 (October 1923): 46.

Paragraph-length review terms novel a failure, a "belated essay in propaganda." Contends Wharton is still too angry to achieve distance. Maintains book will be read for "incomparably vivid accounts" of war-time Paris.

R14.2   Anonymous. "A Father's Heart Is Bared in Mrs. Wharton's New Novel." *Current Opinion* 75 (November 1923): 561-62.

Mentions controversy that rages around the book, but maintains that this is a sign of its vitality. Defines it as primarily a character study, not a war novel, and finds the theme to lie in Campton's spiritual growth. Notes similarity to Wells's *Mr. Britling Sees It Through*.

R14.3   Anonymous. Review of *A Son at the Front. English Review* 37 (November 1923): 664.

Short review terms the novel "remarkably fine," classing Wharton in the Jamesian school of American writers possessing the instinctual politeness of European letters, a dispassionate irony and a "suggestive" completeness.

R14.4   Anonymous. "Two Sides of the War Novel." *Literary Digest* 79 (6 October 1923): 30-31.
Discusses critical controversy: Some say we do not need another war novel--everything has been said; others praise the book's realism.

R14.5   Anonymous. "New Books Reviewed." *North American Review* 219 (January 1924): 139-41.
Contends she presents the "benumbed war-mentality" clearly, but the book is as dreary as most war novels. Judges George unconvincing and Campton too much the eccentric artist, clouding themes expressed through him. Evaluates it as realistic and sincere but not great.

R14.6   Anonymous. "Behind the Line." *Spectator* 131 (13 October 1923): 514.
Maintains that this "vivid picture" of a section of society during the war, with George "exquisitely" the embodiment of youth and true heroism and Campton a convincing study of the artistic temperament, is deeply affecting, a lament for the men killed.

R14.7   Anonymous. "Mrs. Wharton's Novel." *Springfield Republican*, 15 October 1923, p.6.
Praises the novel as true and "charged with sincerity of thought and emotion." Notes its reality, lack of sentimentality and excellent, varied characterization. Argues that though many want to avoid a war novel, this one is important and makes the reader think.

R14.8   Anonymous. "*A Son at the Front*." *Times Literary Supplement*, 20 September 1923, p. 618.

Notes that it seems an inopportune moment for a war novel, but as this has all the characteristics of Wharton's style, "her pliancy and penetration, her leisured, serious beauty" as well as accomplishment and certainty, it will undoubtedly have a permanent value among "minor documents of war."

R14.9 Aynard, Joseph. "Un Fils au front, par Mrs. Edith Wharton." *Journal des Débats*, 29 February 1924, p. 348-50.

In French. Contends EW puts ethical issues in concrete terms; morality is never absent, though. Notes she paints French in their diversity with just sympathy. Calls her descriptions vivid, tangible and expressive. Argues Campton doesn't really understand the tragedy of war; he lives in the small world of art and, from the balcony, comments on what's wrong with the world.

R14.10 Boynton, R.W. "The Incidence of War." *New York Evening Post: Literary Review*, 22 September 1923, p.61.

Objects to returning to the war as material and finds no redeeming value here that would warn men away from war. Believes this is a catharsis for Wharton and, since he had sons at the front, he judges Campton unrealistic.

R14.11 Brulé, A. "Edith Wharton: Un Fils au front." *Revue Anglo-Américaine* 2 (February 1925): 274-75.

In French. Praises description of the French in *A Son at the Front* but wishes Wharton had wider scope in her description of Paris because the focus seems to be what is near the hotels. Notes it is good to see through other than one's own eyes.

R14.12 Chaise, Henry de la. "Edith Wharton: Un Fils au front." *Etudes* 4 (October-December 1924): 374.

In French. One-paragraph review terms the book dense, well thought out, well observed, revealing the complexity of the American soul.

R14.13   DeW., F. H. "Mrs. Wharton Struggles With Masculinity."
          Independent 111 (13 October 1923): 157-58.
                  Mentions surprise among critics that she writes of
          the war at this late date. Yet calls this novel pioneering
          in using the war for art's sake in this study of
          "sensibilities."   However, objects to her men as
          "specimens."   Maintains she cannot create anything
          more than a male type, uninteresting--"at least to men."

R14.14   Egan, Maurice Francis. "Sons and Parents at the Front."
          New York Times Book Review, 9 September 1923, p. 1,
          19, 24.
                  Terms this her best book so far in which she
          "sounds the depths of sentiment without becoming
          sentimental for a moment." Praises the lucid contrast
          of the American and French temperaments. Maintains
          she "pierces easily to the very depths of human joy and
          sorrow." Picture.

R14.15   Farrar, John. "Behind the Lines." *Bookman* 58 (October
          1923): 202.
                  Calls this another "fine and true" war book, a
          powerful study of the artistic temperament, strong
          interpretive reporting of the social background of the
          war.

R14.16   Gould, Gerald. "New Fiction." *Saturday Review*
          (London) 136 (6 October 1923): 390.
                  Complains "the book jars. Its points are not merely
          easy, but cheap." Objects that she adds nothing to the
          understanding of the recent "lesson of reality," in fact,
          argues she "detracts from it." Feels it is useless to
          revive the war unless the theme "can be handled with
          a greatness ... that shall ... attempt to justify the ways
          of God."

R14.17   Lovett, Robert Morss. *"A Son at the Front." New
          Republic* (19 September 1923): 105.
                  Terms her viewpoint myopic, determined by her
          class, creating propagandist fiction, her theme being

American participation in the war. Maintains that the "spurious quality of [her] art does violence to her theme," and, though sincere, her novel is not penetrating.

R14.18   Macy, John. "The American Spirit." *Nation* 117 (10 October 1923): 398-99.

      Review mostly about Lawrence's *Studies in Classic American Literature*. Calls the novel out of date, speculating that she began it five years before, concluding: "It need never have been finished."

R14.19   Mann, Dorothea Lawrence. "Edith Wharton Writes a War Novel." *Boston Evening Transcript*, 15 September 1923, Book Section, p.4.

      Praises the portrait of wartime Paris and brilliant delineation of Campton, arguing that no one else could have written so truthfully and sympathetically of parents during the war.

R14.20   Marcel, Gabriel. "Un Fils au front, par Edith Wharton." *Nouvelle Revue Française* 23 (1 August 1924): 249-50.

      In French. Praises the remarkable evocation of the atmosphere of wartime Paris, yet finds the true focus of the novel to be Campton's gradual awakening to feeling and the relationship of father and son, and therefore wishes the war milieu were not so emphasized to keep a noble simplicity.

R14.21   Mortimer, Raymond. "New Novels." *New Statesman* 22 (13 October 1923): 18.

      Contends the reader faces "some wretched relic of a war-feeling. Maintains that she "has no gift for propaganda" resulting in "the most disagreeable war novel [he has] had the misfortune to read." Terms characters "unpleasant and uninteresting, satire, heavy, and sentiments, undistinguished."

R14.22   Osborn, E.W. Review of *A Son at the Front. New York World*, 9 September 1923, p. 8-E.

Terms this a novel of feeling more than action and praises the depth of sympathy that accompanies her power as a writer.

R14.23   Phelps, William Lyon. "Doctor Edith Wharton Makes a Diagnosis." *Literary Digest International Book Review* 1 (October 1923): 15-16, 90.
Touches on Wharton's career, focusing on *A Son at the Front*, which he ranks among her best. Praises the lack of sentimentalism, even that of patriotism, calling it a book of "rigidly suppressed feeling," held in check both by an aristocratic mind and a conscientious artist. Finds George's characterization excellent and the vacillations in Campton's mind the great triumph of the novel.

R14.24   Priestly, J.B. "Fiction." *London Mercury* 9 (November 1923): 102-03.
Remarks that Wharton is an admirable craftsman who takes the time to structure her work solidly, yet finds this novel dull and disappointing, its war-related pathos "a somewhat cheap trick," its story based on an uninteresting set and not universal. Does balance these criticisms with the observation that it is too soon to judge this type of novel objectively.

R14.25   Rascoe, Burton. "*A Son at the Front*." *New York Tribune*, 9 September 1923, p. 17-18.
Critic wonders that Wharton does not know the contemporary war fiction and does not realize her book is no contribution. Objects that she still seems to plead the French cause, and writes as a woman who does not know the war is over. Maintains that her chill temperament makes her unfit to write a war novel.

R14.26   Reid, Forrest. "New Novels." *Nation-Athenaeum* 34 (6 October 1923): 20.
Comments that she faces the difficulty of covering the very familiar territory of the war, yet finds the plotting "particularly suited" to her talent.

R14.27   Townsend, R.D. "The New Fiction." *Outlook* 135 (26 September 1923): 149.

Argues that although some say no one wants another war novel, this study of the psychology of Paris in war time is a worthy addition to American fiction with both its "interpretation of mass psychology" and its "dissection of individual emotion."

A Son at the Front--Criticism

R14.28   Buitenhuis, Peter. "Edith Wharton and the First World War." *American Quarterly* 18 (Fall 1966): 493-505.

Positive assessment of *A Son at the Front* as another angle of vision on WWI--from a middle-aged perspective. Contends the book is neglected because the disillusioned Lost Generation's truth about the War has been considered the only one. Contains biographical material on Wharton's war work with background of *Fighting France* and *The Marne*. Admits Wharton's Francophilia, but cites lasting value of the concrete detail of *A Son at the Front* and an answer to the artistic problem of portraying the reality of war and giving lasting form to transient emotions in a time of upheaval.

R14.29   Clough, David. "Edith Wharton's War Novels: A Reappraisal." *Twentieth Century Literature* 19 (1973): 1-14.

Seeks reason why Wharton, who had seen so much of the reality of WWI in France, employs sentimental myths of America coming to "save France" and the innocent doughboy in *The Marne* and *A Son at the Front*. He concludes that the two novels are weak because she never attained satisfactory artistic distance. She felt all of Western Civilization was at stake should France fall, and after the way she realized that "inevitable change had come with victory.... [W]hat finally emerges ... is a defiant yet hopeless stand against the course of history."

Old New York--Reviews

R15.1   Alden, Stanley. "Edith Wharton, as Writer of Comedy." *Springfield Republican,* 31 August 1924, p. 7-A.
         Discusses lack of a comedy of manners in America, and determines that Wharton cannot provide it because she cannot create the common American male. Calls these novellas "the most adequate picture yet drawn of New York society of that period." Terms *The Old Maid* the best, with its excellent characterization, and the four a valid criticism of American life.

R15.2   Anonymous. "The New Books." *Outlook* 137 (4 June 1924): 201-03.
         Contends that the worth of the stories is not historical, but in their "merciless, powerful depiction of human suffering under social bondage and the deadly pressure of convention." Notes a new sympathy here, stronger than the irony.

R15.3   Anonymous. "Mrs. Wharton." *Times Literary Supplement,* 11 September 1924, p. 553.
         Considers Wharton's growth as an artist, finding a remarkable increase in strength and security. Maintains her popularity is evidence of greater skill and significance. Objects only that in such an artist we still find melodramatic crises and improbabilities such as exist in *The Old Maid* and *New Year's Day* and *Ethan Frome.* Judges *The Spark* and *False Dawn* simpler and better.

R15.4   Canby, Henry Seidel. "Stories of Our Past." *Saturday Review of Literature* 1 (16 August 1924): 43-44.

Defines collection as a *tour de force* of historical re-creation, with *New Year's Day* a piece of sheer virtuosity equal to *Ethan Frome*. Praises *False Dawn*, reading it as an allegory of "the taste for beauty in America."

R15.5 Chapman, John Jay. "The Atlantic's Bookshelf." *Atlantic Monthly* 134 (August 1924): 6.

Maintains that although she has arrived at a "cold mastership," these sketches are "hasty" and give no idea of her powers. Terms the characters staged not studied and the historic atmosphere "inaccurately splashed in." Doubts Old New York was ever so foolish as this.

R15.6 Douglas, A. Donald. "Mrs. Wharton's Period Novels." *New York Herald Tribune*, 8 June 1924, Book Section, p. 21-22.

Objects to her unrealistic, "doll-like" characters, maintaining that they are not credible because "their lives are determined by one experience" with a "final disastrous extrication," while they move like toys to "the discipline of a heartless social mechanism."

R15.7 Edgett, Edwin Francis. "Edith Wharton Depicts Old New York." *Boston Evening Transcript*, 24 May 1924, p. 4.

Criticizes the novellas as a very narrow, class-bound view of Old New York, somewhat sensational, pessimistic and artificial, with attractive packaging to seduce the reader into an unrewarding experience.

R15.8 Farrar, John. "Authors Remember New York." *Bookman* 59 (July 1924): 590.

Declares these stories among her finest, with their humanity, ironical note, and warmth.

R15.9   Field, Louise M. "Edith Wharton Shows Us Old New
           York." *Literary Digest International Book Review,* II
           (June 1924): 538-39.
                Terms this a composite picture of the society of
           Old New York, except for *The Spark*, which has little
           of the sixties. Praises characterization, craftsmanship,
           and ease, with "no straining after archeological effects."

R15.10   Ford, James L. "Maligning Old New York." *Literary
           Digest International Book Review* 2 (October 1924): 785-
           86.
                Objects to each of the tales as making little
           attempt to render local color. Refutes contention that
           Old New York was unintellectual.

R15.11   Michaud, Régis. "Scènes de la vie New-Yorkaise." *Revue
           Anglo-américain* 2 (February 1925): 275-77.
                Very complimentary review. Asserts that if
           psychoanalysis had not been discovered, she would be
           the first psychoanalyst. Praises round characterization
           and compassion.

R15.12   Morris, Lloyd. "Mrs. Wharton Looks at Society." *New
           York Times Book Review*, 18 May 1924, p. 1, 24-25.
                Defines the theme here as the familiar one in
           Wharton of an individual in conflict with society.
           Praises *The Old Maid* particularly as enduring art, like
           Ethan Frome. Finds *False Dawn* and *The Spark* have
           neither the significance nor the beauty of their
           companions, but they, too, are good and deserve
           popularity.

R15.13   Osborn, E.W. Review of *Old New York.* New York
           World, 25 May 1924, p. 7-E.
                Appreciative review calls each novella an "intensive
           study of a single character," of contemporary meaning,
           each one a "masterpiece of form and conception," with
           New Year's Day the best.

R15.14   Thomas, Gilbert. Review of *Old New York*. *Nation and Athenaeum* 35 (28 June 1924): 416.

Notes the universality of human passion under the period setting. Maintains that this new achievement brings "fresh lustre to American literature" with her art which combines ingenuity, realistic characterization, irony, compassion, bold outline, and exquisite detail.

R15.15   Wilson, Edmund. "Old New York." *New Republic* 39 (11 June 1924): 77.

Maintains that *The Age of Innocence* covers the same material more effectively, contending there is usually not much to admire in her short stories beyond their professionalism. Finds these stories are not realistic enough to be social studies, nor dramatic enough to satisfy as conventional short fiction. Argues her residence abroad makes her novels thin, but she is "probably the only absolutely first-rate literary artist, occupying herself predominantly with New York, that New York has ever produced." Determines she writes the tragedy of the New York soul "caught between ... two eras."

Old New York--Books

R15.16   Rae, Catherine M. *Edith Wharton's New York Quartet*. Introduction by R.W.B. Lewis. Lanham, Maryland: University Press of America, 1984.

Close study of each of the novellas in *Old New York* that provides valuable historical and autobiographical background material. Discusses Wharton's assessment of Whitman.

Old New York--Introductions and Afterwords

R15.17   French, Marilyn. "Introduction." *Old New York*. New
          York: Berkley, 1981. Rpt. London: Virago, 1985.
               Analyzes *Old New York* as an indictment of the
          moral blindness of the wealthy class depicted. Discusses
          the constricted condition of women in this class.

Old New York--Criticism

R15.18   de Montebello, Philippe. "Director's Note." *Metropolitan
          Museum of Art Bulletin* New Series 40.1 (Summer 1982):
          2.
               Short synopsis of *False Dawn* notes Lewis Raycie
          was patterned on Thomas Jefferson Bryan (1800-1870),
          who opened the Bryan Gallery of Christian Art at
          Broadway and 13th Street in 1853.

R15.19   Hays, Peter L. "Correspondence." Letter to the Editor.
          Edith Wharton Newsletter 5.1 (Spring 1988): 9.
               Notes Carlos Fuentes in *The Old Gringo* describes
          character named Lewis in the same situation as Lewis
          Raycie in *False Dawn*.

R15.20   McDowell, Margaret B. "Edith Wharton's *The Old Maid*:
          Novella/Play/Film." *College Literature* 14.3 Edith
          Wharton Issue 14.3 (1987): 246-62.
               General overview of adaptations of Wharton's
          work for film and theater is followed by a detailed
          analysis of the adaptations of *The Old Maid* in Zoë
          Akins' play and Casey Robinson's filmscript for Warner
          Brothers' 1939 film. Notes that several of Wharton's
          most important themes--for example, the power of
          convention, the inutility of sacrifice, conflicts between

passion and social order--are muted or lost in the adaptations, which borrow primarily the basic situation and resulting conflicts. Cites: *EF*, *HofM*, *AofI*.

R15.21   Peterman, Michael A. "A Neglected Source for *The Great Gatsby*: The Influence of Edith Wharton's *The Spark*." *Canadian Review of American Studies* 8 (1977): 26-33.

Suggests that in scene, detail, theme, form and technique, *The Spark* may have influenced Fitzgerald while he was writing *The Great Gatsby*. Notes Wharton's works were readily available, they had the same publisher, she was an insider in the world of the rich which fascinated him and she was held in high literary regard by his friends Gilbert Seldes and Edmund Wilson. Notes similar setting, tone and point of view.

R15.22   Rae, Catherine M. "Edith Wharton's Avenging Angel in the House." *Denver Quarterly* 18.4 (Spring 1984): 119-25.

Reading of *The Old Maid* in terms of the power of women in Old New York through an analysis of the manipulations of Delia Ralston, which are totally unperceived by the men around her, who think themselves in charge.

R15.23   Richards, Mary Margaret. "'Feminized Men' in Wharton's *Old New York*." *Edith Wharton Newsletter* 3.2 (Fall 1986): 2.

Argues Lewis Raycie in *False Dawn* and Hayley Delane in *The Spark* illustrate New York society's stunting and ostracizing of men as well as women, "anyone who wants more or sees more is a danger to the comfort of the familiar."

R15.24   Saunders, Judith P. "A New Look at the Oldest Profession in Wharton's *New Year's Day*." *Studies in Short Fiction* 17 (1980): 121-26.

Insightful discussion of Wharton's technique of challenging basic assumptions in her short fiction in connection with Lizzie Hazeldean's prostitution and the lack of economic alternatives for women in Old New York. Concludes that the subject here is really the cultural degradation of women, and Wharton insists "in defiance of more orthodox views, that prostitution is not the cause of spiritual barrenness, but the consequence."

R15.25 Tintner, Adeline R. "*False Dawn* and the Irony of Taste-Changes in Art." *Edith Wharton Newsletter* 1.2 (Fall 1984): 1.

Contains historical sources for *False Dawn*--notably Thomas Jefferson Bryan's "Gallery of Christian Art," with its collection of early Italian primitives--and enlightening commentary on Wharton's use of art. Cites: *Italian Villas and Their Gardens, GofM, WofF.* [See L10]

R15.26 Tintner, Adeline R. "The Narrative Structure of *Old New York*: Text and Pictures in Edith Wharton's Quartet of Linked Short Stories." *Journal of Narrative Technique* 17.1 (Winter 1987): 76-82.

Analyzes eight narrative devices in the *Old New York* quartet. Discusses models for the quartet from Balzac, James and Crawford, and describes original edition format.

The Mother's Recompense--Reviews

R16.1 Anonymous. "Briefer Mention." *Dial* 79 (November 1925): 431.

Maintains that although the novel has an indulgent, perceptive irony, "a certain quality of thinness is increasingly evident in each of her successive volumes."

R16.2   Anonymous. "New Books in Brief Review." *Independent*
          114 (30 May 1925): 619.
          Terms this work by a tired artist--competent,
          skillful, yet with a sense of artificiality, as if the
          suffering isn't real, which leaves the audience cold.
          Maintains Wharton has written fiction of genuine
          passion and strength and will only injure her fame with
          this "conventional gesture in novel form."

R16.3   Anonymous. "Two American Novels." *Spectator* 134 (6
          June 1925): 940.
          Calls this a "fine sober" novel written from "no
          particular inspiration" with a thin hackneyed plot and
          theme but delightful style.

R16.4   Anonymous. "The Mother's Recompense." *Times Literary
          Supplement*, 14 May 1925, p. 332.
          Praises the book's competence and maintains that,
          although the characters are neither likeable nor
          admirable, they are handled sympathetically and Kate
          Clephane is as living and typical as Lily Bart.

R16.5   Aynard, Joseph. "Le Nouveau Roman de Mrs. Wharton."
          Journal des Débats, 12 June 1925, 986-88.
          In French. Discusses misconceptions foreigners
          have of America as totally free without a class
          structure. Calls this a beautiful book, a study of the
          morals of the new generation, in which we gain a sense
          and taste of the past, but a near, not a faraway, past.

R16.6   Bromfield, Louis. "Mrs. Wharton Sticks to New York
          Life." *New York Evening Post Literary Review*, 9 May
          1925, p. 3.
          Defines novel as the "cold, admirably fashioned
          analysis of an amazing situation."   Compares its
          "glistening efficiency" to *The Great Gatsby*, yet terms
          novel thin with shadowy characterization of all but Kate
          Clephane. Accuses Wharton of lacking the "warmth ...
          curiosity ... sympathy for all of life" of other great
          writers and complains that she "neither understands nor

wants to understand" any but the titled or those who are somehow associated with Old New York.

R16.7   Bullett, Gerald. "New Fiction." *Saturday Review* (London) 139 (30 May 1925): 588.

Calls the novel intelligent and competent, but an underlining of the obvious, in which Wharton allowed herself to be lured "by the attractions of a slick plot."

R16.8   C., E. "Sterile Pain." *Forum* 74 (July 1925): 154-55.

Objects that deft phrasing, the "slap-dash sophistication" of *The Glimpses of the Moon* but little of the vitality of *Old New York* or *The Age of Innocence* can be found here. Claims she has mastered the technique of the bestseller perhaps better than any other American writer.

R16.9   Canby, Henry Seidel. "Pathos Versus Tragedy." *Saturday Review of Literature* 1 (23 May 1925): p. 771.

Objects in a well-constructed analysis that "pathos" is not enough for such a plot, that the novel leaves us cold because Wharton has the elements of a Greek tragedy without the inevitable fifth act. Maintains that Wharton's sympathy for Kate Clephane led her to suggest compromise at the end when her theme demanded a double tragedy.

R16.10   Cook, Sherwin Lawrence. "The Modern Mother's Recompense." *Boston Evening Transcript*, 2 May 1925, Book Section, p. 5.

Cites unity as conspicuous among her literary virtues. Finds similarities here with Pinero's *The Second Mrs. Tanqueray*. Praises Kate's characterization and the description of New York society.

R16.11   Farrar, John. "Society and the Fringe." *Bookman* 41 (June 1925): 469-70.

Maintains this is the best story Wharton has ever written, with a theme as tremendous as any she has explored. "Kate Clephane is so human that she terrifies."

R16.12   Field, Louise Maunsell. "Mrs. Wharton Pictures New York Society of Today." *Literary Digest International Book Review* 3 (June 1925): 463, 466.
　　　　　Calls this one of Wharton's best, with the mental conflict of Kate Clephane more compelling than the theme. Terms the characters shadowy except for Kate, Anne and Fred Landers. Argues Lovett's monograph is condescending, planless and not especially discerning. [See N19]

R16.13   G., Ch. "Les Livres qu'il faut avoir lus: Le Bilan, par Edith Wharton." *Vient de Paraître* 8 (November 1928): 441.
　　　　　* Not seen.

R16.14   G., E.O. "The Bookshelf." *Woman Citizen* 10 (30 May 1925): 24.
　　　　　Notes that Kate Clephane is a usual Wharton type and that the concentration on her viewpoint provides unity but also makes the minor characters rather flat. Contends that here, as elsewhere, the men make little impression.

R16.15   Gorman, Herbert S. "Above Sentimentality." *New York World*, 3 May 1925, p. 7-M.
　　　　　Praises the unity gained through the single intense vision of Kate Clephane, making what might have been sentimental "an affair of lifted tragic intensity."

R16.16   Harwood, H.C. "Books Abroad." *Living Age* 326 (11 July 1925): 123.
　　　　　Strongly appreciative review calls this Wharton's most difficult theme, handled triumphantly, noting that her cool sensibility and strong moral sense enable her to brush away moral implications of incest to concentrate on Kate's jealousy and horror handing her

daughter to a "libertine." States Wharton's purpose as illustrating "the effects of sin upon the sinner."

R16.17   Hawkins, Ethel W. "The Atlantic's Bookshelf." *Atlantic Monthly* 136 (July 1925): 8, 10.

Praises Kate Clephane as one of Wharton's finest portraits of women. Notes distinction of style, wit, emotional intensity, deep preoccupation with the ethical problem and the "sense of the ideal immanent in the actual."

R16.18   Hutchison, Percy. "Mrs. Wharton Brings '*The House of Mirth*' Up to Date." *New York Times Book Review*, 26 April 1925, p. 7, 21.

Finds detachment impressive here. However, in terms of the Aristotelian theory of tragedy, she "evokes horror, but ... fails to arouse the corresponding degree of pity." Calls it her best since *The House of Mirth* with its psychological truth.

R16.19   Kennedy, P.C. "New Novels." *New Statesman* 21 (6 June 1925): 230.

Terms Wharton not at her best, with her tone almost arch and an underlining of "her delicacies of artistic perception." Complains she presents as very important issues which "seem essentially trivial."

R16.20   Lovett, Robert Morss. "New Novels by Old Hands." *New Republic* 43 (10 June 1925): 79.

Argues that the novel is really about the attitudes of different generations and contrasts it with *The Reef*, in which a similar case seemed more important because an issue that once was deeply consequential now seems only a matter of "social adjustment and taste."

R16.21   Martinoir, Francine de. "Un Immense Continent Romanesque." *La Quinzaine Littéraire* 398 (16 July, 1983): 8-9.

In French. Very favorable review of *The Mother's Recompense*. Laments that Wharton, as well as her friend Henry James, is not known or understood in France. Contends that the reissue of the 1928 translation fifty years later allows us to appreciate the novel's modernity. Finds the third person narrator less remote than many, but cites fissures in the narrative in places where certain descriptive details, suspicions about the heroine's sincerity, and a richer faculty for analysis than the character would have, appear. Calls Wharton a forerunner of Rosamond Lehman and Virginia Woolf.

R16.22 Michaud, Régis. "Edith Wharton: *The Mother's Recompense* ... Robert Morss Lovett: *Edith Wharton.*" *Revue Anglo-Americaine* 3 (February 1926): 276-78.

In French. Positive review compliments the vivid characters. Objects that Lovett tends to interject his own social opinions into his book, and argues that the world should remain always compassionate with the older values of an Edith Wharton and not become indifferent to individual suffering. [See N19]

R16.23 Muir, Edwin. "Fiction." *Nation-Athenaeum* 37 (13 June 1925): 328.

Objects that although the style, integrity of imagination in the great scenes and sincerity are praiseworthy, there is no climax. Finds scenes repetitions leading to a sense of monotonous suffering as well as monotony of treatment.

R16.24 Sherman, Stuart P. "Costuming the Passions." *New York Herald Tribune*, 17 May 1925, Section V, p. 1-2. Rpt. *The Main Stream.* New York: Scribner's, 1927.

Summarizes Lovett's view of Wharton's deficiencies, and argues that this "symmetrical, flawlessly finished little masterpiece" challenges his contentions. Finds form and concern with a moral predicament Jamesian. [See N19]

R16.25 Townsend, R.D. "Six Important Novels." *Outlook* 140 (13 May 1925): 69-70.

Terms this an excellent study of a class of Americans abroad which lacks Wharton's lighter, more satiric touch, for that would be out of place.

The Mother's Recompense--Introductions and Afterwords

R16.26   Auchincloss, Louis. "Introduction." *The Mother's Recompense.* New York: Scribner's, 1986.
           Terms *The Mother's Recompense* the last of Wharton's major works. Interprets Kate Clephane as symbolic of Wharton's stance against the chaos of post-WWI society, but finds the central problem of the novel in Kate's making too much of circumstance.

R16.27   French, Marilyn. "Afterword." *The Mother's Recompense.* London: Virago, 1986.
           Feminist analysis of *The Mother's Recompense* notes Kate Clephane is not the conventional virtuous heroine, nor the passionate sinner, but an ordinary woman who, consumed by guilt, lives out a stifling life of "psychic imprisonment." Concludes with the observation she develops in "Muzzled Women" that women writers do not choose women like themselves, who have overcome conventional restrictions, as their heroines.

The Mother's Recompense--Criticism

R16.28   Hansl, Eva J. B. "Parents in Modern Fiction." *Bookman* 62 (September 1925): 21-27.
           Discusses Kate Clephane as a mother in an article on the parent-child relationship. Critic feels Freud has given impetus to the discussion of this question and the changing traditions of family life and the growing independence of women make studies of the problem important. Wharton asks two questions in her novel:

(1) Can a mother run away and hope to gain influence later with her grown child? (Answer is no) and (2) Is there anything more important to parents than the high opinion of their children?

R16.29 Raphael, Lev. "Shame in Edith Wharton's *The Mother's Recompense*." *American Imago* 45.2 (Summer 1988): 187-203.

Striking argument, based on Silvan Tomkins's Affect Theory, is that critics have lacked an understanding of the development of shame and its impact on the formation of identity. Thus, they have grossly misunderstood Kate Clephane's decision to return to France and the key role of shame in her relationships with her husband, Chris Fenno, Fred Landers, her daughter and New York society. Also maintains the novel is one of Wharton's strongest, and the incest motif is not central.

Twilight Sleep--Reviews

R17.1 Anonymous. "Evening Post Guide to Current Books." *New York Evening Post*, 4 June 1927, p. 9.

One-sentence mention terms novel "The Age of Sophistication" portrayed brilliantly.

R17.2 Anonymous. "Fiction." *Outlook* 146 (29 June 1927): 290.

Contends that although Mrs. Manford seems "rather too perfect a specimen," the type is real. As always, Wharton depicts this "sophisticated circle of complex relations" very well.

R17.3 Anonymous. "Among the Very Rich." *Springfield Republican*, 31 July 1927, p. 7-F.

Finds novel, in spite of its vividly clear picture of a certain time and class, disappointing because it lacks a dominant, positive main character and inevitable, arresting or heroic scenes.

R17.4   Anonymous. "*Twilight Sleep.*" *Times Literary Supplement*, 16 June 1927, p. 422.

Cites Pauline Manford as a notable addition to Wharton's gallery of society women, but calls the satire cruel; Wharton appears to find this world of self-delusion so horrible she can scarcely laugh. Terms the writing certain and vigorous.

R17.5   Clark, Edwin. "Six Months in the Field of Fiction." *New York Times Book Review*, 26 June 1927, p. 18.

Thumbnail review terms this novel one of her most perfect, hard, relentless, ironic.

R17.6   Gilman, Dorothy Foster. "In New York with Edith Wharton." *Boston Evening Transcript*, 28 May 1927, Book Section, Part 6, p. 5.

Strongly complains of departure from subject matter of good society, for which, she says, Wharton is justly famous, finding this novel unrealistic, a "disastrous" result of deserting her own class in order to entertain magazine readers.

R17.7   H., S.F. "The Bookshelf." *Woman Citizen* 12 (July 1927): 36.

Praises characterization, plot and style, "told as only Edith Wharton can tell it," but sees it as second rate compared to the brilliance of *Ethan Frome* and *The Age of Innocence*. Classes it with *The Glimpses of the Moon*.

R17.8   Hartley, L.P. "New Fiction." *Saturday Review* (London) 144 (2 July 1927): 24, 26.

Terms novel grim and depressing, but praises organization, coherence, unity of mood and conception, the difficulties faced and overcome even though the medium is "opaque" and the characters and their lives blurred.

R17.9 Hutchison, Percy. "Mrs. Wharton Tilts at 'Society'." *New York Times Book Review*, 22 May 1927, p. 1, 27.

Notes lapses in American diction and finds characters seen somewhat at a distance, but maintains she has never had such refinement of method, creating the subtlest type of realism. Objects that at times Wharton seems to have "assembled a collection of subtly differing psychological mechanisms and then ... grasped at cases ... in which to install them." However, her artistry led to an inevitable ending.

R17.10 Muir, Edwin. "Fiction." *Nation and Athenaeum* 41 (2 July 1927): 452.

Like Wharton's other fiction, this is well written, well constructed, full of understanding, sensible, serious, but not overly so.

R17.11 Paterson, Isabel. "The New Sin." *New York Herald Tribune Books*, 22 May 1927, p. 1-2.

Praises the craftsmanship but maintains that Wharton, a social satirist, interested in manners and contemporary aspects of folly, becomes dated; the texture of her prose is "perishable." Terms characters like Mrs. Manford "mannequins."

R17.12 Phelps, William L. "Edith Wharton." *Forum* 78 (August 1927): 315-16.

Discusses Wharton as a satirist. Terms this novel a "tremendous Puritan sermon" marked by all the qualities of intelligence, knowledge of society, mastery of style and irony that make her the greatest living American writer.

R17.13 Royde-Smith, Naomi. "New Novels." *New Statesman* 29 (2 July 1927): 377.

Argues the focus is on Mrs. Manford, who is exposed with a thoroughness that stops just short of caricature, yet the minor characters are actually stronger thematically, with Lita Wyant's air of disillusioned boredom and Nona Manford's tragic lament for the peace of an unbelieving convent defining post-war American youth and the twilight sleep theme defining rich and hearty American middle age.

R17.14   Taylor, Rachel Annand. "Fiction." *Spectator* 138 (11 June 1927): 1028.

Objects that the material here is not good enough for Wharton's elaborate art.   Terms the novel a "*tranche de vie* ... of a life so muffled and atrophied by wealth it is too dense for her delicate ... entanglements."

R17.15   Walker, Charles R. "Mrs. Wharton Versus the Newer Novelists." *Independent* 118 (11 June 1927): 615.

Analyzing Wharton in light of her contemporaries, critic notes that she was one of the first to write of Americans unfavorably, although it has since become fashionable with Mencken, Sinclair Lewis, Dreiser, and Anderson; however, the sense of immediate reality of these writers is lacking in Wharton.   The inner life, also, lacks the sense of conviction one finds in Virginia Woolf.   Argues that in this novel, the reader has the sense of the beauty of the whole, but has to gain the perspective of the entire work before believing in the details.

R17.16   Webb, Mary. "Irony and Mrs. Wharton." *Bookman* (London): 72 (September 1927): 303.

Defines Wharton's great gifts as irony and interpretation of nature. Objects they are lacking here. Terms this "showing up" of the "fast" life weak because Wharton is not a reformer.   Criticizes ending as squalid.

R17.17   Williams, Orlo. "*Twilight Sleep*." *The Monthly Criterion* 6 (November 1927): 440-45.

The main argument is that she writes well about unimportant things--like America. Contrasts her with James, contending that she balances herself "neatly between Europe and the States ... has remained beautifully on the spot, noting one thing after another ...." However, "what she describes is more practically real, what he describes, more ideally true." Calls this novel "excellently contrived, very amusing, effective ... efficient."

R17.18   Wilson, Edmund. "Twilight Sleep." *New Republic* 51 (8 June 1927): 78.

Notes the lighter touch, the more tolerant attitude as Wharton grows older, but objects that her American scene is too "synthetic" and "shadowy" because she has lived so long abroad. Calls this novel entertaining and distinguished social criticism, if less vivid than her earlier work. Maintains that she has, to a surprising extent, "renewed herself with the new age." [See O91]

The Children--Reviews

R18.1   Amidon, Beulah. "The Family Circus." *Survey* 61 (1 November 1928): 180.

Argues that it would be tempting to "read this book as a tract on modern marriage and divorce." However, it is "not muddled with efforts to raise sociological questions or to answer them with neat formulae." Instead, as a true artist, Wharton "has caught ... the insistent, arresting rhythm of the modern scene."

R18.2   Anonymous. "New Books in Brief Review." *Independent* 121 (22 September 1928): 285.

Objects to the incredibility, with Judith a "sentimental fiction." Maintains that the "shafts of implied indignation pierce oaten dummies."

R18.3   Anonymous. "The Children." *Times Literary Supplement*, 20 September 1928, p. 664.

Mainly plot summary with the objection that so admirable a novelist can find no better theme than the "vagaries and immoralities of ultra-rich Americans."

Admits there are rich, beautiful parts of the book, but finds an element of caricature or a fundamental want of decency weakens artistic treatment. Contends one laughs without thinking or is too angry to be amused.

R18.4   Birrell, Francis. "New Novels." *Nation and Athenaeum* 44 (6 October 1928): 19.

Contends it falls halfway between being a book of information and a work of art. Terms it slick, efficient and readable, but finds Wharton in too much of a temper having lost her sense of proportion.

R18.5   Cook, Sherwin Lawrence. "Edith Wharton and Divorce Problems." *Boston Evening Transcript*, 1 September 1928, Book Section, p. 2.

Praises Wharton's honesty, humor, characterization of the heroic Judith, and the credibility of the ending. Discusses her type of realism, arguing that it is more what realism ought to be than the pessimism of a self-proclaimed realist like O'Neill.

R18.6   Fadiman, Clifton P. "Cable and Fine Wire." *Nation* 127 (10 October 1928): 370, 372.

Compares novel to Morley Callaghan's gangster novel, *Strange Fugitive*. Objects that both are incredible; the complexities of Wharton's universe, he argues, are so foreign to the average reader, they are merely farcical.

R18.7   Frank, Grace. "Bittersweet." *Saturday Review of Literature* 5 (1 September 1928): 84.

Analyzes the novel in terms of two contrasting themes which provide melody and counterpoint and finds the harmony curious and the rhythms strange but cites the poignancy and humor in the contrast and the author's keen observations. Calls Judith Wheater one of Wharton's most unusual and delightful characters.

R18.8   Hartley, L.P. "New Fiction." *Saturday Review* (London) 146 (29 September 1928): 397.

Places Wharton as an artist in the literary line of Flaubert, Turgenev and Henry James--the first aim of her writing, like theirs, is to please, but argues she has the flaws of that school: an absence of vitality and originality, characters more lifelike than living, an overly refined style. Finds *The Children*, as an example, has acute observation but is "too much the deliberate manufacture of the brain, too little the spontaneous creation of the imagination."

R18.9 Hutchison, Percy. "Humor and Satire Enliven Mrs. Wharton's Novel." *New York Times Book Review*, 2 September 1928, p. 2.

Praises the new note of humor here in Wharton, speculating that it will prove her most popular novel. Wonders if she originally planned two novels because the two plots do not always combine harmoniously. Defines Wharton's sermon to be that the problems of children of divorced parents may be insoluble.

R18.10 L., R.M. "Recent Fiction." *New Republic* 56 (26 September 1928): 160.

Sees here an elementary theme--the "conflicting appeal of woman, in the singular, and child, in the plural"--rendered in Wharton's best manner with an epilogue that "rings with the truth of the inevitable."

R18.11 Luhrs, Marie. "'*The Children*' Is Polished Novel." *New York World*, 7 October 1928, p. 11-M.

Terms Wharton here "a veritable Mrs. Grundy-- lace mittens and all--" who has created brilliant surface in a book slight and thin, marred by pale pity which needed "hot rage." Finds faults stem from children as characters and the questionable assumption that "children without home life are ... wretched." Contends *Twilight Sleep* is more convincing.

R18.12 Maurice, Arthur. "Scanning the New Books." *Mentor* 17 (February 1929): 54.

Terms this one of the most distinguished, conspicuous books of the year. Praises its poignant theme, brilliant characterization, rich cosmopolitan background. Calls it Wharton's sermon against irresponsible American divorce practices.

R18.13   Munson, Gorham B. "The Quality of Readability." *Bookman* 68 (November 1928): 337.
Terms it women's magazine fiction, although the Jamesian manner still adds polish to the pages. Cites it as competent but uninspired.

R18.14   O., A.B. "Wealth and Divorce." *Springfield Republican*, 7 October 1928, p. 7-E.
Terms Wharton didactic, "always accurate but hardly profound," with less puppet-like characters than usual here and defines her Jamesian technique as dated. Feels she is most incisively satiric when handling pampered rich women.

R18.15   Roberts, R. Ellis. "New Novels." *New Statesman* 31 (29 September 1928): 760-61.
Terms this Wharton's easier, later manner, less dependent on James. Notes the uncharacteristic seriousness, gravity and genuine indignation.

R18.16   Ross, Mary. "The Children of Divorce." *New York Herald Tribune*, 2 September 1928, Book Section p. 1-2.
Notes that Wharton uncharacteristically "delves quite consciously into the formlessness of contemporary life" here, without didacticism. Praises her catholicity of understanding that she can portray Judith as well as Rose and Martin. Finds a warmer Wharton here, with greater tolerance and sympathy.

R18.17   Slesinger, Tess. "The Innocence of Age." *New York Evening Post Literary Review*, 15 September 1928, p. 5.
Places Wharton as belonging "to an age which looks upon postwar happenings with continuous naive surprise and delighted horror." Maintains Wharton is

out of touch with present problems, treating her "ridiculous, posturing characters" flippantly, furnishing a prewar, sad ending.

R18.18   Taylor, Rachel Annand. "Children Errant." *Spectator* 141 (8 September 1928): 306, 309.
Asserts the charm of the book lies in Judith Wheater. Terms the central situation artificial, created as it is by capricious people. Contends Wharton is best when she is more profound, but notes humor, compassion and style.

The Children--Introductions and Afterwords

R18.19   French, Marilyn. Introduction. *The Children*. London: Virago, 1985.
Interprets the moral conflict, dramatized in Martin Boyne, as the very modern one of "an individual and a world--as participating in a dynamic, shifting interaction" which is not materialistic, for in Wharton "the world is in us as well as without." Includes interesting comment on the Princess Buondelmonte as a satire on the racist eugenics movement.

The Children--Criticism

R18.20   Bruccoli, Matthew. "Hidden Printings in Edith Wharton's *The Children*." *Studies in Bibliography: Papers of the Bibliographical Society of the University of Virginia* 15 (1962): 269-73.
Bibliographical essay that notes "what has passed for the first printing of *The Children* actually consists of two printings from duplicate plates; furthermore, both these printings include two states. Subsequent production of the novel introduced more hidden printings." Notes that two lessons emerge: (1) modern

printing methods do not guarantee uniformity of all copies in a single impression; (2) an attempt to differentiate printings cannot be restricted to an examination of the publisher's code or the copyright page. Collation information follows.

R18.21   Davidson, Donald. "Irony: Edith Wharton, Louis Bromfield." In *The Spyglass: Views and Reviews, 1924-30.* Edited by John T. Fain. Nashville: Vanderbilt University Press, 1963. 83-87. Originally published in *The Nashville Tennessean,* 23 September 1928.

Interprets irony in *The Children* as arising from a conflict between two different kinds of good. Terms Louis Bromfield's irony in *The Strange Case of Annie Spragg* "more artificial" than Wharton's, yet notable.

R18.22   Hamblen, Abigail Ann. "The Jamesian Note in Edith Wharton's *The Children.*" *University Review* 31 (Spring 1965): 209-11.

Traces Jamesian elements in *The Children,* particularly the international theme, the wise but uncorrupted child, characterization of Martin Boyne and Rose Sellars, use of pearls as symbols and a shattered object. Conclusion is that she never really "outgrew" the "tutelage" of the master.

R18.23   Sasaki, Miyoko. "An Approach to a New Value in Edith Wharton's *The Children.*" *The Journal of Tsuda College,* No. 3, Tokyo (April 1971): 109-28.
* Not seen.

R18.24   Sensibar, Judith. "Edith Wharton Reads the Bachelor Type: Her Critique of Modernism's Representative Man." *American Literature* 60.4 (December 1988): 575-90.

Argues *The Children* is Wharton's female revision of mainstream Modernism's idealization of the sexually immature perennial bachelor as Representative Man, whose acute sensibility becomes the prototype for the great creative artist, yet is actually a demonstration of

a stunted emotional life--a homosexual panic. Compares
Martin Boyne both to John Marcher in *The Beast in the
Jungle* and T.S. Eliot's Prufrock and draws biographical
parallels with James, Berry and Fullerton.

Hudson River Bracketed--Reviews

R19.1   Anonymous. "Fiction, Briefs." *Nation* 130 (15 January
         1930): 76.
                Calls this novel one of Wharton's failures.
         Complains Vance Weston is "only the husk of a
         character." Terms the descriptions of the Willows and
         the Spears the best parts, which prove Wharton is "still
         the one fine novelist of that small but tenacious class
         of Americans with a social and cultural tradition."

R19.2   Anonymous. "Hudson River Bracketed." *Times Literary
         Supplement*, 16 January 1930, p. 42.
                Concentrates on analysis of Vance Weston,
         defining *HRB* positively as the "reflection of modern
         American life and its contradictions in the mirror of a
         mind nourished on tradition."

R19.3   Anonymous. "The Bookshelf." *Woman's Journal* 14
         (December 1929): 32.
                Contends that *HRB* lacks the exquisite
         workmanship of her earlier stories, yet finds more
         sympathy and understanding than usual in her
         treatment of the triangular love relationship.
         Emphasizes Wharton's skill in the portrayal of Halo
         and Laura Lou, but finds Vance not clearly delineated.

R19.4   Brickell, Herschel. Review of *Hudson River Bracketed*.
         Bookman 70 (January 1930): 559.
                Synopsis of the novel, terming the contrasts in
         social conditions fairly effective, but characterization

shallow except for Laura Lou. Defines Halo as smug and limited, if well meaning, and Vance as childish.

R19.5   Cook, Sherwin Lawrence. "The Era of Hudson River Bracketed." *Boston Evening Transcript*, 30 November 1929, Book Section, p. 5.

Notes a popular lecturer calls her novels "perfectly marcelled." Although she is meticulous and therefore sometimes lacks spontaneity, reviewer classes her as one of the best contemporary writers. Finds Vance Weston unrealistic and sentimentalized in places, yet one of the most genuine literary types, being neither a great writer nor a bestselling journeyman. Notes greatest interest lies in revelation of the author's own literary contacts, but complains novel is not gripping.

R19.6   F. B. [Fanny Butcher] "New Book by Edith Wharton Full of Skill." *Chicago Daily Tribune*, 16 November 1929, p. 11.

Terms *HRB* "an excellent example of her craft," but Vance is an interesting phenomenon, not understandable, and the novel lacks intensity and reality.

R19.7   Gilbertson, Catherine. "In the Willow Pattern." *Saturday Review of Literature* 6 (7 December 1929): 509.

Cites the spirit of autobiography here, maintaining that she has written nothing either more compassionately just or comprehending than her account of Vance Weston's struggles. Terms novel absorbing with significant background portraits in the best "Comic Spirit." Notes that it does lack clear-cut structure of her other work.

R19.8   Hansen, Harry. The First Reader." *New York World*, 19 November 1929, p. 13.

Concentrates on characterization of Vance Weston, speculating that his background stems from Sinclair Lewis's novels more than observation. Also finds literary life ineffectually portrayed, but the world of publishers and editors realistic. Although Vance is termed "inauthentic" at times, reviewer speculates that she has "rescued for fiction the very man who needed a biographer"--the poet by nature who is not commercial.

R19.9   Hartley, L.P. "New Fiction." *Saturday Review* (London) 149 (1 February 1930): 144-45.

Argues Wharton's vantage point from abroad contributes to the insightful vision of modern America she presents through Vance Weston, and only wishes for a smaller, less inclusive canvas.

R19.10   Hutchison, Percy. "Mrs. Wharton's Latest Novel Has a Mellow Beauty." *New York Times Book Review*, 17 November 1929, p. 4.

Praises characterization, especially the pathos of Laura Lou. Maintains Vance carries conviction. Applauds the book's sanity, and Wharton for holding to human verities in a time of innovations and experiments. Notes a mellower tone here; comments on the breadth and body of the work.

R19.11   Irvine, Lyn. "New Novels." *Nation and Athenaeum* 46 (25 January 1930): 582.

Argues that although the novel is disappointing because the theme and many of the situations are hackneyed, her talents as a writer still make it interesting.

R19.12   Pritchett, V.S. "Warnings." *Spectator* 144 (18 January 1930): 99.

Calls this an old-fashioned novel of huge proportions. Terms Laura Lou's death particularly well done but argues Vance is more a problem than a man although more satisfactory than "geniuses usually are in fiction." Complains the New York literary world is too generalized to be realistic, and the ending with "wholesale tying up of loose ends" is comforting but arbitrary.

R19.13   Proteus. "New Novels." *New Statesman* 34 (1 March 1930): 669.
           Argues that although the characters are unrealistic marionettes, the setting is so real, rich and vital you feel that "you are watching a puppet-show acted in natural scenery."

R19.14   Ross, Mary. "Babbitt's Son." *New York Herald Tribune Books*, 17 November 1929, p. 3.
           Contends that here is her current philosophy of the artist. Maintains that she shows a "deeper absorption in the process of living than in the crystallized patterns of human ways." Terms it her most generous book in scope and sympathy.

R19.15   Seldes, Gilbert. "Notes on Novels." *New Republic* 61 (29 January 1930): 283.
           Terms this one of her "off-year" novels, but finds this of less interest than her other failures, because she has used the theme before but is obviously unfamiliar with the setting here. Argues that once Vance Weston is in the literary world he has no "substantial reality."

R19.16   Shirley, Mary. "A Novel and Some Biographies." *Outlook* 153 (20 November 1929): 465.
           Cites the perfect plot structure and compares novel with the best Wharton has done. Terms Vance Weston "beautifully integrated."

R19.17   Whiting, Lilian. "Mrs. Wharton's Work." *Springfield Republican*, 22 December 1929, p. 7-E.
           Judges this to be a minor work, and argues that Wharton cannot focus modern life outside polite society, yet she recreates that phase of life with powerful realism. Finds too many details of Vance's "literary" experiences, little pathos in Laura Lou's fate and the personal complications uninteresting. Concludes with an interesting flashback to the warm public reaction to the anonymously serialized "Margaret

Aubyn's Letters" which were "hauntingly" Jamesian, and initiated her success.

Hudson River Bracketed--Introductions and Afterwords

R19.18   Auchincloss, Louis. "Afterword." *Hudson River Bracketed*. New York: Signet, 1962.
          Argues Vance is Wharton's first hero "who is also a man" (as opposed to a "cool, self-possessed" dilletante), and is an extension of EW's vision of herself, "freed of the impediments of her sex, generation and background." Contends EW's astonishing intuition makes Vance startlingly like Thomas Wolfe, who published his first novel that year. Argues, despite some heavy-handed satire, the book has some of her finest characters, especially Laura Lou.

R19.19   French, Marilyn. "Afterword." *Hudson River Bracketed*. London: Virago, 1986.
          Feminist. Argues *Hudson River Bracketed* is a "fascinating example of an author working unconsciously against herself." Notes she grants Vance the male prerogatives of arrogance and selfishness but also shows the effect of these on the women in his life. Contends she therefore consciously portrays an admirable, sympathetic hero, but unconsciously subverts the portrait by showing the cruel arrogance and irresponsibility of the egotism which she, like male authors, thought essential to the development of an artist. Maintains, because she was a woman, Wharton had trouble writing about an artist's development and the nature of art.

Hudson River Bracketed--Criticism

R19.20   Bradley, Jennifer. "Valedictory Performances of Three American Women Novelists." Ph.D. dissertation. State

University of New York (Stonybrook), 1981.

Maintains these valedictions--last novels--are divided into two tasks: life review and legacy preparation. This literary appraisal of three long-lived women--Gertrude Atherton, Ellen Glasgow and Edith Wharton--argues Wharton's composing strategy mediates Atherton's "consecutive trying-on of rhetorical masks" and Glasgow's more serious and personal self-rendering; thus maintaining "the tension between conscience and a dramatic version of self. *Hudson River Bracketed* posits the effect of social intercourse and cultural learning on the private person, and *The Gods Arrive* shows how the soul moderates the social being." Discusses Atherton's *Black Oxen* and *The Horn of Life* and Glasgow's *This Our Life* and *Beyond Defeat*. For abstract see DAI 42 (May 1982), 4825A.

R19.21   Buchan, Alexander M. "Edith Wharton and 'The Elusive Bright-Winged Thing.'" *New England Quarterly* 37 (September 1964): 343-62.

Discusses Wharton's purpose in *Hudson River Bracketed*: to give dramatic formulation to her ideas about the creative process and the nature of the making of an artist rather than to give a realistic portrait of a society.

The Gods Arrive--Reviews

R20.1   Anonymous. "Books in Brief." *Forum* 88 (November 1932): viii.

Terms this not her best, maintaining she is not always successful coping with a changed social structure, yet calls novel finished, distinguished, often acute, ironic and moving.

R20.2   Anonymous. "The Gods Arrive." *Times Literary Supplement*, 6 October 1932, p. 708.

Terms the structure one of her most solid achievements. Notes that familiar characters are freshly amusing as they provide background for Halo and Vance. Calls this a "rich and ample" picture.

R20.3   Brande, Dorothea. "Four Novels of the Month." *Bookman* 75 (October 1932): 577, 637-38.

Portrait on 577 from 1905 *Bookman* carries comment on *The House of Mirth* review which praised her lack of moralizing, and contrasts that with later reviews which criticize her "messages, morals and criticisms of life." Review itself objects that Wharton puts artistry aside, becoming journalistic when she writes of literary worlds she loathes. Criticizes caricatures as undermining the novel's importance.

R20.4   Butcher, Fanny. "Skill of New Wharton Book Thrills Critic." *Chicago Daily Tribune*, 17 September 1932, p. 10.

Praises alluring portrayal of the artistic temperament as realistic and profound.

R20.5   Davis, Elmer. "History of an Artist." *Saturday Review of Literature* 9 (1 October 1932): 145.

Objects to unrealistic portrayal of the Midwest and its inhabitants but praises her rendition of the psychology of the artist. Maintains that Vance Weston was more authentic, however, in *Hudson River Bracketed* than he is here. Contends there must be a third volume to show Vance's maturation.

R20.6   Dawson, Margaret Cheney. "False Gods." *New Republic* 73 (23 November 1932): 53.

Argues that behind her sympathy with the torturous irregularities of creativity lies "a relentless belief in the final goodness of her own creative process and her own form of discipline." Contends that although we do not think of Wharton as controversial, here she is squarely partisan, finding the left-wing American literati in Paris basically frivolous.

R20.7   Field, Louise Maunsell. "The Modest Novelists." *North American Review* 235 (January 1933): 65-66.
         Discusses the old novel of "panacea" versus modern ones which present realistic conditions with neither suggestion for nor "any hope of" improvement. Contends this novel offers no realistic solutions because Wharton evades every issue, only making Halo an "honest woman" in eighteenth-century fashion in a totally incredible ending.

R20.8   Hawkins, Ethel Wallace. "The Atlantic Bookshelf." *Atlantic Monthly* 150 (October 1932): 14-15.
         Defines novel as an "effective study of growth through pain." Praises Wharton's "command of the significant detail that makes clear a whole situation or state of emotion."

R20.9   Hutchison, Percy. "Mrs. Wharton Probes a Social Period." *New York Times Book Review*, 18 September 1932, p. 6, 20.
         Discusses this as a "problem novel" and as Wharton's probing, not mirroring, as she did previously, an era. Contends she is seeking to "penetrate that new world in the hope of finding for it standards under which it might attain to ... orderliness" it so conspicuously lacks. Thus, he maintains she conducts a study rather than merely tells a tale.

R20.10   MacAfee, Helen. "Outstanding Novels." *Yale Review* NS 22 (Winter 1933): xxii.
         Brief review contends Halo is more interesting than Vance, and that here Wharton has an "opportunity to exercise her talent" for describing the English and the Americans abroad and the Riviera.

R20.11 Mann, Dorothea Lawrence. "Mrs. Wharton Sees the Gods Arrive." *Boston Evening ·Transcript*, 11 October 1932, Part 4, "Literary World," p. 3.

Finds this novel a distinct, real experience, and praises the psychological insight into Halo and Vance's relationship with an interesting if brief analysis of Halo's unconscious desire for power and management of Vance.

R20.12 Paterson, Isabel. "Egeria on the Left Bank." *New York Herald Tribune Books*, 18 September 1932, p. 3.

Objects to Halo as the embodiment of the nineteenth-century ideal of the inspirational woman, maintaining her function passed with the century. Describes Wharton's satire of the modernists and contends she does not give an inch in either theory or practice to their literary claims.

R20.13 R., W.K. Review of *The Gods Arrive*. *Christian Science Monitor*, 26 November 1932, p. 12.

Defines theme as "the value of marriage as a stabilizer." Although there are rich background, delicate irony and distinguished diction, the characters leave the reader indifferent.

R20.14 Roberts, R. Ellis. "The Woman Novelist." *New Statesman and Nation* NS 4 (22 October 1932): 488, 490.

Terms this not her best but workmanlike with passages of insight, wit and intolerance for pretentious modernity. Feels men should study women's novels to see what women feel must be tolerated, e.g., Halo: Vance.

R20.15 Whiting, Lilian. "Mrs. Wharton's Upper Class." *Springfield Republican*, 9 October 1932, p. 7-E.

Mostly summary of plot and characters. Notes the many acts of this drama may lack unity, but praises her "power of painting a scene."

The Gods Arrive--Introductions and Afterwords

R20.16   French, Marilyn. "Afterword." *The Gods Arrive*. London:
          Virago, 1987.
          Important, insightful analysis of *The Gods Arrive*
          focuses on the relationship between Vance Weston and
          Halo Tarrant as a universal depiction of the problems
          of women's self-effacement in relationships and men's
          insensitive immaturity. Notes the unsatisfying
          son/mother symbolism of the ending to the modern
          reader.

The Gods Arrive--Criticism

R20.17   Becker, May Lamberton. "The Reader's Guide." *Saturday
          Review of Literature* 9 (8 October 1932): 164.
          Brief mention of *The Gods Arrive* as one of twelve
          books recommended for a reading club, with its insight
          into the novelist's process and the creation of a writer.

R20.18   Carroll, Eleanor. "Edith Wharton." *Delineator* 120
          (January 1932): 4.
          Based on an interview conducted because *The
          Gods Arrive* was to appear the next month. Quotes
          Wharton on purpose for the novel: "to portray the half-
          gods that are worshipped by all people--but especially
          by the creative artist."

The Buccaneers--Reviews

R21.1   Anonymous. "Shorter Notices." *Catholic World* 148
          (December 1938): 369-70.
          Classes this as "light fiction" with the end not
          fulfilling the early promise because divorce and

remarriage are presented as a solution. Maintains that "for masterly treatment of the superficial and shallow in life" she has "few rivals."

R21.2   Anonymous. "Mrs. Wharton's Unfinished Novel." *Christian Science Monitor*, 26 October 1938, Weekly Magazine Section, p. 12.

Discusses problems of posthumous publication. Finds novel interesting for certain passages written in Wharton's best manner and as a demonstration of how "that mistress of style and construction worked." However, notes characters sometimes lack depth and actuality and dramatic scenes lack connecting links. Concludes that, completed, it would have stood as one of her richest, most sophisticated novels.

R21.3   Anonymous. "Last Novel." *Time* 32 (26 September 1938): 67-68.

Praises first-rate characterization and sharp social satire, yet notes Wharton's limitation in that the brilliant scenes at Saratoga are followed by magazine-fiction passages. Contends the best thing is the picture of Gilded Age New York society.

R21.4   Anonymous. Review of *The Buccaneers*. *Times Literary Supplement*, 8 October 1938, p. 641.

Notes some scenes are polished and others only lightly sketched. Terms this a return to a Jamesian model and her own background, and contends, though her material and style may seem old-fashioned, she creates living, sympathetic characters.

R21.5   Becker, May Lamberton. "Last of Edith Wharton." *New York Herald Tribune Books*, 18 September 1938, p. 6.

Maintains she did not write well outside of the Gilded Age, but here her hand was never steadier. Contends the outline of the unfinished chapters is so unusually rich in both detail and emotional currents that the reader is not frustrated as with other unfinished works.

R21.6   Bogan, Louise. "The Decoration of Novels." *Nation* 147
         (22 October 1938): 418-19. Rpt. *Selected Criticism: Prose
         and Poetry*. New York: Noonday, 1955.
         Objects that Jamesian form in Wharton becomes
         mere plot, and that although the background has color
         and accuracy, the novel is "dead at the heart." Classes
         Wharton as a bridge from the nineteenth-century novel
         to current magazine fiction where "in a superficially
         arranged scene manners, clothes, food, and interior
         decorations are described carefully." Contrasts her
         unfavorably with James, contending reader loves his
         living people, merely watches her puppets. Maintains
         numbness of her fiction stems from her class and
         feeling for decorum.

R21.7   Brighouse, Harold. "Two Novels." *Manchester Guardian*,
         11 October 1938, p. 7.
         Contends that, though unfinished, and with good
         comedy, but "hardly rational" characterization, its
         "vigorous portraiture of the social comedians of the
         seventies" makes it well worth publication.

R21.8   Hutchison, Percy. "Mrs. Wharton's Unfinished Novel
         and Other Recent Fiction." *New York Times Book
         Review*, 18 September 1938, p. 6.
         Objects that the unfinished nature of the work
         makes the characters mere sketches and the scene
         nebulous at times. Contends Wharton would have cut
         Laura Testvalley, who competes too heavily for interest
         with Nan St. George, one of Wharton's memorable
         women.

R21.9   Morley, Christopher. "Edith Wharton's Unfinished
         Novel." *Saturday Review of Literature* 18 (24 September
         1938): 10.
         Calls this one of her most interesting, shrewdest
         studies. Notes the suavity of turn-of-the century style
         but cautions: "the great old lady knew precisely ... what
         she was doing; her plot structure was as formal and

obvious as the seating of a dinner-party, but she had a merciless eye for character."

R21.10   O'Faolain, Sean. "Edith Wharton's Last Novel." *London Mercury* 39 (November 1938): 88-89.
          Gives synopsis of Wharton's summary, and concludes this is a theme which only a real novelist could conceive. Terms this novel so "real and sincere as to be worth an indeterminate number of completed novels from the generations which ousted Mrs. Wharton from public adoration." Praises her style as decorous, and suitable, her feelings as "refreshingly positive" and wonders if she will eventually prove angry modern realists to be not as realistic as they claim.

R21.11   Tourtellot, Arthur Bernon. "Buccaneers and Snobs." *Boston Evening Transcript*, 24 September 1938, Part 3, p. 1.
          Reviews Wharton's career, classing her as Jamesian, with her dominant claim to fame her craftsmanship. Finds her "repetitious in matter" and "hopelessly uniform" in treatment. Contends she never got beyond "a great concern over trifling conventions." Speculates that she did not trust herself to penetrate deeper without sacrificing unity. Wonders why her executors offer this unrevised, uncompleted work as evidence of her greatness.

R21.12   W., L. "Mrs. Wharton's Unfinished Novel of 'Society.'" *Springfield Republican*, 2 October 1938, p. 7-E.
          Terms the novel too "unfinished," with the London scenes lacking both relation to each other and adequate drama. Nevertheless, finds it interesting.

R21.13   Wilson, Edmund. "The Revolutionary Governess." *New Republic* 96 (26 October 1938): 342-43.
          Contends "mellowness" of her later years "dulled" her "sharpness," yet finds it appropriate that she left "as the last human symbol of her fiction [the governess]

who embodies the revolutionary principle implicit in all her work."

The Buccaneers--Introductions and Afterwords

R21.14   Lapsley, Gaillard. "Afterword." *The Buccaneers*. New York: Appleton-Century, 1938.
           Justifies publication of the incomplete *Buccaneers* and comments on its structure, theme, and the problems of unity and characterization Wharton would have had to solve in the finished version.

The Buccaneers--Criticism

R21.15   Wershoven, Carol. "Edith Wharton's Final Vision: *The Buccaneers*." *American Literary Realism 1870-1910* 15.2 (Autumn 1982): 209-20.
           Critic analyzes *The Buccaneers* as Wharton's "final vision of a world to come, one which blends that part of the past worth saving with the vitality of the future, and which is formed by those with the courage to embrace it." In this novel, women are friends and help each other. Positive change is possible, unlike the fate of the earlier heroines. Compares and contrasts Laura Testvalley, Nan St. George and Fulvia (*VofD*). Here, the hero is a positive force. See Wershoven's *The Female Intruder* for detailed discussion of women in Wharton. [See N27]

Chapter 10

Reviews of the Short Story Collections

Chapter lists reviews of the short story collections which are cited in chronological order. Anonymous reviews are alphabetized by journal or newspaper.

The Greater Inclination

S1   Anonymous. Review of *The Greater Inclination. Academy* 57 (8 July 1899): 40.

      Praises craftsmanship and a control rare in women writers. Cites Jamesian influence but concludes she is less subtle and more articulate.

S2   Anonymous. Review of *The Greater Inclination. Athenaeum* (London) No. 3745 (5 August 1899): 189.

      Comments that Wharton takes a "dreary view" of humanity, but although she is an American writing about Americans, she does have a command of good English.

S3   Anonymous. "The Rambler." *Book Buyer* 18 (June 1899): 355.

Calls this a remarkable first book, containing "some of the most skillful and finished writing ... of recent years."

S4   Anonymous. "Recent Fiction." *Critic* 35 (August 1899): 746-48.

Discusses realism and concludes that the Jamesian influence here is very strong, not only in method, but in substance and titular phrase as well. Objects to the unconscious plagiarism which it becomes the reviewer's duty to point out, particularly "in proportion as the work considered is more clever."

S5   Anonymous. Review of *The Greater Inclination*. *New York Times Saturday Review*, 24 June 1899, p. 408.

Notes that Wharton's short stories emphasize modern morals and manners. Objects to the lack of "more joyous incidents of existence." Questions if the writer implies that the greater inclination is to "moral failure" to the exclusion of all brighter beliefs.

S6   Anonymous. Review of *The Greater Inclination*. *Saturday Review* (London) 88 (15 July 1899): 82.

Praises Wharton as subtle, introspective, sympathetic with a "scholarly grace of style, a vividness of phrase and a mastery of language."

S7   Barry, John D. Review of *The Greater Inclination*. "New York Letter." *Literary World* (Boston), 1 April 1899, p. 5-6.

Laments Jamesian influence, remarking that "some of his worst faults of style she reproduces." Concludes she has not yet mastered her technique, but does show promise. Objects to condescending tone toward characters in "The Coward." Praises her insight into masculine mind, unusual in a woman.

S8   Barry, John D. Review of *The Greater Inclination*. "New York Letter." *Literary World* (Boston), 13 May 1899, p. 152-53.

Cites praise he is hearing for *The Greater Inclination*. Mentions Wharton dislikes comparisons with James--so he thinks her "next book will probably not be marked by a slavish adherence to the methods of a very questionable literary model." Remarks she ought to be able to write studies of leisure class Howells is asking for in *Literature*.

S9   Earle, Mary Tracy. "Some New Short Stories." *Book Buyer* 18 (June 1899): 399-401.
      Favorable review with the comment that Wharton "writes of worldly people and commands a technique so perfect that once in a while the interest of the story is not quite vivid enough to sustain it."

S10   G., F.J. "Mrs. Wharton and Her Use of the Epigram." *Book Buyer* 18 (June 1899): 395-96.
      Praises Wharton's ability to weave epigrams into the texture of her prose so that they serve as an integral part of character development.

S11   Gorren, Aline. "Studies in Souls." *Critic* 37 (August 1900): 173-76.
      Praises Wharton's revelation of feminine psychology and her realistic portrayal of both women and New Yorkers. Applauds her for showing that New Yorkers, as well as New Englanders, have souls.

S12   Payne, William Morton. "Recent Fiction." *Dial* 27 (1 August 1899): 76-77.
      Finds stories all realistic. Praises Wharton's ability to bring subjective reality "into the field of vision," noting the great gulf between these stories and ordinary, entertaining ones.

S13   Peck, Harry Thurston. "The Great Inclination." *Commercial Advertiser* 102 (20 May 1899): 12.
      Praises psychological insight, style, depth, and "the fine intuition of a woman with the firmness and precision of a man."

S14   Peck, Harry Thurston. "A New Writer Who Counts."
        Bookman 9 (June 1899): 344-46.
             Notes Jamesian influence, but comments that,
        although she has "caught" his latest manner, she has
        improved upon his "workmanship" and deserves
        independent criticism.

                              Crucial Instances

S15   Anonymous. "Art and Life." *Academy* 61 (27 July 1901):
        75-76.
             Criticizes Wharton's narrow scope; claims she has no
        elemental quality.   Objects that her writing reflects a
        decadent age; dialogue is "extraordinary jargon" and her
        "little art" is very limited. Contends that when she takes
        for her theme art itself, it is like embroidering an
        embroidery, and turning to great art we see the "instability
        of the whole Wharton fabric."

S16   Anonymous. Review of *Crucial Instances*. *Athenaeum*
        (London) 3850 (10 August 1901): 186.
             Cites "subtlety and strenuousness" as the most notable
        qualities here, which are "characteristic of many American
        writers gifted with a fine dramatic instinct." Notes she
        exhibits an intimate knowledge of Italy and the Italians.

S17   Anonymous. "The Editor's Easy Chair." *Harper's Monthly
        Magazine* 103 (October 1901): 823-24.
             Cites Jamesian influence but argues that in poetic
        moments she writes on her own authority.

S18   Anonymous. "Literature." *Independent* 53 (6 June 1901):
        1322-23.
             Decides the appreciation of these stories rests on the
        reader's "culture and mental endurance" for she "works out
        her really difficult conceptions without the risk of
        inspiration." Notes that in writing of Italy, however, from
        the tourist's viewpoint, she sees everything with "startling

vividness." Asserts her genius consists "in a delicate perception of forms and color."

The Descent of Man

S19   Anonymous. Review of *The Descent of Man and Other Stories*. *Academy* 67 (3 September 1904): 163.

      Praises *The Valley of Decision*. Finds Wharton "most successful when not fantastic," asserting her skill lies in devising "unheard-of" situations as much as in style. Mentions her ability to reveal us to ourselves. However, "The Lady's Maid's Bell" and "A Venetian Night's Entertainment" are unworthy of inclusion. Critic applauds himself for omitting "all allusion to the particular King Charles' head" of Wharton reviewers.

S20   Anonymous. Review of *The Descent of Man and Other Stories*. *Athenaeum* (London) 4001 (2 July 1904): 13-14.

      Calls Wharton original with "hints" of James. Several of the motives are so good, critic wishes one or two of them could have been developed by a true master of the short story.

S21   Anonymous. "Mrs. Wharton's Short Stories." *Bookman* (London) 26 (July 1904): 140-41.

      Extensive synopsis of "The Descent of Man" and "The Other Two." Notes Wharton's irony. Contends she is as rare an artist as James, with all his insight and subtlety of thought and a simple directness that he lacks.

S22   Anonymous. Review of *The Descent of Man and Other Stories*. *Independent* 56 (9 June 1904): 1334-35.

      Categorizes Wharton as the best interpreter among American writers of those, such as the very rich and scholars, who live "a purely artificial existence." Asserts she has made "a literary art of casuistry," and her "characters have conscientious scruples that rarely deal with the real issues of life." Notes that, like James, she can present a revolting scene with delicacy.

S23   C., H. Review of *The Descent of Man and Other Stories*.
        Reader Magazine 4 (July 1904): 226.
              Asserts that this volume will have wider appeal than
        her others because she has added humor and humanity,
        and they are less subtle in thought and expression while
        retaining a general artistic perfection.

S24   Dunbar, O. H. "Mrs. Wharton at High Water Mark." *Critic*
        45 (August 1904): 187.
              Cites "Lady's Maid's Bell," "The Dilettante" and "The
        Mission of Jane" as particularly well done, noting that
        Wharton supplies theme as well as plot. "She is a finely
        interpretive artist with a just sense of proportion; an
        inveterate satirist who is yet incapable of extravagance or
        over-emphasis."

S25   Pyke, J.R. "Two Novels of Cynicism." *Bookman* 19 (July
        1904): 512-15.
              Praises "The Other Two" for its understanding of
        moral implications. Finds that "knowledge of the world,
        a sure psychology and a well-bred cynicism are here
        united." Notes that her cynicism is "an intellectual
        attitude, the result of wide experience and careful
        observation."

The Hermit and the Wild Woman

S26   Anonymous. Review of *The Hermit and the Wild Woman*.
        Athenaem (London) 4230 (21 November 1908): 644.
              A short review praising "The Hermit and the Wild
        Woman," "The Last Asset" and "The Potboiler"
        particularly, noting the careful, conscientious craftsmanship
        throughout and the "broadmindedness" which attains a
        "sympathetic comprehension of the Ages of Faith" in the
        title story.

S27   Anonymous. Review of *The Hermit and the Wild Woman*. *Nation* 87 (26 November 1908): 525.

        Reviewer finds the title story "interesting" rather than moving, notes Wharton's "growing preoccupation with the irony of things" and the lack of any "touch of cheerfulness."

S28   Anonymous. "Short Stories by Mrs. Wharton." *New York Times Saturday Review*, 3 October 1908, p. 541.

        Praises Wharton's craftsmanship, style and insight. Contends she is "above all a delineator of character," and her setting in "The Pretext" is too obviously negative. Objects that the heroine of "The Last Asset" is not sufficiently realized. Also notes: "The Potboiler," "The Verdict," "The Trust."

S29   Anonymous. "Comment on Current Books." *Outlook* 90 (17 October 1908): 362.

        Praises Wharton's workmanship, but feels these stories are not as novel or interesting as others of hers and are inclined to "a certain form of preciosity from which Mrs. Wharton will do well to deliver herself."

S30   Anonymous. "The Hermit and the Wild Woman." *Spectator* 101 (28 November 1908): 886-87.

        Criticizes the lack of gaiety for contrast in the stories and finds that the themes of failure, disappointment and disillusionment become monotonous and depressing. "The Best Man" termed an exception.

S31   Repplier, Agnes. "A Sheaf of Autumn Fiction." *Outlook* 90 (28 November 1908): 698, 702.

        Praises these stories, their "sentences ... cut like gems" with "inimitable descriptions of people and places." Argues these "clear-sighted expositions of ... ordinary, every-day failures..., come within reach of us all."

Tales of Men and Ghosts

S32   Anonymous. Review of *Tales of Men and Ghosts*.
        Athenaeum (London) 4336 (3 December 1910): 700.
        Terms Wharton's ghosts the "subtle suggestion of an
        unseen world in which our subconscious selves continually
        move." Finds that Wharton "never forgets that power of
        pure human love which ... has indeed the element of
        immortality."

S33   Anonymous. Review of *Tales of Men and Ghosts*. *Bookman*
        (London) 40 (Spring Supplement 1911): 14.
        Calls these "keen little studies of temperament" which
        have more to do with men than ghosts, which is termed
        fortunate because Wharton excels at studies of human
        nature. Notes that characters seem to inherit fortunes
        conveniently.

S34   Anonymous. "Some Notable Books of the Year."
        Independent 69 (17 November 1910): 1089.
        Brief notice finds them of "strangely unequal merit"
        with "The Bolted Door" the most ingenious. Notes a
        "cramping influence."

S35   Anonymous. "A Guide to the New Books." *Literary Digest*
        41 (19 November 1910): 949.
        Terms her ghost stories thrilling but not spooky
        because they symbolize tangible facts. Praises her
        psychology, but finds her appeal to the head not the heart.

S36   Anonymous. Review of *Tales of Men and Ghosts*. *Nation*
        91 (24 November 1910): 496.
        Cites uncertainty of style and objects that they are too
        "trumped up out of the author's fancy." Notes "Afterward"
        and "The Letters" are in her earlier manner reminiscent
        of Bourget, when they do not go further, and fare worse,

becoming reminiscent of James, but the rest are commonplace, magazine fiction style.

Xingu and Other Stories

S37   Anonymous. Review of *Xingu and Other Stories*. *Athenaeum* (London) 4612 (December 1916): 598.

Calls her ghost stories Jamesian, but finds Wharton's style pleasanter for subtle psychological analysis than later James.

S38   Anonymous. Review of *Xingu and Other Stories*. *Independent* 88 (25 December 1916): 552.

Thumbnail review calls the tales admirable.

S39   Anonymous. "Some Recent Short Stories." *Nation* 104 (4 January 1917): 20.

Names Wharton the most popular practitioner of the "lettered ... scriptive" style, but finds "Xingu" different, with its delightful, exuberant humor.

S40   Anonymous. "Xingu." *New York Times Book Review*, 5 November 1916, p. 465-66.

Contends she wants to escape the "hothouse atmosphere" of her other volumes and thus there is deeper humanity here. Mentions all the stories, citing "Coming Home" and "Bunner Sisters" as particularly notable-- because not typical Wharton--although there is a loss of "sureness of touch" in the latter caused by her abandoning her accustomed environment. Cites: "Kerfol," "The Triumph of Night," "Autres Temps...," "The Choice," "The Long Run."

S41   Anonymous. "Novels and Short Stories." *Review of Reviews* 54 (December 1916): 679.

Brief review praises literary craftsmanship, calling
"Autres Temps..." one of the best studies of changing
social conditions ever written.

S42   Anonymous. "Xingu." *Spectator* 117 (30 December 1916):
       836-37.
       Comments on mixed emotions approaching Wharton,
       a reverence fo her subtlety and style tempered by sense of
       the inhuman in her detachment and "absolute self-
       effacement." Argues that she is not "glacially cruel" as
       Huneker claims, but still finds "she has a peculiar talent
       for the dissection of disillusioned, unhappy, uncomfortable,
       or disagreeable matters." [See R9.24]

S43   Anonymous. "'Xingu' by Mrs. Wharton." *Springfield
       Republican*, 14 January 1917, Section II, p. 15.
       Contends that Wharton is the only living American
       writer "with a sense of cosmopolitan values, flawless
       craftsmanship, and artistic principles which do not truckle
       to the popular appetite." Here, finds "Xingu" an amiable
       farce, "Coming Home" the most remarkable with its
       emotional suspense and "Bunner Sisters" pervaded with an
       "almost spiteful morbidity."

S44   Anonymous. "Xingu." *Times Literary Supplement* (London),
       30 November 1916, p. 572.
       Praises the variety of class and locale, ironic comedy,
       dramatic portraiture and romantic legend and her keen
       versatile imagination, lucidity of *Bunner Sisters*,
       unforgettable quality of "Coming Home" and the ironic
       comedy of manners of "Autres Temps..."--calling the latter
       Wharton's best.

S45   Edgett, Edwin Francis. "Edith Wharton and the Short
       Story." *Boston Evening Transcript*, 28 October 1916, p. 8.
       Warm praise for the style and substance of *Xingu and
       Other Stories*. Contends that, although not one of the eight
       is "based upon anything but a commonplace theme,"
       Wharton gives each life and distinction. Terms *Bunner
       Sisters* proof of what melodrama can become "in the hands

of an expert literary workman" who can bring old tales to life and "make something new." Calls "Xingu" the best.

S46   Gould, Gerald. "New Novels." *New Statesman* 8 (9 December 1916): 234.
         Terms "Bunner Sisters" the best, "Xingu" trivial, "Coming Home" trite and sensational, "Autres Temps..." perfect of its kind, "The Choice" melodramatic, "Kerfol" something new in the ghost story and "The Triumph of Night" even more successful "in the same gloomy view."

S47   H[ackett], F[rancis]. "Mrs. Wharton's Art." *New Republic* 10 (10 February 1917): 50-52. Rpt. *Horizons, A Book of Criticism*. New York: Huebsch, 1918.
         Finds volume almost completely gratifying though deficient in comedy which would shed other lights on her landscape which is "acid, cold and bleak." Argues she does best women "among well-off people in a given time and sphere." Cites "The Long Run" as the "flower of a career." Believes Wharton is interested in a restricted world with its chance for intense relationships because marriage and love are her primary themes.

S48   Hale, Edward E. "Recent Fiction." *Dial* 61 (28 December 1916): 586-87.
         Cites James and de Maupassant as the realists who influenced Wharton to employ the short story form, but contends she is best in her novels. Terms "Coming Home" the best story, here; while the subject explored in "Xingu" has been over-done and isn't worth her attention.

Here and Beyond

S49   Anonymous. "New Books in Brief." *Independent* 117 (7 August 1926): 164.
         Review cites her original, "extremely subtle variety" of the ghost story which has her "familiar grace of phrase and structure" but not always "her old conviction of reality."

S50   Anonymous. Review of *Here and Beyond*. *Nation and Athenaeum* 39 (19 June 1926): 325.
        Finds Wharton "undoubtedly" old-fashioned with her pity, sentiment, satisfying plots and realistic characters "rather than sequences of reaction, stimuli, and complexes." Praises "The Seed of the Faith" as "tender, powerful, ironic."

S51   Anonymous. "Edith Wharton's Finely Fashioned Tales in *Here and Beyond*." *New York Times Book Review*, 2 May 1926, p. 9.
        Notes Wharton's high place in American and English literature, with particular praise here for "Bewitched." Brief commentary on stories in collection.

S52   Anonymous. "New Books at a Glance." *Saturday Review* (London) 141 (29 May 1926): 653.
        Short notice finds three stories mundane, three, psychic.

S53   Anonymous. "Here and Beyond." *Times Literary Supplement*, 2 September 1926, p. 578.
        Maintains that "Bewitched" is the only story which contains an "unrationalized" ghost, and that throughout, the manner and technical accomplishment are more remarkable than the matter. Terms "The Seed of the Faith" the best.

S54   Edgett, Edwin Francis. "Here and Beyond with Edith Wharton." *Boston Evening Transcript*, 8 May 1926, Book Section, p. 4.
        Begins with strong, detailed praise for *Ethan Frome*, goes on to criticize the stories with supernatural overtones as lacking reality and concludes with praise for "The Seed of the Faith" and Wharton's style.

S55   Field, Louise Maunsell. "Here and Beyond." *Literary Digest International Book Review* 6 (June 1926): 450-51.

Very favorable review cites Wharton's depth and praises "Bewitched" as the "most notable" with its superb portrait of Mrs. Rutledge.

S56   Frank, Grace. "Grave Tales." *Saturday Review of Literature* 2 (29 May 1926): 822.

Contends that though the "gentility may seem old-fashioned," her themes are timeless, made even more poignant with the absence of stridency and "flashy virtuosity" so often found in magazine fiction. Praises "The Temperate Zone," "The Young Gentlemen" and "The Seed of the Faith" as models of construction. Maintains that if she is detached, she is understanding.

S57   Hartley, L.P. Review of *Here and Beyond*. *Saturday Review* (London) 141 (19 June 1926): 754.

Contends the architectural quality of Wharton's work avoids the uncertain structure of modern fiction and that it is natural in her work for people to be haunted and to have psychic powers and premonitions. "[S]he accepts the psychic world as our alternative to the real world and binds herself to obey its rules."

S58   Kennedy, P.C. "New Novels." *New Statesman* 27 (19 June 1926): 266.

Finds only "The Seed of the Faith" strong and skillful. The rest are "half-ghost-stories" and light social comedy in which the manner is "too grand for its matter."

S59   Leech, Margaret. "Edith Wharton's New Book of Short Stories." *New York World*, 9 May 1926, Book Section, p. 6-M.

Summarizes stories, calling "The Temperate Zone" the best. Feels these are the "late flowering of a distinguished talent, reflecting the facility, the worldly wisdom and the urbane detachment of [her] work. No flame burns here; but there is an art refined, urbane and unfailingly sure."

S60   Meadows, George. Review of *Here and Beyond*. *Catholic World* 123 (August 1926): 715-16.

Short review praises psychological analysis, style, diversity, and her handling of the "psychic" medium, which he compares to the surety of Emily Bronte.

S61   Newman, Frances. "Deserves Pulitzer Prize Every Year." *New York Evening Post Literary Review*, 22 May 1926, p. 2.
        Comments on Wharton's advantages of birth and discipleship to James. Finds these stories add nothing to James in terms of the short story's evolution, compares her with Mansfield, and contends she deserves the Pulitzer for "presenting the higher standard of American manhood and manners." Praises her suave, pleasant writing and brilliant, successful phrases.

S62   Pearson, Edmund. "Fiction." *Outlook* 143 (2 June 1926): 186.
        Briefly summarizes each story.

S63   Rodgers, John T. "An Age of Innocence." *North American Review* 223 (June-July-August 1926): 375-76.
        Negative review terming the stories "silly inconsequential, irrelevant bits of flubdubbery." Reviewer calls Wharton's "gay repartee" merely "padding."

S64   Woolsey, Dorothy Bacon. "Short Stories." *New Republic* 47 (21 July 1926): 262-63.
        Argues that this volume, published by an unknown writer, would be received with praise; however, Wharton is unfairly expected to live up to the heights of *Ethan Frome* and *The Fruit of the Tree*. Comments on separate stories.

Certain People

S65   Anonymous. Review of *Certain People*. *New Statesman* 36 (29 November 1930): 250.

Argues only in "After Holbein" is she at her best, but contends that there is much mastery even in her weakest work compared to her juniors.

S66   Anonymous. Review of *Certain People*. *Saturday Review* (London) 150 (6 December 1930): 747.
       Contends that theme of "After Holbein" has been done too often and she is "over-generous with her effects." Terms "Bottle of Perrier" more successfully grim, while Wharton is at ease with the satire of "The Refugees."

S67   Anonymous. "Short Stories of Varying Themes by Edith Wharton." *Springfield Republican*, 28 December 1930, p. 7-E.
       Positive review notes these stories carry on the Wharton tradition and demonstrate her versatility. Mostly plot summary, particularly of "After Holbein," termed "far and away the best."

S68   Anonymous. "Certain People." *Times Literary Supplement*, 27 November 1930, p. 1010.
       Praises collection as evidence of Wharton's vitality, "a quality without which the school of fiction to which she belongs is apt to seem wilfully remote." Contends she maintains the integrity which James prized.

S69   Chamberlain, John. "The Short Story Muddles On." *New Republic* 65 (7 January 1931): 225.
       Brief review contends her prejudices cause "an orientation toward a dead life." Feels she practices "a dexterous but perfunctory technique upon anything that comes to hand out of the past." Analyzes problems of the short story in a time when behaviorist (e.g., Hemingway) and Freudian tendencies have eschewed moral choice and plot, motive and purpose.

S70   Codman, Florence. "Short Stories by Novelists." *Nation* 131 (10 December 1930): 654.
       Terms volume "shockingly third rate" with "After Holbein" the one exception with its "perfect imprint of a

vanishing race" fashioned with "mature grace and rich understanding."

S71   Gilman, Dorothy Foster. "Certain People." *Boston Evening Transcript*, 13 December 1930, Book Section, p. 2.
        Judges "After Holbein" the masterpiece and comments on her assurance when describing the traditional life of her own generation. However, contends her insights are tinged with acidity, and her ability to convey irony transcends her capacity to move readers. Terms her writing beautiful, but "chilly."

S72   Gilman, Dorothy Foster. "Some Distinguished Stories." *New York Herald Tribune Books*, 2 November 1930, p. 5.
        Praises Wharton as the best social historian America has ever produced, while maintaining that she must remain with her own generation where she is strongest. Terms these stories the product of a novelist, not a short story writer, yet judges "After Holbein" in some respects the best American short story in a decade.

S73   Hutchison, Percy. "Mrs. Wharton's Mastery of the Short Story Revealed in Six New Tales." *New York Times Book Review*, 9 November 1930, p. 7.
        Contends that one of the Jamesian school cannot abandon the short story, and praises this collection, terming "After Holbein" a "miniature masterpiece" and equating Nora Frenway with Ibsen's Nora as an important literary figure.

S74   Lieber, Maxim. "Edith Wharton and Zona Gale." *New York World*, 23 November 1930, p. 3-E.
        Contrasts Wharton with Zona Gale, finding that Wharton is like a virtuoso on the platform playing with flawless technique, whereas Gale is like that virtuoso doing beloved encores. Main point is that Wharton carefully composes her work and therefore at times fails to move her readers.

S75 Pritchett, V.S. "Clashes--Mental and Physical." *Spectator* 145 (22 November 1930): 804.

Terms Wharton's "entertaining ideas" like Kipling, but contends the short story is "too mechanical, too reticent" for her talent and "though [she is] expert in inventing ingenious situations," the ingenuity seems more apparent than the art.

Human Nature

S76 Anonymous. "Les Lettres et le théâtre." *Le Mois* 29 (May 1933): 167.

In French. Complains that the volume, though artistic, doesn't touch the reader--as if this is an "objet d'art" in a deluxe shop window.

S77 Anonymous. "New Stories by Edith Wharton." *New York Times Book Review*, 2 April 1933, p. 7.

Praises Wharton's many excellencies, terming her "almost the last of those elder craftsmen whose motto was 'If a story is worth writing at all, it is worth writing in as nearly perfect a manner as is humanly and artistically possible.'" Comments on the predominant note of irony unrelieved by humor or romance, and finds the fundamental crudeness of "extrusion of" human nature to be the foundation of this collection.

S78 B., A. "New Novels." *Saturday Review* (London) 155 (29 April 1933): 414.

Speaks of Wharton's long apprenticeship which laid the foundation for the commanding maturity here. Mentions her knowledge, in terms of human nature, of the selfishness of men. Notes these short stories tend toward the ironic and tragic.

S79 Britten, Florence Haxton. "The Perfection of Technique." *New York Herald Tribune Books*, 26 March 1933, p. 6.

Contends Wharton has grown complete master of
herself and her materials with the years.   Terms her
unsentimental, cool as a scientist and as precise of vision.
Maintains she chooses death as a theme because "around
it people seem to be most themselves." Calls "The Day of
the Funeral" extraordinarily impressive.

S80   Cestre, Charles. "Edith Wharton: Human Nature." *Revue
        Anglo-Américain* 11 (April 1934): 378.
            In French. Very favorable review calls the volume
        Wharton's "best manner." Cites her skeptical view of
        human feelings. Notes she is interested not in youthful
        romantic love but in mature passion with its unconscious
        egotism. Terms the rhythm of the narration so rapid and
        capricious it gives the impression of being both delightfully
        artificial and human at the same time.

S81   Greene, Graham. "Fiction." *Spectator* 150 (5 May 1933):
        654.
            Greene mentions the Jamesian influence and finds the
        prevailing theme to be the Jamesian one of deception.
        Notes she has the surface ingenuity and wit of James, but
        her sentimentalities are unlike James. He calls her attitude
        "cool, aloof, a little withering."

S82   Mortimer, Raymond. "New Novels." *New Statesman and
        Nation* NSV (22 April 1933): 507.
            Finds the situations often improbable: the "patterns of
        human behavior neater than they would be in actuality."
        Complains that Wharton seems intent on shaping her
        stories into objects, but praises her psychological insight.
        Contends young writers could learn from studying her
        technique.

S83   Purdy, Theodore Jr. "Character Studies." *Saturday Review
        of Literature* 9 (22 April 1933): 549.

Terms these highly artificial in choice of subject and setting with a "limited and familiar Whartonian gallery." Appealing to those who accept her world. Contends that her perfected formula results in lost vitality, if greater clarity.

The World Over

S84   Anonymous. Review of *The World Over*. *Nation* 142 (27 June 1936): 852.
    Paragraph-length review cites the impeccable style, but wonders how she allowed "these slick little bits to be exhumed from the files of the ladies' magazines."

S85   Anonymous. "Cultivated Garden." *Time* 27 (4 May 1936): 80.
    Notes the younger generation may find her quaint, but for the older she has "nostalgic charm." Contends the characters are not completely realistic, but "her eye for formal effect has lost none of its cultivated keenness."

S86   Anonymous. "Mrs. Wharton." *Times Literary Supplement*, 25 April 1936, p. 353.
    Praises her mastery as of an older tradition which delights the intelligent and shows what "ease, finish and lightness" mean in fiction. Notes these stories are not exceptionally brilliant for her, but are admirable examples of an art.

S87   Butcher, Fanny. Review of *The World Over*. *Chicago Daily Tribune*, 25 April 1936, p. 10.
    Praises structural and stylistic beauty, and her "incomparable skill," noting "Roman Fever," "Charm Incorporated" and "Confession."

S88   Greene, Graham. "Short Stories." *Spectator* 156 (22 May 1936): 950.

Brief critique terms these tales suave and well bred, but essentially trivial and unlike the author of *The Children* or "A Bottle of Perrier."

S89   Hutchison, Percy. "Mrs. Wharton's New Stories and Other Recent Works of Fiction." *New York Times Book Review* 26 April 1936, p. 6.

Contends her mastery of the short story form is unimpaired, maintaining that few equal her "getting under the skin of a character ... or a reader." Calls "Roman Fever" like a diamond--hard and brilliant, in which social satire is pushed to a more demolishing conclusion than ever before.

S90   Quennell, Peter. "New Novels." *New Statesman and Nation* NS 11 (2 May 1936): 670.

States "Mrs. Wharton belongs to a tradition of American life that has now almost disappeared." Though competent, these stories are not up to the standard of the novels which have established her as a minor master of early twentieth-century fiction, although the tone of "dry worldliness" makes her "insidiously readable."

S91   R., F. "Mrs. Wharton." *Manchester Guardian*, 15 May 1936, p. 7.

Objects to the occasionally slick effects and the "well-made" story which give the sense of "literature masquerading as life." Contends that "Pomegranate Seed" fails because it seems "an intention of the intellect."

S92   R., W.K. "Bittersweet." *Christian Science Monitor* "Book News of the Day," 27 April 1936, p. 16.

Notes that Wharton has always shown interest in shorter fiction, and these stories are examples of her skill, but they do not strike deeply into universal qualities and emotions. Terms plots dependent on "something strange and out of the way." Finds her wealthy characters gain importance through her realism, wit, subtlety and precision.

S93   Reilley, Joseph. Review of *The World Over*. *Catholic World*
       144 (December 1936): 367-68.
           Praises artistic conscience, unfailing artistry, and
       striking talent of her long career, noting that she reached
       genius once in *Ethan Frome*.   Maintains "Charm
       Incorporated," "Confession" and "Roman Fever" are among
       the best she has done.

S94   S., G. "New Books." *Saturday Review of Literature* 14 (2
       May 1936): 19.
           Praises construction and good story-telling, noting
       these stories are not deep, but dramatic and entertaining.

S95   Simonds, Katherine. "Edith Wharton's Evocative Stories."
       New York Herald Tribune Books, 26 April 1936, p. 5.
           Contends there is intellectual excitement here for
       those who think of the short story as an "elaborate
       pattern" and admire phrasing and technique.   Yet,
       maintains that in spite of artistry stories have "thinness of
       an echo," and seem "not true ... even to a vanished
       present" in a way James still seems true.

                              Ghosts

S96   Anonymous. "Briefer Mention." *Commonweal* 27 (5
       November 1937): 55.
           Two-sentence comment praises Wharton's outstanding
       qualities in the use of different methods of short story
       writing.

S97   Anonymous. "Ghosts and Ghost Stories." *Times Literary
       Supplement*, 6 November 1937, p. 823.
           Brief discussion of Wharton in a review of four
       anthologies, contends that the reader is sometimes
       befogged here and left to choose an ending for himself,
       and finds Wharton's justification in her Preface, in which
       she terms reading a creative act.   Nevertheless, the three

best are all ghostless: "All Souls'," "Mary Pask" and "Bewitched."

S98   B., W.R. "Fiction." *Saturday Review of Literature* 17 (6 November 1937): 19.
        Praises the charm of the Preface and contends that this is the book for lovers of ghost stories because Wharton knows her craft.

S99   Greene, Graham. "Short Stories." *Spectator* 159 (24 December 1937): 1155.
        Feels Wharton fails to give the ghost story its physical sense except for "A Bottle of Perrier," although, like James, she is good at the "moral twist."

S100   Moult, Thomas. "Short Stories." *Manchester Guardian*, 19 November 1937, p. 7.
        Contends Henry James would have approved of her kind of ghost story, the "vividly imagined." Calls Wharton one of the few first-class living writers of fiction, and finds the subtlety, strength and beauty of these twelve stories make them "near-masterpieces."

S101   Shawe-Taylor, Desmond. "New Novels." *New Statesman and Nation* NS 14 (6 November 1937): 758.
        Short paragraph terms these tales not hair-raising, but with a "half-eerie, half cozy charm" of their own.

Chapter 11

The Short Stories Criticism

Chapter cites critical discussions of the short stories. For reviews of the individual short story collections, see Chapter 10. For citations of contents of the individual collections, consult the primary bibliography, Chapter 1. For discussions of individual stories, refer to the Works Index.

T1   Anonymous. "Their Pictures." *Woman's Home Companion* 46 (September 1919): 55.
        Issue contains "Writing A War Story" and Wharton's picture bears the caption that she is the foremost among American novelists and, though living in France, has not lost her American humor or knowledge of American life.

T2   Bell, Millicent. "A James 'Gift' to Edith Wharton." *Modern Language Notes* 72 (March 1957): 182-85.
        Quotes letter 8 January 1908 in which James gave Wharton the donnée for "The Pretext," and discusses the story with the conclusion that her dry treatment seems to

relish the "joke" as much as the reverberations within the characters and illustrates her preference for anecdote over psychology.

T3   Bendixen, Alfred. *Haunted Women: The Best Supernatural Tales by American Women Writers.* New York: Ungar, 1985.
          Contains "The Fullness of Life" and "Pomegranate Seed." Introduction contends women found the conventions of supernatural fiction particularly suited to exploring their aspirations and frustrations. Wharton comments note that her tales "attempt to shock the reader into recognizing the inadequacy of conventional views," and she recognized the potential for "probing examinations of love and marriage" in this genre.

T4   Caws, Mary Ann. "Framing in Two Opposite Modes: Ford and Wharton." *The Comparatist* 10 (May 1986): 114-20.
          Contrasts framing narration in Ford Madox Ford's *The Good Soldier* and Wharton's "The Other Two." Notes in setting and class the works are alike, but shows they offer a structural contrast with stable framing narration in Ford and shifting, in Wharton.

T5   Chu, Li Min. "The Ghostly Stories of Edith Wharton." *Bulletin of National Taiwan University* 26 (1977): 417-48.
          In English. Analyzes all the stories in *Ghosts*, with plot summaries. Argues Wharton excels in maintaining a ghostly atmosphere with a feeling of doom permeating each work. However, contends that her ghost stories are essentially moral, showing her regard for human dignity, and that the Chinese reader can find her a model of clear, graceful English as well as a moral measure.

T6   Downey, June E. "Comparative Discussion." In *Creative Imagination: Studies in the Psychology of Literature.* New York: Harcourt Brace and Co., (1929): 202-08.
          Argues understanding of "a peculiarly atrocious murder" comes most objectively from literature, not journalism. Cites "The Duchess At Prayer" as the most objective of three masterpieces (Poe's "The Cask of

Amontillado" and Balzac's "La Grande Breteche," the others) with its detached introduction and distant setting.

T7   Dwight, Eleanor. "Edith Wharton and 'The Cask of Amontillado.'" In *Poe and Our Times: Influences and Affinities*. Edited by Benjamin Franklin Fisher IV. Baltimore: Edgar Allan Poe Society, 1986.

Traces influences of Poe's "The Cask of Amontillado" on "The Duchess at Prayer." Notes differences in Poe and Wharton in that her supernatural world is logical and orderly, without raving and obsession. Notes Poe's influence on "The Eyes" and speculates on his influence on "Kerfol."

T8   Edel, Leon. "The Nature of Literary Psychology." *Journal of the American Psychoanalytic Association* 29: 447-67. Also incorporated within *Stuff of Sleep and Dreams*. New York: Avon, 1982.

Discusses "All Souls'" (February, 1937) as an attempt (however unconsciously) to deal with the "panic and terror" of approaching death. Also briefly mentions *HofM* as a coming to terms with the social imprisonment she felt and argues nothing she wrote afterward had the same emotional intensity, although it freed her to go on to realize herself as a woman of letters. Also discusses: *AofI*, *EF*.

T9   French, Marilyn. "Introduction." *Roman Fever and Other Stories*. London: Virago, 1985.

Feminist critical commentary on "The Other Two" and "Autres Temps ...". Contends reader must "probe within the language, beneath the genteel ironic surface to find the author's moral stance." Terms one of Wharton's "profoundest themes ... the demonstration of sexual and emotional constriction, especially through the proscription of honest dialogue." Argues the stories are not merely social commentaries, but "penetrating moral analyses." [See B13.1]

T10   Funston, Judith E. "'Xingu': Edith Wharton's Velvet
        Gauntlet." *Studies in American Fiction* 12 (Autumn 1984):
        227-34.
              Argues "Xingu" is "Wharton's repaying James in kind
        for all his honest though tactless criticism of her work, as
        well as for his sketch of 'la Princesse Lointaine' in 'The
        Velvet Glove.'"

T11   Going, W. T. "Wharton's 'After Holbein.'" *Explicator* 10
        (November 1951): Item 8.
              Argues that the title "refers to the elaborate series of
        woodcuts by Holbein, the *Dance of Death*," and traces
        motifs from the woodcuts in the story.

T12   Hicks, G. "Intense Aristocrat." *Saturday Review* 51 (3
        August 1968): 17-18.
              Occasioned by the publication of the complete short
        stories edited by R.W.B. Lewis [B14]. Notes that he
        appreciated her more than formerly after reading the
        volume, but it "was not a major literary experience."
        Comments on the effect of snobbishness, the growth of
        her power in the genre over the years, the Jamesian
        influence, the marriage theme.

T13   Howells, William Dean. *Great Modern American Stories*.
        New York: Boni and Liveright, 1921.
              Howells's short explanation of his choice of "The
        Mission of Jane" to reprint here is that it was such a
        family favorite, portraying the dull Jane so perfectly,
        unsurpassed artistically.

T14   Kozikowski, Stanley J. "Unreliable Narration in Henry
        James's 'The Two Faces' and Edith Wharton's 'The
        Dilettante.'" *Arizona Quarterly* 35 (1979): 357-72.
              Valuable analysis of the difference in narrative
        technique in relation to point of view and the use of the
        reflector and reliable and unreliable narration in the two
        stories. Concludes that Wharton "achieves telling ironies
        more clearly and coherently than does James's 'The Two
        Faces' in a similar plot which uses a reliable narrative

account of an unreliable reflector." Contends that in Wharton the action is under "a firmer aesthetic control," has a more intact artistry and greater thematic integrity.

T15   Kronenberger, Louis. "Mrs. Wharton's Literary Museum." *Atlantic Monthly* 222 (September 1968): 98-102.

     Review of *Complete Short Stories* edited by R.W.B. Lewis [B14]. Finds they resemble "a crowded, very reputable antique shop which yields only a few really valuable pieces." Attributes this datedness to the stranglehold of her class and conformist society which makes every character a type. Also finds more artifice here than either art or life. Cites: *HofM, CC, EF, Children, Summer, Reef*, "The Other Two."

T15.1   Lawson, Richard. "Edith Wharton." *Dictionary of Literary Biography.* Vol.78. *American Short Story Writers 1880-1910.* Detroit: A Bruccoli Clark Book, 1989. 308-323.

     General survey of EW's short stories. Paragraph-length synopses, presented in chronological order, include brief critical commentary on most entries. Notes constancy of theme of entrapment, beginning with "Mrs. Manstey's View." Thematic concerns of imprisonment, the artist and his role in society, the problem of marriage and divorce and "the woman's social or socially conditioned plight ..." are highlighted. Contends that, although not an innovator, "Wharton can lay just claim to first rank as a short story writer." Notes earlier critics overestimate her literary parallels with Henry James and Hawthorne. Cites most of the short fiction with particular commentary on: *GI, CI, DofM, Sanctuary, H&WW*, "The Letter," "The House of the Dead Hand," "The Introducers," "Les Metteurs en Scène," *Tales of Men and Ghosts, Xingu, M'sR, Here and Beyond, Certain People, Human Nature, The World Over, Ghosts,* "A Venetian Night's Entertainment." Includes primary list with first printing date, short secondary bibliography of book-length titles.

T16   Lawson, Richard H. "Nietzsche, Edith Wharton and The
        Blond Beast." In AN 80-1-0000196 (1980): 169-72.
        Festschrift in Milan V. Dimic and Juan Ferranté, eds.
        Proceedings of the 7th Congress of the International
        Comparative Literature Association. Stuttgart: Bieber, 1979.
            Reading of "The Blond Beast" in terms of Wharton's
        interest in Nietzsche. Speculates that in Nietzsche she
        appreciated the idea that the breaking of convention is
        exhilarating and returning to a basis of natural instinct is
        "salutary"--particularly in light of her marital difficulties.
        [See N16].

T17   Lewis, R.W.B. "Introduction." *The Collected Short Stories
        of Edith Wharton*. New York: Scribner's, 1968. Introduction
        reprinted in *Women Writers of the Short Story*. Edited by
        Heather McLane. Englewood Cliffs, New Jersey: Prentice-
        Hall, 1980.
            Defines Wharton's concept of the short story, and
        finds within her best stories, although she did not
        significantly modify the genre, the situation "gradually
        revealed in all its complexity and finality" so that each
        gains the stature of a "paradigm of the human condition."
        Contends she was the first American writer to make
        almost exclusively her own the exploration of the marriage
        question. Discusses marriage in the short stories, her use
        of the ghost story, the feminine and masculine aspects of
        her art, Old New York and illegitimacy. Suggests grouping
        of the short stories: Marriage Question, Ghost Stories,
        Romance and History, Crime, Art and Human Nature,
        Culture and Comedy, Old New York and Illegitimacy, but
        cautions other groupings would be instructive and several
        stories fall into more than one group. See discussion of:
        "Souls Belated," "The Long Run," "The Letters," "The
        Reckoning," "Autres Temps...," "The Other Two,"
        "Pomegranate Seed,""All Souls'," "Kerfol," "The Hermit and
        the Wild Woman," "The Eyes," "The Pelican," "The
        Descent of Man," "After Holbein," "Roman Fever," "His
        Father's Son," "Her Son." [In B14]

T18   Lewis, R.W.B. "Powers of Darkness." *Times Literary Supplement* (London) 13 June 1975, p. 644-45.

Written on the occasion of Constable's issuing a collection of Wharton's ghost stories, this article praises her work in the genre, and adds significant biographical material that contributes to an understanding of the psychological dynamics behind her ghost stories. As he says, "[L]ike other Victorian and Edwardian writers of ghost stories, [she] deployed the supernatural as a way of getting at certain aspects of human nature and experience ... the aberrant, the perverse, the lawless, the violently sexual--which could not be dealt with in realistic fiction." Cites: "Kerfol," "Eyes," "All Souls'," "The Lady's Maid's Bell," "Life and I."

T19   McDowell, Margaret B. "Edith Wharton's 'After Holbein': A Paradigm of the Human Condition." *Journal of Narrative Technique* 1 (1971): 49-58.

Discussion of Wharton's technique and artistry in the short story form, contending she "so consummately suggests the general in and through the particular that" the situation can be seen as a paradigm of the human condition. Valuable examination of "After Holbein" that draws parallels between allegorical elements in Holbein's intentions and realism and Wharton's.

T20   McDowell, Margaret B. "Edith Wharton's Ghost Stories." *Criticism* 12 (1970): 133-52.

Insightful appreciation of the ghost stories. Contends that Wharton's "finest efforts in this mode are notable precisely because they are more than adroit evocations of the otherworldly" and "reveal her extraordinary psychological and moral insight." Argues she explores, in her best ghost stories, "human situations of considerable complexity" and that she is able, from this "unusual angle of penetration" to achieve a "new perspective from which to review the mundane and the perhaps unfamiliar problems of human beings." Important readings of: "The Eyes," "Miss Mary Pask," "Pomegranate Seed," "The Triumph of Night," "Kerfol," "Bewitched." Contrasts these excellent stories with others like "Mr. Jones," "Afterward," "The Lady's Maid's Bell," "A Bottle of Perrier," "All Souls.'"

T21   Murray, Margaret P. "The Gothic Arsenal of Edith Wharton." *The Journal of Evolutionary Psychology* 10.2 and 3 (August 1989): 315-21.

Contends that through the myth of the *femina alba* in "Pomegranate Seed" EW is able to rework the theme of the displaced wife in *Fruit of the Tree*. Maintains Charlotte and Elsie are manifestations of the Aphrodite/Persephone myth.

T22   O'Brien, Edward. *The Advance of the American Short Story*. New York: Dodd, Mead, 1923.

In chapter titled "The School of Henry James," Wharton's "arctic frigidity" is mentioned, and opinion given that she has "assimilated every lesson that her master can teach except tenderness and ease, and in sheer craftsmanship it may even be held that she has occasionally surpassed him." Long quote from Van Wyck Brooks on the intellectual quality of her characters who do not grow. Contends most American writers influenced by James are "indirectly derivative" through Wharton. [See O14]. Bibliography.

T23   Pattee, Fred Lewis. *The Development of the American Short Story: An Historical Survey*. New York: Harper, 1923.

Draws parallels with James, finding she surpasses him in "simplicity and naturalness of style." Praises *MdeT* highly. Also cites: *EF*, "Pot-boiler."

T24   Pattee, Fred Lewis. "Introduction." "The Choice." In *Century Readings in the American Short Story*. New York: The Century Company, 1927.

Brief introduction to "The Choice" with notes on Wharton's theory of the short story. [See T23]

T25   Petry, Alice Hall. "A Twist of Crimson Silk: Edith Wharton's 'Roman Fever.'" *Studies in Short Fiction* 24.2 (Spring 1987): 163-66.

      Argues "Roman Fever," Wharton's late short story, is a complex work of art worth serious critical attention. Examines knitting imagery closely as a clue to the psyches of both women.

T26   Plante, Patricia R. "Edith Wharton as a Short Story Writer." *Midwest Quarterly* 4 (Summer 1963): 363-70.

      Detailed analysis of critical response to Wharton's short stories, emphasizing that Wharton felt the situation should occupy the center of interest, her openings contain the germ of the story, and her skillful dialogue contributes greatly to her presentation of the situation. Notes critical objections to her irony, often cited as creating a monotonous tone, and her coldness. Deplores her decline and the lack of contemporary appreciation of her stories. Cites: "Recovery," "The Other Two," "Father's Son," "Daunt Diana," "Xingu," "Bewitched," "After Holbein," "Her Son."

T26.1   Price, Alan. "Edith Wharton's War Story." *Tulsa Studies in Women's Literature.* 8.1 (Spring 1989): 95-100.

      Reviews the biographical background to EW's war story "Coming Home."

T27   Quinn, Arthur Hobson. "Mrs. Wharton as a Writer of Short Stories." *Book News Monthly* 26 (November 1907): 179-81.

      Praises the unity of Wharton's short stories. Contends her real mission is to portray modern American life. Brief criticism of *FofT*.

T28   Robillard, Douglas. *Supernatural Fiction Writers.* Volume II. Edited by E.F. Bleiler. New York: Scribner's, 1984. 783-788.

      A compendium of supernatural fiction writers. Volume II is a series of essays on individual authors. In Wharton chapter, analysis of her supernatural tales is for the most

part summary. Concludes: "She has a keen sense of how
the world of the spirit can impinge upon the mundane,
and one of her effective contributions to the field is the
reality of that world." Cites: "Fullness of Life," "Lady's
Maid's Bell," "Eyes," "Afterward," "Miss Mary Pask,"
"Pomegranate Seed," "Mr. Jones," All Souls'," "Triumph of
Night," "Kerfol," "Bottle of Perrier," "Bewitched."

T29   Ross, Danforth. *The American Short Story*. Minneapolis:
         University of Minnesota Press, 1961.
              Pamphlet on the American short story briefly
         introduces Wharton as a disciple of James and then
         summarizes "The Mission of Jane" in a paragraph--noting
         the lack of sentimentality.

T30   Sasaki, Miyoko. "The Dance of Death: A Study of Edith
         Wharton's Short Stories." *Studies in English Literature* 51.1-
         2 (1974): 67-90. Tokyo: The English Literature Society of
         Japan.
              In English. Analysis of the "dance of death" in "A
         Journey," "The Duchess at Prayer," "Atrophy," "After
         Holbein," "Joy in the House," "Diagnosis," "The Day of the
         Funeral," "Permanent Wave," "The Looking Glass," and
         "Roman Fever." Notes ironies and contrasts with the
         juxtaposition of the dance of love. Analyzes the tragic,
         comic and tragi-comic aspects of the characters' reactions
         to both approaching death and bereavement.

T31   Saunders, Judith P. "Ironic Reversal in Edith Wharton's
         'Bunner Sisters.'" *Studies in Short Fiction* 14 (1977): 241-
         45.
              Analyzes "Bunner Sisters" as an educative process in
         reverse in which Ann Eliza learns that reliance on
         traditional female principles of self-sacrifice and
         renunciation is "dangerous" and that seeming selflessness
         can cover a "fatal egotism." Therefore, Wharton poses
         "complicated questions about the morality of self-
         abnegation."

T32   Scarborough, Dorothy. *The Supernatural in Modern English Fiction*. New York: Putnam, 1917.

Short commentary on several of Wharton's ghost stories used to illustrate characteristics of modern supernatural stories, as they have developed and changed from earlier forms. Mentions use of animals, doubles, and modern humans as ghosts. Cites: "Triumph of Night," "Afterward," "Duchess at Prayer," "Eyes," "Kerfol."

T33   Schriber, Mary Sue. "Darwin, Wharton and 'The Descent of Man': Blueprints of American Society." *Studies in Short Fiction* 17 (1980): 31-38.

Discusses Darwin's theories of human motivation, the development of conscience and the relationship between the sexes in terms of the cultural and intellectual condition of American society at the turn of the century, as illustrated by Wharton in the characterization of the Linyards in "The Descent of Man." Article has a feminist orientation, noting that Wharton saw the dangers in the sharp male-female social divisions of the time. Cites: *HofM*, *FW&M*.

T34   Smith, Allan Gardner. "Edith Wharton and the Ghost Story." In *Gender and Literary Voice*. Edited by Janet Todd. New York and London: Holmes and Meier Publishers, 1980.

An analysis of the collection *The Ghost Stories of Edith Wharton*. Contends that "In the genre of the ghost story ... she was able to penetrate into the realm of the *unseen*, that is, into the area that her society preferred to be unable to see, or to construe defensively as super (i.e., not) natural." Cites: "All Souls'," "Looking Glass," "Bewitched," "Miss Mary Pask," "Triumph of Night," "Afterward," "Mr. Jones," "Pomegranate Seed," and "Eyes."

T35   Tintner, Adeline R. "The Hermit and the Wild Woman: Edith Wharton's 'Fictioning' of Henry James." *Journal of Modern Literature* 4 (1974): 32-42.

Predates Lewis biography, so does not take account of Fullerton role, but offers fascinating reading of "The

Hermit and the Wild Woman" and the narrative poem "Ogrin the Hermit" as containing hermits that can be identified with aspects of James. Detailed explication of the story as an *histoire à clef.* [See also T17]

T36 Williams, Blanche. *Our Short Story Writers.* New York: Moffat Yard, 1920.

Chapter on Wharton has biographical data. Notes art of her stories, and argues the Jamesian influence is not excessive. Answers charges that she has not changed since 1899, that her viewpoint is too literary, that she is merely clever. Covers her published work to date. Cites: *DofM, MdeT, Xingu, Touchstone, Reef, EF,* "Debt," "Duchess at Prayer," "Afterward," "Daunt Diana," "Letters," "Bolted Door," "Triumph of Night," "Eyes," "Confessional," "Muse's Tragedy," "Journey," "Pelican," "Souls Belated," "Moving Finger," "Copy" and "Kerfol."

T37 Wolff, Cynthia Griffin. "Introduction." *Roman Fever and Other Stories by Edith Wharton.* New York: Collier Books, 1987.

Argues Wharton's universality and timelessness in that the major characteristic of her work is a "profound concern with the ever-changing relationships between individual liberty and social context." Notes that her stories often end with a dilemma stated as she probes the "timeless implications" of the necessity of social order versus the equally compelling needs of individuals in pain. Discusses: "After Holbein," "Angel at the Grave," "Xingu," "Souls Belated," "Autres Temps ...," "The Last Asset."

T38 Woollcott, Alexander. "An Afterword on 'The Lady's Maid's Bell.'" In *Woollcott's Second Reader.* New York: Viking, 1937.

Short Afterword attributes the heightened effect of "The Lady's Maid's Bell" to the point of view "below stairs" which also gives *Wuthering Heights* "the priceless flavor of an old wives' tale." Quotes from the Preface to *Ghosts.* [B1]

T39 Wright, Austin McGiffert. *The American Short Story in the Twenties*. Chicago: University of Chicago Press, 1961.

Purpose is to define the modern short story (1919-1931), using earlier short stories (1890-1919) as contrasts. Discusses differences in subject matter, form and treatment. Wharton classed as of the earlier tradition. Cites: "Reckoning," "Long Run."

T40 Zilversmit, Annette. "Edith Wharton's Last Ghosts." *College Literature* 14.3 Edith Wharton Issue (1987): 296-305.

Psychological analysis of Wharton's late ghost stories, "Pomegranate Seed" and "All Souls'" in terms of the relationships of the women within them, their self-defeating fears and lack of self-knowledge, and, in the latter, the "long denied isolation and loneliness" of Mrs. Clayburn. Also cites "The Fullness of Life."

Chapter 12

Poetry

Chapter lists reviews of the poetry volumes which are cited in chronological order followed by articles on the poetry. See the Works Index for discussions of individual poems and collections. Anonymous reviews are alphabetized by journal or newspaper.

Artemis to Actæon

U1 Anonymous. Review of *Artemis to Actæon and Other Verse*. *Athenaeum* (London) 4268 (14 August 1909): 178.

    Applauds her excellent blank verse, but finds the rhymes less successful with the sonnets lacking inspiration and the lyrical pieces, spontaneity.

U2 Anonymous. Review of *Artemis to Actæon and Other Verse*. *Nation* 89 (15 July 1909): 55.

    Terms volume "musky," full of "unrest and strain," with an itch to "allegorize" in "strange effective fashions." Judges "Life" the best.

U3 Anonymous. "Books of Poems by Two Writers." *New York Times Saturday Review* 14 (8 May 1909): 33.

Contends book "has all the grace and loveliness of the intellect, but it is on the whole an academic production." Argues it "makes no appeal to the emotions because it has not drawn from them."

U4   Anonymous. "New Books Reviewed." *North American Review* 190 (November 1909): 702-03.

Praises her dramatic monologue "Vesalius in Zante" and finds her best in the sonnet. Notes her prose craftsmanship and feels it sometimes lends the halting quality of prose to the poetry, yet she is a poet "we could not spare."

U5   Anonymous. "The New Books: Recent Volumes of Poetry." *Review of Reviews* 40 (July 1909): 123.

Brief review notes the high seriousness and fine quality, but objects to the lack of emotional appeal.

U6   Anonymous. "Recent Verse." *Spectator* 103 (3 July 1909): 20.

Praises the vigor of her blank verse, points out her classical form, concluding that her poetry, beautiful and perfect in its way, "makes its chief appeal to the intellect."

U7   Hooker, Brian. "Some Springtime Verse." *Bookman* 29 (June 1909): 365-72.

Wharton reviewed pp. 367-68. Objects that at times her thought absorbs feeling, leaving "her language dry." Praises craftsmanship and "Margaret of Cortona." Concludes that although she is not a born poet, as a thoroughly cultured prose artist she can attain a high quality of verse.

U8   Payne, William Morton. "Recent Poetry." *Dial* 47 (16 August 1909): 101.

Objects to the lack of spontaneity and intellectual quality, finding the poetry "too sicklied o'er with the pale cast of thought" with a "song" that does not "well straight up from the heart."

Twelve Poems

U9 Anonymous. "Twelve Poems." *Times Literary Supplement*, 17 March 1927, p. 183.
    Maintains that Wharton the novelist, not Wharton the poet, is the one who can show us "the heart of wonder in familiar things." Laments the absence of surprise, of new vision which make these more verse than poetry, yet there is music in them.

Poetry--Articles

U10 Bell, Millicent. "'Eadgyth' Wharton in the New York *World* 1879." *Yale University Library Gazette* 30 (October 1955): 64-69.
    Details of publication of EW's poem, "Only a Child," under the penname of "Eadgyth" in the NY *World* May 30, 1879. Written in response to the suicide of a twelve-year-old boy in a reformatory, the poem, Bell argues, was more important to her than the privately printed *Verses* and displays her "response to a bit of 'real life' and her imaginative, if sentimental, reconstruction of the event."

U11 Golden, Arline. "Edith Wharton's Debt to Meredith in 'The Mortal Lease.'" *Yale University Library Gazette* 53 (1978): 100-08.
    Demonstration of structural and thematic similarities between Wharton's sonnet sequence, "The Mortal Lease," and George Meredith's Sonnet XXIX of *Modern Love*. Contends that not only her title, but her theme and much of the language are derived from Meredith, and "[e]ven her choice of poetry rather than

fiction follows Meredith, who also turned from the novel to the sonnet sequence for intimate disclosure." Interesting note that the neglect of her poetry may stem from critical inability to reconcile a poetry of adultery and intense sexuality with the author's public image. Discusses "The Mortal Lease" in terms of her affair with Fullerton.

U12   Nevius, Blake. "'Pussie' Jones's Verses: A Biographical Note on Edith Wharton." *American Literature* 23 (January 1952): 494-97.

Cites manuscript data for Wharton's adolescent volume *Verses*. Concludes the poems are "derivative, full of echoes--sometimes pure, sometimes adulterated--of Keats, Wordsworth, Browning, Rossetti, and the German romantics." Although a dominant elegiac mood somewhat unifies the collection, Nevius finds an authentic personal note lacking.

U13   Sencourt, Robert. "The Poetry of Edith Wharton." *Bookman* 73 (July 1939): 478-86.

Deplores fact her poetry is forgotten. Terms her the best American woman poet. Finds her theme is "competent will, working with intricate and sensitive reason and the subtlest social sense to dominate the disorder of passion..., not in the act, but in the psychology of adultery." Cites: "Two Backgrounds," "Vesalius to Zante," *Artemis to Actæon* and "The Mortal Lease."

U14   Tintner, Adeline R. "An Unpublished Love Poem by Edith Wharton." *American Literature* 60.1 (March 1988): 98-103.

Gives text of a 5-line love poem in Edith Wharton's handwriting at the back of a copy of Romain Rolland's *Vie de Tolstoi* (1911) from Henry James's library, given to James by Walter Berry. Speculates that the poem was actually meant for Fullerton.

Chapter 13

Nonfiction

Chapter is divided into two sections: (1) Reviews of the nonfiction volumes. Volumes appear chronologically. Anonymous reviews are alphabetized by title of journal or newspaper. (2) Discussions of the nonfiction appearing in books and articles. Refer to the Works Index for material on individual nonfiction titles.

The Decoration of Houses--Reviews

V1   Anonymous. "The Decoration of Houses." *Architect and Building News*, 22 January 1898, p. 28-29.

        Wishes Wharton and Codman were not so severe on American architecture, but terms this "far ahead of anything of the kind we know of within the last half-century." Calls book straightforward and sensible, and maintains that although there is nothing new here to the trained architect, presenting this volume to "a rich client" can be an aid to taste and style.

V2   Anonymous. "Hints for Home Decoration." *Critic* 32 (8 January 1898): 20.

          Defines focus as the emphasis on the separation of principles of decoration for palaces and grand houses from decoration of simpler residences. Contends "[m]uch reading, travel in Italy and France and independent thinking" are evident and make it, if not practical for everyone, worthwhile as a study of both modern architecture and European buildings.

V3   Anonymous. Review of *The Decoration of Houses*. *Nation* 65 (16 December 1897): 485.

          Finds book signifies the reaction against doctrines of "constructive virtue, sincerity, and the beauty of use," and is an example of reversion to "quasi-classical styles and methods." Calls it intelligent and sensible, bringing attention to the artistic aspects of decoration, but objects that "architectural fitness [here seems to] mean agreeable proportions and combination of lines, and no more."

V4   Berry, Walter. Review of *The Decoration of Houses*. *Bookman* 7 (April 1898): 161-63.

          Berry organized and edited the book, and his review emphasizes its central thesis "that the true expression of interior decoration rests not in superficial application of ornament, but in architectural proportion." The purpose of the book, Berry stresses, is to remedy abuses in decoration with a return to classical simplicity.

V5   Blashfield, Edwin H. "House Decoration." *Book Buyer* 16 (March 1898): 129-33.

          States that the authors enunciate principles clearly, addressing themselves to the moderately well-to-do and wealthy. Contends their emphasis on harmony and proportion in the decoration of the private house is particularly important in a country in its aesthetically formative period, which has no compelling sense of tradition, to act as a corrective against extravagance.

Italian Villas and Their Gardens--Reviews

V6   Anonymous. "Pen and Pencil in Italy." *Critic* 46 (February 1905): 166-68.

Objects to Wharton's approach, finding the illustrations much more instructive than the text. Complains of the lack of history and description of the life of the people who occupied the villas which would restore them to life.

V7   Anonymous. Review of *Italian Villas and Their Gardens*. *International Studio* 25 (April 1905): 179.

Paragraph-length review concentrates on praise of Parrish's landscape paintings. Calls the text well-written and informative.

V8   Anonymous. Review of *Italian Villas and Their Gardens*. *Nation* 79 (24 November 1904): 423.

Finds Wharton's comments closer to the truth than the paintings, with their at times "overstrained scheme of color." Praises her taste, love of Italy, appreciation for garden art and intimate knowledge of it, which make this one of the best books on the subject.

V9   McMahan, Anna Benneson. "Italian Country Houses." *Dial* 37 (16 December 1904): 419-21.

Points out the difficulty the American has understanding the Italian villa and garden because the Italian garden is meant to be lived in. Finds the work analytic enough for the exacting and beautiful enough for the most artistic taste. With an American audience in mind, reviewer suggests general use Americans can make of Italian principles.

Italian Backgrounds--Reviews

V10   Anonymous. Review of *Italian Backgrounds*. *Academy*
           69 (5 August 1905): 798-99.
               In this informal, reflective essay, reviewer
           takes issue with "the wooded island of San Giuliano,"
           but praises the book's knowledge, sympathy, and
           excellent English.

V11   Anonymous. "Wharton--Italian Backgrounds." *Critic* 47
           (September 1905): 287.
               Judges that this book, though better, will
           attract less attention than *The Valley of Decision,*
           although here she has "descriptive felicities" and a
           "glow of ... genuine enthusiasm."

V12   Anonymous. "Literature." *Independent* 48 (8 June
           1905): 1311-12.
               A positive, thumbnail review which praises
           Wharton for finding new places in Italy to write about
           and giving the familiar new interest.

V13   Anonymous. Review of *Italian Backgrounds*. *Nation* 80
           (22 June 1905): 508.
               Defines Wharton's qualifications as "brilliant
           style, historic research, and a catholicity of taste."
           Finds her main emphasis to lie on the blend of
           literature, art, nature and history as they go into the
           making of each city.

V14   Anonymous. "Backgrounds of Italy." *New York Times
           Saturday Review,* 22 April 1905, 265.
               Primarily a day-of-publication announcement
           detailing the contents. Notes book will contain phases
           of art and architecture overlooked by the conventional
           tourist.

V15   Anonymous. "Book of the Week." *Outlook* 80 (8 July 1905): 643.

Classes the book as one of the few books of observation which is also one of artistic and spiritual interpretation, which not only describes places in Italy, but conveys a sense of society. Praises her thorough knowledge, original research, respect for different types of art and style.

V16   Anonymous. "Italian Backgrounds." *Spectator* 95 (30 September 1905): 470-71.

Finds Wharton's studies, in contrast to much modern Italian observation, not "self-conscious" chatter but charming. Praises her knowledge of art, real love of Italy, and clear conception of what gives Italy eternal beauty. Notes the San Vivaldo find. Criticizes the slight sneering at old devotions, however.

V17   Anonymous. "Pictures From Italy." *Times Literary Supplement*, 7 July 1905, p. 215.

After warm praise for her classical style and discriminating, observant eye, reviewer adds that her taste in Italian art is too inclusive. She seems wanting in selectivity and prejudices, although a few do surface.

V18   Carpenter, G.R. "Mrs. Wharton's 'Italian Background'." *Bookman* 21 (August 1905): 609-10.

Negative review accuses Wharton of being hypnotized by Italian art and thus she has "denationalised, defeminised" herself. Objects to her writing as not that of an American or a woman, but of an "art-antiquarian." Does praise the style, but terms the thought "pedantic and inhuman."

V19   Littlefield, Walter. "Italian Backgrounds and Views." *New York Times Saturday Review*, 9 September 1905, p. 588.

Calls Wharton a priestess who has formed the liturgy for the cult of academic investigators who dislike tourists and guidebooks and bring to the surface hitherto hidden meanings.

V20   McMahan, Anna Benneson. "Italian By-Ways." *Dial* 38 (16 May 1905): 352-53.
            Calls this travel book literature and notes distinction of style, "scholarship, savoir-faire, cosmopolitanism." Analyzes the vision of Italy as "a stream of impressions and memories that is much more inspiring than any mere observation." Mentions San Vivaldo find.

A Motor-Flight Through France--Reviews

V21   Anonymous. "Books of Travel and Description." *Dial* 41 (1 December 1908): 409.
            Recommends the book to those who enjoy style, automobiles, and have an interest in the art, architecture or landscape of rural France.

V22   Anonymous. "Travel in Many Lands." *Independent* 65 (19 November 1908): 1180.
            Brief review praises the delicate observations of a "keen, well-stored mind, eager for new impressions" and her lively interest in nature, man, society, architecture and literature.

V23   Anonymous. "Fifty of the Year's Best Books." *Literary Digest* 37 (12 December 1908): 911-12.
            Praises Wharton's familiarity with France, and cites her brilliant sketches as lending a piquancy rare in travel books.

V24   Anonymous. Review of *A Motor-Flight Through France*. *Nation* 87 (12 November 1908): 469.
            Claims it has the marks of a pot-boiler and cites a sense of indifference in the enormous surplus of material, crude arrangement and abrupt ending.

Concludes it can give pleasure to those who know the places, but is too wide, crowded and hasty for the untravelled. Still, she is ever the artist in detail and style.

V25   Anonymous. "Intimate France." *New York Times Saturday Review*, 31 October 1908, p. 637.
         Warmly appreciative short review mentions her insight which presents an intimate, back-door view. Praises pictures and makeup of book.

V26   Anonymous. Review of *A Motor-Flight Through France*. *Review of Reviews* 38 (December 1908): 760.
         Brief review praises keen observation and delicate descriptive style.

V27   Anonymous. Review of *A Motor-Flight Through France*. *Spectator* 101 (5 December 1908): 947.
         Praises book for its evocation of the "almost magic" power of the automobile, and asserts that "no one can read the book without having his eyes ... opened to much that is beautiful and ... newly discovered."

Fighting France--Reviews

V28   Anonymous. "Les Livres de la Guerre." *L'Illustration* 147 (24 June 1916): 574.
         In French. Paragraph praises Wharton's French and her clear-sighted sympathy for the French cause.

V29   Anonymous. "Mrs. Wharton and Kipling on the War." *New York Times Book Review*, 5 December 1915, p. 490.
         Maintains she depicts both trench life and psychological realities with intelligence and grace

which makes her a "peculiarly apt interpreter of the French temperament."

V30 Anonymous. Review of *Fighting France*. *Springfield Republican*, 5 December 1915, Section II, p. 7.

Compares volume with Arnold Bennett's account of his experiences in France. Brief summation, with conclusion praising her style.

V31 Bellaing, Jacques de. "Edith Wharton: Voyages au front de Dunkerque à Belfort." *Etudes* 150 (January-March 1917): 531-32.

In French. Warm appreciation for the book which brings the savage beauty of the struggle of WWI and the horror of the disasters to life with fascinating descriptions and fine psychological observations. Is thankful that an English-language author could recognize the French during the war as "the most intelligent people on earth" and also "the most sublime." Has only one regret: She has drawn a splendid picture of the noble qualities of the French but has forgotten that French traditions and particularly religious faith form anew the character and spirit of the people.

V32 Edgett, Edwin Francis. "Edith Wharton in Fighting France." *Boston Evening Transcript*, 8 December 1915, p. 26.

Edgett's long review is for the most part a celebration of the attempt of writers to "bring about the downfall of the twentieth century barbarians." Extensive quoting and synopsis ends in homage to France, the "most powerful partner in the struggle ... against the great German conspiracy." Typographical error subtitles book "From Dunkerque to *Belfast*."

V33 Hirsch, Charles. "Les Revues." *Mercure de France* 115 (1916): 128-29.

In French. Explains that Edith Wharton has published, in the *Revue des Deux Mondes*, her impressions of a trip to the Front, and that she has gone to Argonne, Lorraine and les Vosges. Contains extended quotes from the book; the only critical comment is: "extremely moving."

V34   Kelly, Florence Finch. "Fighting France." *Bookman* 42 (December 1915): 462-63.
       Terms this a realistic narrative of the daily life of the French people--civilian and soldier, illuminating for Americans the figure of France at war.

V35   Le Cardonnel, George. "Ouvrages sur la Guerre Actuelle." *Mercure de France* 117 (1916): 361-362.
       In French. Synopsis with conclusion that Wharton captures the feelings of the French people and that she understood the French soul better than anyone else as the storm was coming.

V36   R., L. "Les Livres. Edith Wharton. Voyages au front de Dunkerque à Belfort." *Nouvelle Revue* 26 (November 1916): 78.
       *Not seen.

French Ways and Their Meaning--Reviews

V37   Anonymous. Review of *French Ways and Their Meaning*. *Catholic World* 110 (February 1920): 688.
       Contends, in a paragraph-length review, that this is probably a more realistic picture of French life than that given in *Madame de Treymes*, and that it leaves the reader with profound respect for a "heroic, disciplined race."

V38   Anonymous. "Books of the Fortnight." *Dial* 67 (20 September 1919): 272.
       Short review finds "Wisdom enough in some of its single sentences to furnish the raison d'etre of a more pretentious volume."

V39   Anonymous. "Notes on New Books." *Dial*, 67 (4 October 1919): 322.

        Contends this book "does in fact discover the direction which any study of France should take" and promotes understanding.

V40   Anonymous. Review of *French Ways and Their Meaning*. *Nation* (London) 26 (6 December 1919): 368.

        Finds chapter on Intellectual Honesty the keynote. Calls this an interesting, sympathetic analysis of the French, and notes the case she makes for their "less lovable qualities." Regrets omission of "growing spirit of internationalism among the workers."

V41   Anonymous. "Mrs. Wharton's Study of French Ways." *New York Times Book Review*, 28 September 1919, p. 497.

        Notes that she has set a difficult task for herself. Terms the book "desultory," but mentions interesting chapters on marriage, continuity of French culture and on "The New French Woman."

V42   Anonymous. Review of *French Ways and Their Meaning*. *New Republic* 20 (24 September 1919): 241.

        One paragraph satiric review notes that some American "snobs" adopt England; others ... France." Asks: "Can it be possible that America will survive this apologist and France this defender?"

V43   Anonymous. "Travel and Description." *Outlook* 123 (12 November 1919): 308-09.

        Calls this brilliant, intimate and penetrating, yet notes some disappointments, such as when the author defends the French ideal of marriage against the American.

V44   Anonymous. "Mrs. Wharton on the French." *Springfield Republican*, 14 September 1919, Magazine Section, p. 17-A.

Summarizes main points, with the contention that though the reader may not always agree, "he will find them always clear and appreciative, though perhaps over friendly, and always pungently and suggestively phrased." Objects that she tends to estimate the taste of France by the standards of cultured Parisians.

V45   Anonymous. "Latin and Anglo-Saxon." *Times Literary Supplement*, 4 December 1919, p. 710.

Objects to her lack of a "purely philosophic spirit," defends the Anglo-Saxon, and hopes that there can be an amalgamation of the West in both civilizations. Feels her ardent Francophilia is not objective, and takes issue with several of her conclusions.

In Morocco--Reviews

V46   Anonymous. "Briefer Mention." *Dial* 70 (February 1921): 231.

Terms this another of her "swiftly-told, graceful, vivid ... informative" travel books.

V47   Anonymous. Review of *In Morocco*. *Independent* 104 (13 November 1920): 242.

Finds the book recreates atmosphere and scene without authorial intrusion. Comments that she had many opportunities not open to the average tourist.

V48   Anonymous. "Travel." *New York Evening Post, The Literary Review*, 13 November 1920, p. 18.

Defines this as not only a travel book, but also an interpretative history of Morocco which brings back the romance of the Arabian nights because she is at home there--past or present.

V49   Anonymous. "A New Touring Ground." *Saturday Review* (London) 130 (23 October 1920): 339.

Speculates that with the new French roads, Morocco will become "the new touring-ground of Europe." Classes this as not a guide but an "eager, vivid description of people, places, buildings, customs, and finds that her "nervous style" always conveys her chosen effects.

V50   Anonymous. Review of *In Morocco*. *Spectator* 125 (23 October 1920): 541.

Finds the book vivid and entertaining. Mentions her tribute to General Lyautey.

V51   Anonymous. Review of *In Morocco*. *Times Literary Supplement*, 7 October 1920, p. 649.

Finds it fortunate that she did not, as was her original intention, write a guidebook because that "would have lost in broad suggestiveness far more than it would have gained from precision in detail." In this volume, she gives sensitive, vivid descriptions which strongly convey "what was revealed to her."

V52   Hervier, Paul-Louis. "Courrier des lettres anglo-américains." *Nouvelle Revue* 51-52 (January-April 1921): 92.

In French. Paragraph-length review notes *Au Maroc* shows Mrs. Wharton's sympathies for the French.

V53   Mann, Dorothea Lawrence. "*In Morocco*." *Boston Evening Transcript*, 22 December 1920, Part 3, p. 4.

Discusses General Lyautey's achievements, the political situation in Morocco and the circumstances surrounding its new openness to travellers.

V54   Redman, Ben Ray. "Mrs. Wharton Visits Morocco." *New York Times Book Review*, 31 October 1920, p. 9.

         Praises Wharton's remarkable ability to translate "color, line and form into their perfect verbal equivalents." Contends the subject matter here is perfect for her descriptive pen.

V55   Van Doren, Irita. "A Country Without a Guide Book." *Nation* 111 (27 October 1920): 479-80.

         Finds the qualities of an Arabian Nights tale. Notes that she accepts the general theory of imperialism, as she regards General Lyautey's "pacification" of Morocco as an act of accommodation to the Moroccans and the French occupation as benevolent.

The Writing of Fiction--Reviews

V56   Anonymous. "New Books in Brief Review." *Independent* 116 (2 January 1926): 23.

         Argues book is not pedantic and, written neither for beginners nor masters, it will delight anyone interested in the technique of writing.

V57   Anonymous. Review of *The Writing of Fiction*. *New Statesman* 26 (12 December 1925): supplement xxii.

         Terms these essays "well thought out and expressed with ... masculine brevity and clearness," but finds the Proust essay might be more thorough.

V58   Anonymous. Review of *The Writing of Fiction*. *Outlook* 142 (6 January 1926): 34.

         Maintains aspiring novelists should read this book because it emphasizes art and stresses the responsibility of the artist both as craftsman and as critic of life.

V59   Anonymous. "This Week's Books." *Spectator* 135 (7 November 1925): 836.
            Terms the book direct, thoughtful and well-knit.

V60   Anonymous. "The Writing of Fiction." *Times Literary Supplement*, 17 December 1925, p. 878.
            Notes book is addressed to the writer, not reader. Although much of her advice is negative, it is still very helpful. Comments on her emphasis on form and style, praises her examples and analysis of Proust. Compares book with Lubbock's *The Craft of Fiction*.

V61   Aynard, Joseph. "L'Art du roman d'après Mrs. Wharton." *Journal des Débats* 3 (22 January 1926): 119-21.
            In French. Calls this a penetrating critique of writing. Restates her principles. Describes Wharton's novels as like court trials with a long introduction, then inquiries, followed by an understanding of the obscurity of the situation. Contends she has greater finesse in analysis than the British, approaching the Russians--a realist of the best standing.

V62   Cross, Wilbur L. "Mrs. Wharton on Her Art." *Yale Review* 15 (April 1926): 600-03.
            Summarizes Wharton's discussion of the two points of departure for the novelist: situation or character. Praises her study of Proust and feels that her perceptions give us new insight into the art of fiction.

V63   M., A. "Mrs. Wharton Discourses on the Novelist's Art." *Springfield Republican*, 3 January 1926, p. 7-A.
            Summarizes Wharton's main points, commenting on her obvious expertise and the good humor with which she dismisses younger novelists "perhaps a little cavalierly."

V64   Matthews, Brander. "A Story-Teller on the Art of Story-Telling." *Literary Digest International Book Review* 3 (October 1925): 731-32.

Argues book is thoughtful and worthwhile, with the comment that, although many writers have theorized about the novel and most argue that their way is the only one, luckily, the novel has managed to remain free from rigid rules.

V65   Morris, Lloyd. "Mrs. Wharton Discusses the Art of Fiction." *New York Times Book Review*, 15 November 1925, p. 2.

Finds no new ideas here and was disappointed that a novelist of her distinction has not further enriched our knowledge of narrative art further. Objects to her criticism of stream of consciousness fiction. Contends Lubbock's *The Craft of Fiction* is better on some points; however, recommends book as an introduction to problems of narrative art.

V66   Peyre, Henri. "Edith Wharton: The Writing of Fiction." *Revue Anglo-Américaine* 3 (April 1926): 366-68.

*Not seen.

V67   Priestley, J.B. "The Novelist's Art." *Spectator* 135 (5 December 1925): 1047.

Objects that, although this study is very sensible and contains really valuable comments on the novel, particularly her analysis of the stunt-like nature of stream-of-consciousness literature, overall it is slight and more a bundle of notes than an argument.

V68   Smith. "III. The Writer and His Readers." and "IV. Nothing New Under the Spotlight." *Literary Digest International Book Review* 3 (November 1925): 784.

Part III questions the wisdom of Wharton's statement that one should ignore editors, publishers and readers and write only for "that *other* self" because Shakespeare, Homer and others concerned themselves with their readers. Part IV discusses Wharton's essay on Proust and argues that Proust's knowledge of letters made him able to experiment without becoming a slave to innovation, as have many modern dramatists.

V69   Wallerstein, Helen. Review of *The Writing of Fiction*. *New York Evening Post Literary Review*, 28 November 1925, p. 11.
       Concise summary, urging this as a textbook on the writing of fiction.

A Backward Glance--Reviews

V70   Anonymous. "Les Lettres et le théâtre." *Le Mois* 49 (January 1935): 171-72.
       In French. Short paragraph notes she observed life of society in Europe with great insight. Notes she deals with friendship with James and that she made him read Proust.

V71   Anonymous. "Reminiscences." *Saturday Review* (London) 157 (21 July 1934): 863.
       Notes charm of her style. Cites Henry James and Roosevelt reminiscences.

V72   Anonymous. "The Last Survivor." *Time* 83 (5 June 1964): 101-104.
       Occasioned by the reprint. Blames her failure to become a truly first-rate novelist on her lack of understanding of the breakup of preindustrial America, which she was the first to use as material for fiction. General orientation is of Wharton as a lady survivor from an earlier, vanished world.

V73   Anonymous. "A Backward Glance." *Times Literary Supplement*, 17 May 1934, p. 359.

Summarizes contents, noting that she humanizes James, and that it is more about her friends and the "general business of living fully, wisely and vividly" than her literary work. Terms book wise, gracious, witty and charming.

V74   Arvin, Newton. "The Age of Innocence." *New Republic* 79 (6 June 1934): 107.

Maintains her background harmed her in that she has been unable to look any further inward than the foibles of her set. Contends she would have "towered higher in American letters" if she could have overcome the obstacles of her class and her consequent vision of the world.

V75   Baxter, Annette K. "What Is Not Said Illuminates What Is So Gracefully Said." *New York Times Book Review*, 9 August 1964, p. 4.

Occasioned by the reprint of *A Backward Glance*. Speculates lack of true Wharton revival stems from her interest in manners 'and from her own life, about which the autobiography furnishes little in terms of conflict and struggle. Wonders if a revival will stem from opening of Yale papers.

V76   Brown, E.K. "A Backward Glance." *American Literature*, 6 November 1934, p. 474-75.

Terms this "[p]recious as a memorial to a few exquisitely civilized beings who have left a deep impression upon Mrs. Wharton," but regrets the absence of information on her creative activity. Contends that the impression here is that the center of her interest was her friends, not her books. Notes different accounts of the British renaming of *The Touchstone*, and the material on her youth in Old New York as furnishing background for *The Age of Innocence* and *Old New York*.

V77   Butcher, Fanny. "Edith Wharton is Herself in Memoir Book." *Chicago Daily Tribune*, 28 April 1934, p. 15.

Terms memoirs not intimate, but a "rich ... warm re-creation of ... many modes of life which are lost to the world." Notes that here James "lives deeply," that "never before has he seemed like someone one would have liked knowing!"

V78   Cross, Wilbur. "A Happy Chronicle." *Yale Review* NS 23 (June 1934): 817-20.

Calls the mind and temper revealed here both feminine and charming. Notes that she has lived two lives--one with family and friends, one with her imagination. Terms this autobiography delicately psychological, related more to her second life. Comments on new *Ethan Frome* material.

V79   Edgett, Edwin Francis. "Edith Wharton Takes a Backward Glance." *Boston Evening Transcript*, 28 April 1934, Book Section, p. 1.

Terms volume a valuable contribution to American literary history in her account of her own work and its reception. Calls her one of the leading women novelists of the world, more a cosmopolite than an American. Although he terms her unfair to New England in *Summer* and elsewhere, he praises her "clear-sighted vision" of American life and her style, depth and broad outlook.

V80   Forster, E.M. "Good Society." *New Statesman and Nation* NS 7 (23 June 1934): 950, 952.

Notes that her "constant prosperity" makes for a certain autobiographical monotony. Contends she is best on her art, James and Sturgis. Mentions that she belongs to a tradition which is ending, realizes it, and surveys without bitterness the succeeding chaos.

V81   Hutchison, Percy. "Mrs. Wharton Recalls an Era." *New York Times Book Review*, 6 May 1934, p. 1, 13.

Summarizes parts of the book, finding that this memoir is foremost the record of her friendships. Notes the volume contains the "pageant" of a lost era, and skillfully differentiates the social life in New York, London and Paris.

V82   Loveman, Amy. "The Life and Art of Edith Wharton." *Saturday Review of Literature* 10 (28 April 1934): 662.
        Calls this "the recollections of a singularly happy life." Contends that although personalities take up the majority of the volume, the sidelights on her art, such as in "The Secret Garden," give it "a significance beyond" reminiscences.

V83   M., L.H. "Reviews." *America* 51 (28 July 1934): 378.
        Calls her "our most distinguished contemporary writer of fiction" and maintains she has achieved that status without concession to the times and one finds here the same aloofness as in her novels and short stories. Cites moving war material.

V84   Paterson, Isabel. "Edith Wharton Recalls the Age of Innocence." *New York Herald Tribune Books*, 29 April 1934, p. 7.
        Terms reserve the book's keynote, noting she gives tribute to the past age she once satirized. Calls portrait of James unconsciously devastating. Finds here "the pathos of distance; the authentic, if faded charm, of the past."

V85   Sloper, L.A. "Mrs. Wharton Recalls." *Christian Science Monitor* "Book of the Day," 28 April 1934, p. 14.
        Cites the pleasing anecdotes and James material, but objects there is no more about her literary labors.

V86   Sorani, Aldo. "Edith Wharton: *A Backward Glance.*" *PAN* (Rome) 3 (January 1935): 147-50.
        In Italian. Cites Wharton's interest in Italy and her knowledge of Italian art, furniture and gardens as an important part of her literary personality. Calls *A Backward Glance* a refined, tranquil conversation with Wharton, who is not

attempting to startle the world, like some contemporary female autobiographers, but is sincere and a great lady.

V87   T., R. "Two Literary Lives." *Current History* 40 (September 1934): vii, xii.
            Dual review of *A Backward Glance* and E.M. Forster's biography of G. Louis Dickinson terms both literary memoirs deserving of exceptional praise. Notes Wharton's artistry and her delicate, if incomplete, picture, with its gratifying emphasis on James.

V88   Troy, William. "Flower of Manhattan." *Nation* 138 (23 May 1934): 598.
            Discusses Wharton as a member of her class and notes she became a novelist because of her early perception of its "flatness and futility." Lays blame on her class for weaknesses of her writing, but contends strengths are her own. Finds dramatic thread in volume to be her struggle for emancipation. Maintains there is an ambiguity in her work and here of greater interest than dogmatism.

V89   Walton, Edith H. "The Book Parade." *Forum* 92 (July 1934): iv.
            Contends that she "crystallizes for all time the *Age of Innocence*." Calls volume charming, correctly reticent, dignified, yet humorous and urbane.

V90   West, Edward Sackville. "War and Peace." *Spectator* 152 (15 June 1934): 929.
            Recommends volume as well-written and "exquisitely mannered," noting that those interested in Old New York will find the early pages of greatest interest, but speculates Europeans will prefer James and war material.

V91 Whiting, Lilian. "Mrs. Wharton's Life On Two Continents." *Springfield Republican*, 17 June 1934, p. 7-E.

Summarizes content, concentrating on descriptions of New York society. Speculates that such a background might be as great an obstacle to overcome as poverty. Praises Wharton's achievements. Cites interest of James material.

Nonfiction--Criticism

V92 Anonymous. "Fair Vagabonds on Varied Highways." *Travel Magazine* 38 (February 1922): 16.

Article consists of captioned photographs noting women travellers, briefly recounts Wharton's visit to Morocco.

V93 Anonymous. "The Garden Calendar for June." *House and Garden* 43 (June 1923): 84.

Very brief mention, calling *IV&G* "one of the best books on Italian gardens in existence."

V94 Auchincloss, Louis. "Introduction." *A Backward Glance*. New York: Scribner's, 1964.

Appreciative, balanced introduction which notes her memoirs are as tidy as other details of her life were, and terms her life a revolution against the restrictive ideas of what a lady should be. But notes in her memoirs there is almost an apologetic attitude toward Old New York, of which she was a precise, superb historian.

V95 Bayley, John Barrington. "The Decoration of Houses as a Practical Handbook." In *The Decoration of Houses* by Edith Wharton and Ogden Codman, Jr. New York: Norton, 1978.

Subjective, discursive attack on Modern Art and Architecture frames extensive quotations from the text meant to illustrate Wharton and Codman's notion of "suitability" based on classical architecture as the only one which expresses "human dignity and greatness."

V96   Coles, William A. "The Genesis of a Classic." In *The Decoration of Houses* by Edith Wharton and Ogden Codman, Jr. New York: Norton, 1978.

Offers high praise for the authors' "triumphantly" authoritative point of view of "house decoration as a branch of architecture," whose values are proportion and symmetry. Notes the book appeared in a period of American cultural evolution and helped overcome the gap between architecture and decoration, as well as overpowering Victorian style. Corrects Wharton's reminiscences in *A Backward Glance* about working on the book, surveys Wharton's and Codman's expertise, discusses their collaboration. Examines the book's "classical" structure, using the chapter on Walls as an example of the authors' method.

V97   Fryer, Judith. "Edith Wharton's 'Tact of Omission': Harmony and Proportion in *A Backward Glance*." *Biography* 6.2 (Spring 1983): 148-60.

Analysis of the persona created in the autobiography as an attempt to reconcile the disturbing opposites in her life--the conflict between the inner creative self and the outer public person. Notes that what is left out is considerable: "adolescence, marriage, divorce, love affair, pain, isolation, self-doubt"--and what she does is to conduct "her last performance: choosing actors, set, language, she can call us back to witness the presentation of a final, perfected version of her life."

V98   Funston, Judith E. "*In Morocco*: Edith Wharton's Heart of Darkness." *Edith Wharton Newsletter* 5.1 (Spring 1988): 1.

    Describes Wharton's tour of Morocco in 1917, her fascination with the fairy-tale nature of the contrast-filled alien land, and her repulsion at the enslaved condition of women, rendering the book both an expression of Wharton, the artist, and the "most unadorned statement of her feminism." Notes effect of this trip on *AofI*, with its tribal rituals.

V99   Masson, Georgina. *Italian Gardens*. London: Thames and Hudson, 1961.

    See pp. 83, 141, 149, 242. Contrasts gardens as Wharton saw them with their present condition.

V100   Price, Alan. "Writing Home From the Front: Edith Wharton and Dorothy Canfield Fisher Present Wartime France to the United States: 1917-1919." *Edith Wharton Newsletter* 5.2 (Fall 1988): 1-5.

    Explains that both Edith Wharton and Dorothy Canfield Fisher "set themselves the task of explaining French customs to an American audience" during WWI. In the context of their war work, attitudes toward France, and the impact of their work on American audiences, analyzes Fisher's *Home Fires in France* and EW's *French Ways and Their Meaning*. Contends that "rather than writing a handbook for AEF soldiers trying to understand France, Wharton has written her own defense for preferring France to the United States."

V101   Sapora, Carol Baker. "Wharton Acts As Guide." *Edith Wharton Newsletter* 4.2 (Fall 1987): 1-2.

    Describes contemporary family motor trip following Wharton's route in *A Motor-Flight Through France*, maintaining the 1908 work is enduringly fresh and insightful, offering an awareness of history and the "continuity of human experience, implicit in the art and architecture of France." Also cites: *FF*.

V102   Schriber, Mary Suzanne. "Edith Wharton and Travel Writing as Self-Discovery." *American Literature* 59.2 (May 1987): 257-267.

Discusses reasons for Wharton's expatriation as revealed through her travel writings and "the process of self-discovery they initiated." Concentrates on *Motor-Flight Through France* and *Italian Backgrounds*, noting her selectivity, craftsmanship, the process of composition, and her discovery of "an avatar in the character of her narrator" who conceives of travel as a sacred quest. Analyzes metaphor, dialogue, strong verbs, allusions and the denigration of America. Concludes: "Wharton recognized in the narrative version of herself a woman who had undertaken a spiritual quest and had found her most authentic self."

V103   Tintner, Adeline R. "Wharton's Forgotten Preface to Vivienne de Watteville's *Speak to the Earth*: A Link with Hemingway's 'The Snows of Kilimanjaro'." *Notes on Modern American Literature* 8 (Autumn 1984): Item 10.

Speculates that Wharton's Preface to *Speak to the Earth* influenced Hemingway's appreciation of the book and therefore was a link between that work and his short story, "The Snows of Kilimanjaro," which contains striking similarities to de Watteville's thought. Cites evidence Hemingway knew and admired Wharton.

V104   Wilson, Richard Guy. "The Decoration of Houses and Scientific Eclecticism." *Nineteenth Century* 8.3-4 (Autumn 1982): 193-204.

Discusses *The Decoration of Houses* in terms of the changes in American visual culture in the 1890's, particularly the development of scientific eclecticism; i.e., a wide ranging selection of models from the past based on a rigorous and accurate methodology of classification and cataloguing. Argues the book is "central to understanding of the American Renaissance and the eclectic methodology of the period," for it was the first to explain to Americans "the artistic principles of the Renaissance and how they could be used."

V105 Wilson, Richard Guy. "Edith and Ogden: Writing, Decoration and Architecture." In *Ogden Codman and the Decoration of Houses*. Edited by Pauline C. Metcalf. Boston: David R. Godine, 1988.

  Examines EW's difficult friendship with Codman and their important influence on each other's careers. Detailed discussion of Codman's remodelling of Land's End and EW's New York home; their at times uneasy collaboration on *The Decoration of Houses*; the book's "scientific eclecticism" and its impact on society and other architects and designers; Wharton's work on the Mount. Analyzes sources of EW's almost professional knowledge of architecture and the role interiors and buildings play in her fiction. Contends: "Without an understanding of her architectural enthusiasms, much of her fiction remains only half understood."

Chapter 14

The Collections, Translations, Manuscripts and Miscellaneous Work

Chapter is divided into two sections: (1) Reviews of *The Book of the Homeless*; (2) Articles on the collections, translations and manuscripts. Anonymous reviews are alphabetized by name of journal or newspaper. See the Works Index for material pertaining to a particular work.

The Book of the Homeless--Reviews

W1   Anonymous. Review of *The Book of the Homeless*. *Dial* 60 (13 April 1916): 386.
       Describes circumstances of publication. Terms it of imposing beauty in every external detail, the contents, a varied feast. Praises the quality of her English renditions of French poetry.

W2   Anonymous. "War Relief." *Independent* 86 (3 April 1916): 29.

Terms this the most beautiful of all the war relief books, a brilliant mosaic.

W3   Anonymous. "Famous Writers Aid War Sufferers." *New York Times Book Review,* 30 January 1916, p. 37.
Warm praise for the volume, along with mention of its purposes.

W4   Anonymous. "Book of the Homeless." *Springfield Republican,* 30 January 1916, Section II, p. 15.
Applauds the excellent workmanship in writing, illustration and printing as well as the worthy purpose. Includes detailed list of charities which the book will support, Wharton's part in establishing these charities, and a complete list of contributors, and text (translated) of letter from General Joffre which opens book. Notes Theodore Roosevelt's introduction.

W5   Anonymous. "The Book of the Homeless." *Times Literary Supplement* (London), 9 March 1916, p. 116.
Praise for the collection and brief summary of its purposes and contents.

Editions, Translations and Manuscripts--Criticism

W6   Lauer, Kristin Olson. "Is This Indeed 'Attractive'?: Another Look at the 'Beatrice Palmato' Fragment." *The Journal of Evolutionary Psychology* 11.1 and 2 (March 1990): 1-8.
Uses personality theories of Karen Horney to argue that the "Beatrice Palmato" fragment is not the attractive scene of incest supposed by Lewis and Wolff, but actually is another instance of the ubiquitous rescue motif in Wharton in relationships between men and women. Also argues that although the scene may seem to be about sexuality, it actually demonstrates the type of disturbances between men and women throughout her fiction that are not primarily sexual but arise from neurotic development.

Also cites rescue motifs in *EF* and *HofM*. [See N17 and N28]

W7   Lawson, Richard H. "Edith Wharton, Gaylord Wilshire and Hermann Sudermann." *South Atlantic Bulletin* 44.2 (1979): 83-92.

Discussion of Wharton's translation of Sudermann's *Es lebe das Leben* and of H. Gaylord Wilshire's socialist criticism of the play. Surmises Wharton became so involved in the translation because of the failure of her earlier *Manon* and her personal identification with the heroine, who was also forty, aristocratic, trapped in a loveless marriage and in love with another man. Regrets that Wilshire, with his socialist orientation, could not judge the play on its merits and, unlike Wharton, did not appreciate the theme of the social constriction of the heroine. [See N16]

W8   Leach, Nancy R. "Edith Wharton's Unpublished Novel." *American Literature* 25 (November 1953): 334-53.

Contends that the incomplete manuscript of *Literature* gives insight into Wharton's work methods and points out autobiographical elements as well as similarities between *Literature* and *HRB* and *Gods Arrive*. Concludes she did not "abandon her earlier novel but rather utilized its characters and situations in the subsequent ones, modifying and changing them as the intervening fifteen years modifed and changed her own ideas."

W9   Leach, Nancy. "New England in the Stories of Edith Wharton." *New England Quarterly* 30 (March 1957): 90-98.

Analyzes three unpublished fragments set in New England--*Mother Earth*, *The Cruise of the Fleetwing* and *New England*. Concludes there are many slips in detail and characterization. Argues her "impressions are all part of the regional picture ... but they are essentially literary impressions and are handled, for the most part, superficially and conventionally." Cites: *EF, Summer,* "Bewitched," "Pretext," "Angel at the Grave," "Coward," "Young Gentlemen."

W10   Price, Alan. "The Making of Edith Wharton's *The Book of the Homeless*." *Princeton University Library Chronicle* 47.1 (Autumn 1985): 5-21.

Recounts the history of *Book of the Homeless* with excerpts from Wharton's letters about the project. Summarizes her charitable work. Includes accounts from Scribner's letters and description of the auctioning of the contributions. Reproduces Léon Bakst's Portrait of Jean Cocteau and Theo van Rysselberghe's Portrait of Andre Gide. Issue reprints Wharton's "The Tryst" (pp. 41-42).

W11   Puknat, Siegfried B. "Mencken and the Sudermann Case." University of Wisconsin *Monatshefte* (April-May 1959): 183-89.

In a discussion of H. L. Mencken's appraisal of the German playwright, novelist and short fiction writer, Hermann Sudermann, notes that Wharton's appraisal was, like Mencken's, one of "attraction and repulsion." Comments on the unfortunate circumstances surrounding her translation of Sudermann's play, *Es Lebe das Leben*, and that she found his novel, *Es War* (The Undying Past), "the greatest of modern German novels."

W12   Winner, Viola H. "Convention and Prediction in Edith Wharton's Fast and Loose." *American Literature* 42 (1970): 50-69.

Analysis of Wharton's adolescent novella *Fast and Loose*, tracing beginnings of the characteristic style, theme, tone, approach, fatalism, pessimism and irony of her later work. [See A22]

Chapter 15

Dissertations

Published dissertations are listed in Chapter 5. Dissertations referring to a particular work are entered under that title. Bibliographical dissertations are listed in Chapter 2. If a dissertation has been revised and/or renamed for publication, cross reference is given here.

X1   Ammons, Elizabeth Miller. "Edith Wharton's Heroines: Studies in Aspiration and Compliance." Ph.D. dissertation. University of Illinois (Urbana-Champaign), 1974.
      Feminist. Study of Edith Wharton's heroines as their lives are influenced by their culture. For abstract see DAI, 35 (1975), 7292A. [See her book, N1]

X2   Anderson, Linda Carlene. "Edith Wharton's Heroes." Ph.D. dissertation. Kansas, 1982.
      Study of Wharton's attitude toward male characters in *The House of Mirth*, *The Custom of the Country*, *The Age of Innocence*, *The Fruit of the Tree*, *The Reef*, *The Children*,

Hudson River Bracketed, *The Gods Arrive*. For abstract see DAI, 43 (1983), 2664A.

X3   Andrews, Maridella Elizabeth. "Initiation and Growth in Edith Wharton's Fiction." Ph.D. dissertation. University of Texas (Austin), 1979.
        Traces theme of initiation and growth in the fiction. For abstract see DAI, 40 (1979), 1463A.

X4   Antush, John Vincent. "Money in the Novels of James, Wharton, and Dreiser." Ph.D. dissertation. Stanford, 1968.
        Discussion of the importance of money in Wharton's work, with particular emphasis on *The Custom of the Country*. For abstract see DAI, 29 (1968), 558A.

X5   Askew, Melvin Wayne. "Edith Wharton's Literary Theory." Ph.D. dissertation. Oklahoma, 1957.
        Explores Wharton's critical theory and similarities between her thought and that of her friends, particularly James, Bourget, Berenson and Vernon Lee. Discusses the artist in *Hudson River Bracketed* and *The Gods Arrive*. For abstract see DAI, 17 (1957), 3009.

X6   Beauchamp, Andrea Louise Roberts. "The Heroine of Our Common Scene: Portrayals of American Women in Four Novels by Edith Wharton and Henry James." Ph.D. dissertation. University of Michigan, 1976.
        Discusses the determinism of Wharton's heroines versus the self-determination of James's. For abstract see DAI, 37 (1976), 965A.

X7   Bell, Millicent L.. "Edith Wharton: Studies in a Writer's Development." Ph.D. dissertation. Brown, 1955.
        For abstract see DAI, W1955.

X8   Bose, Mita. "Fictional Conventions in the Novels of Henry James and Edith Wharton." Ph.D. dissertation. Kent, 1980.
        Contrasts James and Wharton in, first, *The Portrait of a Lady* and *The House of Mirth* and then in *The Ambassadors* and *The Age of Innocence* to demonstrate the

two realistic modes involved--James's "poetic realism" and Wharton's more immediate and practical "prosaic or literal realism." For abstract see DAI 42, (1981), 212A.

X9   Bratton, Daniel Lance. "Conspicuous Consumption and Conspicuous Leisure in the Novels of Edith Wharton." Ph.D. dissertation. Toronto, 1983.
       Discusses particularly *The House of Mirth, The Custom of the Country* and *The Age of Innocence* in light of Thorstein Veblen's *Theory of the Leisure Class.* For abstract see DAI, 44 (1984), 2765A.

X10   Carlson Constance H. "Heroines in Certain American Novels." Ph.D. dissertation. Brown, 1971.
       Wharton, Fitzgerald and Updike are the core of this discussion of heroines in the American novel. For abstract see DAI, 32, 5175A.

X11   Colavecchio, Barbara Marie. "Edith Wharton and the Re-Shaping of Legend." Ph.D. dissertation. University of Rhode Island, 1985.
       Studies use of legends in *The House of Mirth, The Custom of the Country, The Age of Innocence,* and *The Reef* to examine the theme of the ideal and the real woman. For abstract see DAI, 47, 529A.

X12   Collins, Alexandra. "The Death of the Soul: A Study of Edith Wharton's Fiction." Ph.D. dissertation. Calgary (Canada), 1979.
       In *American Doctoral Dissertations.*

X13   Colquitt, Clare Elizabeth. "Composing the Self: Edith Wharton and the Economy of Desire." Ph.D. dissertation. University of Texas (Austin), 1986.
       Examines the dilemma of passion in Wharton's life and fiction through study of the Fullerton correspondence and pertinent works, particularly, "The Letters," *The House of Mirth, Summer, The Age of Innocence* and *The Mother's Recompense.* For abstract see DAI 47, 4388A. [See L34]

X14   Dupree, Merrily Ellen. "Edith Wharton's Business-
        Feminism." Ph.D. dissertation. Syracuse University, 1986.
             Traces development of Wharton's struggle as a woman
        to overcome "anxiety of authorship"--first, in identification
        with liberalism, then (after disillusionment) from liberalism
        to business as a means of survival, and, after WWI, to
        advocacy of women's achieving equality through traditional,
        maternal roles. For abstract see DAI, 47, 3426A.

X15   Dwight, Eleanor. "The Influence of Italy on Edith
        Wharton." Ph.D. dissertation. New York University, 1984.
             Discussion of the influence of Italy on Edith
        Wharton's fiction and nonfiction with biographical
        information on her relationship to Italy. Demonstrates that
        her early short stories with Italian subjects treat the
        inhibited, frustrated young woman. For abstract see DAI,
        45, 520A.

X16   Fedorko, Kathy Anne. "Edith Wharton's Haunted House:
        The Gothic in her Fiction." Ph.D. dissertation. Rutgers,
        1987.
             Analyzes Gothic in Wharton as a means to express the
        socially unacceptable: sexuality, ambition, anger, death.
        Defines Gothic elements in short stories and novels.
        Explains transformation of the Gothic in the novels into
        imagery creating an alternative text, "the other side of the
        social pattern." For abstract see DAI, 48, 1769A.

X17   Finn, Helena Kane. "Designs of Despair: The Tragic
        Heroine and the Imagery of Artifice in Novels by
        Hawthorne, James and Wharton." Ph.D. dissertation. St.
        John's, 1976.
             Examines tragedy of the heroines in Wharton's fiction
        and imagery associated with it. Studies concepts of tragedy
        in Christian, Western and classical philosophy as they have
        bearing on Wharton's art. For abstract see DAI, 37 (1977),
        5827A.

X18   Fritz, Alphonse Joseph. "The Use of the Arts of
        Decoration in Edith Wharton's Fiction: A Study of her

Interests in Architecture, Interior Decoration and Gardening and of the Landscape in Which She Exploited Them." Ph.D. dissertation. Wisconsin (Madison), 1956.

Contends the dominant principle in Wharton's fiction and literary theory is "taste"--based on standards of suitability, fitness and proportion. Discusses problems of the later fiction in terms of a decline in moral, social and aesthetic standards. Examination of the various decorative arts in her fiction. For abstract see DAI, 16 (1956), 2161.

X19   Gleason, James Joseph. "After Innocence: The Later Novels of Edith Wharton." Ph.D. dissertation. Ohio State, 1969.

Study of the later novels and Wharton's search for a theme in the post-war world. See discussion of Vance Weston as Wharton's resolution of the problem of a character to express the times. Also discusses *The Children* and *The Buccaneers*. For abstract see DAI, 30 (1969), 1564A.

X20   Godfrey, David Allen. "A Real Relation to Life: Self and Society in Edith Wharton's Major Novels." Ph.D. dissertation. Kentucky, 1982.

Discussion of the search for community in Wharton's fiction, particularly *The Valley of Decision*, *The House of Mirth*, *The Reef*, *The Custom of the Country*, *The Age of Innocence* and *The Buccaneers*. For abstract see DAI, 44 (1983), 168A.

X21   Goldberg, Raquel Prado-Totaro. "The Artist Fiction of James, Wharton, and Cather." Ph.D. dissertation. Northwestern, 1975.

Discussion of Wharton's treatment of the artist, contending she departs from James in important respects. For abstract see DAI, 36 (1976), 4475A.

X22   Goodman, Debra Joy. "The Scapegoat Motif in the Novels of Edith Wharton." Ph.D. dissertation. New Hampshire, 1976.

Discusses modifications of the theme of the scapegoat in Wharton's fiction, defining scapegoat in Wharton to mean one who seems to suffer inordinately while seeking happiness. For abstract see DAI, 37 (1977), 5121A.

X23   Gray, Patrice K. "The Lure of Romance and the Temptation of Feminine Sensibility: Literary Heroines in Selected Popular and 'Serious' American Novels, 1895-1915." Ph.D. dissertation. Emory, 1981.
Discusses *The House of Mirth* and *The Custom of the Country*. For abstract see DAI 42 (1981): 2130A.

X24   Greenwood, Florence Joan Voss. "A Critical Study of Edith Wharton's Short Stories and Nouvelles." Ph.D. dissertation. Stanford, 1962.
Argues the importance of serious consideration of the shorter fiction. [See Q31, Q32, Q33] For abstract see DAI, 23 (1962), 234.

X25   Greenwood, Walter Brewster. "Edith Wharton: Her Materials and Methods." Ph.D. dissertation. Cincinnati, 1941.
DAI, W1942, 105. In *American Doctoral Dissertations*.

X26   Hemmer, Jean Marie. "A Study of Setting in the Major Novels of Edith Wharton." Ph.D. dissertation. Fordham, 1964.
Study of Wharton's theory and use of setting based on *The Writing of Fiction*. For abstract see DAI, 25 (1964), 3571.

X27   Henry, Mary Joanne. "The Theme of Success in the Writings of Edith Wharton." Ph.D. dissertation. Harvard, 1976.
In *American Doctoral Dissertations*.

X28   Hewitt, Rosalie. "Aristocracy and the Modern American Novel of Manners: Edith Wharton, F. Scott Fitzgerald, Ellen Glasgow and James Gould Cozzens." Ph.D. dissertation. Purdue, 1970.

Chapter on Wharton defines her as a novelist of manners and points out the deterministic elements in her work. Discusses *Old New York, The House of Mirth, The Custom of the Country, The Age of Innocence* and *The Buccaneers*. For abstract see DAI, 31 (1971), 4163A.

X29　Horton, Rod William. "Social and Individual Values in the New York Stories of Edith Wharton." Ph.D. dissertation. New York University, 1945.

Argues Wharton's faithful realism in response to charges she is dated and class-bound. Notes her naturalism. Valuable historical information of period 1870-1914. For abstract see DAI, W1945, p. 57.

X30　Huh, Joonok. "Shifting Sexual Roles in Selected American Novels, 1870-1920." Ph.D. dissertation. Indiana, 1983.

Discusses Alcott, Norris, Chopin, James and Wharton in the context of changes from a male-dominated society. Explores *The House of Mirth, The Custom of the Country* and *The Age of Innocence*. For abstract see DAI, 44 (1983), 752A.

X31　Jacoby, Victoria Ann Dowling. "A Study of Class Values and the Family in the Fiction of Edith Wharton." Ph.D. dissertation. Stanford, 1972.

Exploration of the meaning of the family in Wharton's work--particularly as she saw the family as an important source of continuity and order and argued the role of the family in a society was an important key to its values. For abstract see DAI, 33 (1972), 2379A.

X32　Jones, Ann Maret. "Three American Responses to World War I: Wharton, Empey, and Bourne." Ph.D. dissertation. Wisconsin (Madison), 1970.

Explores Wharton's response to WWI as it grew from the pre-war situation and demonstrates her belief that the war would save Western culture. Discusses *Fighting France*, "Coming Home," *The Marne* and *A Son at the Front*. For abstract see DAI, 31 (1970), 1802A.

X33   Joslin-Jeske, Katherine Harriet. "The Social Thought and
        Literary Expression of Jane Addams and Edith Wharton."
        Ph.D. dissertation. Northwestern, 1984.

        Traces "connection between content and form" in the
        writing of Jane Addams and Wharton, particularly in
        relation to their redefinition of the female role. Considers
        both writers' responses to the Woman Question, capitalism
        and WWI. Discusses many of Wharton's novels, including
        The House of Mirth, *The Fruit of the Tree*, *The Custom of
        the Country*, *The Marne* and the nonfiction books, *Fighting
        France* and *French Ways and Their Meaning*. For abstract
        see DAI, 45, 2102A.

X34   Kimbel, Ellen. "Chopin, Wharton, Cather and the New
        American Fictional Heroine." Ph. D. dissertation. Temple,
        1980.

        Feminist. Examines the new tradition of the female
        heroine stemming from Chopin's *The Awakening*,
        Wharton's novels--*The House of Mirth* and *The Custom of
        the Country* are analyzed here--and Cather's frontier fiction.
        Discusses departures from traditional patterns and the
        suggestion throughout these works that women take
        responsibility for themselves. For abstract see DAI, 42
        (1981), 703A.

X35   Klampferer, Helga. "Die New Yorker Aristokratie in den
        Werken Edith Whartons." Ph.D. dissertation. Vienna, 1951.
        *Not seen.

X36   Koprince, Susan Jean Fehrenbacher. "The Fictional Houses
        of Edith Wharton." Ph.D. dissertation. University of
        Illinois (Urbana-Champaign), 1981.

        Explores houses as metaphors in Wharton, both as
        extensions of the owners' personalities and as bearers of
        emotionally charged atmosphere. Discusses *The Decoration
        of Houses* as a point of departure. [See Q43, R4.65] For
        abstract see DAI, 42 (1981), 2677A.

X37 Kraft, Stephanie Barlett. "Women and Society in the Novels of George Eliot and Edith Wharton." Ph.D. dissertation. Rochester, 1973.

Traces similarities in Wharton and George Eliot. For abstract see DAI, 34 (1973), 2632A.

X38 Krupnick, Mark L. "Stephen Crane and Edith Wharton: Two Essays in the Literature of Disinheritance." Ph.D. dissertation. Brandeis, 1969.

Discusses Wharton's characters' struggles for emotional liberation and the forces that inhibit them. For abstract see DAI, 30, 1567A.

X39 Leach, Nancy Rafetto. "Edith Wharton: Critic of American Life and Literature." Ph.D. dissertation. Pennsylvania, 1952.

Exploration of Wharton's social criticism in the context of a cultural and historical study of her times. Argues Wharton's importance as a critic of American literature and her dislike for materialism and provincialism. For abstract see DAI, 12 (1952), 303.

X40 Leder, Priscilla Gay. "'Snug Contrivances': The Classic American Novel as Reformulated by Kate Chopin, Sarah Orne Jewett, and Edith Wharton." Ph.D. dissertation. University of California (Irvine), 1981.

Exploration of women's use of the classical American theme of the individual in flight from society and its restrictions into either physically or psychologically freer space. Analyzes the pattern in *Summer* and *Ethan Frome* as well as *The Awakening* (Chopin) and *The Country of the Pointed Firs* (Jewett). Concludes "spaces in women's texts hold forth the possibility of a liberating redefinition of cultural structures." For abstract see DAI, 42 (1982), 4000A.

X41 Leerabhandh, Sivaporn. "A Study of Women Characters in Edith Wharton's Fiction, 1905-1920." Ph.D. dissertation. Michigan State University, 1985.

Study of Wharton's women characters, 1905-1920, as representing women at the beginning of the twentieth century, particularly in terms of the "old" dependent, innocent woman and the "new" independent and mature woman. Analyzes *The House of Mirth, The Reef, The Age of Innocence, Ethan Frome, Summer, The Custom of the Country, Madame de Treymes*. For abstract see DAI, 46, 3719A.

X42   L'Enfant, Julia Chandler. "Edith Wharton and Virginia Woolf: Tradition and Experiment in the Modern Novel." Ph.D. dissertation. Louisiana, 1974.

Discusses contributions of Wharton and Virginia Woolf to the modern novel. Examines *The Reef, The Age of Innocence, Hudson River Bracketed* and *The Gods Arrive*. For abstract see DAI, 35 (1975), 4531A.

X43   Lewis, Katherine Ann. "Satire and Irony in the Later Novels of Edith Wharton." Ph.D. dissertation. Stanford, 1968.

Argues Wharton's neglected post-war novels--*Glimpses of the Moon, Twilight Sleep, The Children, Hudson River Bracketed* and *The Gods Arrive*--deserve critical attention for their insight and the standards they set. For abstract see DAI, 29 (1968), 608A.

X44   Lischer, Tracy Kenyon. "The Passive Voice in American Literature: Vehicle for Tragedy in Brown, Hawthorne, O'Neill, Wharton and Frost." Ph.D. dissertation. Saint Louis, 1977.

Analyzes *The Age of Innocence* and *Ethan Frome* in context of the polarization of the sexes. For abstract see DAI, 39 (1978), 1573A.

X45   Logue, Marie Theresa. "Edith Wharton and the Domestic Ideal." Ph.D. dissertation. Rutgers, 1983.

Contends that Wharton held to the domestic ideal, seeing "the domestic circle as the source of the greatest fulfillment and satisfaction." Traces this ideal within *The House of Mirth, The Custom of the Country, Summer, The*

Age of Innocence, Hudson River Bracketed and *The Gods Arrive*. For abstract see DAI, 44, 3685A.

X46 Lowy, Julius. "Edith Wharton and her Relationship to France." Ph.D. dissertation. Vienna, 1949
* Not seen.

X47 Maynard, Moira. "The Medusa's Face: A Study of Character and Behavior in the Fiction of Edith Wharton." Ph.D. dissertation. New York University, 1971.
Studies Wharton's work from *Sanctuary* through *The Buccaneers* in the context of the characters' maturation and the problems they have in love relationships. Argues the importance of the novels after *The Age of Innocence* for the understanding they provide of Wharton's vision. For abstract see DAI, 32 (1971), 2096A.

X48 McCall, Raymond George. "Attitudes Toward Wealth in the Fiction of Theodore Dreiser, Edith Wharton and F. Scott Fitzgerald." Ph.D. dissertation. Wisconsin (Madison), 1957.
Contends Dreiser, Wharton and Fitzgerald "pierced through the illusions generated by wealth and illuminated areas of American experience in ways that historians and sociologists cannot." Argues Wharton believed that wealth both increases responsibility and frees the individual. For abstract see DAI, 17 (1957), 2269.

X49 McManis, Jo Agnew. "Edith Wharton's Treatment of Love: A Study of Conventionality and Unconventionality in her Fiction." Ph.D. dissertation. Louisiana, 1967.
Contends Wharton is unconventional in writing of romantic love as a destructive force. Explores Wharton's treatment of the failure of love in light of her own marital and love difficulties. For abstract see DAI, 28 (1968), 2689A.

X50 Miller, Carol Ann. "Natural Magic: Irony as a Unifying Strategy in the Fiction of Edith Wharton." Ph.D. dissertation. Oklahoma, 1980.

[See R4.74] For abstract see DAI, 41 (1981), 4400A.

X51   Molley, Chester Norman. "The Artemis-Athene and Venus
        Polarity in the Works of Edith Wharton: A Mythological
        Dimension with Psychological Implications." Ph.D.
        dissertation. Pennsylvania, 1971.
            Contends the basic dichotomy in Wharton's
        characterization of women is that of the Artemis-Athene
        (intellectual, rational) ideal as the epitome of the civilized
        woman versus the Venus antithesis of beauty, promiscuity
        and uncontrolled emotion. For abstract see DAI, 32
        (1972), 6442A.

X52   Morante, Linda Maria. "Edith Wharton: The House of the
        Past." Ph.D. dissertation. New York University, 1979.
            Argues the importance of tradition to both culture
        and artist. Analyzes *Ethan Frome*, *The House of Mirth*, *The
        Age of Innocence* and *The Custom of the Country*. For
        abstract see DAI, 40 (1979), 2684A.

X53   Papke, Mary Elizabeth. "'Abysses of Solitude': The Social
        Fiction of Kate Chopin and Edith Wharton." Ph.D.
        dissertation. McGill, 1983.
            Feminist. Contends the work of Chopin and Wharton
        "is part of the first modern female literary discourse in
        America" because, although they worked within forms
        defined by male discourse, they also spoke to the woman
        question and offered "both realistic and critical portrayals
        of American women in search of selfhood." For abstract
        see DAI, 44 (1983), 1451A.

X54   Parker, Jeraldine. "'Uneasy Survivors': Five Women
        Writers: 1886-1923. Ph.D. dissertation. University of Utah,
        1973.
            Argues Wharton is one of a group of women writers,
        Jewett, Freeman, Cather and Glasgow the others, who
        bridge the "sentimentalism of the genteelists and the
        factualism of the naturalists." Contends these writers'
        experimental techniques contributed to a world changed
        by Darwinian biology, Freudian psychology and the

Industrial Revolution, yet they "became, paradoxically, the guardians of the traditional values that were being displaced." For abstract see DAI, 34 (1973): 1927A.

X55 Patterson, Eric Haines. "The Most Stately Mansions: An Analysis of the Social Functions of Domestic Architecture Among the Affluent in America in the Later Nineteenth Century and a Discussion of the Manner in which Edith Wharton, Henry Blake Fuller, and Theodore Dreiser Interpreted the Domestic Architecture of the Affluent as a Social Artifact in Fiction." Ph.D. dissertation. Yale, 1977.

Study of the interior decoration and architecture in Wharton's fiction in the context of social history. For abstract see DAI, 39 (1978), 1680A.

X56 Peterman, Michael Alan. "The Post-War Novels of Edith Wharton 1917-1938." Ph.D. dissertation. Toronto, 1977.

Study of the post-war novels concludes they have been unjustly neglected, and that, in them, Wharton seeks "to celebrate growth and inner development in her characters, particularly those of middle age." Analyzes: *Summer, The Age of Innocence, Old New York, The Children, The Mother's Recompense, Hudson River Bracketed, The Gods Arrive, The Glimpses of the Moon, Twilight Sleep, The Buccaneers*. For abstract see DAI, 39, 4248A.

X57 Pitlick, Mary Louise. "Edith Wharton's Narrative Technique: The Major Phase." Ph.D. dissertation. Wisconsin (Madison), 1965.

Defines Wharton's major phase as the six novels written from 1905-1920. Focuses on the classical aspects of her theory, technique and vision. For abstract see DAI, 26 (1965), 3347.

X58 Price, Richard Alan. "The Culture of Despair: Characters and Society in the Novels of Edith Wharton and Theodore Dreiser." Ph.D. dissertation. University of Rochester, 1976.

Explores both isolation and materialism in *The House of Mirth, The Custom of the Country,* and *The Age of*

Innocence. For abstract see DAI, 37 (1976), 315A. [See R4.84, R9.27]

X59   Rice, Charles. "Edith Wharton: The American Novelist and American Christianity." Ph.D. dissertation. Duke, 1967. For abstract see DAI, 28, 3760A.

X60   Rice, Mary Lund. "The Moral Conservatism of Edith Wharton." Ph.D. dissertation. Minnesota, 1953.
          Contends that Wharton always remained a conservative moralist. Explores works written between 1905-1920. Parallels drawn with George Eliot. For abstract see DAI, 14 (1954), 521.

X61   Ruthchilds, Geraldine Quietlake. "The Whartonian View." Ph.D. dissertation. Johns Hopkins, 1983.
          Discusses *HofM*, *Reef*, *AofI*, *HRB*, and *GA*, seeking to correct distortions that have occurred when critics overlook EW's conception of the relationship between the individual and his/her social, material surroundings--which is not one of opposition. Argues this "Whartonian view" can uncover a previously unrecognized coherence in her work. For abstract see DAI 44, (1984), 3384A.

X62   Sapora, Carol Baker. "Seeing Double--the Woman Writer's Vision: Doubling in the Fiction of Edith Wharton." Ph.D. dissertation. University of Maryland, 1986.
          Argues Wharton used "literary doubling" to deal with the problems of expressing female experiences as well as post-war disillusionment. Examines: *The Valley of Decision*, *The Fruit of the Tree*, *The House of Mirth*, *The Custom of the Country*, *Ethan Frome*, *The Reef*, *Summer*, *The Age of Innocence*, *A Son at the Front*, *The Mother's Recompense*, *Hudson River Bracketed*, *The Gods Arrive*. For abstract see DAI, 47, 3041A.

X63   Sasaki, Miyoko. "The Sense of Horror in Edith Wharton." Ph.D. dissertation. Yale, 1973.
          Explores the Gothic in Wharton's ghostly tales, her moral perspective in them as well, her treatment of the

supernatural throughout her fiction, and the horror underneath the social convention. See her discussion of the grotesque in *The House of Mirth*. For abstract see DAI, 34 (1974), 7244A. [See Q67, Q68, Q69, R4.91, T30]

X64 Saunders, Thomas. "Moral Values in the Novels of Edith Wharton." Ph.D. dissertation. Pittsburgh, 1954.

Defines and classifies moral categories in the longer works of fiction. Finds ideal morality most often in women. For abstract see DAI, 14 (1954), 2352.

X65 Schaible, John A. "Incidents Grasped and Colored: The Indirect Interior Monologue in the Fiction of Edith Wharton." Ph.D. dissertation. Wayne State, 1983.

Argues the indirect interior monologues in Wharton "portray characters searching for lasting values in a society increasingly separated from such values." Contends these monologues account for the episodic structure of her novels and stories. See analysis of *The House of Mirth*, *The Reef*, *The Age of Innocence*, and *Twilight Sleep*. For abstract see DAI 44, 3687A.

X66 Sears, Sue Ellen. "Edith Wharton and a Modernist Reappraisal: Three Critical Essays." Ph.D. dissertation. University of North Dakota, 1986.

Refutes Wharton's reputation as a dated novelist of manners through three critical essays--first, traces her development as "social historian;" second, explores feminist themes; third, examines the ghost stories. For abstract see DAI, 48, 650A.

X67 Seifert, Charlene Simo. "Houses of Mirth: Edith Wharton's Hieroglyphic World." Ph.D. dissertation. Chicago, 1980.

For abstract see DAI, X1980.

X68 Semel, Ann. "A Study of the Thematic Design in the Four Major Novels of Edith Wharton." Ph.D. dissertation. Notre Dame, 1971.

Studies devices used to develop theme of the individual versus society, particularly as it relates to "the tragedy of life which results from the failure of love" in *The House of Mirth, The Reef, The Custom of the Country* and *The Age of Innocence*. For abstract see DAI, 32 (1971), 2707A.

X69   Shelton, Frank Wilsey. "The Family in the Novels of Wharton, Faulkner, Cather, Lewis and Dreiser." Ph.D. dissertation. North Carolina (Chapel Hill), 1971.

Study of the family in Wharton concludes that it is a positive force ensuring continuity, demanding responsibility, with spiritual dimensions. For abstract see DAI, 32 (1972), 5244A.

X70   Showalter, Shirley Hershey. "A Triumph of Comedy: Edith Wharton, Ellen Glasgow, Willa Cather, and a Professional Coming-of-Age." Ph.D. dissertation. University of Texas (Austin), 1981.

Feminist. Argues the work of Wharton, Glasgow and Cather demands reinterpretation in light of feminist criticism. Explores strategies each employed to reconcile professionalism and femininity. Concludes "each found hope for the triumph of the spirit over social limitations." Examines *Ethan Frome, Summer* and *The Age of Innocence* in detail. For abstract see DAI, 42, 1223A.

X71   Singley, Carol J. "The Depth of the Soul: Faith, Desire, and Despair in Edith Wharton's Fiction." Ph.D. dissertation. Brown, 1986.

Study of Wharton in terms of Calvinism, Platonism, and Catholicism traces her developing moral vision and places her in a tradition including Hawthorne, the New England local colorists, Whitman, and T.S. Eliot. For abstract see DAI, 47, 1730A.

X72   Smith, Herbert W. "Some American Fiction Writers and Their Reviewers: A Study of the Reviews and Reviewers in Connection with Eight Representative Fiction Writers. 1918-1941." Ph.D. dissertation. University of Pennsylvania, 1949.

Study that undertakes examination of reviews to determine if reviewers tend to be abusive or supportive. For abstract see DAI, 10-03 (1950), 151.

X73   Stephenson, Gloria Sue. "Romanticism in the Fiction of Edith Wharton: A Concept of Continuity." Ph.D. dissertation. University of Missouri, 1986.

Examines relationship between personal freedom and cultural tradition in Wharton, arguing that 1891-1906 she created a Romantic protagonist, morally superior to society, but 1907-1920 she defends cultural tradition and abandons previous Romanticism, only to return 1922-1937 to the Romantic protagonist with an intuitive knowledge of truth. For abstract see DAI, 48, 1205A.

X74   Thompson, Paula Carlene. "The Decline of Daisy: Fiction and American Womanhood." Ph.D. dissertation. Ohio State, 1983.

Study of Lily Bart and Undine Spragg in the context of the effect of the new materialism on the individual, as "products of a culture increasingly ruled by the lust for money and often unhampered by the scruples that once ordered American life." Contends Wharton, Dreiser and Fitzgerald took James's representative American girl as a point of departure and traced the decline of American culture through the manners of American women. For abstract see DAI, 44, 2768A.

X75   Trechsel, Gisela Brigitte. "The Single Parent in the Fiction of Henry James and Edith Wharton." Ph.D. dissertation. The American University, 1983.

Explores "diverse single-parent situations" in James and Wharton, concluding these situations "depict conflicts between individual and environment brought about by deviations from the norm" and function "to reflect society in the process of alteration and change." For abstract see DAI, 44, 491A.

X76   Turner, Jean. "The Ideology of Women in the Fiction of
       Edith Wharton 1899-1920." Ph.D. dissertation. Wisconsin,
       1975.
            Study of the conflict between the individual and
       society in Wharton's women. For abstract see DAI, 36
       (1976), 5307A.

X77   Tuttleton, James Wesley. "Edith Wharton and the Novel
       of Manners." Ph.D. dissertation. North Carolina (Chapel
       Hill), 1963.
            Valuable definition of the novel of manners in
       America. Defines Wharton's principal theme as the decline
       and fall of Old New York. For abstract see DAI, 24
       (1964), 3345. [See P53]

X78   Tyree, Wade. "Puritan in the Drawing-Room: The Puritan
       Aspects of Edith Wharton and her Novels." Ph.D.
       dissertation. Princeton, 1979.
            Traces decline of Puritan values in *The Custom of the
       Country*, *The Age of Innocence* and *Twilight Sleep*. DAI, 40
       (1980), 4047A.

X79   Van Klooster, Jantine H. "Moderne Amerikaansche
       Letterkunde: Edith Wharton." Ph.D. dissertation.
       Gronnigen, 1924.
            *Not seen.

X80   Weir, Sybil Barbara. "The Disappearance of the
       Sentimental Heroine Characterization of Women in
       Selected Novels by Robert Herrick, Edith Wharton, and
       Theodore Dreiser 1898-1925." Ph.D. dissertation. California
       (Berkeley), 1972.
            For abstract see DAI, X1972.

X81   Weissman, Leopoldine. "Edith Wharton's Romankunst und
       Ihre Beeinflussung Durch Henry James." Ph.D.
       dissertation. Vienna, 1947.
            * Not seen.

X82   Welling, Evalynn Beatrice. "Edith Wharton and Ellen Glasgow: A Critique of the Small Society." Ph.D. dissertation. Harvard, 1977.

          For abstract see DAI, X1978.

X83   Whaley, Ruth Maria. "Landscape in the Writing of Edith Wharton." Ph.D. dissertation. Harvard, 1982.

          Explores the meaning of landscapes in Wharton. Finds them representative of an American vision and traces three recurring scenic compositions: "expansive vistas of a natural wilderness, enclosed houses of a metropolitan world, and Arcadian visions of country estates. Examines landscapes in "The Fullness of Life," "Mrs. Manstey's View," *Ethan Frome*, *Summer*, *A Son at the Front*, *The Reef*, *The Custom of the Country*, *The Age of Innocence*, *Hudson River Bracketed*, *The Gods Arrive*, *The Buccaneers*. For abstract see DAI, 43, 2995A.

X84   White, Charles J. "'The Intelligent Acceptance Of Given Conditions': Moral and Social Attitudes, and Their Relationship to Social Change, in the Novels of Edith Wharton, John P. Marquand and James Gould Cozzens." Ph.D. dissertation. Pennsylvania, 1973.

          Explores weakness of the later novels as stemming from social change. For abstract see DAI, 34 (1973), 1943A.

X85   Williams, Barbara Maria. "Edith Wharton's Independent Woman and the Social Matriarch in Old New York." Ph.D. dissertation. Kent, 1983.

          Studies the conflict between the individual and society in Wharton in two types of female characters: the Social Matriarch and the Independent Woman. Feminist. For abstract see DAI, 44, 2769A.

X86   Wolfe, Robert Francis. "The Restless Women of Edith Wharton." Ph.D. dissertation. Columbia, 1974.

          Examines Wharton's changing view of the role of women over a fifty-year period. Contends that Wharton is ambivalent toward her "restless women"--at times praising the unconventional and at times criticizing it. See discussions of *The Valley of Decision*, *The Custom of the Country*, "The Last Asset," *The Age of Innocence*. For abstract see DAI, 35, 1130A.

X87   Zilversmit, Annette Claire Schreiber. "Mothers and Daughters: The Heroines in the Novels of Edith Wharton." Ph.D. dissertation. New York University, 1980.

Psychological study contends Wharton's heroines are defeated by their "own internal fears and anxieties" stemming from emotionally impoverished childhoods. Defines the narrative pattern in Wharton as "[w]inning ... [the] man but subverting the victory and asserting the claims of the other woman." See discussions of *The House of Mirth*, *The Age of Innocence*, *Ethan Frome*, *The Fruit of the Tree*, *Twilight Sleep*, and *The Mother's Recompense*. For abstract see DAI, 41, 5104A.

X88   Zlotnik, Jan. "The Virgin and the Dynamo: A Study of the Woman as Hero in the Novels of Edith Wharton, Ellen Glasgow and Willa Cather." Ph.D. dissertation. Syracuse, 1977.

Discusses Wharton's women in the light of a deterministic universe. For abstract see DAI, 39 (1978), 878A.

Author Index

Title Index

"The Abode of the Fool's Heart." R4.6

"Above Sentimentality." R16.15

"'Abysses of Solitude': The Social Fiction of Kate Chopin and Edith Wharton." X53

"The Achievement of Edith Wharton." Q40

"Addenda to the Bibliographies of Boyle, Conrad, DeForest, Eliot, Ford, Hemingway, Huxley, Wharton and Woolf." K10

The Advance of the American Short Story. T22

"The Advance of the English Novel, X." O64

"After Holbein." C1

"After Innocence: The Later Novels of Edith Wharton." X19

After the Vows Were Spoken: Marriage in American Literary Realism. Q76

Afternoon Neighbors: Further Excerpts from a Literary Log. L54

"Afterword." C2

"Afterword." *The Buccaneers.* R21.14

"Afterword." *Ethan Frome.* R7.17

"Afterword." *The Gods Arrive.* R20.16

"Afterword." *Hudson River Bracketed.* R19.18

"Afterword." *Hudson River Bracketed.* R19.19

"Afterword." *The Mother's Recompense.* R16.27

"An Afterword on 'The Lady's Maid's Bell.'" T38

"The Age of Edith." Q3

THE AGE OF INNOCENCE. A12

427

"Deserves Pulitzer Prize Every Year." S61

"Designs of Despair: The Tragic Heroine and the Imagery of Artifice in Novels by Hawthorne, James and Wharton." X17

"The Desolation of Charity Royall: Imagery in Edith Wharton's *Summer*." R10.25

"Desperate Women: Murderers and Suicides in Nine Modern Novels." R4.79

"The Destruction of Lily Bart: Capitalism, Christianity, and Male Chauvinism." R4.42

"Determinism and Point of View in *The House of Mirth*." R4.57

The Development of the American Short Story: An Historical Survey. T23

"Diagnosis." C26

Die amerikanische Dichtung der Gegenwort. O17

"Die New Yorker Aristokratie in den Werken Edith Whartons." X35

"Dieu d'Amour." C27

"The Dilettante." C28

"Director's Note." R15.18

"The Disappearance of the Sentimental Heroine Characterization of Women in Selected Novels by Robert Herrick, Edith Wharton, and Theodore Dreiser 1898-1925." X80

"The Divided Conflict of Edith Wharton's *Summer*." R10.27

"Divided Selves and the Market Society: Politics and Psychology in *The House of Mirth*." R4.93

"Doctor Edith Wharton Makes a Diagnosis." R14.23

"The Domestic Orientation of American Novels, 1893-1913." R9.21

Doubles. Q54

"The Drama II. Plays of Some Importance." R12.23

"Dramatizations of American Novels 1900-1917." R4.70

The Dream of Arcadia: American Artists and Writers in Italy 1760-1915. Q12

Subject Index

See Chapter 5 for all-encompassing general treatments of Wharton's life and work. These book-length studies are well-indexed. Also see H1 and separate entries in the primary bibliography for pertinent biographical material.

Academics, as characters O92

Adams, Henry L100, L105

Adaptations, *AofI* R12.21, R12.22, R12.23, R12.24, R15.20; *Drama* N24; *EF* R7.37; *HofM* G4, R4.70, R4.71

Addams, Jane L93, X33

Adolescence L38, R10.28, W12

Adolescents, *Summer* R10.19

Adultery L83, Q54, R15.24, U13. *See also* Marriage

Aesthetics X64

Affect Theory R1.7, R3.8, R8.14, R11.7, R16.29. *See also* Psychological criticism

Age, references to EW's L124, R9.10, R16.2, R17.18, R18.17, R20.1, R21.9, R21.10, R21.13, S72, V80, V83, V84

Aguilar, Grace Q79

Akins, Zoe R15.20

Alcott, Louisa May R10.27, X30

Alienation P33, R4.74

Works Index

Consult indexes of the volumes in Chapter 5, Book-length Studies, for critical interpretations of individual works covered.